Self- forgetfulness

I Have Found God

Complete Works
Elizabeth of the Trinity

VOLUME II

The being of God absorbs the soul.

Meditate with feeling w/ attention
at the eye center; repeat simiran
and rememt thia

D1294281

Complete Works
of
Elizabeth of the Trinity

Centenary Edition
(1880–1980)
in three volumes

Volume I
MAJOR SPIRITUAL WRITINGS

Volume II
LETTERS FROM CARMEL

Volume III
DIARY — PERSONAL NOTES
LETTERS OF HER YOUTH — POEMS

Edition realized, presented, annotated
by Conrad De Meester, Carmelite

ICS Publications
Institute of Carmelite Studies
Washington, DC
1995

Elizabeth of the Trinity
Carmelite

I Have Found God

Complete Works
VOLUME II

Letters from Carmel

Translated by Anne Englund Nash

ICS Publications
Institute of Carmelite Studies
Washington, DC
1995

I Have Found God, Complete Works II—Letters from Carmel
is a translation of Elisabeth de la Trinité,
J'ai trouvé Dieu, Oeuvres Complètes, Tome I/B
(Les Éditions du Cerf, 1980)
Copyright © by Washington Province of
Discalced Carmelites, Inc. 1995

ICS Publications
2131 Lincoln Road NE
Washington, DC 20002-1199

Typeset and produced in the U.S.A.

Photos used with permission of Dijon Carmel

Library of Congress Cataloging-in-Publication Data

Elizabeth of the Trinity, Sister, 1880–1906.
I have found God.

Translation of J'ai trouvé Dieu.
Includes bibliographies.
Contents: v. 1. General introduction. Major spiritual
writings — v. 2. Letters from Carmel.
1. Spiritual life—Catholic Church. I. De Meester,
Conrad. II. Title.
BX2350.A1E45   1984   271'.971'02   84-3748
ISBN 0-935216–01–4 (pbk. : v. 1)
ISBN 0-935216–54–5 (v. 2)

Contents

Translator's Preface

Born in 1880, Elizabeth Catez entered Carmel in 1901 and lived as a Carmelite for only five years before her death in 1906, at the age of 26. Though never intended for publication, her letters and writings for friends and family, in which she shares the secrets of her soul, have come to inspire countless Christians searching for a deeper relationship with the "divine Three," the indwelling Trinity.

This volume of letters, written by Blessed Elizabeth of the Trinity from Carmel, is the second of three volumes in the ICS translation of her *Complete Works*. The first volume, which contains the general introduction, biographical sketch, and major spiritual writings, was published in 1984, translated by Sr. Aletheia Kane, O.C.D. Every effort has been made to translate the present volume in a style that accords with that of the first.

In his General Introduction to the *Complete Works*, Fr. Conrad De Meester, O.C.D., editor of the original French edition, explains the idiosyncracies of Elizabeth's style and his own preference for close fidelity to the original texts rather than cosmetic changes that might have made the texts more "readable" (see Vol. I, pp. 63–68). We have followed his practice of keeping Elizabeth's punctuation, capitalization, run-on sentences, and long paragraphs, assuming that the reader would like as close a picture as possible of Elizabeth's personal style of writing. For that reason, we have also included her many ellipses, which indicate a pause or an unexpressed thought rather than an actual omission in the letter.

Readers should be aware that the *Esquisse biographique* (biographical sketch) of Elizabeth's life prior to her entry into Carmel, which appears in this volume in the French edition, was already transferred to the first volume for the ICS edition. Likewise the indices to the *Complete Works,* which appear in this volume in the French edition, will appear later in the third and final volume of the English-language translation (which will also include the 83 extant letters Elizabeth wrote before entering Carmel).

I am deeply grateful to Fr. Donald Kinney, O.C.D., and Mrs. Helen Anne Taylor for their extensive and significant help in editing this translation, and to Fr. Salvatore Sciurba, O.C.D., and Sr. Patricia Veale, D.C.M., for reading an earlier draft. I am also indebted to Jeffrey A. Mirus, of Trinity Communications, for an excellent job of scanning the typescript into the computer, to Jude Langsam, O.C.D.S., for her editing and desktop publishing skills, to Michele Koch for preparing the floor plans of the Dijon Carmel, and to Frs. Conrad De Meester, O.C.D., John Sullivan, O.C.D., and Steven Payne, O.C.D., for their invaluable advice and deeply appreciated encouragement.

Anne Englund Nash

Abbreviations

ACD   Archives of the Carmel of Dijon.

AL   *Elisabeth ou l'Amour est là,* by C. De Meester (cf. Foreword, Vol. I).

Ang   *Le livre des visions et instructions de la bienheureuse Angèle de Foligno* (The Book of the Visions and Instruction of Blessed Angela di Foligno), DDB, 1895, third ed.

CE   Composition Exercises by Elizabeth of the Trinity, in PAT.

Circ   *Obituary Circular of Elizabeth of the Trinity* (1906).

D   *Diary* (cf. Vol. III).

Exc   *Excursions in the Jura* by Elizabeth of the Trinity, in PAT.

GV   *The Greatness of Our Vocation,* Major Spiritual Writing II (cf. Vol. I).

HA   *Histoire d'une Ame* (Story of a Soul), by Thérèse of Lisieux, 1899.

HF   *Heaven in Faith,* Major Spiritual Writing I (cf. Vol. I).

K-RJ   *The Collected Works of St. John of the Cross,* trans. Kieran Kavanaugh and Otilio Rodriguez, rev. ed. Washington, DC: ICS Publications, 1991 (cf. LF and SC).

K-RT   *The Collected Works of St. Teresa of Avila,* trans. Kieran Kavanaugh and Otilio Rodriguez, 3 vols. Washington, DC: ICS Publications, 1976-1985.

L   *Letters* of Elizabeth of the Trinity (cf. Vols. II and III).

LC   St. Thérèse of Lisieux, *Her Last Conversations,* trans. John Clarke. Washington, DC: ICS Publications, 1977.

LF   *La vive flamme d'amour* (Living Flame of Love), by St. John of the Cross, in *Vie et oeuvres...* (Life and Works ...), Paris: Oudin, 1892, third ed., Vol. IV (see K-RJ).

LL   *Let Yourself Be Loved,* Major Spiritual Writing IV (cf. Vol. I).

LR   *Last Retreat,* Major Spiritual Writing III (cf. Vol. I).

LT   Letters of St. Thérèse, in St. Thérèse of Lisieux, *General Correspondence,* trans. John Clarke, 2 vols. Washington, DC: ICS Publications, 1982–1988. (The enumeration of the letters in the ICS edition is the same as that in the French critical edition of the *Correspondance général.*)

P   *Poems* (cf. Vol. III).

PA   Procès apostolique (Apostolic Process) followed by the number of the paragraph in the Summarium of the cause of beatification of Elizabeth.

PAT   *Elisabeth de la Trinité. Paroles, annotations personnelles et premiers témoins oculaires* (cf. Foreword, Vol. I).

PN   *Personal Notes* (cf. Vol. III). [This should not be confused with the "PN" used in the French critical edition of St. Thérèse of Liseux's poetry for the enumeration of her poems.—Tr.]

PO   Procès de l'Ordinaire (Bishop's Process). (Cf. PA.)

PS   Philipon Survey, in PAT.

RB   Récit biographique (Biographical account), in PAT.

Ru   *Rusbrock l'Admirable* (Oeuvres choisies), Paris: Perrin, 1902.

S   *Soeur Elisabeth de la Trinité. Souvenirs,* Carmel of Dijon, first edition of 1909.

SC   *Cantique spirituel* (Spiritual Canticle), by St. John of the Cross, in *Vie et oeuvres ...* (Life and works ...), Paris: Oudin, 1892, third ed., Vol. IV (cf. LF and K-RJ).

SS   *Story of a Soul: The Autobiography of St. Thérèse of Lisieux,* trans. John Clarke, second ed. Washington, DC: ICS Publications, 1976 (cf. HA).

SRD   *Semaine religieuse de Dijon* (revue).

The French editions of Sts. Teresa of Avila, John of the Cross, and Thérèse of Lisieux available to Elizabeth of the Trinity do not always conform to the modern critical editions on which current ICS translations are based. Nevertheless, wherever possible, we have tried to indicate the corresponding passages in available ICS translations. Thus the numbers following "K-RT" and "K-RJ" indicate the appropriate chapter and section in the Kavanaugh-Rodriguez translations of Sts. Teresa and John of the Cross, respectively; those following "SS" and "LC" indicate the page number in the Clarke translation of St. Thérèse's *Story of a Soul* and *Last Conversations*.

For Elizabeth's writings, the number following the abbreviation refers to the paragraph numbers in the present edition of the *Complete Works;* but for other books, the number refers to the *page,* except for PA and PO (cf. *supra*).

On terrace near infirmary, August 5, 1901, three days after Elizabeth's entrance into Carmel. In front (l.r.): Elizabeth (wearing postulant's black cape and veil); Mother Germaine of Jesus (holding copy of Thérèse of Lisieux's autobiography, *Story of a Soul*); Geneviève of the Trinity. Standing (l.r.): Marie of the Trinity; Hélène of Jesus (novice); Agnes of Jesus and Mary.

I

A New Path
August 2, 1901–January 10, 1903

At the entrance of the cloister, the Sub-Prioress, Germaine of Jesus, and several Sisters greeted the young girl who was entering Carmel. She went up to her cell and put on her postulant's dress with the cape and black veil.

This is how we see her [Elizabeth] dressed in a group photograph taken three days later. Her face betrays the suffering of the last few days but also her decision to go forward. The next day, Sister Thérèse of Jesus sent several photographs to the Carmel of Lisieux (to Sister Geneviève, Thérèse's sister), and in her long commentary, we come across this astounding phrase: "a postulant of three days but one who has desired Carmel since the age of seven,[1] Sr. Elizabeth of the Trinity, who will turn out to be a Saint, for she already has remarkable dispositions for that." The Sisters were in fact struck by her virtues and her recollection, although some wondered if this were not too good to be true.

The Carmel and Its Novices

Elizabeth's cell (without electricity, heat, or running water), off the large corridor, looked out on the courtyard where a large cross without a corpus stood in the midst of greenery. The three wings of the monastery on the southwest side received the sun; over the cloister with neo-Gothic ribbing, Elizabeth saw the trees of one of the three gardens that surrounded this spacious convent.[2]

On August 2, 1901, the date of her entrance, twenty-four Sisters lived inside the monastery and two extern Sisters in the out-quarters. Elizabeth was the seventh young one in the novitiate,

1

where they remained for three more years after profession (there were no temporary vows at the time). In the following months, five Sisters went to join the six Carmelites (one an extern Sister) who had already left for the new foundation at Paray-le-Monial; among them was Marie of Jesus, still Prioress of the Dijon Carmel, where she returned from time to time.

The elections of October 9 placed two very young superiors, both from Dijon, at the head of the community. Germaine of Jesus (31 years old) became Prioress. Marie of the Trinity (26 years old) was the new Sub-Prioress, who, as [Elizabeth's] "Angel," was responsible for initiating the postulant into the monastic customs. With Elizabeth in the novitiate were Sister Hélène (Cantener), a novice who would leave Carmel the following June, and Sister Geneviève of the Trinity, a professed Sister. Because they were so few in number, and because the Prioress also held the office of Mistress of Novices, the novices remained in the midst of the professed.

Each morning they saw their Mistress of Novices for a few minutes to give her an account of their prayer. In the afternoon, they gathered after Vespers in the novitiate where, for half an hour, the Mistress of Novices explained the *Rule* and *Constitutions* to them, corrected and encouraged them, or read to them.

Because of her fatigue, Elizabeth at first had to rest more than the others, but she was soon following the complete horarium.[3] The Eucharist, two hours of silent prayer, the Office recited *recto tono* [i.e., on a single note] in Latin, and two examinations of conscience took about six and one-half hours. An hour of free time, several hours of silent work, two meals and two recreations completed the day harmoniously. This hidden life, at the service of the Church, is both communal and solitary; it unfolds to the rhythm of liturgical feasts and has a fairly invariable horarium, in a contemplative monotony where the great surprise is God, present for faith and love in prayer.

Events

What was there to relate, then, in the 69 letters and notes that Elizabeth addressed during this period to 23 correspondents? The various events are hardly sensational: her first contact with her new cell and rough straw mattress, the unexpected visit of Mother Marie of Jesus, a bat at night during the Grand Silence, the wash done in common and the little tasks in choir, a veiling ceremony with songs to be sung, the elections, an adoration and a procession, a visit to the parlor and a letter received, and frosted windowpanes in the cloister and her cell.

Elizabeth made five retreats during this period: (1) eight days in November 1901 (preached by P. Vergne, S.J.); (2) from December 5 to 7, in preparation for her clothing; (3) the annual days of silence between Ascension and Pentecost, from May 9 to 17, 1902; (4) from October 7 to 14, 1902 (preached by P. Vallée); (5) from January 1 to 10, 1903, in preparation for her profession; this was her first long personal retreat in solitude.

Two very important dates should be highlighted. After barely four months of postulancy, Elizabeth was allowed to receive the habit on Sunday, December 8, 1901, the feast of the Immaculate Conception of Mary. She spent the morning with her family and girlfriends in the outquarters of the extern Sisters. In the afternoon, wearing her white wedding dress and flooded with joy, radiant in her union with God, she entered the outer chapel where the Bishop of Dijon, Msgr. Le Nordez, presided at the ceremony; P. Vallée preached the sermon. After entering the choir she received the habit of Carmel she had so desired to wear. The first rumors about Bishop Le Nordez, which would soon cause great divisions in the diocese, had already reached the convent. All over France the sky was very dark for religious communities threatened with expulsion; the Carmel of Dijon wondered whether they would have to leave the country. In November 1902, Mother Germaine traveled to Switzerland for this reason.

On January 11, 1903, the feast of the Epiphany, after thirteen months of novitiate, Sister Elizabeth of the Trinity, unanimously accepted by her community, was consecrated to God for eternity through her profession.

A Hard Novitiate

If the four months of her postulancy were spent in joy and light, the year of her novitiate was all the more hard and painful.

Prayer became dry; for the second time, Elizabeth was regularly afflicted by scruples, partly because of her desire to do everything to perfection; her health vacillated; her oversensitivity (her dominant character trait, she said during her postulancy, cf. PN 12) stirred painfully. But no one knew of this suffering except her two Superiors. On the eve of her profession she was "overwhelmed with anguish" (L 152), and Mother Germaine even thought it necessary to call P. Vergne that day to examine her final commitment closely.

To complain was not in Sabeth Catez's nature. Nothing betrayed her suffering in her letters to her family and girlfriends. She may have thought Mme. Catez still had a lingering hope that her daughter would turn back (a letter from Canon Angles to [Elizabeth's] mother shortly before her clothing confirms this). What she stresses is her real happiness despite the sufferings, which she does not mention. Long years before, she had learned to forget herself, to suffer for her Jesus, and to live in faith and abandonment. Mother Germaine helped her in this path. After her clothing her letters speak especially of her joy at being in Carmel, living in community, in silence, in the presence of God, listening like Magdalene to her Master, surrendering herself to the life of "the Three" within her. More than her letters, the seventeen poems of this period and the single *Personal Note* 13 ("To Be the Spouse of Christ") reveal her interior life to us.

To reassure her mother, she often tells her how she has found a new mother in the person of the Prioress, Germaine of Jesus. And this was true! A Carmelite of high caliber, Mother Germaine had the gift of putting into practice the golden rule St. Teresa of Avila gave to her prioresses: "Seek to be loved in order to be obeyed." Under Germaine's leadership, the Carmel of Dijon was a happy, fervent community. Elizabeth helped maintain this good atmosphere: she was willing and helpful, she loved her Sisters and was loved by them.

Before the Mystery of Suffering

We would like to make a few remarks here about suffering that are valid for all Elizabeth's writings. In the midst of very great happiness, suffering was a reality in her very brief life. Meeting it with faith and contemplating it in the mystery of the "One crucified by love," she accepted, even loved and desired, suffering.

But it is important to distinguish between the way Elizabeth *expresses* the mystery of suffering and her *lived attitude* toward it.

Her presentation of this mystery does not differ much from what was commonly offered at that time. To summarize this briefly: suffering, if it is not the effect of our own acts, is sent by God, who always remains our Father; it is God who wounds in order to heal, who punishes in order to educate. A trial gives us an opportunity to expiate our sins and those of the world, but above all to grow in love; it is even a proof of the love of God, who sends it to his best friends so he can reward them afterward. By accepting it, we prove our abandonment, our trust, our generosity. Jesus is the great example of this: by embracing the Cross, he reconciled the world to his Father. Following him, we can be "co-redeemers" through suffering, as we can through intercessory prayer and by generous sacrifice. There is even reason to desire suffering; the saints all emphasize its necessity and benefits.

We can recognize several aspects of this doctrine in the sermons of the great Mission of 1899 in Dijon that Elizabeth summarized in her *Diary,* which is a *good record* of the popular catechesis then in vogue. The preacher summarized: "Suffering is the ladder that leads us to God, to Heaven" (D 65).

Although suffering remains an inevitable reality for everyone, on the personal as well as the collective level, it seemed closer and more ordinary in the centuries preceding our own era of medical, social, and economic progress; it was a fate one had to be resigned to, having few means to remedy it: life was like that. From the acknowledgment of this inevitability, one ascended to the image of a supreme "Dispenser"; and, having faith in this love proclaimed by Scripture and made visible by the life of Jesus, one considered suffering a disposition of that Love, in view of our good. To this was added a doctrine inherited from romanticism about the usefulness of suffering that made world-weariness, afflicted hearts, and human misery into privileged subjects for poetic meditations and the like. Finally, an ever-present Jansenist mentality that emphasized God's justice, the vengeful anger of an offended honor, gave suffering a character of necessary expiation: one had to merit one's salvation;

sacrifices were the small change. All this marked, and distorted, the language of the period. In comparison, note the very positive manner in which Elizabeth *lived* suffering.

Her attitude was essentially *oblative*. To accept and even to desire suffering was to *offer oneself*. Elizabeth (whom two people had to accompany when she went to the dentist) was not animated by a hidden masochism. She really wanted to suffer "for you, with you" (PN 5). She accepted, even desired, suffering because it put her in a more *radical* situation (one of the reasons Teresa of Avila wanted her Carmel to be so demanding), in which to fight against the sluggishness in us, the fear of making progress, and all forms of egoism. Elizabeth knew the quickening power of self-forgetfulness, which directs our attention toward the One for whom we are forgetting ourselves and strengthens the will through generosity. The repeated demand of the young laywoman: "Break, burn, tear out all that displeases you in me" (D 105; PN 4 and 5) is nothing but a more active expression of her mystical prayer as a Carmelite: "O consuming Fire, Spirit of Love, 'come upon me,' and create in my soul a kind of incarnation of the Word ..." (PN 15).

Elizabeth's suffering had a *relational* perspective. She carried her cross in obedience to Jesus, who invited his disciples to "follow him" (Mk 8:34). "I cannot say that I love suffering in itself, but I love it because it conforms me to Him who is my Bridegroom and my Love" (L 317). It was through love of his Father and fidelity to the ideal and the message the Father was asking him to live in the midst of humanity that Jesus agreed to carry the Cross and drink the cup of sin, trusting that God would save him beyond death. It was through love of Jesus and fidelity to his Gospel that Elizabeth agreed to suffer, while preserving charity with respect to her mother and to all those close to her. She maintained the peace of abandonment, faith in the hours of darkness, courage and hope during her terrible illness at so young an age. To love Jesus, to live his Gospel, to attain union is to give oneself completely—and this entails suffering and the self-forgetfulness that alone makes one totally free: "He is also drawing me very much toward suffering, the gift of self; it seems to me that this is the culmination of love" (L 298). These three equations, to begin with the last, reveal here absolutely everything that follows from Jesus' example: "Love, to be true, must be sacrificed: 'He loved me, He gave Himself for me,' there is the culmination of love" (L 278). In the course of her last illness, Elizabeth developed the eucharistic context even more fully, as she entered entirely into the sacrifice of the "One crucified by love"; her passion was wholly for the church. Along with Christian tradition, Elizabeth believed that self-forgetfulness, whether lived in charity within community, in prayerful attention to God, or in crucifying fidelity to the least demands of the Gospel, was assumed into the redemptive Passion of Christ and became a preparation for the outpouring of the Spirit over the world.

The saints live a tradition in the church, but they also share more profoundly in a mystery that they then speak to us about in a necessarily limited way. The *attitude* that Elizabeth of the Trinity assumed in human suffering contained an evangelical and prophetic aspect translated into the *language* of her time. If one recognizes the tree by its fruits, how can we fail to discern the presence of the Spirit in the intense joy that shines on every page of the work of this young saint?

[1] To be precise, she had desired *religious* life since that age. Her Carmelite vocation evolved later.

[2] See Plans 1 and 2 at the end of this volume and Plan 4 in Vol. III.

[3] See the horaria on pp. 371–372 of this volume.

Note: Letters 1–83, from Elizabeth's youth, will appear in the third and final volume of her *Complete Works*.

Elizabeth in traditional wedding dress, for reception of Carmelite habit on December 8, 1901.

L 84   To Françoise de Sourdon   [August 4, 1901][1]
       J.M. + J.T.[2]   Dijon Carmel, August 4

My dear little Françoise,
    If you knew how happy your Sabeth is, you couldn't cry any more, but on the contrary, you'd be thanking God for me! You are wondering, perhaps, how I can find so much happiness, since in order to enter this dear solitude I had to let go of those I loved. But you see, my darling, in God I have everything. Close to Him, I find once again all those I left. Ah! how I entrust my little Framboise to Him. I will always be her little mother, nothing will be changed between us, don't you see? Tell yourself that the grilles will in no way be a separation and that I'll always keep your place for you in my heart. I have many things to tell you, but I'm in a bit of a hurry, yet I've rushed to send you this little note to tell you my heart is always close to yours. I caught a glimpse of my dear Mama and Guite Saturday[3] and they're to come see me today. Ask them to tell you all I haven't time to say. Thank your good mother and Marie-Louise for all you're doing for my darlings!
    If you knew how good everyone is here.... It seems like I've been among them for a long time. Mother Sub-Prioress[4] is a true little mother—Friday she came to my little bed to give me a kiss; I've already spoken to her of my Framboise! I leave you now, darling, but my heart remains so close to those I love and whom I'll never forget.... Give your mother a big kiss for me, with all my gratitude. Tell her I'm not forgetting her intentions, and thank Marie-Louise for taking my place with Guite.
                         Your great friend Sabeth.
Abbé Courtois[5] came to see me.

---

[1] Two days after she entered Carmel, "Friday," August 2. Françoise (whom Elizabeth nicknamed affectionately "Framboise" [Raspberry]), then 14 years old, and her older sister, Marie-Louise, were the daughters of Mme. de Sourdon, a widow and a close friend of Mme. Catez. [Françoise] was very saddened by the entrance of Elizabeth, "her little mother." Just as Elizabeth had done before she entered (e.g., Vol. III, L

43, 45, 63, 65, 66, 67, 69, 74), she continued to guide her young friend with her letters and conversations in the parlor. This was also a consideration shown to Mme. de Sourdon.

[2] Abbreviations for "Jesus, Mary, Joseph, Teresa" used in Carmel. Elizabeth almost always omits the period after the M.

[3] Monday, August 5, her sister Guite writes to Mlle. Forey: "We were permitted to see her Saturday and Sunday, and we are returning there tomorrow" (cf. PAT).

[4] Mother Germaine of Jesus, who would soon become Prioress (cf. L 97) and would remain so during the five years Elizabeth spent in Carmel. [Germaine] would be her Mistress of Novices at the same time.

[5] Jules-Bernard-Edmond Courtois, then 50 years old, chaplain of the Carmel; he said Mass there every day and heard the confessions of the Sisters every week.

L 85   To her mother   [August 9, 1901][1]
       J.M. + J.T.   Dijon Carmel, August 9

My darling little Mama,

    What happiness it is to come and have a little chat with you. Oh! if you knew how much I love you; it seems to me that I will never be able to thank you enough for letting me enter this dear Carmel where I am so happy. It's partly to you as well that I owe my happiness, for you surely know that if you had not said "yes," your little Sabeth would have stayed close by you. Oh! my little mother, how the good God loves you, if you could see with what tenderness He looks on you!...

    Since you want me to tell you about myself, I'm going to make you happy. My health is perfect, my appetite has returned to normal, and I'm doing credit to the cooking of Carmel. Alice[2] told me you would like me to drink a little wine; don't you recall that I can't digest it? I sleep like the blessed on our[3] straw mattress; it's been a long time since I've had that happen. The first night, I didn't feel very secure, and I wondered if I weren't going to roll out; by the next morning, I had already gotten used to our bed. I go to sleep before 9 o'clock, and I wake up at 5:30, isn't that *great?* So I'm recovering.[4] Tonight Mother Sub-Prioress is letting me go to Matins, and I'm delighted. You can rest assured, I won't do too much; this good little Mother cares for me like a real baby. My heart is with you there,[5] tell me everything you're doing, I'll be very happy to hear all your news. Really enjoy that beautiful country you love so much, and when you

think of your little Sabeth, thank God, for He has chosen so beautiful a part for her, oh! if only you knew!...
I kiss you, hold you tightly in my arms, just like before. If you knew how I love you and how I thank you!

Your Elizabeth[6]

[1] This first letter to her mother is dated August 9, not 19, as formerly thought. (The 1 of this presumed date is the upper bar of the t in "avant" at the end of this letter, written across the first horizontal lines....) Mme. Catez and Guite had left for Switzerland on "Wednesday," August 7 (cf. the letter from Guite quoted in L 84, note 3).

[2] Probably her friend Alice Chervau (cf. Letters of Her Youth [in Vol. III]), "the poor little one" (the same expression in L 96) who came yesterday (L 86).

[3] Elizabeth first writes "my" but corrects it to "our," following the Carmelite custom of considering all possessions as held in common.

[4] "I assure you that she has also suffered from leaving everything, she was wasting away from it, and it was better to have that end" (letter from Guite quoted in L 84, note 3).

[5] According to the letter quoted from Guite, to the Hôtel Beau Site, Fleurier, Canton de Neuchâtel in Switzerland.

[6] Mother Germaine adds this postscript: "Dear Madame, I have really wanted to write to you, to speak to you at greater length about our dear little Sister, but time has been lacking; besides, you know my heart so well with regard to her and also to you. Elizabeth is doing *very well* in all ways, is looking well again and is perfectly happy. We love her more and more."

L 86   To her sister   [August 9, 1901][1]
J.M. + J.T.

My darling Guite,
Don't be sad at seeing this tiny little scrap of a letter. Mother Sub-Prioress said this wouldn't count,[2] and I'll write you soon. How is my little one? Tell me *everything*, do you hear?
I saw Alice yesterday,[3] the poor little one was quite nervous. Jeanne Sougris came for a moment with her, and I confess that I don't understand how she happened to be there.
Tuesday we will have a veiling,[4] I'll tell you about this ceremony. If you knew how well I am, it seems to me that I have changed bodies! But then, you see, I have found what I was searching for, Oh, my darling, how good God is! Would you like us to have but one soul and one heart to love Him? Thank Him every day for your Sabeth who loves you very much and who kisses you with all her heart.

Tell Marie-Louise[5] that I am thinking of her very especially, as well as Madame Hallo.

[1] The paper on which this letter is written is one-fourth of a leaf of which L 85 is one-half. This "tiny little scrap of a letter," with no greeting to Mme. Catez, thus accompanied L 85.
[2] The custom was one letter or one parlor visit per month for parents, brothers, and sisters. Elizabeth wrote to Guite again on August 30.
[3] Cf. L 85, note 2.
[4] Of Sister Madeleine of Jesus, Tuesday, August 13.
[5] Marie-Louise Hallo, whom the Catezes were going to meet in Switzerland, as L 87 suggests. Marie-Louise, one month younger than Elizabeth, was her close friend. She is to be distinguished from Marie-Louise de Sourdon and Marie-Louise Maurel, to whom these letters often refer. The reader will meet four other Louises: Recoing (L 93), Demoulin (L 291), a friend of her aunts from Carlipa, and Sister Louise de Gonzague in Carmel.

L 87   **To her mother**   [August 13–14, 1901][1]
        J.M. + J.T.   Dijon Carmel, August 13

My darling little Mama,
    I send you my whole heart as a feast-day bouquet.[2] Oh! we have not left each other, have we, and you do feel your little child very close to her dear Mama. If you knew how we speak of you with my Beloved, it seems to me that you must feel it! I am so glad that you are receiving Communion more often. It is there, my little Mama, that you will find strength. It is so good to think that after Communion we possess all of Heaven within our soul except the vision![3]
    Your letter, or rather the letters from *all* of you, have made me so happy…. Perhaps I've been too glad, but the good God, whose Heart is so tender, understands me well, and I don't believe He holds it against me at all. All your details interested me, but I nearly got angry with that fellow Koffman who relegated you to that chalet! Do enjoy that beautiful country, nature carries one to God. I used to love those mountains so much, they spoke to me of Him. But you see, my darlings, the horizons of Carmel are even more beautiful, it is the Infinite!…
    In God, I have all valleys, all lakes,[4] all perspectives. Oh! thank Him every day for me, my part is too beautiful and my heart melts

away with gratitude and love. Don't be jealous, I love you both so much; I'm asking Him to take hold of you as He takes hold of me! I have so many things to tell you that I don't know where to begin. Monday evening, during recreation, our Mother[5] arrived unannounced, you can imagine the sensation! I only saw her for a few moments, for she left again the next day at 2 o'clock, taking away two of our Sisters; she is to return on Monday, and you will find her on your return. She came only to give the veil to one of our Sisters yesterday. Do you see this little jealousy: I was quite pleased that it was not Mother Sub-Prioress who performed the ceremony, for I want to be her first, she is so good, I love her so much. We speak of you together; you don't have to worry, I assure you she looks after me. This morning, for my first fast,[6] they made me take something, which, to be sure, I would not have done if I had not been here. This morning, my good little Mother allowed me to go to prayer. So I got up at the first calling, at a quarter to 5, I was afraid I wouldn't be ready in 15 minutes, and you can imagine how pleased I was when I arrived in choir and saw that I was the first one!...

I am Jesus' little chambermaid: every morning before Mass I clean the choir.[7] Today I decorated a little altar of the Virgin which is in the preparatory.[7a] As I was putting some flowers at the feet of this good Mother of Heaven, I spoke to her of you; I asked her to gather all these flowers, to make a beautiful bouquet of them, and to bring it to you on behalf of your Sabeth.

As a *terrible trial*, I had to compose some verses for the veiling and sing them[8] last night at recreation. I was shaking...which is really ridiculous, for our Sisters are so charitable that they found my work a great success. Marie-Louise, who so loves to see me blush, would have some chances to see my timidity tested. Mother Sub-Prioress is letting me send you my verses, that will amuse you! A Dieu, darling Mama, I think you'll be pleased with this long letter. In closing, I sleep like the blessed, my appetite is excellent, the food is very nourishing and suited to my constitution. Oh! my little mother, how happy I am! *Thank you* again for having given me to the good God. I hold you close to my heart and I kiss you near the good Jesus, who smiles when He sees us.

Your Sabeth.

My Angel[9] asks me to tell you she will also offer Holy Communion for you tomorrow. She would like to have written you, but she doesn't have time. I will give you my verses later, I don't have time. My darling Guite won't be jealous that Marie-Louise has taken her place today.[10] I keep her in my heart and ask God to tell her all I can't tell her myself; she knows where I keep my rendez-vous with her.[11]

[1] Begun on the 13th ("yesterday"), the letter was completed on the 14th. The envelope, which has been preserved (and cancelled on the 14th), is addressed to Fleurier (cf. L 85, note 5).
[2] August 15th, the feast day of Mme. Catez, Marie Rolland.
[3] Several days earlier, Elizabeth expressed the same conviction (cf. PN 12); a eucharistic context is added here. If this conviction did not result from reading *L'Histoire d'une Ame [Story of a Soul]* by Thérèse of Lisieux, it surely found support there. Thérèse states it ("heaven was in my soul") in the account of her first Communion (HA 58 [SS 78]), a text Elizabeth loved very much (cf. Vol. III, *Diary*, note 149). Elsewhere Thérèse repeats that, by means of the Eucharist, the Lord wants "to find another heaven: the heaven of our soul in which He delights" (HA 78 [SS 104]).
[4] Cf. the poem "Ce que j'aimais" ["What I Loved"] (Poem 18 in the French critical edition of St. Thérèse of Lisieux's *Poetry)*: in God "I have the beautiful lake, I have the valley" (HA 436).
[5] Mother Marie of Jesus, still Prioress before founding the Carmel of Paray-le-Monial. The preparations obliged her to be absent on numerous occasions.
[6] For the vigil of the Assumption.
[7] She had been given the duty of cleaning the choir.
[7a] ["Avant-choeur," outer choir, where the Sisters assembled before entering the choir—TRANS.]
[8] P 73. The music, written in Elizabeth's hand, has been preserved.
[9] The "Angel" was the Sister charged with initiating the new postulant into the customs of the monastic life. For Elizabeth, this was Sister Marie of the Trinity, the future Sub-Prioress; she had known Elizabeth before she entered.
[10] I.e., a letter (lost) to Marie-Louise Hallo accompanied the letter to Mme. Catez.
[11] Perhaps an allusion to the crucifix she had given to Guite and that she had proposed as the site for their "rendez-vous" (L 80a)? Or to the interior "little cell" (L 89)? Mother Germaine adds as a postscript: "Our little Sister enchants us more and more. She looks well and is more than happy."

L 88   To Françoise de Sourdon   [August 22, 1901][1]
    J. M. + J. T.   Dijon Carmel, Thursday

My good little Françoise,
    Our dear Mother, who has been back for two days, is letting me come to you. You know, my darling, a Carmelite hardly ever

writes, and this is a favor they have given to my little Framboise. But, you see, if my pen remains silent, ah! how I think of you; every day I speak to the good God of my darling, it's so sweet to entrust to Him those one loves and has left for His sake. But what am I saying? We have not been separated, the grilles will never exist for our hearts, and the heart of your Sabeth will always be the same. Tell your good mother that I pray every day for her and the intentions she recommended to me, as well as for Madame d'Anthès;[2] I am not forgetting anyone; you see, in Carmel the heart expands and knows how to love even more!

The good God has completely restored me without powders or quinine. My health grows stronger every day, I devour food, if you could see what I consume! They are taking good care of me, you can set your mind at rest on my account. I sleep deeply on our straw mattress, something I never experienced before. The first night I didn't feel very secure, and I thought that before morning I would roll out one side or the other, but nothing happened, and now I've gotten used to our bed and it seems delightful to me. Oh! my darling, if you knew how good everything is in Carmel, your Sabeth cannot find words to express her happiness. When you all think of me, don't cry, but thank God, I am so happy! Since you're so eager for details, I'll tell you, like an egoist, just about myself! Our cell, this little nest loved above all others, is exactly like my bedroom[3] in size, with the bed and the window in the same place, with the door where my chest of drawers was and, in the corner where my dressing room was, our desk, on which I'm writing to you, with the *Combat spirituel [Spiritual Warfare]*[4] beside me: it is right there on my little board, and I use it every day. Your little heart never leaves me, it is attached to my rosary that I wear on my belt: you see, I have not left all your mementos behind, and it is especially in the depths of my soul, very close to God, that I find you and put you. My days are not always the same, for they treat me like a baby, and I get up and go to bed more or less early. If you only knew how quickly time passes in Carmel, and yet it seems to me that I've always lived in this dear house. Don't be jealous, you know very well that you will always have your place in my heart, since I will always be your *little mama;* only, you know, I want a Françoise who is entirely good!

A Dieu, I gather you all together, even Madame d'Anthès if she'll allow me, to send you my deepest affection.

M.[5] Elizabeth of the Trinity

I saw Mama this morning; Switzerland didn't agree with her. Poor dear Mama, pray for her. I recommend my little Guite to Marie-Louise, thanking her again for all she has done. A Dieu, my heart remains very faithful to you, let's love the good God, let's be saints. Forward to Heaven![6]

---

[1] 1901: date deduced from the trip taken by the Catezes in Switzerland and from the health report.
[2] Françoise's maternal grandmother, who was living in Avallon. Elizabeth will write several letters to her.
[3] At rue Prieur-de-la-Côte-d'Or.
[4] By Lorenzo Scupoli. The copy that Françoise gave her has not been preserved.
[5] Abbreviation for Marie. This is her complete religious name.
[6] Reminiscent of a maxim by Teresa of Avila: "Forward, my daughters, to eternal Life!"

L 89   To her sister   [August 30, 1901][1]
      J. M. + J. T.   Dijon Carmel, Friday

My good little Guite,
      You can imagine how grieved I was to learn of your misfortunes. Poor dear Mama, take good care of her.... You didn't tell me what the doctor said before you left.[2] Saint [Mary] Magdalene will cure her. All your details interested me very much; thanks for the holy cards, they pleased me greatly. I put mine in our *Manual* [3] that I use every day. I so love to look at her, this dear saint at the feet of the Master, she is the Carmelite's model. Oh! how good it is to stay there, silent, like a little child in the arms of its mother, no longer seeing or hearing anything but Him. It is there, you know, that you will always find your Sabeth again; then there is no more separation, the trio[4] is reunited in His Heart!
      Since you like me to tell you lots of things, here is something very interesting: we've done the wash. For the occasion I put on my nightcap, my brown dress[5] all turned up, a large apron over that and, to complete the outfit, our wooden shoes. I went down like that

to the laundry room where they were scrubbing for all they were worth, and I tried to do like the others. I splashed and soaked myself all over, but that didn't matter, I was thrilled! Oh, you see, everything is delightful in Carmel, we find God at the wash just as at prayer. Everywhere there is only Him. We live Him, breathe Him. If you knew how happy I am, my horizon grows larger each day.

Today, four weeks since I left you, my darlings, I have never loved you so much. Thank my dear Mama again for having given me to God. Thank my little one for her generosity; I am not forgetting all that she has done, but above all, *He* knows it. Oh! may He give you all that He gives me; may He take you both and make you all His!

My health is still excellent. I eat so much food, I don't think you would be able to fill me up any more. I am asleep as soon as my head hits the pillow; these days that's around 10 P.M., for our Reverend Mother is letting me go to Matins. Except that on the night of our washday, my good Angel made me take a nap beforehand; so I stretched out on our bed without being afraid of messing it up (one advantage of a straw mattress) and I slept a good half-hour before going down to choir for Matins. Oh, you see, at that hour when God is so alone, it is so good to unite with Heaven to sing His praises. It seems then that Heaven and earth are one and sing the same hymn.

Our dear Mother[6] comes to the novitiate every day from 2:30 to 3 o'clock. If only you knew how good that is.... I wish my little Guite were in a little corner so she could be fed along with me!...

These days I'm going to prayer, too. So I get up at a quarter to 5. I hurry as fast as I can and almost always get to choir first; you can imagine how pleased I am!... Oh! it is good to have God so close here, under the same roof!...

A Dieu, my darling little Guite, take good care of our dear Mama, tell me about her. Tell her with a special kiss that I pray for her fervently, I love her with all my heart. I don't think my writing you will upset her; she has permitted it. Continue to receive Jesus often!

Elizabeth of the Trinity

I have received a long letter from Madame de Montléau, from Anne-Marie, and from Madame de Vathaire, who is still sick;[7] she sent me the book[8] she had promised me.

If Monsieur le Curé[9] has kept the Noël [Christmas carol] that I composed for him, bring it back!

Our Mother loves you very much, we speak of you together; my good Angel thanks you for your holy card, and Mother Sub-Prioress was very touched that Mama wrote something on her holy card, which is in her breviary.

Do you think about the little cell?[10] I am keeping my rendezvous with you there every day at 8 o'clock.

---

[1] "Today, four weeks since I left you": this "Friday" is therefore August 30, 1901.
[2] Just back from Switzerland (at least since August 21, cf. L 88), the Catezes set off again for the South of France. Perhaps they visited the shrine of Saint Magdalene at Sainte-Baume.
[3] Cf. L 64, note 3.
[4] Her mother, Guite, and herself.
[5] Her postulant's dress was dark brown in color. For dusty or heavy work, the postulant put on a white nightcap instead of the veil we see Elizabeth wearing in her photograph as a postulant.
[6] Again Mother Marie of Jesus.
[7] This refers to the young Mme. de Montléau (née Elisabeth Auburtin) whom Elizabeth met at the Château Chesnel in September 1900 (cf. L 34, note 2; see her "long letter" in PAT), to Anne-Marie d'Avout, and to Mme. de Vathaire, aunt of Antoinette de Bobet, who will be one of Elizabeth's correspondents.
[8] Unidentified.
[9] Georges Tescou, Curé of Carlipa. We do not know which "Noël" this refers to.
[10] "The little cell" (of the heart): perhaps Elizabeth's personal interiorization of her cell in Carmel of which she had long dreamed before entering (cf. *Diary*, note 136)? Or the influence of St. Catherine of Siena, who recommended "how often" to Blessed Raymond of Capua: "Make yourself a cell in your soul and never leave it" (Raymond of Capua, *Vie de Sainte Catherine de Sienne [Life of Saint Catherine of Siena]* [Paris: Sagnier et Bray, 1853], p. 25). Elizabeth could have been familiar with this anecdote from several sources.

L 90   To her Rolland aunts[1]   [August 30, 1901][2]

J. M. + J. T.   Dijon Carmel, Friday

My dear little Aunts,

I don't want this mail to arrive without bringing you a memento from your little Elizabeth, who thinks of you so much. If you could read my soul and see all the happiness that Jesus puts there, you who love me so much would be happy too! My heart is still the same, nothing has changed, I am always yours. You see, in Carmel the heart expands, and it knows how to love even better! My good Aunt doesn't understand that perhaps, tell her that I am praying fervently for her. I commend my dear Mama and my little Guite to you, thank you for your goodness, for your affection; you know how I love you. Tell Monsieur le Curé that he is remembered very especially in my prayers and that I ask him to pray fervently for me so that I may be a Carmelite through and through, which is to say, holy, for it is all the same thing! I am writing to you during grand silence at night, I don't know what I'm scribbling for I can hardly see with our little lamp. If you knew how nice it is in this little cell.... Ah, you see, Carmel is not yet Heaven, nor is it still earth. How good God is to have brought me here. Don't be jealous, my heart is very big, and you will always have your place. You are in my thoughts, my heart is close to you; can't you feel me there among you in that dear Carlipa with its beautiful Serre?[3] But the horizons of Carmel are even more beautiful, it is the Infinite. A Dieu, I kiss you with all my heart. I am leaving you to go to Matins, and I carry you in my soul close to God.

Your little Elizabeth of the Trinity

In Carmel we also have great devotion to Saint Roch. On his feast day,[4] we had a procession all over the monastery. If you could only be here in a little corner for our Offices! It is so beautiful on feast days that it makes you think of Heaven.

Greetings to good Anna.[5]

[1] In reality, unmarried cousins of Mme. Catez. "Aunt" Mathilde Rolland was 43 years old, "Aunt" Francine nearly 42. Their mother, Catherine Saignes, Mme. Catez's real aunt, lived with them at Carlipa. She is "my good Aunt" of whom the letter speaks, or "Aunt Catherine."

[2] This letter was part of the "mail" sent to Guite on "Friday," August 30 (L 89). It was the only mail sent during those weeks to Carlipa.

[3] A hill, cf. P 30, note 1.

[4] August 16. After an influenza epidemic in 1893, the community made a vow to St. Roch to implore his protection: "Since that time, every year on August 16, coming out of Vespers, we go in procession through the different parts of the monastery reciting various prayers used in such circumstances" (Chronicles of the Dijon Carmel for the year 1893).

[5] Unidentified.

L 91   To Canon Angles[1]   [September 11, 1901]
        J. M. + J. T.   Amo Christum![2]
                                            Dijon Carmel, September 11

Dear Monsieur,

Our Reverend Mother is letting me come to you, and I come with all my heart to thank you for your kindness to my dear Mama. I am not at all surprised by everything she tells me. You know how grateful I am to you: not a day passes without my praying for you. Oh! you see, I feel that all the treasures enclosed in the soul of Christ are mine, so I feel so rich; and with what happiness I come to draw from this source for all those I love and *who have done good to me.*

Oh! how good God is! I can't find words to express my happiness, every day I appreciate it more. Here there is no longer anything but Him, He is All; He suffices, and we live by Him alone. We find Him everywhere, at the wash just as at prayer! I love the hours of grand silence above all others, and it is during one of those that I am writing to you. Just picture your Elizabeth in her little cell that is so dear to her; it is our sanctuary, just for *Him* and me alone, and you can imagine the happy hours I spend there with my Beloved!

Every Sunday we have the Blessed Sacrament exposed in the oratory.[3] When I open the door and contemplate the divine Prisoner who has made me a prisoner in this dear Carmel, it seems to me that it is almost the gate to Heaven that is opening! Then I place before my Jesus all those who are in my heart, and there, close to Him, I find them again. You see that I think of you very often, and I know that you do not forget me, that every morning when you offer the Holy Sacrifice you remember your little Carmelite who confided her secret to you a *very long time ago.* I do not regret those years of waiting, my happiness is so great it really had to be paid for. Ah! how good God is!...

We are not leaving. Ah! how I love living in this time of persecution;[4] we must be saints! Ask for me that holiness I thirst for. Yes, I would like to love like the saints, like the martyrs.

I am delighted to think that my dear Mama is going to meet you again.[5] What a soul, isn't she? Tell her that I have never loved her so much and that I thank her again for having given me to God.

And my little Guite, what generosity! She does not give up easily, but
if you could look and see how completely she has let go of her big
sister! Sometimes I wonder if God will not take her too!
A Dieu, dear Monsieur, in union always, to live only by Him.
Ah! let us leave the earth, it is good to live above.[6] I ask you to bless
me with all your soul.

Marie Elizabeth of the Trinity

[1] Emilien Isidore Angles, then 66 years old and Canon at Carcassonne. Previously
Curé of Saint-Hilaire, where the Catez family had regularly visited him. As a child
Elizabeth had confided to him her first secrets about her religious vocation. She had
written him five letters in the last months before entering.
[2] "I love Christ!" The beginning of a response sung at the veiling ceremony. The
words *Amo Christum* are engraved on the crossbeam of Elizabeth's profession crucifix.
[3] Cf. Plan 1 (no. 3) of the Dijon Carmel. Behind the altar in the chapel was a large
tabernacle that faced the oratory.
[4] On July 1, 1901, the President of the Republic, Emile Loubet, signed the "Law of
Associations," primarily aimed at religious congregations, which had to ask (before
October 3, 1901) for legal authorization.
[5] At Carcassonne, or in his former parish of Saint-Hilaire, or else, as in 1900, at
Labastide at the home of the Maurels and Victor Angles (cf. L 17, note 1).
[6] Perhaps this is an echo of a thought of St. Ignatius found in Elizabeth's notebooks
of quotations (cf. PAT): "Sursum corda! Let us leave the earth! In rising, one breathes
one's native air."

L 92   To her mother   [September 12, 1901]
     J.M. + J.T.   Dijon Carmel, September 12

My darling little Mama,
     Oh! how I think of you! How I pray for you! How is your dear
health? The latest news distressed me, I wish so much that you were
better, and I assure you that your little Sabeth is fervently commending you to God. You remember in the past when you used to be sick
at night, I was always the one you awakened and who quickly ran to
you? Well, call me again now and I'll really feel it, for my soul is so
close to yours. I dearly love to speak to God of this dear little Mama
whom I love so much and whom I left for Him!...
     I saw Père Vallée last week; he was very nice. We spoke of you,
and he told me you should go to see him on your return; he will do
you a lot of good, my good little Mama.

Oh, you see, if I could just give you a little of my appetite: I devour my food; and they say I look wonderful. Madame d'Avout, who came to see me the other day, declared on seeing me that she was going to ask them to take Anne-Marie into Carmel to fatten her up, for she really looks bad. I eat everything, and things I couldn't swallow before now seem delicious to me.[1] Lately I've been going to Matins all the time, and sometimes I even stay for Lauds.[2] I'm also up at the first calling, but I assure you, I don't waste any time in bed: I have only to put my head on the pillow and I'm asleep. Beginning on Saturday, we are going to rise an hour later, for that is the rule for winter.[3] I find I'm doing housework. The blouse that I had made for entering was in such a state that Mother Prioress told me to mend it; fortunately I had some material, I did my best to patch it. When you return, I'll ask you for some black cloth to re-cover all my books, for otherwise they'll be ruined; but our Mother has told me that I can wait all the same. Oh, if you knew how good she is, she is quite *maternal,* and then she knows the little heart of her Elizabeth! The other night I had quite a scare, and I think if my little Mama had been in my place she wouldn't have been any braver. I had gone back up to our cell at 8 o'clock with our lamp. Usually I close the window when I have a light, but since I was only going in for a moment, I left it open when, all of a sudden, I felt something over my head. What did I see? A bat playing about in our cell! The good God gave me the grace not to cry out, I fled into the hallway, and I really wanted to knock on the door of Mother Sub-Prioress, who is my neighbor. But, getting up all my courage, I went back in and, since I'd removed the light, it had flown away! Kiss my very dear Aunt Sabine, my good Uncle Jules,[4] and tell them I'm praying for them every day, that I don't forget all their kindness, all their treats, and that I keep a very special place for them in my heart: I love them so much, they are so good…. A Dieu, my darling little Mama, I think this long letter will please you. Our Reverend Mother spoils you!

I send you all my love, it seems to me your big girl is on your shoulder and she's allowed to cuddle as before. Take courage, I am so happy, that doesn't make you jealous, does it? Oh, you see, if you knew how God loves you! It is there, close to Him, that Sabeth and her dear little Mama find each other again and *are made one.* Madame de Rostang and Yvonne[5] have written me. Framboise too.[6]

[1] Cf. the testimony of Mother Germaine: "In the refectory, we would never have suspected that such food disagreed with her if her mother had not informed us of it later" (PO 61).

[2] At this time, they recited Lauds the night before, immediately after Matins (see the horaria at the end of this volume, pp. 371–372).

[3] From September 14, the feast of the Exaltation of the Cross, until Easter.

[4] Unidentified. They could only be the cousins of Mme. Catez in any case.

[5] Yvonne de Rostang, another close friend from Elizabeth's youth. Her family had lived in Dijon from April 1889 until summer 1896, when she settled in Tarbes; Elizabeth visited her friend there (cf. L 11 and 14). Mme. de Rostang and Yvonne came to see her in Dijon shortly before she entered (cf. L 74).

[6] Several words that follow this have been very firmly crossed out; they probably read: "I've written to Abbé Angles." Perhaps Elizabeth was afraid of putting her mother in a bad mood.

L 93   To her sister   [September 12, 1901][1]
         J. M. + J. T.

My good little Guite,

   You are such a good little sister, and I know that my little notes make you so happy that I'm slipping one of them into Mama's letter, hoping to please you. I can't tell you enough how much I am praying for my little one, for I'm sure there are some very sad moments seeing our Mama so tired, and no more Sabeth to pour out that poor little heart to. Oh, my darling, when you're sad, tell Him, the One who knows everything, who understands everything, and who is the Guest of your soul: realize that He is within you as in a little Host.[2] He loves His little Guite so much, I am telling you for Him.... During the day, sometimes think of Him who lives in you and who so thirsts to be loved. It is close to Him that you will always find me!

   My Angel is on retreat.[3] I don't talk to her any more, and I don't even see her any more, for she goes around with her veil lowered. How envious she makes me! But she promised to take me with her, and I do in fact sense it! You see, the union of souls is so good! We must love each other above every passing thing, then nothing can separate us any more. Let's love each other like that, my Guite, let's love Him above all! And meditation? I would advise you to simplify all your reading, to fill yourself a little less, you will see that this is much better. Take your Crucifix, look, listen. You know our rendez-vous is there,[3a] and don't be troubled when you are occupied like you are now and can't do all your exercises: you can pray to God while working, it's enough to think of Him. Then all becomes sweet and easy since you're not working alone, since Jesus is there. Do reassure Mama. Several Carmels are in fact leaving, but we are staying. Our Reverend Mother is getting authorization,[4] so be at peace. A Dieu, my little darling. I'm going down to Matins and I'm carrying you in my soul close to God. Oh! how good it is to love Him, that is our calling in Carmel, you see how very sweet it is! Thank Him every day for your big sister.

Elizabeth of the Trinity

Greetings to Gabrielle.[5] If she only knew how I have the better part!...

---

[1] By the process of elimination, we conclude that this letter, "slipped" into mail addressed to Mme. Catez, could only have accompanied L 92 of September 12.

[2] Is this idea, already expressed in L 54 of May 16, 1901, indebted to the "Act of Oblation to Merciful Love" of Thérèse of Lisieux, a prayer that Elizabeth had copied at least four times? Thérèse says: "Remain in me as in a tabernacle and never separate Yourself from Your little victim" (HA 251 [SS 276]). [Here, as elsewhere, the French word *hostie* carries the meaning of both "victim" and "host"—TRANS.]

[3] Sister Marie of the Trinity. This refers to her annual private retreat.

[3a] Cf. L 80a.

[4] Actually this plan seems not to have been carried out. In any case, the Carmel was never "authorized" (cf. L 91, note 4).

[5] Undoubtedly Gabrielle Montpellier from Limoux (cf. L 11).

L 94   To her mother   [September 17, 1901][1]
       J. M. + J. T.   Dijon Carmel, Tuesday evening

My dear little Mama,
       Since my letters make you so happy, our good Mother, who understands a mother's heart so well, is letting me come to you. So I am preparing a whole packet of mail for Labastide,[2] but as I don't have much time, I'm starting it early, and every day I'll come to chat a moment with you. So don't be surprised when you see the date of my letter.
       Sunday, the feast of Our Lady of Seven Sorrows, I thought it

was a little like your own feast, my dear little Mama, so I prayed for you with such fervor! You did feel that, didn't you? I placed your soul in that of Our Lady of Sorrows and asked her to console you. At the back of the cloister we have a statue of [the] Mater Dolorosa,[3] to whom I have a great devotion. Every night I go to speak to her of you; tonight I said my little word to her before coming up to write you. I love those tears of the Virgin so much, I unite them to those my poor Mama sheds when thinking of her Elizabeth. Oh, you see, if you could read my soul, if you saw all the happiness I enjoy in Carmel, happiness so profound that I understand better each day, happiness that God alone knows! Ah! what a beautiful part He has given to His poor little one! If for one instant you could see all that, oh! my little Mama, you would have to rejoice. Since I had to have your "fiat" to enter this corner of Heaven, thank you again for having pronounced it so courageously. If you knew how God loves you! and how your daughter cherishes you more than ever!

Last week I had a visit from Madame Recoing and from Marcelle, I was surprised not to see Louise, who stayed at La Cloche[4] with her grandmother. Claire de Chatellenot, who spent several days in Dijon, also came; she couldn't get over my beautiful cheeks. Mother Sub-Prioress claims they are elastic, for they're more *filled out* every day. Ah! if you could only do as I do, my dear little Mama. Eating and sleeping well, they say, are the conditions for making a good Carmelite; in that I leave nothing to be desired. I even ask God to give me a little less sleep. I had a first-rate humiliation at Matins: it seems I'd fallen half asleep. Mother Sub-Prioress, who was watching me, saw my head go off to one side, our breviary to the other, so she came to signal me to go off to my little bed, which woke me up completely. Very edifying, wasn't it? I'm delighted about your stay at Labastide. tell Monsieur Angles that I mention him to God every day, that I unite myself to him when I recite the Divine Office and that I ask him to say it in union with his little Carmelite, who is so grateful for all that he is doing for my dear Mama. The bell is about to call me to Matins, I leave you without leaving you, for I carry you in my soul, close to the One who is all Love.[5] Ah! how sweet it is to be His, if only you knew all my happiness!

A Dieu, darling little Mama, I place myself in your arms to be cuddled. Your little Sabeth who loves you more than ever.

Aunt Francine has written to me and gives me much better news of your health, which has made me very happy. *Let* our good little Guite *take care of you.*

---

[1] "Sunday," the feast of Our Lady of (Seven) Sorrows, which at that time was celebrated on the third Sunday of September, was thus the 15th in 1901. The "Tuesday" of the letter is September 17.

[2] For the guests of the Maurel family, as in 1900 (L 33). The other letters in this "whole packet" of mail have been lost except for L 95. There was probably one for Marie-Louise Maurel, who would be married on September 30.

[3] Cf. Plan 1 of the Dijon Carmel, no. 8, in this volume.

[4] The main hotel in Dijon. The Recoings, friends of the Catezes, had left Dijon in 1899 for Romans.

[5] The first appearance in the letters from Carmel of this characteristic expression of Elizabeth, already used previously in P 57, L 57, L 58. Perhaps it is an echo of a quotation from St. Ignatius (cf. PAT): "Let us give all the love we can to the God who is all Love."

L 95   **To her sister**   [around September 20, 1901][1]
          J. M. + J. T.   Amo Christum!

How happy I am, my dear little one, to think that this letter is going to find you at Labastide, where you'll have a big sister[2] to replace your Sabeth; but you do know, don't you, that she is quite close to you, our souls are so united in the One who is all Love. Oh! how good it is to be His! On October 2nd we will be united very specially to pray for our dear Papa.[3] You see, I think he is so happy when he looks down from Heaven on his little one in Carmel. Ever since I've been here, I have felt so much closer to him. Oh! how good it is in Carmel! Don't be afraid that my happiness will pass, for God is its sole object, and "He never changes"![4]

Mother Sub-Prioress is on retreat[5] with her veil lowered, and I don't say a word to her anymore, but I'm so happy to see her all lost in God that I'm not sorry at all, that's how we must love each other. My two neighbors in the cells next to mine[6] are on retreat, if you knew how envious that makes me!

Madame Massiet[7] wrote me a few lines to ask my prayers for her brother, the one who has been at Carcassonne; he just underwent a very serious operation on his throat, and the doctors were afraid they couldn't save him. Our Reverend Mother let me write a few lines right away. Oh! my Guite, how good it is in our dear cell! When I return to it, how I feel that I'm there all alone with my Bridegroom in whom I have everything, which is to say, my little one, that I can't say how happy I am. I spend some very pleasant hours there: I settle down with my Crucifix[8] in front of our little window, then I sew fervently while my soul stays close to Him. A Dieu, I'm going down to choir to say Matins and, I hope, Lauds.[9] I send you all my love, thanking you again for all that you've done for your big sister.

M. E. of the Trinity

I don't have any more stamps, when will you return?

I haven't hurt you by telling you of my happiness? Don't be jealous, I think so much about you, my darlings whom I love so much!

[1] The letter, sent to "Labastide" like the preceding one, was a part of that "whole packet of mail" that Elizabeth wrote at intervals over several days (cf. L 94). It can only be dated approximately. See also note 5.
[2] Marie-Louise Maurel.
[3] This was the anniversary of his death in 1887.
[4] Teresa of Avila. Cf. D 92, note 88.
[5] Mother Germaine speaks in a letter to Abbé Jaillet, dated "September 1901," of her next ten-day retreat, which would take place during the period of September 24, 29, and 30.
[6] On her left, Sister Aimée of Jesus; on her right (cf. L 92), Mother Germaine of Jesus (until her next election as Prioress).
[7] Wife of General Massiet, friends of the Catezes. The letter Elizabeth wrote has been lost.
[8] Her large profession crucifix that she brought with her when she entered (cf. L 156, note l).
[9] Cf. L 92, note 2. Elizabeth "hopes" that she will not be sent to rest after Matins.

L 96   To Alice Chervau   [September 29, 1901][1]
J. M. + J. T.   Dijon Carmel, Sunday

My very dear Alice,

I cannot believe what they just told me, and my heart is with you constantly. I have gone through this anguish, so I understand your sorrow and know how tender, how sensitive is the heart of my poor little Alice whom I love so much!

I have been close to the Blessed Sacrament, which we have in the oratory; I have placed your dear patient close to the good Master and said to Him, "Lord, the one you love is sick."[2] Trust Him, my dear Alice, He is all-powerful and we are praying with all our soul! I have not forgotten all the goodness and consideration you showed my dear Mama when she too was so sick, and I am asking my Bridegroom to return all that to you. Courage, your poor mother must need you very much to cheer her up. Tell her, won't you, how much I am uniting myself to you both and that my heart does not leave you. I kiss you with much affection, my very dear Alice, remember that you are not alone, that God is with you to sustain you. Abandon yourself into His arms, He is all Love.

M. Elizabeth of the Trinity

In Carmel we are praying fervently for your dear patient.

[1] In a letter to the Dijon Carmel on May 12, 1963, Alice Chervau, who had become Mme. de Confévron, testified that she received this letter at the moment of her father's death (September 30, 1901). On that "Sunday" M. Chervau was not yet dead but very sick; thus it was September 29, 1901.
[2] Jn 11:3.

L 97   To her sister   [October 10, 1901][1]
        J. M. + J. T.   Dijon Carmel, Thursday

My darling little Guite,

We're having a holiday in Carmel, for our elections took place yesterday. Oh! if you knew how, in taking away our good Mother whom I loved so much,[2] God has given me two others who are so good, so good! You see, it is delightful, and that makes me love still more this good Master who spoils His little one so much. Our dear Mother Sub-Prioress was elected Prioress, and my good Angel, Sub-Prioress; this good news is really going to delight my dear little Mama, and I've been anxious to announce it to you. Because of the elections we're having a free day, that is, we can have little visits with each other during the day. But, you see, the life of a Carmelite is silence, so she loves that above all! Oh, how good Carmel is; I can't find words to say this enough! Tuesday[3] we're going to celebrate the feast of Saint Teresa, and I'm already delighted about it. We'll have the Blessed Sacrament in choir, and on that day I think I can stay there as much as I want; so you can imagine how I'm going to indulge myself! You'll be there with me, my darlings. I so love to speak of you to God.... There, close to Him, I find you again, for there is no separation for souls. Ah! how I love you! I have never felt it so much!...

As for interesting things, we've done the wash. I set about it with such ardor that I had blisters that night, but in Carmel everything is delightful, for we find God everywhere. More and more this seems like a corner of Heaven to me. Ah! how I thank my little Mama for having said her "fiat" that opened the prison of love to me.[4] Thanks too to my little one who has done so much for her big sister. God knows all that. Ah! how He loves you! You see, it does me good to see all the love that surrounds you, my darlings whom I love so much!

What happiness that our little Mama is better! I'm so pleased to know that you're at dear Madame de Guardia's house; I'm sure she hasn't forgotten this little Elizabeth who keeps so good a place for her in her heart. Thank Marguerite and Jeanne[5] for all their goodness to you; I'm so grateful to them for the affection they've lavished on my little one.... It seems you talk about me together, but if you knew how I, too, behind my dear grille, speak of you with my Beloved, with the One who is all Love....

A Dieu, my little one, I'm leaving you to go to Matins, and I'm carrying you in my soul. Kiss my dear little Mama, tell her that I love her *very much, very much.* All my affection to Marguerite and Jeanne, a very special remembrance to my dear Madame Berthe whom I love so much.[6] Thank them for their goodness to Mama. Keep the best of my heart for yourself.

E. of the Trinity

Tuesday, even closer union.

---

[1] According to the Book of Elections of the Dijon Carmel, it was indeed "yesterday," on October 9, 1901, that Mother Germaine of Jesus (who also held the office of Mistress of Novices) was elected Prioress and Sister Marie of the Trinity (who remained Elizabeth's "Angel" during these first days), Sub-Prioress. The two religious, aged 31 and 26 respectively, bore the title "Mother" by virtue of their office.

[2] Mother Marie of Jesus, who had become Prioress at Paray-le-Monial.

[3] October 15. We do not know who preached on this occasion.

[4] By adding the word "love," Elizabeth changes the perspective of the classic comparison of Carmel with a prison (because of the cloistered life and the grilles), a comparison she must have heard often. The image of the "prisoner," which we meet for the first time in Elizabeth's writings on October 15, 1899, in P 72, is surely due in part to Thérèse of Lisieux. Elizabeth had copied (cf. PAT) the passage in which Thérèse dreams of becoming a "prisoner in Carmel" (HA 95 [SS 125]); see also HA 110 and 137 [SS 141 and 175]). When Elizabeth says that the grilles of her monastery seem "all golden" (L 109), she is again using an expression borrowed from Thérèse (poem "La volière" [The Aviary]—referring to Carmel—"de l'Enfant-Jésus" [of the Child Jesus], HA 366.

The term "prisoner" (of love) appears in L 111, 116, 137, 243, 303, P 74, and 123, a comparison sometimes paired with that of Jesus or God as "prisoner" (L 91, 108, 109, 198). As early as 1898 (P 57), the *Tabernacle* is a "prison of love," where Jesus is held "captive" (P 56, 57, 67). Elizabeth was surely touched by another image of Thérèse of Lisieux in "Vivre d'amour" [Living on Love] (HA 330); we found in her breviary (how long had it been there?) one stanza from that poem written around the picture of Thérèse holding a harp: "O Trinity! You are Prisoner / Of my love!..." Elizabeth also read the poem "Mon ciel à moi" [Heaven for Me] (HA 354), in which Thérèse expresses this profoundly "Elizabethan" idea: "I've found my heaven in the Blessed Trinity / Which dwells in my heart, my prisoner of love."

We can also link with the image of the Carmelite prisoner the words "to take captive" (cf. L 110, note 2) and "to chain": Elizabeth refers to St. Paul, "the one chained by Christ" (cf. L 179, note 14). P. Vallée—among others—often used these expressions, which fostered their use in the Dijon Carmel. The expression "all His" (cf. L 99, note 2) also belongs to the "Valléen fund" [of expressions].

Finally, we should note that the image of the prisoner also contains for Elizabeth the spirituality of the religious *vows* (which bind one to the Lord: "the vows that will unite me to Him forever," L 149), in the climate of the "persecution" of religious in France at that time: the example of the Carmelites of Compiègne, prisoners and finally martyrs, was then very current. They were to be beatified in 1906.

[5] Daughters of Mme. Gout de Bize (cf. the following note).

[6] Mme. Berthe Gout de Bize, whom we meet again in the correspondence of 1906. She was the sister-in-law of Mme. de Guardia.

L 98   To Françoise de Sourdon   [October-November 1901][1]
        J. M. + J. T.   Dijon Carmel, Sunday

My dear little Françoise,

        Since our Mother has given me leave to write you, I'm taking advantage of this Sunday to come to you. I think they're spoiling you, my darling, but you know on what condition!...

        I see my Framboise has hardly been converted. This certainly grieves me. In the past I overlooked these fits of temper, but now you're no longer a baby and these scenes are ridiculous. I know that you'll allow your Sabeth anything, so I'm telling you what I think! You absolutely must get to work on this! You see, my darling, you have my nature,[2] I know what you can do. Ah, if you knew how good it is to love God and to give Him what He asks, especially when that costs, you wouldn't hesitate for so long to listen to me. Of course in the beginning you feel only the sacrifice, but you will see, my Framboise, how after that you experience a delightful peace! If you knew how I think of you.... You see, nothing has changed, I am always your little mother. Ah, I would like you to be so good. I'm going to tell you something: since I'm not there to receive the overflowing of your little heart at every moment: each time you feel the need to confide in me, run off to your room and there, between your Crucifix and my picture, since you love it so much, recollect yourself for a moment and imagine that I am there with the good Jesus and my Framboise. Every time you avoid a scene or an argument with Marie-Louise,[3] or when you feel in too ugly a mood, you'll come there, won't you? Is that agreed?

I did as you asked that very night. I think since I'm being nice, you can really make me happy. I love you so much, my darling, you know you're my little child and I don't love anyone else as I do you. Do you want to continue our rendez-vous at 8 P.M. as at Mont-Dore?[4]

A Dieu, darling, I leave you without letting you go, for I keep you in my soul. Thank Jesus for me, for I am so happy. You don't understand that, but if you knew how good it is to live only in Him.... I'm asking Him with all my soul to teach you that.

Your Sabeth

Tell your good mother that I pray every day for her intentions. Greetings to Marie-Louise. Kisses to my Guite.

---

[1] Handwriting from 1901. The "kisses to Guite" implies that she had returned from her long trip in the South of France. On the other hand, it was not yet December 1, when correspondence stopped because of Advent.

[2] Proud and energetic, but sensitive and thin-skinned. "You have such an ardent heart" (L 182).

[3] Her sister.

[4] Cf. L 65. This refers to a rendez-vous of prayer. The time of grand silence began at 8 P.M., after Compline.

L 99   **To Canon Angles**   [December 1, 1901]
        J. M. + J. T.   Dijon Carmel, December 1

Very dear Monsieur,

    I am so very happy to announce to you my immense happiness, to which, I know, you have contributed a large part. Do I need to express my profound gratitude to you? You know the heart of your little Elizabeth and you know how she repays all her debts to those she loves!

    On the 8th, that beautiful feast of her Immaculate Conception, Mary is going to clothe me in my dear Carmelite habit.[1] I will prepare myself for the beautiful day of my betrothal by a three-day retreat. Oh! you see, when I think about it, I already feel as if I am no longer on earth! Pray much for your little Carmelite, that she may be wholly surrendered, wholly given, and that she may give joy to her Master's Heart. On Sunday I would like to give Him something special, for I so love my Christ.... Oh! how happy I would have been to have you very close to me, I know that if you could, you would not refuse me this great joy. Your soul, I know, will be completely in communion with that of the happy betrothed who is finally going to give herself to Him who has been calling her for so long and who wants her to be all His.[2] Ask Him that I might live no longer but that He might live in me,[3] then with all your soul, bless your happy and grateful little child.

                                      Elizabeth of the Trinity

    Thank you for your kind feastday wishes.[4] I cannot write to my dear Marie-Louise,[5] please tell her of my happiness.

---

[1] In the afternoon. The bishop, Msgr. Le Nordez, presided at the ceremony; P. Vallée preached.

[2] "All His": an expression familiar to P. Vallée that we meet again in L 54, 81, 89, P 82. The use of "tout," meaning "all" or "wholly," before an adjective (often several times, e.g., "wholly surrendered, wholly given") has the same origin and becomes quite natural to Elizabeth; besides, it suited her absolutist temperament very well.

[3] Cf. Gal 2:20.

[4] On the feast of St. Elizabeth, November 19.

[5] Maurel, who had become Mme. Ambry.

L 100   To Sister Marie-Xavier of Jesus   [December 3, 1901(?)]¹
+

The whole soul of your little sister celebrates with yours. Listen to what rises for you from her heart to the heart of Christ.... Then let us lose ourselves in Him.

E.²

¹ This little note must have accompanied a poem that has been lost, perhaps on the occasion of the feast of St. Francis Xavier. The writing is certainly from 1901 or 1902.
² Elizabeth encloses the capital letter within a triangle, the symbol of the Trinity.

L 101   To Mother Germaine   [December 25, 1901]¹

O my adored Word, in silence whisper softly to Our Mother what the very grateful heart of her novice cannot express. Then carry us away into those realms of peace, light, and love where the "One" is consumed in the Three!

Christmas 1901 +

¹ Written in pencil on the back of a lace-trimmed holy card representing the Infant Jesus seated on the manger before a cross and holding a chalice with a host in one hand, and in the other a book with the inscription *Ego sum vita* and several little crosses.... On the back is a printed meditation on "Jesus, our Emmanuel, through the Incarnation and through the Eucharist."

L 102   To Sister Marie of the Trinity   [December 25, 1901]¹

The whole soul of Christ is in this Little One. It is there that your Tobias² awaits you. Let us allow ourselves to be caught and carried away in His brightness. He comes to say all, to show all.

Christmas 1901 +

¹ In pencil, on the back of a holy card identical to that of L 101.
² In reference to Tb 5, the new religious was called "Tobias," helped by her "Angel."

L 103   To her mother   [December 25, 1901][1]
          J. M. + J. T.   December

My darling little Mama,
      God has not separated us. Nothing has changed, and your
little Sabeth comes as always to be cuddled and to tell you with a big
kiss that she loves you very much, very much! So no sadness today, if
you knew how close I am to you! It is so good to meet again close to
God, it seems to me there is no more separation there, no more
distance, "in Him, we have all."[2] O darling Mama, if you knew how
the Master loves you, how He blesses your sacrifice…. He has said
that "Whoever does the will of my Father is my father, my mother,
my sister."[3] It seems to me that it is to you He is addressing these
words; the little Jesus in the manger holds out His arms to you with
love and calls you His "mother." You have given Him your daughter
to be His little bride, and now He has become your beloved child.
You see, He has taken me in order to give Himself more to you. Listen to Him, be very quiet, He will deliver all my messages to you. It
is to this Christ, my adored Fiancé, that I entrust my wishes, my affection, my thanks for my dear Mama and my little Guite whom I
love with all my heart.
                          Elizabeth of the Trinity,[4]
                          very happy in her Carmel.

[1] This letter of "December" (1901, judging from the handwriting) was written at
Christmas (after the long silence of Advent), as the particular style of this "today,"
the wishes, and "the little Jesus in the manger holding out His arms" suggest.
[2] The quotation marks that Elizabeth places at the end (but not at the beginning)
indicate a quotation, perhaps Rom 11:36 or the "Prayer of a Soul Taken with Love,"
by St. John of the Cross (*Oeuvres*, t. I, 1894 ed., p. 477 [K-RJ 668-69]): "Yours is all of
this, and all is for you…." This prayer is very well known in Carmel. The passage is
quoted in HA 308.
[3] Mt 12:50. Elizabeth writes "father" instead of "brother" as used in the Gospel text.
Cf. L 143, note 4.
[4] This is the first time Elizabeth signs a letter to her mother with her religious name.

L 104   To her sister   [January 7(?), 1902][1]

      May God teach my little Guite the secret of happiness: it con-
sists in union, in love!… No longer being anything but "one" with

Him, that is to have one's Heaven in faith while awaiting the vision face to face!...

January 1902.   Elizabeth of the Trinity +

¹ The autograph has disappeared. The Process and Notebook 4 indicate "January 1902" as the date. A loose-leaf copy made during Mother Germaine's lifetime (there are notes in her handwriting) and preserved in the ACD summary specifies: January 7, 1902, and: "Text on the back of a picture." Philipon's dossier, without specifying the date, gives some detailed information about the autograph: "On a picture with New Year's greetings."

L 105   To Françoise de Sourdon   [January 28, 1902]¹
         J. M. + J. T.

My darling Françoise,
    I'm sending you my whole heart as a feastday bouquet. You can really feel, can't you, that it's quite close to yours and that nothing has changed between us? It seems to me that the grilles cannot be a separation between two souls as united as those of Framboise and her Sabeth, and if you don't know how to find me, it's really *your fault,* for I've indicated where our "Rendez-vous"² is, and I assure you that I don't hold back from going there to find you!...
    Our good Mother, to whom I often speak of my little Françoise, is going to let a pretty little Carmelite³ out of the cloister, and she will carry all my feastday greetings to you: don't make too much noise around her; remember that she is coming from the solitude of Carmel, and don't scare her away!
    O my Framboise, may she bring you a little of the sweetness of your holy patron; may she teach you the secret of true happiness. You see, I love you so much, I would like you to be so good.... Ah! what fine words I say for you to God!
    A Dieu, darling Framboise, don't forget what you promised me. I love you very much and I send you the best in my heart.
                                      Sr. Elizabeth of the Trinity

    I send all my gratitude to your good mother. I don't know how to thank her for her kindnesses to my dear Mama. Remember me

respectfully to Madame d'Anthès, tell her that I am praying with all
my soul and am full of confidence: it seems to me that my prayer is
all-powerful, for it is not I who am praying but my Christ *who is within
me!* [4]

Love and thanks to Marie-Louise.

[1] For her feast (St. Francis de Sales), January 29.
[2] Cf. L 98, note 4.
[3] A doll.
[4] A Pauline background. Cf. Gal 2:20 (already quoted in L 99) and Rom 8:15 and 26.

L 106   To Madame de Bobet   [February 10, 1902]
        J. M. + J. T.   Dijon Carmel, February 10

Very dear Madame,
        I don't know how to thank you, you have spoiled me so much;
if you knew how much pleasure you have given me! I so desired this
beautiful *Canticle* of Saint John of the Cross, and, given by you with
this pretty thought on its first page,[1] it is doubly precious to me. It is
right here beside me on my little board in our dear little cell; but
will I tell you that I need to look at it in order to think of you, dear
Madame? Oh no, of course not, for my thoughts and my heart, or
rather my soul, find you in the One near whom there is neither separation nor distance and in whom it is so good to meet. Would you
like Him to be our "Rendez-vous," our Meeting Place, dear Madame? Our souls have certainly made an impact on each other: we
know each other very little and we love each other so much. Oh! it
is Jesus who has done that; may He thus bind us together and may
He consume us in the flames of His love.
        A Dieu, dear Madame, know that behind the grilles of Carmel
you have a little heart that keeps a very faithful memory of you, a
soul wholly united to yours and deeply fond of you. Thank you
again. I don't know how to say it, it is He who will bring it to you on
behalf of His little fiancée.
                                        Elizabeth of the Trinity

A kiss to dear little Simone.[2]

[1] The book *Vie et oeuvres de saint Jean de la Croix*, vol. 4, *Le Cantique spirituel et La vive Flamme d'amour [Life and Works of Saint John of the Cross*, vol. 4, *The Spiritual Canticle and The Living Flame of Love]*, 1892, 3d ed., autographed on February 3, 1902, by Mme. de Bobet, carries this thought: "Jesus gave us the Cross so the Cross might give us Love."
[2] Her daughter.

L 107   To Mother Marie of Jesus

[February 11 (or a little before), 1902][1]

J.M. + J.T.   Amo Christum!

My good Mother,
    You must find your little Elizabeth very silent. If her pen is quiet, her soul and her heart at least do not keep from going to find you in Him who always remains while all passes and all changes around us! Oh! my good Mother, offer a few prayers that the little "house of God"[2] might be wholly filled, wholly invaded by the Three! I have set off into the soul of my Christ, and there I am going to spend my Lent. Ask Him that I might live no longer, but that He might live in me,[3] that the "One" might be consumed more every day, that I might always remain beneath[4] the great vision! It seems to me that this is the secret of sanctity, and it is so simple! Oh my good Mother, to think that we have our Heaven within us, that Heaven for which I am sometimes homesick…. How good it will be when the veil is lifted at last, and we have the joy of being face to face with Him whom alone we love! In the meantime I live in love, I am immersed in it, I am lost in it.[5] It is the Infinite, that infinity for which my soul is starving. But you know the soul of your Elizabeth, for whom you have done so much. She does not forget all that; you know God has given her a grateful heart, a heart that is loving and full of tenderness for the good Mother who taught her to love the Master for whom she would like to die of love! Permit your little one to kiss you, bless her with all your soul and keep her in it, very close to Him!…

Elizabeth of the Trinity

[1] Handwriting of 1902; lacks the "r.c.i." used after her profession. Written a little before "Lent," which began on February 12.
[2] This is the meaning of the Hebrew name "Elizabeth." Mother Marie of Jesus had revealed this to her on the day of her first Communion, April 19, 1891 (cf. AL).

[3] Cf. Gal 2:20.
[4] To be "beneath," a turn of phrase often used by P. Vallée, as were the words "to invade" or "to possess" and "vision," and the expressions "soul of Christ" and "to be consumed in the One." It should be noted that Marie of Jesus, the former Prioress of Dijon, had P. Vallée as a spiritual director from January 1895 until January 1901. P. Vallée was the prior of the Dominicans at Dijon.
[5] "To be lost," cf. L 110, note 3.

L 108   To her Rolland aunts   [February 11, 1902][1]
         J. M. + J. T.

My good little Aunts,

        Lent already, I can't believe it.... Time passes so quickly in Carmel, where for six months I have had the happiness of being the little prisoner of Him who made Himself a prisoner for us![2] I don't forget you, and I pray for you every day, you can really feel that, can't you? We had the Blessed Sacrament exposed for Forty Hours, and it was very good to come console Him. It's even so good that you would like to stay there forever, don't you agree, Aunt Francine? Do you remember when my little Aunt Mathilde used to tease the two Magdalenes[3] who had begun to pray instead of decorate the chapel?[4] Fortunately, while being Martha[5] one can remain like Mary Magdalene always near the Master, contemplating Him with a wholly loving look. And that is our life in Carmel, for, although prayer is our principal and even our unique occupation, for the prayer of a Carmelite never ceases, we also have works, external acts. I wish you could see me at the wash, with my habit turned up and splashing around in the water. You doubt my ability in this field, and with good reason, but with Jesus I tackle everything, and I find everything *charming*, nothing is difficult or boring. Oh! how good it is in Carmel, it is the best country in the world, and I can say that I am as happy as a fish in water. My Aunt[6] has difficulty believing me; kiss her for me and keep for yourselves what is best in the heart of your little one who loves you so much and will never forget you.

                                        Sr. Elizabeth of the Trinity

My respects to Monsieur le Curé.

[1] "Forty Hours" are over. It is therefore the evening of February 11, the night before "Lent" (1902, according to the handwriting and the absence of "r.c.i." after Elizabeth's signature, indicating that she was still a novice).

[2] On the two prisoners, see L 97, note 4.

[3] Probably Aunt Francine and Elizabeth; perhaps Elizabeth and Guite.

[4] In 1875 the maternal grandfather of the two Rolland aunts gave the white marble altar of the chapel of the Blessed Virgin as well as the painted terra cotta statue of Mary that is still on that altar. Mathilde and Francine Rolland were sacristans or churchwardens for the church of Carlipa and until their death took jealous care of that chapel.

[5] Cf. Lk 10:38–42.

[6] Their mother, Aunt Catherine.

L 109   To her sister   [February 16, 1902][1]

       J. M. + J. T.   Dijon Carmel, Sunday

My darling Guite,

What a happy surprise, a letter from Sabeth in Lent! You see, God is very good, and our Mother too, and they are the ones who are sending me to tell my little one that on Thursday my prayer will be very intense and that the two of us will be *one*, besides that won't be anything new, will it, for we never leave each other? You know very well the prayer that Christ made to His Father: "I want them to be one, as you and I are one."[2] Well, when that "oneness" has been achieved between souls, it seems to me that separation is no longer possible; you really feel that, don't you? Saturday[3] I was following you, my darlings, I saw that train that took you away, but it seemed to me that you were not moving farther away, for that is how it is with the One who is Unchanging, He who always remains and in whom we always find each other!...

I'm sending my letter to you in Lunéville; I imagine you're there right now. Give all my love to good Mademoiselle Adeline,[4] tell her the grilles of Carmel, which made her freeze and seemed so somber to her, seem all golden to me. Ah! if we could only raise the curtain, what a beautiful horizon we would see on the other side! It is the Infinite, that is why it expands every day. Darling Guite, don't cry for your Sabeth, if you knew what a good little nest my Beloved is preparing for me here. Ah! this Carmel, this being alone[5] with Him whom we love, if you knew how good it is! Yes, it is an anticipated Heaven. Don't be jealous, my darlings, He *alone* knows what

I've sacrificed in leaving you, and if His love had not sustained me, if He had not held me very tight in His arms, ah! I really feel I could not have done it; I love you both so much, and it seems to me that this love grows every day, for He is divinizing it!

I had a delightful, *divine* Shrovetide. Monday and Tuesday we had the Blessed Sacrament in the oratory and on Sunday in the choir; I spent nearly my whole day close to Him, and my Guite was there with me, for it seems to me that I *keep her in my soul.* It was very nice, I assure you. We were in darkness for the grille was open,[6] and all the light came from Him. I so love to see this great grille between us: He is a prisoner for me, and I am a prisoner for Him!

Since Mama is interested in news of my health, tell her I am doing quite well. Lent isn't tiring me; I don't even notice it, and then I have a good little Mother who watches over me with a quite *maternal* heart. My dear Mama may be at peace, her little one is well cared for, well loved. As for the cold, I wouldn't know it was winter if I did not see the beautiful curtains God has hung at our little window. If you could see how lovely our cloister is with its frosted panes! Have you learned of the death of Mademoiselle Galmiche, the one who was with the *Dames de la retraite?* [7] Her friend Mademoiselle Rouget is very ill; Madame Sagot has written me to ask for prayers. Darling Mama, don't you think it is better for her to give her daughter to God and to enjoy her happiness than to let her be taken by Him?

A Dieu, darling Guite, may Christ bring my love to you, along with all my soul would like to tell you. Don't leave Him, live in His intimacy; it is there that we are made one.

All my affection, darling Mama, and thank you. God is so pleased; if you could see with what love He looks at you![8]

Thank Mademoiselle Adeline for her affection for us, and thank Madame Cosson. Tell Madame Massiet that her little Carmelite is very united to her.

---

[1] Lent has begun. This "Sunday" is February 16, before the "Thursday [when her] prayer will be very intense," for on February 20 Guite will celebrate her 19th birthday.

[2] Quoting from memory, Elizabeth mixes Jn 17:24 and 22.

[3] Yesterday, February 15.

[4] Adeline Lalande, a close friend of Mme. Catez. On her "sudden chill" when faced

with the grilles, cf. L 64. Mme. Cosson, named farther down, was her sister.
[5] "Alone with the Alone" (cf. L 162, 297, etc.; LR 23): an old maxim in Carmel originating with Teresa of Avila, who in closing her *Life* (chap. 36, p. 543 in the de Bouix trans., 1857 ed. [K-RT, Vol. 1, 36:29]), said of her Sisters at San José: "This is what they must always have as their aim: to be alone with Him alone."
[6] That is, the interior wooden grille, covered with a light black veil; they then closed the shutters of the choir windows.
[7] The person and institute are unknown.
[8] Cf. L 85. An allusion to Mk 10:21: "Jesus looked at him with love." For the second time, Elizabeth reverses the perspective here by applying Jesus' look, not to the one who is leaving her family, but to the family who is permitting their child to leave them. She does the same thing with the "hundredfold" promised by Jesus (cf. L 196, note 6).

L 110   To her sister   [February 16(?), 1902][1]

May Christ take my darling Guite captive,[2] put her in chains and invade her, that she may be lost in Him like a drop of water in the ocean![3]

Let us remain in His Love,[4] for that is where He keeps a rendez-vous with the two little sisters in order to fuse them into unity.

Elizabeth of the Trinity

[1] Written on the back of a little holy card representing Mary Magdalene kissing the feet of the Crucified. This text can be placed in this period with some certainty both by the ink and by the handwriting. Perhaps it accompanied L 109 for Guite's birthday.
[2] Perhaps an echo of Teresa of Avila's Exclamation 17, [K-RT, Vol. 1, Soliloquies 17] which Elizabeth will later copy (cf. L 255)? Already in 1899, Elizabeth had found this expression in Thérèse of Lisieux in transcribing "La Volière de l'Enfant-Jésus" [The Aviary of the Child Jesus] (HA 366). The expression is found again in L 121, 128, 130, 133, 171, 199; P 77, 84, 88. This term was also part of P. Vallée's vocabulary in the passive form "captivated."
[3] The same series of images in L 190; we find here the influence of the account of Thérèse of Lisieux' first Communion (HA 57 [SS 77]), which she had copied (cf. PAT) and had already used at least three times (cf. *Diary*, note 149 and 157). Let us underline in Thérèse the images that reappear in this text of Elizabeth's: "... a *fusion*. We were no longer two; Thérèse had vanished *as a drop of water is lost* in the immensity of the *ocean*."
The image of the ocean is found in Elizabeth in L 129, 177, 190, 293; HF 13; P 115. Cf. also L 292: "[the heart] of the Three, the immense sea." The image of "waves" and "to overflow" also appears a number of times, following Thérèse's example; she asks, in her "Act of Oblation" (often used by Elizabeth), that God allow "the waves of tenderness shut up within [Him] to overflow into my soul" (HA 251 [SS 277]), and

describes the effects of her offering as "oceans of graces that flooded" her soul (HA 144 [SS 181]).

The ocean image returns twice, explicitly in "chapter 11" of HA (which played an undeniable role in Elizabeth's life): "the soul who plunges into the shoreless ocean of Your Love" (HA 196 [SS 254]) and Thérèse's love, which "is not even like a drop of dew lost in the Ocean!" (HA 198 [SS 256])—and implicitly in the image of the "navigator perceiving [love's luminous] beacon that must lead him to the port" (HA 208-209 [SS 195]); Elizabeth takes up this series of images again in P 98.

At the end of her life, Elizabeth also appreciated St. John of the Cross's description of the death of love: "Then the rivers of love escape from the soul and go to be lost in the ocean of divine love" (LF 478 [K-RJ 1:30]). In John of the Cross, however, the image of fire dominates that of water.

The words "to be lost" and "abyss" are connected to the image of the ocean (cf. L 292, note 2).
4 Cf. Jn 15:9.

L 111   To Canon Angles   [April 7, 1902][1]

         J. M. + J. T.   Dijon Carmel, April 7

Dear Monsieur le Chanoine,

If you only knew how good it is to spend Lent, Holy Week, and Easter in Carmel—it is something unique! With what joy I sang Alleluia, wrapped in the white mantle, clothed in the dear habit that I have so longed to wear. It was quite wonderful, I assure you, to spend Holy Thursday close to Him, and I would have spent the night as well, but the Master wanted me to rest. But that does not matter, does it? We find Him in our sleep just as we do in prayer, since He is in everything, everywhere, and always! At 2 o'clock I went down to choir; you can guess what a *glorious* time I had, and also what I said on your behalf! More and more I love the dear grilles that make me His prisoner of love. It is so good to think that we are prisoners, in chains for each other; more than that, that we are but one victim, offered to the Father for souls, so that they may be wholly consummated in Unity.

When you think of your little Carmelite, thank Him who has given her so beautiful a part. Sometimes I think that it is an anticipated Heaven: the horizon is so beautiful, it is He! Oh! what will it be like above since here below He already makes our union so intimate? You know my homesickness for Heaven, it does not diminish, for I already live in that Heaven, since I carry it within me; in Carmel it seems that we are already so near. Won't you come to see me some day and continue through the grille the fine conversations you used to have with your little Elizabeth? Do you remember the first time I confided my secret to you in the cloister of Saint-Hilaire?[2] I spent some happy moments with you and I am asking God to reward you for the good you have done me. I still remember my joy when I was able to have a little conference with you and entrust my great secret to you. I was only a child, but you never doubted the divine call!

I have not seen my dear Mama yet; I am expecting her at the first opportunity. My little Guite came last week. It had been nearly two months since we had seen each other, so you can guess what a meeting it was! I am overjoyed to see all the good God is doing in the souls of my darlings. He has taken me in order to give Himself more, and I can see I am doing them much more good in my dear Carmel than when I was near them; oh, how good God is! I am leaving you to go to prayer where we have the Blessed Sacrament exposed every Sunday. I only have time to ask your blessing; I know it is a fatherly one for your little Carmelite.

                                        M. Elizabeth of the Trinity

Thank you very much for your pretty holy card. Please give my greetings to my dear Marie-Louise. Tell her she has certainly not been forgotten!

[1] This letter, dated April 7, is surely from 1902, in which "Sunday" actually fell on April 6. But perhaps Elizabeth confused Sunday with the Annunciation, a feast that was deferred that year because of Holy Week and celebrated on April 7, a day when the Blessed Sacrament was also exposed.
[2] Cf. RB 5 of Canon Angles in PAT. Abbé Angles was Curé of Saint-Hilaire when Elizabeth, at seven years of age, confided to him her desire for religious life.

L 112   To Berthe Guémard   [April 22, 1902][1]
        J. M. + J. T.   Dijon Carmel, Tuesday

My dear little Berthe,
        My heart is rejoicing and united to the joy of yours, and along with you I count the days that separate you from the first visit of your Beloved Jesus. Ah! how He too is waiting for that blessed day when

He will finally give Himself to His little Berthe and make her, like the beloved Apostle, rest on his heart![2] When you are there, my darling, don't forget your Angel who loves you so much: behind her dear grilles, she will be very united to you. I will offer Holy Communion for you, and it is there, close to the good God, that we will meet, both of us beneath our white veils, since He has given me the veil of the betrothed, of the virgins who follow the Lamb everywhere.[3] You will come to see me, and on that day I will be able to open the curtain[4] for you and read in the eyes of my little Berthe all the joy that her Jesus has left. More than that, it will be He Himself I will see in the dear communicant, for it is not for only a few moments that He comes to her, but in order to remain in her always; remember that well. And when the beautiful day is over, tell yourself that it has not ended, but a union has begun between Jesus and His little communicant that is to be a foretaste of Heaven.

Tell your dear Mama I will be very close to her, sharing all her feelings. A special remembrance to the dear patient,[5] the little victim whom God has chosen because He loves her with such a special love. And all the best in my heart for you and my[6] Madeleine.

Sr. Elizabeth of the Trinity

---

[1] A letter of "April 22, 1902, several days before [my] first Communion," wrote Berthe Guémard in 1931 on a copy preserved in the ACD. "Tuesday" was in fact the 22nd, and the first Communion took place on April 27, 1902 (holy card memento).
[2] Cf. Jn 13:25.
[3] Cf. Rev 14:4.
[4] The interior grille of the parlor was covered with a black veil that was normally opened only for parents, brothers, and sisters.
[5] Perhaps Madeleine.
[6] Elizabeth was the godmother of Berthe's sister, Madeleine (cf. P 50).

L 113   To her sister   [May 25, 1902][1]
       J. M. + J. T.

My little Guite,

How happy your surprise made me. I almost had my mouth open to sing when I heard the first sounds of the harmonium and my heart *guessed it all.* The heart of your Sabeth was moved, the thoughtfulness of her little one really touched her, and her whole soul was in communion with hers. Give all my gratitude to the lovely voices that came to celebrate the Holy Trinity, particularly to my Marie-Louise. Tell her that I recognized her very well, and Alice too, and that I'm praying fervently for her.

Oh yes, my Guite, this feast of the Three is really my own, for me there is no other like it. It was really nice in Carmel, for it is a feast of silence and adoration; I had never understood so well the Mystery and the whole vocation in my name. I've given you to the Three, my Guite, you see how I dispose of you. Yes, it is in this great Mystery that I keep my rendez-vous with you. May He be our Center, our Dwelling Place. I leave you with this thought of Père Vallée, which will be your prayer.... "May the Holy Spirit bring you to the Word, may the Word lead you to the Father, and may you be consumed in the One, as was true of Christ and our saints."[2] I kiss you, my two darlings. I'll keep my rendez-vous with you every day of the octave from *noon* to *1 o'clock.*[3]

[1] Handwriting of 1902. Guite and her friends came to celebrate the "Holy Trinity" (May 25th), Elizabeth's second feast day. She is apparently thanking them the same evening.

[2] Borrowed from the 10th instruction, on "The Most Holy Trinity," from the retreat preached by P. Vallée at the Dijon Carmel in 1900. The Notebook of the sermons, preserved in the ACD in Sister Agnès's handwriting, repeats the verb "emmène" (to lead or take [away or out]) twice instead of "emporte" (to carry away) and "conduise" (to lead or guide). Elizabeth recopied her own version in her notebooks in 1902 or 1904 (cf. PAT). We should note that "to carry away" is a typically "Valléen" expression.

[3] The hour of adoration indicated for Elizabeth. The octave of the Blessed Sacrament (the feast was the 29th) lasted from May 30 to June 6. The Blessed Sacrament remained exposed.

L 114   To Sister Marie of the Trinity   [May 25, 1902(?)][1]

May the *One* be consumed in the very depths of our souls with the Father, the Son, and the Holy Spirit.

[1] Text recorded by Marie of the Trinity (PO 184); it had been written for her "on the back of a holy card." The phrase fits well into the spiritual context of 1902. Perhaps this was in honor of the feast of the Sub-Prioress, the Holy Trinity, on May 25 in 1902. Elizabeth gave her P 79 on this occasion.

L 115   To an unidentified correspondent   [1902][1]

May the Three fuse our souls into the unity of one single faith and one single love.

Elizabeth of the Trinity

[1] At the bottom of a copy made by Elizabeth of the prayer "O Eternal Trinity" by St. Catherine of Siena. The black ink suggests the period of May–September of the year 1902. The recipient may have been Sister Geneviève of the *Trinity.*

L 116   To Cécile Lignon   [May 29, 1902][1]
       J. M. + J. T.   Dijon Carmel, May 29

My dear little Cécile,

Your great friend was truly united with you today, her heart made one with yours. I met you close to the Beloved Jesus, we were both on His Heart: my Cilette wrapped in her communion veil and I in the white mantle of the Blessed Virgin and the veil of the betrothed, for I am the one my Christ has put in chains, His little prisoner of love. Ah! if you knew how good it is on the mountain of Carmel. I left everything to be able to climb it, but my Jesus came to meet me. He took me in His arms to carry me like a little child,[2] and to take the place of all I had left for Him. For I gave Him my dear Mama and my little Guite, then all those I loved, and my Cilette is certainly one of them. I no longer go to see her or her dear mama whom I love so much, but I keep a rendez-vous with them near the Tabernacle: when they think of me, they should go there, they will always meet me close to God; let Him be our Rendez-vous, shall we, Cécile? If He came this morning into your little heart, it was not to pass through it and go away, but to remain there always; keep Him well, my darling, and keep me also in that dear little sanctuary. Kiss your little mama for me, tell her that my heart keeps a faithful memory of her.

Sr. M. Elizabeth of the Trinity

[1] Date furnished by the holy card, a memento of this first Communion.
[2] We can recognize in this passage the "elevator" or the "little way" of Thérèse of Lisieux, a doctrine that Mother Germaine would not have failed to inculcate in her

novice. We see all the images in HA 147-48 [SS 207-8]: mountain, ascent, arms, carrying, little one, child. The image of the child in the arms or the hand in that of her mother (or father) reappears often from now on (cf. L 89, 123, 129, 160, 169, 172, 186, 200, 208, 209, 222, 224, 231, 239, 263, 301, 305; HF 34. (See also L 129, note 4.)

L 117   To her sister   [May 30, 1902][1]
  J. M. + J. T.   Friday night

My little Guite,
      You told me you really loved for me to ask you for things, so I'm coming to say how nice it would be if you could sing for us at Benediction next Friday, the feast of the Sacred Heart, at 5 P.M. Perhaps it will be difficult for you to join our friends because of the Saint Ignatius procession,[2] but I hope you will be able to; do you have something pretty to sing as a solo? Paule de Thorey could perhaps come, and Marie-Louise will be very happy to do that for the Sacred Heart; as for Alice, she surely won't go to the Fathers since she is in mourning.[3] In short, my Guite, try to arrange it. I can feel you in the chapel from noon to 1 o'clock, it is the *fusion* of our two souls in Him, oh! if you knew how close we are! Continue to live in communion with the Three through everything, that is the center where we meet. I love you very much, my Guite; my Communion on Sunday will be for you, then I'll spend the day in choir and you'll be there with me. Isn't it good to be close to Him? You see, He is my Infinite, in Him I love, and am loved, and have everything. A close and profound union. Tell Mama that I've received her little note.
      Please excuse this paper, I put it close to our lamp so that it would dry more quickly and I burned the bottom of the page.
                                          Your Sabeth,
                                    who is "one" with you.

Tell Madame d'Avout that I am praying for her intention.

---

[1] The "Friday" before the "Friday … of the Sacred Heart" was May 30. The handwriting and black ink are typical of 1902. Moreover, in 1903, the chapel had already been closed for public worship for political reasons.
[2] The Saint Ignatius College of the Jesuit Fathers (cf. L 63, note 3).
[3] Alice had lost her father eight months before (cf. L 96).

L 118   To her sister   [(shortly before) June 15, 1902][1]

My Guite,

Could you copy the music of the following hymns for me, along with the words of one verse so I can figure out the meter:

O Saint Autel [O Holy Altar], two parts;

Le Trio by Saint Saëns, two parts;

Le petit air de la médaille miraculeuse [The Little Song of the Miraculous Medal].

If you have any pretty ballads whose verses are easy to do, send them too.

(It was our good Mother who gave me that pretty holy card.) As soon as possible if you can. Thanks.

[1] The two notes that follow, hurriedly written, relate to the preparation for the Prioress's feast on June 15th. The handwriting and black ink are sufficient to indicate the period.

L 119   To her sister   [(shortly before) June 15, 1902]
           J. M. + J. T.

My little Guite,

I'm coming again to ask a favor of you. Would you be so very kind as to give me as soon as possible some white glove (glacé kid) leather; you could give me the cuffs of your long gloves. Please clean it so it will be neat. You'd be doing me a great favor. Tell our Sisters not to deliver it to Our Mother, for I'll be using it to make something for her feast. Could you also copy the *Salutaris* by Gounod for me? Thank you, my darling Guite, I am keeping my rendez-vous with you in the mystery of the Three, pray for your Sabeth who loves you much and feels her soul to be very close to yours.

L 120   To her sister   [(shortly before) June 15, 1902][1]

My little Guite,

The melody Mademoiselle de Benoit chose is quite disjointed, and I was unable to do anything with it. Our Sisters love very much the melody of the "Martyrs" that we sang at Saint-Bénigne.[2] Mother Sub-Prioress has the music that she's lending you, so that will be the melody you'll sing the verses to; I have three of them,[3] I think that's what you told me. Would you please send me during the next few days the muslin that's left from our first Communion dresses, and if there's not very much of it, that dotted muslin that's in a box in the attic (still to be delivered to Mother Sub-Prioress). It's for Saint Germaine, I'll tell you about it (I'll return it to you afterward).

Adieu, I only have time to kiss you before going to sleep. In union, we have our Heaven within us, *let's live it.* I love you much, my Guite.

[1] This still relates to the preparation for the feast of St. Germaine. June 15 fell on a Sunday in 1902, so there would be Benediction during which Guite would also sing.
[2] The cathedral of Dijon.
[3] This refers to P 81.

L 121   To Sister Agnès of Jesus-Mary   [June 11, 1902][1]

+

Let us go to the Father [2]

Yes, dear Sister, like that great passionate, illuminated Magdalene, let us pass through everything, lost in His Infinity! "Many sins will be forgiven her because she has loved much!" [3] That is what He asks of us: Love that no longer looks at self, but leaves itself and ascends higher than its own feelings, its own impressions; Love that gives itself, surrenders itself, Love "that *establishes Unity.*" [4] Let us live like Mary Magdalene through everything, day [and] night, in light or darkness, always beneath the eyes of Unchanging Beauty that wishes to fascinate us, to captivate us, more than that, to deify us!

Oh my Sister, "*to be Him,*" that is my whole dream; then, do you believe that the Father, who contemplates His adored Word in us, can resist the powerful prayer that one glance, one desire can become? Oh yes, let us be *Him,* and "Let us go to the Father" in the movement of His divine soul.

June 11, 1902

[1] Sister Agnès said in 1963 that this was "the first note she wrote me after the first free day we had" (PA 834). The "free day," a day when the Sisters could meet freely, anticipated the Prioress's feast the following Sunday. Agnès continues: "There are several expressions in it that were dear to us, coming as they did from P. Vallée." It is very difficult to assess here the importance of the Valléen vocabulary precisely. Undoubtedly Sister Agnès overlooked the tone of John of the Cross that is already perceptible in this letter (cf. note 4). According to our reading, we would retain as truly typical of P. Vallée (but not of him alone) only the words: Magdalene, great, illuminated, surrender itself, light, beneath, unchanging, take captive, contemplate, His Word, movement, His soul.

[2] Reminiscent of Jesus's words: "I am going to the Father" (Jn 14:12, 28 and 16:10, 16). (It refers to a movement of Jesus's soul, as Elizabeth says farther on.)

[3] Lk 7:47.

[4] Elizabeth could have found the idea in P. Vallée's sermon on charity (1900 retreat), quoting Aristotle: *"Union is the work of love.* Love establishes a mutual compenetration between two souls." But Elizabeth is quoting John of the Cross from the French here (*Spiritual Canticle,* st. 36, p. 383 [cf. K-RJ 36:1] "Love establishes unity" (unity, not union as in Vallée's text). In 1906, she explicitly attributed this word to John of the Cross (cf. L 274); even in 1903 she quoted the rest of the same phrase of the Mystical Doctor (cf. L 184, note 8). At the end of the *Spiritual Canticle* and the beginning of *The Living Flame of Love,* Elizabeth found a wonderful description of her "dream" of "being Him" (quotation marks do not necessarily indicate a quotation in her writing; sometimes they are representative or condensed expressions: "God grants her the favor of uniting her with the Most Blessed Trinity, in which she becomes deiform and God through participation" (SC 422 [K-RJ 39:4]). The Holy Spirit "penetrates ever more deeply the substance of the soul it deifies"—that is also the term Elizabeth uses—"and renders, so to speak, completely divine. The Being of God absorbs the soul..." (LF 484 [K-RJ 1:35]). We should recall that four months earlier Elizabeth said how much she had "desired" to have this book (cf. L 106). P. Vallée had also been influenced by John of the Cross (cf. AL).

L 122   To Madame de Sourdon   [shortly after June 15, 1902][1]
J. M. + J. T.

Very dear Madame,

It was with a child's joy that I offered those good madeleines[1a] to our Reverend Mother on your behalf; she was showered with things from all sides and was very touched by your tender care. Please allow me to express my gratitude for this as well as for all your kindnesses to my dear Mama, who tells me of all your thoughtfulness each time we visit in the parlor. I can assure you that I am praying fervently for you, since by this divine trade I can acquit myself of all my debts of gratitude. Oh yes, dear Madame, let us live with God as with a friend, let us make our faith a living faith in order to be in communion with Him through everything, for that is what makes saints.[2] We possess our Heaven within us, since He who satisfies the hunger of the glorified in the light of vision gives Himself to us in faith and mystery, it is the Same One! It seems to me that I have found my Heaven on earth, since Heaven is God, and God is [in] my soul.[3] The day I understood that, everything became clear to me. I would like to whisper this secret to those I love so they too might always cling to God through everything, and so this prayer of Christ might be fulfilled: "Father, may they be made perfectly one!"[4]

I caught a glimpse of Marie-Louise this morning and I imagined my Framboise must have had a big disappointment at having missed this good opportunity. Let her be consoled: I send her the best part of my heart, and let her meet me in Him who never fails us.

A Dieu, dear Madame, please tell Madame de Maizières[5] that I am praying fervently concerning the lawsuit, and keep for yourself the most tender affection of your very grateful little friend.

Elizabeth of the Trinity

Our Reverend Mother, to whom I often speak of my Framboise, gave me this photograph of O. L. of Mount Carmel for her.

[1] She is sending her thanks after the feast of June 15.
[1a] [A small, rich French cookie or cupcake baked in a distinctive fluted shape— TRANS.]
[2] "What makes saints" and the frequent mention of "saints": typical expressions of P. Vallée.
[3] Reminiscent of Lacordaire, already quoted in L 75.
[4] Jn 17:23.
[5] Her sister.

L 123   To Françoise de Sourdon   [June 19, 1902][1]
          J. M. + J. T.   Carmel, Thursday night

Yes, my darling, I am praying for you and I keep you in my soul quite close to God, in that little inner sanctuary where I find Him at every hour of the day and night. I'm never alone: my Christ is always there praying in me, and I pray with Him. You grieve me, my

Framboise; I can well see that you're unhappy and I assure you it's your own fault. Be at peace. I don't believe you're crazy yet, just nervous and overexcited, and when you're like that, you make others suffer too. Ah, if I could teach you the secret of happiness as God has taught it to me. You say I don't have any worries or sufferings; it's true that I'm very happy, but if you only knew that a person can be just as happy even when she is crossed. We must always keep our eyes on God. In the beginning it's necessary to make an effort when we're just boiling inside, but quite gently, with patience and God's help, we get there in the end.

You must build a little cell within your soul as I do.[2] Remember that God is there and enter it from time to time; when you feel nervous or you're unhappy, quickly seek refuge there and tell the Master all about it. Ah, if you got to know Him a little, prayer wouldn't bore you any more; to me it seems to be rest, relaxation. We come quite simply to the One we love, stay close to Him like a little child in the arms of its mother, and we let our heart go. You used to love sitting very close to me and telling me your secrets; that is just how you must go [to] Him; if only you knew how well He understands.... You wouldn't suffer any more if you understood that. It is the secret of life in Carmel: the life of a Carmelite is a communion with God from morning to evening, and from evening to morning. If He did not fill our cells and our cloisters, ah! how empty they would be! But through everything, [we] see Him, for we bear Him within us, and our life is an anticipated Heaven. I ask God to teach you all these secrets, and I am keeping you in my little cell; for your part, keep me in yours, and that way we will never be parted. I love you very much, my Framboise, and I'd like you to be completely good and completely in the peace of the children of God.

Your Elizabeth of the Trinity.

I was really delighted with the Benediction,[3] thank Marie-Louise very much for me. I've been praying fervently concerning the lawsuit.[4]

---

[1] The autographs of L 122 and 123 are two halves of the same sheet of paper (L 123 adds another piece of paper). If the letters were not sent in the same envelope, they

were in any case very close. "Thursday" would thus have been June 19, which notes 3
and 4 confirm.
² Cf. L 89, note 10.
³ Of June 15, cf. L 120, note 1.
⁴ Cf. L 122.

L 124   To Abbé Beaubis   [June 22, 1902]¹
         J. M. + J. T.   Dijon Carmel, June 22

Monsieur l'Abbé,

    Do you not find that, for souls, there is no distance or separa-
tion? This is really the fulfillment of Christ's prayer: "Father, may
they be made perfectly one."² It seems to me that the souls on earth
and those glorified in the light of vision are so close to each other,
since they are all in communion with the same God, the same Father, who gives Himself to the former in faith and mystery and satisfies the others in His divine light.... But He is the Same One, and
we carry Him within us. He bends over us with all His charity, day
and night, wanting to communicate with us, to infuse us with His
divine life, so as to make us deified beings who radiate Him everywhere. Oh, how powerful over souls is the apostle who remains always at the Spring of living waters;³ then he can overflow without his
soul ever becoming empty, since he lives in communion with the
Infinite! I am praying fervently for you, that God may invade all the
powers of your soul, that He may make you live in communion with
His whole Mystery, that everything in you may be divine and marked
with His seal, so that you may be another Christ working for the
glory of the Father! You are praying for me too, aren't you? I want
to be an apostle with you, from the depths of my dear solitude in
Carmel, I want to work for the glory of God, and for that I must be
wholly filled with Him; then I will be all-powerful: one look, one desire [will] become an irresistible prayer that can obtain everything,⁴
since it is, so to speak, God whom we are offering to God. May our
souls be one in Him, and, while you bring Him to souls, I will remain, like Mary Magdalene, silent and adoring, close to the Master,
asking Him to make your word fruitful in souls. "Apostle,
Carmelite," it is all one! Let us be wholly His, Monsieur l'Abbé, let
us be flooded with His divine essence, that He may be the Life of

our life, the Soul of our soul, and we may consciously remain night and day under His divine action. Yours faithfully in Our Lord,

Sr. Elizabeth of the Trinity

Thank you for your kind letter. Yes, may God unite our souls in Him for His glory. Union, communion!...

[1] Henri Joseph Beaubis, at that time 24 years old, had left the Dijon seminary in 1902 to go to China, working with the Lazarist missionaries. Mother Germaine must have put him in contact with Elizabeth before his departure. The letter is from 1902: the handwriting, black ink, and the absence of "r.c.i." after the signature testify to this.
[2] Jn 17:23.
[3] Cf. Rev 7:17.
[4] For the influence of Thérèse of Lisieux, cf. P 81, notes 4 and 5.

L 125   To Hélène Cantener[1]   [after June 21, 1902]

... May Christ bring us into those depths, those abysses where one lives only by Him. Would you like to be united[2] to your little sister in order to become wholly loving, wholly listening, wholly adoring?

To love, to love all the time, to live by love, that is, to be surrendered, to be His prey!...[3]

Would you like to give me your soul, and we will meet as before at the feet of the Master, who wants to show us His whole mystery. I kiss you very affectionately.

Your little sister,

Elizabeth of the Trinity.

[1] Twenty-one years old, she had been a novice (under the name of Sister Hélène of Jesus) with Elizabeth until June 21, 1902, the day she left Carmel (PO 341). Only fragmentary copies of the following two letters have been preserved. The expression "as before" presupposes that Hélène had already left Carmel.
[2] "Listening": a "Valléen" term.
[3] The image surely comes from Thérèse of Lisieux (cf. L 41, note 7). "The Divine Eagle," the complement of the comparison that we find in L 41, seems to be missing in all of P. Vallée's pages that have been preserved (although he does sometimes use the image of the prey). "Prey" is seen again in P 88; L 169, 171 (in each case it is the prey of love), 269 (his little prey); GV 7; PN 15. For the "Eagle," cf. L 269, note 4. Also note the Thérèsian expression "to live by love" (cf. PN 12, note 2).

L 126   To Hélène Cantener   [after June 21, 1902]

… Let us remain in His love.[1] May He virginize,[2] may He imprint His divine beauty in us, and, wholly filled with Him, may we be able to give Him to souls.…

[1] Cf. Jn 15:9.
[2] Cf. Thérèse of Lisieux, HA 99 (Ms A, 61v) and particularly the poem "Jésus, mon Bien-Aimé, rappelle-toi" [Jesus, My Beloved, Remember] (HA 343), in a stanza that leaves its mark on L 199 (see note 11). "To virginize" is repeated during this period in P 84 and 85.

L 127   To Françoise de Sourdon   [July 1902][1]
         J. M. + J. T.

I would be very grateful to you, my Framboise, if you could lend me your little collection of Botrel; the melodies are so pretty that I would like to make some verses for them, and I'd hurry to copy a few of them before you leave. Marie-Louise told me I could send this little note to your mother who would have the goodness to send it in one of her letters. Tell her I'm praying fervently for her intentions. As for you, my Framboise, I keep you in my soul and I ask Him who lives there to make you *wholly good*. I love and kiss you.

                                                            Elizabeth[2]

[1] Typical handwriting and black ink. "Before you leave": before the vacation that usually began around the end of July.
[2] A triangle, the symbol of the Trinity, follows her name.

L 128   To Françoise de Sourdon   [July 24, 1902][1]
         J. M. + J. T.   Carmel, Thursday, July 24

My dear little Framboise,

I still have the long letter you wrote me before you left; I've read it over and over again, asking the Divine Ideal to captivate and wound that dear little heart that He is seeking and surrounding and that is trying to escape from Him, to live in things so far below the end for which it was created and placed in the world! My Framboise,

I understand that you need an ideal, something that will draw you out of yourself and raise you to greater heights. But you see, there is only One; it is *He*, the *Only Truth!* Ah, if you only knew Him a little as your Sabeth does! He *fascinates*, He sweeps you away; under His gaze the horizon becomes so beautiful, so vast, so luminous…. You see, I love Him passionately, and in Him I have everything! It is through Him, by His radiance, that I must view and do everything! My dear one, do you want to turn with me toward this sublime Ideal? It is no fiction but a reality, it is my life in Carmel. Rather, look at Mary Magdalene: was she captivated? Since you need to live beyond yourself, live in Him; it's so simple. And then be good; you make me so sad by causing such suffering to the one who loves you *more than you know*. Perhaps one day you'll realize how mean you're being, and then what regrets [you'll have], my Framboise! You don't know what is in the hearts of mothers like the ones God has given us; remember there is nothing better in this world, and I believe my Master could ask nothing more from me than to give Him mine. I want you to be *polite* and submissive, completely in the peace of God. Let's remain *in* Him,[2] Framboise, whom I love so much; the more I see you misbehaving, the harder I work for your soul, for the Master wants it. And then in a way you're like my own little child, and it seems to me that I'm a bit responsible for you. So don't make a conversion too difficult; let yourself be taken in the Master's nets, it is so good to be there.

Your great friend and little mother,

> Elizabeth of the Trinity
> (captivated by Christ)

---

[1] "Thursday" and "July 24" coincide in 1902.
[2] Cf. Jn 15:4. The expression recurs often.

L 129   To Madame de Sourdon   [July 25, 1902][1]
    J. M. + J. T.   Dijon Carmel, July 25

Very dear Madame,
    Your nice long letter made me sad, for I feel the deep sorrow of your soul. I have prayed much for you; I have been in commun-

ion with the Word of Life,[2] with Him who came to bring consolation to all in distress and who, on the eve of His passion, in that discourse after the Last Supper in which He gave all His soul, said in speaking of those who were His own: "Father, I want the fullness of My joy to be in them!"[3]

Abandonment, dear Madame, that is what allows us to surrender to God. I am quite young, but it seems to me that I have really suffered at times. Oh, then, when everything was dark, when the present was so painful and the future seemed even more gloomy to me, I used to close my eyes and abandon myself like a child in the arms of this Father[4] who is in Heaven. Dear Madame, would you allow this little Carmelite who loves you so much to tell you something? These are the words that the Master addressed to Saint Catherine of Siena: "Think of me, and I will think of you."[5] We look at ourselves too much, we want to see and understand, we do not have enough confidence in Him who envelops us in His Charity.[6] We must not stop before the Cross and regard it in itself, but, recollecting ourselves in the light of faith,[7] we must rise higher and recognize that it is the instrument that is obeying Divine Love. "One thing alone is necessary: Mary has chosen the better part, which shall not be taken from her."[8] This better part, which seems to be my privilege in my beloved solitude of Carmel, is offered by God to every baptized soul.[9] He offers it to you, dear Madame, in the midst of your cares and maternal concerns. Believe that His whole desire is to lead you ever deeper into Himself. Surrender yourself and all your preoccupations to Him and since you find me a good advocate to the Court of the King, I ask you also to confide to me all that is close to your heart; you can guess how *eagerly* your cause will be *pleaded!* When my dear Mama used to confide her concerns for my Guite to me, I would tell her not to think, that I would think for her, and you can see that God has thought for me.[10] Do you want me to make the same prayer for you; you've said *yes,* haven't you?

Yesterday I saw my happy Mama, who recognizes now that God is really good; one day you too will see everything become clear and light!

Monsieur Courtois came home today, and I am going to see him to speak to him about you. Would you be kind enough to thank

Madame d'Anthès for her good letter, which was so full of faith? I
have prayed much; God has plans that we do not always understand
but that we must adore! Would you also express to Miss[11] my complete union with her. I sense that her soul is lost in the Infinity of
God, before the Ocean that speaks so well to the soul that longs for
Him!

A Dieu, dear Madame, I enfold Marie-Louise and Framboise
in my prayer, and if you would like, I will keep a rendez-vous with
you in Him who is *All*, asking Him to make you feel the sweetness of
His presence and His divine intimacy!

Sr. Elizabeth of the Trinity

[1] 1902, according to the handwriting, black ink, and the absence of "r.c.i." after the
signature.
[2] "Word of Life": 1 Jn 1:1.
[3] Jn 17:13.
[4] Again, the influence of Thérèse of Lisieux; in addition to the account of her discovery of the "little way" (cf. L 116, note 2), passages come to mind in which the notion
of abandonment is expressed more by the image of a sleeping child: cf. the poems
"Jésus, mon Bien-Aimé, rappelle-toi" [Jesus, My Beloved, Remember], st. 31 (HA
345); "L'Abandon" [Abandonment] (from which Elizabeth copied the introductory
quotation from St. Augustine in her notebooks), st. 3 (HA 378); "Jésus seul" [Jesus
Alone] (which Elizabeth copied), st. 3 and 5 (HA 362-63).
[5] *Life*, by Raymond of Capua, I, chap. 10.
[6] "Enveloping" and "Charity" were often used by P. Vallée.
[7] The same is true for "recollecting oneself," "beneath," "light of faith."
[8] Lk 10:42.
[9] Before her entrance, Elizabeth had already relativized the monastic dimension of
the "better part" of contemplation, which she extends here to all believers, by applying it to the concrete will of God in our life (cf. AL).
[10] An allusion to Guite's coming marriage. The "pain" and concern of Mme. de
Sourdon for the future undoubtedly relate to her daughter Marie-Louise's difficulty
in finding a husband, as we see throughout this correspondence.
[11] Probably Miss Skelton, her former English professor. (Cf. L 19, note 6.)

L 130   To her mother   [August 2, 1902][1]
J.M. + J.T.

Darling Mama,

One year ago I gave the best of mamas to God, but that great
sacrifice could not separate our two souls; today more than ever they
are but *one;* you feel that, don't you? Oh! let me tell you that I am

happy, *divinely happy*, that God has been *too good* to me; it's all a wave that overflows in my soul, a wave of gratitude and love toward Him and toward you: thank you for having [given] me to Him. He is pleased with you, and up above, our dear departed are so happy. In looking back on those heartrending hours,[2] I thank Him who has so sustained and enveloped us! I was delighted with the photographs; Monsieur Chevignard[3] shows up better than my Guite. How radiant she was the other day, I haven't seen her like that for a year; her little heart has been taken. Ah, don't you see that when a heart has been taken captive by Christ, it must then give itself wholly? My Fiancé is so handsome, Mama, I love Him passionately and in loving Him, I am transformed in Him. And then it's so good, for He is always with me, He consumes me into One with Him, and we love each other so much!! Ah, if it weren't for that I would still be with you! I kiss you, darling Mama, I feel the sacrifice just as you do, but I'm divinely happy.

Your daughter Sabeth

Tell the engaged couple that *the Carmelite envelops them with prayer.*

[1] "One year" since her entrance.
[2] Elizabeth wrote "ces heureuses déchirantes" [those heartrending happy] instead of "ces heures déchirantes" [those heartrending hours].
[3] Georges Chevignard, then nearly 32 years old, who had recently become Guite's fiancé.

L 131   To Canon Angles

J. M. + J. T.

[August 2, 1902][1]

Amo Christum

Dear Monsieur le Chanoine,

How quickly time passes in Him! One year ago He brought me into the holy ark,[2] and now, as my blessed Father Saint John of the Cross says in his *Canticle:*

> "The turtledove
> has found its longed-for mate
> by the green river banks."

Yes, I have found Him whom my soul loves, that One Thing

Necessary that no one can take from me. Oh! how good He is, how beautiful He is. I wish to be wholly silent, wholly adoring so I may enter into Him ever more deeply and be so filled with Him that I can give Him through prayer to those poor souls who are unaware of the gift of God.[3]

I know that you are praying for me every day at Holy Mass. Oh, won't you please place me in the chalice so my soul may be wholly bathed in this Blood of my Christ for which I so thirst! so as to be wholly pure, wholly transparent, so that the Trinity can be reflected in me as in a crystal.[4] The Trinity so loves to contemplate its beauty in a soul; this draws it to give itself even more, to come with greater fullness so as to bring about the great mystery of love and unity! Ask God that I may live *fully* my Carmelite life, my life as a bride of Christ! This presupposes such a profound union! Why has He loved me so much?... I feel so little, so full of misery, but I love Him; that is all I know how to do, I love Him with His own love, it is a double current between He who is and she who is not![5] Ah, when I feel my God invade my whole soul, as I pray to Him for you, it seems to me that it is a prayer He cannot resist, and I want Him to make me all-powerful! How I would like to come pour out my soul to you as before, but it is from soul to soul, isn't it, that we communicate?

A Dieu, Monsieur le Chanoine, bless the one who always loves to call herself your child.

Sr. Elizabeth of the Trinity

Madame Angles has written to me without giving me her address. So I am entrusting my letter to you.[6]

---

[1] "One year" since her entrance.

[2] The comparison of Noah's "ark" (Gen 6-7) with Carmel is also found in Thérèse of Lisieux (cf. HA 111, 157 [SS 143, 216]). The comparison of the ark with God is in John of the Cross (SC 372 [K-RJ 34:4]), in st. 34 of the *Spiritual Canticle*, which Elizabeth then quotes (SC 373 [K-RJ 34:1]).

[3] "The gift of God": cf. Jn 4:10. The expression occurs again in Elizabeth, e.g., L 138.

[4] The comparison of the "soul" with a crystal, already made in P 79 of May 25 and again in P 82 and 95, comes from Teresa of Avila (cf. *The Interior Castle*, I, 1 Bouix trans., Vol. 3, p. 334), as Elizabeth attests in L 136. The influence of John of the Cross (LF 466 [K-RJ 1:13]) and the Book of Revelation (cf. P 104, note 2) will be added.

[5] "He who is," "she who is not": expressions of Catherine of Siena, sometimes used by P. Vallée, for example in the 16th sermon of the 1897 retreat and the third and tenth

of the 1900 retreat. But Elizabeth had already quoted this phrase in 1901 (cf. L 73 and PN 12).
[6] Lost.

L 132   To Sister Marie of the Trinity   [August 6, 1902][1]
+

May this anniversary truly be a day of *illumination* for my little Mother.[2] May the rays of the whole Divinity be reflected in her soul, so that through everything, day and night, she may begin her face-to-face [encounter] with the Unchanging One, the radiant Beauty who will satisfy our hunger during eternity and who already here below wants to plunge us ever deeper into the infinite depths, into the *"great vision!"* [3]

[1] The "anniversary" of her profession five years before. Elizabeth also composed P 84 for this same day. It was the feast of the Transfiguration, "truly a day of *illumination*," the reason for the language of light.
[2] "Mother" because Marie of the Trinity was her Sub-Prioress.
[3] "Great vision," an expression dear to P. Vallée, an echo of the Book of Revelation.

L 133   To Germaine de Gemeaux   [August 7, 1902][1]
J.M. + J.T.   Dijon Carmel, August 7

My dear little Germaine,
     Thank you for your nice letter; it made me happy. I was really glad about Albert's success, which I had not doubted, and then glad too that you took me as your confidante. The other day in the parlor I could sense your soul so well that if I hadn't been afraid of frightening your dear mother,[2] I would have kept you a few minutes, and like little sisters we could both have spoken of Him whom our soul loves! I still remember the first secret you shared with me at Gemeaux,[3] you were very little, but already the Master had taken your little heart captive, and my soul felt drawn toward yours!… A Carmelite,[4] my darling, is a soul who has *gazed on the Crucified*, who has seen Him offering Himself to His Father as a Victim for souls and, recollecting herself in this great vision of the charity of Christ,

has understood the passionate love of His soul, and has wanted to give herself as He did!... And on the mountain of Carmel, in silence, in solitude, in prayer that never ends, for it continues through everything, the Carmelite already lives as if in Heaven: "by *God alone*." The same One who will one day be her beatitude and will fully satisfy her in glory is already giving Himself to her. He never leaves her, He dwells within her soul; more than that, the two of them are *but one*. So she *hungers for silence* that she may always listen, penetrate ever deeper into His Infinite Being. She is identified with Him whom she loves, she finds Him everywhere; she sees Him shining through all things! Is this not Heaven on earth! You carry this Heaven within your soul, my little Germaine, you can be a Carmelite already, for Jesus recognizes the Carmelite from *within*, by her soul. Don't ever leave Him, do everything beneath His divine gaze, and remain wholly joyful[5] in His peace and love, making those around you happy!

A Dieu, my good little Germaine. I've asked our Reverend Mother for a blessing for you, and I'm delighted to send it; our Mother is so good! Like you, she is called Germaine "of Jesus."[6]

Please give my respectful and very affectionate greetings to Monsieur and Madame de Gemeaux. A big kiss to Yvonne, and for you, the best of my soul.

Elizabeth of the Trinity

If you have any message for me, you can entrust it to Marguerite.[7] She is a *good confidante*.

---

[1] Elizabeth knew the De Gemeaux family well. They lived in the chateau of the village of the same name, in which she had spent part of her vacation in 1893 (cf. L 6, note 3). She went there every year for Corpus Christi (cf. Germaine's testimony in PAT). Germaine was at this time almost 14 years old. Albert was her brother and Yvonne her sister. The handwriting and black ink place the letter in 1902.

[2] Mme. de Gemeaux was opposed to the idea that her daughter might enter Carmel.

[3] Germaine relates (PA 668) this, on June 4, 1896: "One afternoon on Corpus Christi, we were going for a walk together in Gemeaux. She was sixteen years old and I was eight. She asked me, 'Germaine, what will you do when you grow up?' 'I'll be a Carmelite'; which filled her with joy. She immediately ran to her mother in the drawing room: 'Mama, Germaine says she wants to be a Carmelite!' Mme. Catez wisely answered, 'Be quiet.' "

[4] In the way in which it is stated, this personal definition, which comes from a very Thérèsian and deeply lived inspiration, retains some traces of P. Vallée, from whom,

before she entered Carmel, Elizabeth had copied this thought in her notebooks (cf. PAT): "A religious ... is one who recollects herself at the feet of Christ, who has seen Him pass, a permanent victim, as an offering to His Father for the whole human race ...: there was, on God's part, an endless love ... a passionate need to associate us with His own life.... And then there are souls who understand that the great work of their life is to be redeemed and, like Christ, to redeem all the other souls around them" *(Madame Louise de France,* Saint-Cloud, Impr. Belin et fils, 1888, pp. 20-22). P. Vallée developed the same ideas using other words in his *Discours prononcé au Carmel de Dijon pour la prise de voile de Mlle B. F., en religion Soeur Marie de la Trinité, le 9 août 1897* [Address delivered at the Carmel of Dijon for the veiling of Mlle. B. F., known in religion as Sister Marie of the Trinity, on August 9, 1897], s.l., 26 p. Elizabeth, who had not heard this sermon (cf. L 13), certainly became acquainted with it in Carmel. The expression "prayer that never ends" comes from the *Discours pour la fête de Notre-Dame du Mont-Carmel* [Address for the feast of Our Lady of Mount Carmel], July 16, 1900, manuscript copy ACD, p. 32, which Elizabeth read in 1901 before she entered (cf. L 54).

[5] "Longs for silence" and especially "wholly joyful" are expressions from the same source.

[6] The name that the young Germaine dreamed of having as a religious.

[7] Elizabeth's sister. The Gemeaux visited the Catezes every year.

L 134   To Marie-Louise Ambry (née Maurel)

J.M. + J.T.   [around the end of August 1902][1]

My very dear Marie-Louise,

I learned of your great sorrow through a note from Mama, and my heart needs to tell you right away that it is one with yours and asks Him who inflicted the wound to heal it, for only He can do so! I understand so well the grief of your heart, my dear little Marie-Louise, that I won't try to bring you human consolation; you should take refuge in a Mother's heart, the heart of the Virgin. It knew all the breaking, all the tearing, and it always stayed so calm, so strong, for it always stayed leaning on the heart of her Christ! My darling, you have sent a little angel on high, and she will never know our miseries; look at her among those spirits that are so pure they can contemplate the Face of God; she smiles on her little mother; she wants to lure her whole heart, her whole soul into those celestial regions where suffering is transformed into love! Tell your whole family how closely I am united with them, and, my very dear Marie-Louise, believe in the deep affection of your friend.

                    Sr. Elizabeth of the Trinity

[1] Marie-Louise Maurel, the wife of Joseph Ambry since September 30, 1901, had lost her daughter Suzanne on August 25, baptized privately the same day (Parish Register of Labastide). Living in Carcassonne, Marie-Louise had returned to her paternal home to give birth.

L 135   To her sister   (before September 14, 1902)[1]
          J. M. + J. T.   Amo Christum.

I am going through you, my little Guite, to reach your fiancé, the pearl of brothers-in-law! I am deeply touched that my wish has been fulfilled, and I'm truly happy that Saint Teresa will bless my Guite's marriage[2] for which I've prayed so much! We will have the Blessed Sacrament in the chapel that day, and while the Church consecrates your union, the Carmelite, the happy one chained by Christ, will spend the day at His feet becoming wholly praying, wholly adoring, for those "two" whom God wishes to be "one"![3] Wouldn't you like me to envelop you in my prayer, or rather in that of my Christ who lives in me!

I had a very holy visit in the parlor with Abbé Chevignard;[4] I believe there has been a *fusion* between the soul of the priest and that of the Carmelite!

I bring the fiancés together to send them the best of my heart. At night, when they hear the clock chime, may they be united to a fiancée who is the happiest of creatures; in singing the praises of Him she loves, her heart does not forget the *duo*, the *trio* of rue Prieur.[5]

                                        Elizabeth of the Trinity

[1] In L 137 of September 14, Elizabeth speaks of the same visit with Abbé Chevignard.
[2] Set for October 15, the feast of Saint Teresa.
[3] Cf. Gen 2:24.
[4] André Chevignard, a seminarian then 23 years old, Georges's brother.
[5] The "duo": Guite and Georges, or Guite and her mother. Guite was still living at that time on rue Prieur-de-la-Côte-d'Or.

L 136   To Germaine de Gemeaux   (September 14, 1902)[1]
        J. M. + J. T.   Dijon Carmel, September 14

My dear little Germaine,

This letter will reach you for the 17th. I will receive Holy Communion for that day and, if you'd really like to give me your soul, I will consecrate it to the Holy Trinity so that it may introduce you into the depths of the Mystery, and so that those Three whom we both love so much may truly be the Center in which our life passes! Saint Teresa says that the soul is like a crystal in which the Divinity is reflected.[2] I love that comparison so much, and when I see the sun invade our cloisters with its rays, I think that this is how God invades the soul that seeks only Him! My darling, let us live in intimacy with our Beloved, let us belong wholly to Him, as He belongs wholly to us. You are deprived of receiving Him as often as you wish, and I understand your sacrifice so well. But remember that His Love does not need a sacrament to come to His little Germaine: communicate with Him the whole day since He is living in your soul. Listen to what our holy Father Saint John of the Cross says to us; since you are so completely my little sister, he is your Father as well: *"Oh, soul, most beautiful of creatures who desires so ardently to know the dwelling place of your Beloved in order to seek Him and be united with Him, you are yourself the refuge where He takes shelter, the dwelling place in which He hides Himself. Your Beloved, your Treasure, your one Hope is so close to you as to live within you; and, actually, you cannot be without Him!"*[3]

That is the whole life of Carmel, to live in Him. Then all sacrifices, all immolations become divine, for through everything the soul sees Him whom it loves, and everything leads it to Him; it is a continual heart-to-heart! You see you can already be a Carmelite in soul. Love silence and prayer, for that is the essence of Carmelite life. Ask the Queen of Carmel, *our Mother,*[4] to teach you to adore Jesus in profound recollection; she so loves her daughters in Carmel, her privileged order, and she is our foremost patron.

Pray also to our seraphic Mother Saint Teresa, who loved so much that she died of love! Ask her for her passion for God, for souls, for the Carmelite must be apostolic;[5] all her prayers, all her sacrifices tend to this! Are you familiar with Saint John of the Cross?

He is our Father who went so far into the depths of the Divinity! Before him, I should have spoken to you of Saint Elijah, our first Father; you can see that our order is very ancient since it goes back to the prophets.[6] Ah, I wish I could sing all its glories!

Let us love our Carmel, it is incomparable! As for the Rule, my little Germaine, one day you will see how beautiful it is; live the spirit of it now! Our Reverend Mother herself is going to reply to what you asked her; I can just see your happiness! You will see how good she is, so thank God for having given her to me! A Dieu, my little sister, I pray fervently for you. It is a communion between my soul and yours: I do everything with you, at prayer, at the Divine Office, everywhere you are with me, for I keep you in my soul very close to Him; together we are lost in the Holy Trinity!...

I am still called Elizabeth, but I also bear the name of the Holy Trinity.

Sr. Elizabeth of the Trinity

Isn't it a beautiful name?

My affectionate greetings to your dear parents and a kiss to good Yvonne. Marguerite said that in seeing the two of you, she found herself once again with me.

[1] Handwriting of 1902. "The 17th," Germaine will celebrate her fifteenth birthday.
[2] Cf. L 131, note 4.
[3] SC 26-27 [K-RJ 1:7]. Elizabeth wrote the quotation in smaller letters.
[4] Carmel is the "Order of Our Lady of Mount Carmel."
[5] Cf. L 179. A desire that Teresa of Avila expresses especially in the first three chapters of the *Way of Perfection:* "And when your prayers, desires, disciplines, and fasts are not directed toward obtaining these things I mentioned [i.e, the good of the Church and her ministers], reflect on how you are not accomplishing or fulfilling the purpose for which the Lord brought you here together." ([K-RT Vol. 2, 3:10]).
[6] According to legend.

L 137   To her aunt Francine Rolland   [September 14, 1902][1]
J. M. +J. T.   Dijon Carmel, September 14

My dear Aunt Francine,

Yes, time passes very quickly in my blessed Carmel. It is an oasis in the desert of this life, a corner of Heaven, or at least a channel between Heaven and earth. You who understand all the beauty, the greatness of my vocation, thank Him who chose the better part for me and ask Him that I may respond to so much love!

What a shame you won't be coming to Guite's wedding! I am so very happy it will take place on Saint Teresa's day, Carmel's great feast, and while the Church consecrates the union of my Guite, I, a thousand times happier, will spend the day close to the Blessed Sacrament; if you knew how good it is in choir! When the Blessed Sacrament is exposed in the chapel, the large grille is open and, so people on the outside can't see us, we are in complete darkness. When I open the door to go in, it seems to me that it is Heaven I am entering, and it really is just that in reality, since the One I adore in faith is the same One the glorified contemplate face to face! If you'd like to send me your soul, we can both be Magdalenes! On the vigils of feasts, I can see you decorating your dear little church I love so much. I imagine you're really busy and that you wouldn't mind having your little helper even though she didn't do much of anything! Here I clean the choir every day. I don't have the consolation of coming quite close, *right* against the Tabernacle, like I did at Carlipa. I don't even see the altar since everything is shut,[2] but still it is much better to be a Carmelite. I cherish this thick grille that hides my Beloved from me at the same time as it makes me the prisoner of His love!

During the month of the Rosary, we have Benediction every day. It is a month I particularly love, for it is also that of our holy Mother Teresa. We are making a special novena to her and I promise to pray fervently for you; you will see how she'll lead you here for the day when I have the happiness of making my profession. For your part, my little Aunt, pray to her a bit for me, so that I may become a true Carmelite, which is no more and no less than a saint! Then pray too for our little Guite, so that God may be well loved in that little household, and I do believe it will be so, for both are so pious. I thank God for having chosen so serious a young man for my little sister; his family is so deeply Christian. The other day I had a visit from his brother, who is a seminarian,[3] quite an angelic soul, completely filled with God!... A Dieu, I only have room to kiss all three of you.[4] Tell my aunt that I pray for her every day. Please give my respectful greetings to Monsieur le Curé. Doesn't he want to come and get acquainted with Carmel? I pray very particularly for him and I ask him not to forget me at the Holy Sacrifice of the Mass. Tell him that the muse is getting through to Carmel,[5] but that I really need his lights as before in order to correct my verse.

Sr. Elizabeth of the Trinity

Hello to Anna.

[1] 1902: before Guite's marriage.
[2] Cf. L 109, note 6.
[3] Cf. L 135, note 4.
[4] Although addressed to only one aunt, the letter concerns the other two as well.
[5] Cf. P 73 to 84.

L 138   To Madame Angles   [September 29, 1902][1]
    J. M. + J. T.   Dijon Carmel, September 29

Very dear Madame,
    I have been sharing your feelings and your grief; please tell our dear Marie-Louise that I am praying fervently for her, that God may console the sorrow that is breaking her tender and loving heart. I am also praying fervently for you, dear Madame, and I believe that the Master wants to consummate His union with you on the Cross. There is no wood like that of the Cross for lighting the fire of love in the soul! And Jesus so needs to be loved and to find in the world, where He is so offended, souls that are given, wholly surrendered to Him and His good pleasure! "My food is to do the will of Him who sent me."[2] Our Lord was the first to say this, and, by living in communion with Him, the soul enters into the movement of His divine soul, and its whole ideal is to fulfill the will of this Father who has loved us with an eternal love.[3] Since you allow me to talk intimately with you and to read a little of your soul, let me tell you, dear Madame, how much I see a "*will* of God" in your sufferings. I can tell you on His behalf that He is taking away your capacity to act, to find things to distract yourself, to keep yourself busy, so the sole occupation of your heart may be to love Him and to think of Him! He thirsts for your soul. You have been particularly consecrated to

Him,[4] to my great joy. You would like to be wholly His, although in the world, and that is so simple: He is always with you, be always with Him, through all your actions, in your sufferings, when your body is exhausted, remain in His sight, see Him present, *living* in your soul. If I did not have my dear Carmel, I would be jealous of your solitude! You are so well secluded in your beautiful mountains, it seems to me like a little Thebaid. It is so nice to go off alone into your vast woods, and then to leave the books and work, and to remain with God in a wholly intimate heart-to-heart, in a gaze full of love. Taste this happiness, it is divine, and take the soul of your little friend with you! Now I am going to ask your prayers, too, for on October 6th we will be going into retreat until the feast of Saint Teresa. The Rev. P. Vallée, who preached at my clothing, is going to give this retreat.[5] He is so profound, so luminous, please pray that I may profit from the gift of God! Then, on the 15th, pray for Guite, too. I recommend her to you very especially. Pray too for my dear Mama, who will feel the loss of all those who are absent that day, but, in Heaven and on earth, they will be quite close to her. I know that your health does not permit the long trip, though that would have made many happy! Dear Madame, let us meet in Him who is Love, and may our lives be consecrated to His greater glory!

I kiss you very affectionately, without forgetting the others at Labastide. My greetings to Monsieur Angles.[6]

Your little friend profoundly united in Our Lord.

Sr. Elizabeth of the Trinity

I find my dear Mama very tired and I am concerned about that long trip for her;[7] I would have loved so much to think of her being near you, what a shame that it's so far away!

---

[1] 1902: the year determined by reference to P. Vallée's (L 145, note 2) retreat (cf. note 5). For Mme. Angles, née Marie Metge, aunt of Marie-Louise Maurel and sister-in-law of Canon Angles, see L 17, note l. Forty years old at this time, married to the Notary of Mas-Chabardès, Victor Angles, she had no children. She entered the Visitation Convent of Orthez at the age of 75. One of her former companions in the novitiate later said (in a communication to the Dijon Carmel, September 8, 1974) that "Sister Elizabeth Marie (Mme. Angles's name in religion) confided some things to her about the early days of her marriage, and that made it possible for her to understand the anxious and timid state of soul you point out, which is probably related to the period of her life when she underwent a serious operation (with insufficient

anesthesia, from which she was traumatized for several years). Her husband, completely engrossed in the duties of his profession, left her somewhat alone ... for she continued to suffer physically and spent her days on a chaise longue at the bottom of a meadow. That led to a painful withdrawal into herself.... Fortunately her brother-in-law, Canon Angles, cheered her up and helped her turn toward God in this trial." This information sheds light on Elizabeth's correspondence with Mme. Angles, whom she had already met several times in the South of France before she entered.

² Jn 4:34.
³ Cf. Jer 31:3.
⁴ She was a member of the Franciscan Third Order.
⁵ Cf. L 145, note 2.
⁶ Her husband.
⁷ A trip planned to the South of France with Guite and her husband. As a matter of fact, Mme. Catez remained home.

L 139   To her aunt Mathilde Rolland
J. M. + J. T.   [around the beginning of October 1902][1]

Dear Aunt Mathilde,

I am more and more convinced that the grilles have not separated us at all and that souls who are really united, for whom God is the Bond and the Rendez-vous, always know where to meet. Don't you feel my soul in that dear little church where, morning and evening, I so loved to come pray beside you? Do you also recall our walks on the Serre in the evening by the moonlight, when we heard the lovely carillon? Oh, how beautiful it was, my little Aunt, that starlit valley, that immensity, that infinity. It all spoke to me of God.... Never will I forget those vacations spent with you; they will always be among my fondest memories, and you will always be in the best part of my heart; you feel that, don't you?

As for me, I have found my Heaven on earth in my dear solitude in Carmel, where I am alone with God alone. I do everything with Him, so I go to everything with a divine joy; whether I'm sweeping, working, or at prayer, I find everything good and delightful since it is my Master whom I see everywhere! I really wish I had your skill for linen and could make pretty petit points like you, though I don't lack for work.

Please give my respectful greetings to Monsieur le Curé; tell him that I love the Divine Office passionately and ask him to unite himself to the little Carmelite when he says it.

A Dieu, dear Aunt Mathilde. I'm delighted to think that my darlings are going to see you. I know I don't need to commend them to you, you're both so good for them! I kiss you both, and my aunt as well; tell her I pray for her every day.

Your little one who loves you very much.

Sr. Elizabeth of the Trinity

Hello to Anna.

[1] A little before Guite and Georges's honeymoon in the South of France. Mme. Catez ("my darlings" in the plural) was to accompany them to Carlipa.

L 140   To her sister   [October 14, 1902]
J. M. + J. T.   Dijon Carmel, October 14

My dear little Guite,

On the eve of that great day,[1] your Elizabeth sends you her whole heart, her whole soul, and she is one with you, and tonight, in thinking of her little one whom she loves so much, she feels so deeply moved and can't speak any more; you understand, don't you, my Guite! This morning I offered Holy Communion for you, and during the 8 o'clock Mass my soul was really united *to both of yours*.[2] You can guess how fervently I have prayed for the engaged couple and how I am asking God to pour out His sweetest blessings on them. He loves you, my Guite, your union is wholly blessed by Him!

I am delighted to send you this beautiful Saint Teresa. Marthe Weishardt[3] had the thoughtfulness to paint it; you'll recognize her touch. Our Reverend Mother, who loves you very much, my little Guite, chose the words that are written around our two saints:[4] you'll see that both of us are blessed, each in the way our Master calls us and wishes us to be. Until tomorrow, my Guite, meanwhile receive all the best that your big sister has in her heart. She is asking Him who collected all the tears you shed in giving her to Him to transform them into sweet dew, into a shower of blessings, into a sweet outpouring of His peace and His love.

Your Elizabeth of the Trinity

[1] Her wedding.
[2] This may have been a Mass for their intentions.
[3] Elizabeth spelled it "Weisa." Marthe Weishardt was a friend and former novice of the Dijon Carmel.
[4] The painting, which has not been preserved, represents St. Margaret of Scotland and St. Elizabeth of Hungary, who both followed the path of marriage.

L 141   To her mother   [October 14 or 15, 1902][1]
J.M. + J.T.

My dear little Mama,

Those in Heaven and on earth who are absent are very close to you, can't you feel it? Oh, darling Mama, you are not alone, He is there, *He,* and those who have left you for Him![2] Tonight, in the silence of this dear little cell, alone with Him I love, my soul and my heart go to find you; and I think that if, in reality, I were there with you, I would be less so, for you can really feel there is no distance for hearts, and that of your Elizabeth is always yours. Oh, Mama, He to whom you gave me is Love and Charity, and He is teaching me to love as He does, He is giving me His love to love you with!

My heart could go on talking to you for a long time more, it's so good to be close to her Mama, but it's time for Matins and I'm going to go down to the choir to speak to you right next to Him, which will be even better.

I kiss you as the best of mamas! How is your poor heart doing? Mine is really full of emotion and I've wiped some tears from my eyes! I am happy; He has chosen the better part for me. Oh! thank our great Saint Teresa, whom you love so much, for the happiness of your

                                        Elizabeth.

[1] L 140 and 141 form two halves of the same sheet (the handwriting is also of the same period). Elizabeth is consoling her mother, who is left alone now that Guite is getting married on "Saint Teresa's" day.
[2] Her deceased husband and Elizabeth in Carmel: "those in Heaven and on earth who are absent."

L 142   To Marie-Louise Ambry (née Maurel) [October 26, 1902]
J. M. + J. T.   Dijon Carmel, October 26

My dear Marie-Louise,

Yes, I have prayed much for you and I still do so every day; prayer is the bond between souls, don't you feel it? I am asking God Himself to console the heart of His[1] Marie-Louise. He is the supreme Consoler who loves us with a love we will never be able to understand! Jesus wept when He was on earth; unite your tears to His divine tears, adore with Him the will of Him who wounds only because He loves, then turn your soul toward that abode of peace and light toward which your angel has flown. Oh! if you knew how close He is to you, how you can live with Him in sweet intimacy, for this whole invisible world draws near to us in the light of faith, and communion is established between those above and those below!

Actually, I think you will have a visit from Guite; she told me that the last time I saw her, and the prospect delighted her. I will be there with you in my heart. What good times we've spent together, dear Marie-Louise! I will never return again to your beautiful mountains, but there is One in whom I meet you always. When you pray to Him, speak to Him of your Elizabeth and imagine that she is there quite near you. Ah, if you knew how Carmel is a corner of Heaven! In silence and solitude, we live here alone with God alone. Everything speaks of Him here, we feel Him everywhere, so living, so present. Prayer is our principal, I should say our sole, occupation, because for a Carmelite it must never cease. You are not forgotten during those hours spent close to Him; I am going to leave you now to go to Matins, and I will carry you in my soul to sing God's praises with you, if you'd like. I'm writing to you in our little cell; it's a true paradise to me, an intimate sanctuary for Him and me alone: no one except our Reverend Mother can come into it. If you knew how good it is to live there in the Master's sight in a sweet heart-to-heart with Him! A Dieu, I'm going to ring the bell. I only have time to send you all my affection. Don't forget me at Labastide and at Mas[2] when you write. My greetings to Monsieur Joseph.[3] Union always.

Sr. Elizabeth of the Trinity

Would you go to see Monsieur le Chanoine [Canon Angles] for me and tell him to pray fervently for his Carmelite. You will see my Guite before I do, give her a kiss for me and tell her to do the same to my dear Marie-Louise.

¹ Elizabeth had written "my" first. Cf. L 134, note 1.
² At Labastide: her parents; at Mas-Cabardès: M. and Mme. Angles.
³ Joseph Ambry, her husband.

L 143   To her mother   [November 1, 1902]
          J. M. + J. T.   Dijon Carmel, November 1

My dear little Mama,
        Our Reverend Mother is so good that she understands the loneliness of your heart and is letting me come tell you that my soul will be even more closely united with yours right now, and that, in the unity of the same faith and love, we'll find in God those dear departed ones who have gone on ahead of us. Never have I felt them so present; you see, my dear Mama, they're so happy that I'm in Carmel, for Carmel is so close to Heaven, it's Heaven in faith! When you hear the bell ring for the Office of the Dead, let your soul be united with mine; do everything I do with me, it's all arranged with God! Today the Master said, "Blessed are those who weep for they will be comforted,"¹ in Heaven, "He will wipe every tear from their eyes."² Dear Mama, I've seen you weep so often, your life has been sown with sorrows and sacrifices, but you know, the more God asks, the more He provides and gives!
        That Lamb whom the blessed adore in the [Beatific] Vision is the One to whom your Elizabeth is betrothed and the One whose bride she so longs to become. Oh! Mama, how beautiful my part is. The whole divine world is mine, for it is the center in which I must live and, already here below, I must follow my Lamb everywhere.³ If you knew my happiness, you would thank Him who chose me; then listen to what He says: "Whoever does the will of my Father is my father, my mother, my brother, my sister"!⁴ Remember that you are not alone, that the divine friend is with you, and your Elizabeth with Him!...

May He bring you all the tender affection of my heart. I've left you for Him, but I love you more than ever, you are so good a mama!

Eliz. of the Trinity

If you're not too tired, you should go to hear Père Menne[5] at Saint-Michel during the Octave of All Souls; they say he is a true son of Père Vallée.

[1] Mt 5:4
[2] Rev 7:17.
[3] Cf. Rev 14:4.
[4] Mt 12:50. Cf. L 103, note 3. Elizabeth adds "father" here to the Gospel text.
[5] From November 3 to 10, 1902, at 8 P.M. (cf. SRD, 17, p. 690). This is what determines the year of the letter. Elizabeth spells it "Maine."

L 144   To her sister   [November 1, 1902]
J. M. + J. T.   Dijon Carmel, November 1

My dear Guite,

Your sweet letter really made me happy. I think so often about you and, for my heart, Dijon and Sainte-Maxime[1] are very close, I assure you. I'm delighted by your happiness; I thank God (and Saint Teresa), asking them that this happiness might always increase and my little sister might be as happy as I!

I saw Mama on Monday;[2] she told me what joy your good letters are bringing her. She really needs that, for time passes less quickly for her than for us, but in her solitude she is enjoying our happiness, for you know she has always lived only for us. Thursday morning, too, she had to accompany our dear Alice to the Little Sisters.[3] I had a visit with her several days before she left, I thought she was very likable.

Thank Georges[4] for his kind (and clever) note that really touched me; I think my thanks will be better received if it goes by way of his dear Marguerite, so I confide it to you. Isn't it true that one never tires of gazing at that beautiful sea? Do you recall the last time we saw it together on the Rock of the Virgin at Biarritz?[5] What wonderful hours I spent there. Those waves sweeping over the rocks were so beautiful, my soul thrilled before such a magnificent sight!

Really enjoy it with Georges and remember that in Carmel I have all those vast horizons. Don't forget me at Carlipa, at Limoux[6] and in all your visits with friends; I'll follow you everywhere. We'll see each other in two weeks, but we haven't left each other, have we? If you knew how I enfold you in my prayer! You, too, my little one, pray for your Sabeth, that she may soon become a bride,[7] for she is longing for that so much!

I join you both to send you much affection, and thank Georges for so pampering my Guite whom I myself loved to pamper so much.

Your Sister Elizabeth of the Trinity

You should ask Marie-Louise to take you to the Carmel of Carcassonne.[8]

[1] On their honeymoon.
[2] October 28. "Tired" (L 143 and 145), Mme. Catez gave up the idea of accompanying her daughter in the South of France.
[3] The Little Sisters of the Poor who kept a house for the elderly on the Boulevard de Strasbourg. It is not known which Alice is referred to here.
[4] Her brother-in-law. Elizabeth wrote "genil" and then wrote "gentil" over it ("gentil" = kind).
[5] Cf. L 30 of August 12, 1900.
[6] With the Le Soujeole family, where Elizabeth had surely gone in 1900 (L 33) and 1896 (L 11, 12).
[7] By her profession.
[8] This Carmel had had to move because of political difficulties. Mother Germaine wrote in a postscript, "The aforesaid Carmel is in London!"

L 145   To Madame Angles   [November 9, 1902][1]
         J. M. + J. T.   Dijon Carmel, November 9

Very dear Madame,

I imagine you have seen Guite these past few days and that she has given you all the messages my heart had entrusted to her; but above all it is from "soul to soul" that I love to come to you beneath the gaze of Him we love and whom alone we seek. Thank you for your good prayers; we have had so beautiful, so profound, so divine a retreat. Père Vallée spoke to us the whole time on Jesus Christ[2] and I wish I could have had you very close to me so that your soul could have been carried away with mine. Dear Madame, through everything, let us constantly live in communion with this Incarnate Word, with Jesus who dwells in us and who wishes to tell us the whole Mystery. On the eve of His Passion, He said to His Father in speaking of those who were His own: "The words which you gave me, I have given to them; the brightness that I had in you before the world began, I have given to them."[3] He is always living, always at work in our souls; let us allow ourselves to be formed by Him; may He be the Soul of our soul, the Life of our life, so that we may say with Saint Paul: "For me, to live is Christ."[4] Dear Madame, He does not want any sadness in your soul about what was not done solely for Him. He is the Savior, His mission is to pardon; and Father told us during his retreat: "There is only one impulse in the Heart of Christ: to wipe out sin and to lead the soul to God."[5] I am praying fervently for you, for I feel that the Master loves you so much, and I ask Him to take you, to draw you more and more to Himself, so that through everything you will enjoy His presence. May your soul be another Bethany where Jesus may come to rest,[6] and where you serve Him the banquet of love. Dear Madame, let us love as Magdalene loved; then, for your little friend, thank Him who chose the better part for her!...

Yesterday[7] I saw my good Mama, who is looking forward to Guite's return. She is very tired, but God is at work in the midst of all that, and when this dear Mama opens her soul to me, I am overjoyed to see all that is being done by Him for whom I left her. A Dieu, dear Madame, I am leaving you to go to Matins, or rather I am going to meet you in Him who unites our souls. Continue always to pray with me, that Jesus may absorb and possess us.

Your very affectionate little friend,

Elizabeth of the Trinity

I wrote to Marie-Louise.[8] I hope my letter reached her, for I'm afraid I may have addressed it wrong.

---

[1] 1902: cf. the following note.

[2] The retreat lasted from October 7th (they went into retreat on the 6th, according to L 138, therefore in the evening) until the 14th (up to the feast of St. Teresa, according to L 138, therefore the 15th; on the latter date, P. Vallée preached in the afternoon in the chapel during "solemn Benediction sung to music" [SRD, 17, p. 642] in honor of St. Teresa—the text of the sermon has been preserved).

P. Irénée Vallée, a Dominican, was at that time 61 years old. The entire text of the

14 sermons for these eight days has been preserved (there was undoubtedly no sermon for Sunday, October 12). P. Vallée announced that "I would like to preach this whole retreat for you on Our Lord Jesus Christ." In the morning, he treated more speculative subjects: 1. Our Lord Jesus Christ; 2. Grace in Jesus Christ; 3. Infinite grace in Jesus Christ (continued); 4. Christ, *Caput Ecclesiae*; 5. Christ, Head of the Angels; 6. The light of vision in the soul of Christ; 7. Infused knowledge in the soul of Christ. In the evening, the themes were more concrete: 1. St. John the Baptist, the Precursor; 2. The temptation; 3. The apostles; 4. Christ's word to the multitude; 5. The word of Jesus Christ in the temple; 6. The Divine Office; 7. Christ's word to the Blessed Virgin and St. Joseph.

　　　P. Vallée had announced euphemistically, "In the morning, I will be asking you to work a little." To judge from her quotations, Elizabeth seems to have profited much more from her reading of the 1900 retreat, which was simpler and closer to concrete life. The 1902 audience passed through some difficult moments, as attested by this admission from the Book of the Chronicles of the Dijon Carmel (pp. 201–202): "The morning topics treated the riches of grace in the soul of the Incarnate Word with great loftiness.... Notes were taken as the preacher spoke; but the young Sister charged with this work [Sister Agnès, according to tradition] let more than one error slip into her account; in spite of her intense desire not to let anything be lost from this celestial feast, being a stranger to those lofty studies, she committed several little heresies.... The Reverend Father kindly corrected these long summaries; thanks to his fatherly goodness, we have a perfect copy of it...." This copy in an unknown hand is kept in ACD. As for the notes taken by Elizabeth, they have been collected in PAT. Finally, let us remark that this retreat, in its outline and general themes, is completely different in its elaboration from that published under the title *L'Ame du Christ [The Soul of Christ]* (Lyon: Les Editions de l'Abeille, 1943, 265 p.). The printed retreat is more polished (and at the same time simplified). It would therefore be incorrect to present it as the one Sister Elizabeth heard (cf. the preface of the book cited). After becoming in 1904 the first Prior of Saulchoir in Belgium (cf. A. de Pitteurs, *Le R. P. Vallée: Un grand Prêcheur, [Rev. Fr. Vallée: A Great Preacher]* Cerf, 1934, pp. 188–200), the author undoubtedly put his conferences in their final form at that time.

³ Cf. Jn 17:8, 22–24.
⁴ Phil 1:21.
⁵ Elizabeth quotes here her own summary of the beginning of the fifth morning sermon (cf. PAT).
⁶ Cf. Lk 10:38-42.
⁷ Saturday, November 8.
⁸ L 142.

L 146　　To Madame de Sourdon　　　　　[November 19, 1902]
　　　　　J. M. + J. T.　　　　　　Wednesday, November 19

Very dear Madame,

　　　I cannot tell you how much I have appreciated your kind feastday wishes[1] and all your treats. Your heart will read between these lines what mine cannot express; you have always been so good to your little friend and to her dear Mama, and there are some memories that cannot be forgotten! Dear Madame, I so love to meet you close to God. In Him there is no distance or separation; I feel that so clearly since I have been in Carmel. It seems to me that such real, intimate encounters can be made from one soul to another, and just as we can live with the dear departed ones[2] who have gone before us, we also have contact with souls who are deeply united to us; it is God who does that! Really believe, dear Madame, that the grilles have not separated us at all, and the heart of your little Carmelite is always yours, for it is God who guards it, and you know, as Saint Paul says, "He is faithful,"[3] and what He guards is well guarded. When you write to Madame d'Anthès, would you tell her I am praying for her in a special way and I do not forget her intention. Yours, dear Madame, are not forgotten either. You know my heart well enough to know that those who have entered it can never leave it, and where better to meet them than in Him who is the source and the indissoluble bond of true and profound affection, which neither time nor distance can alter. Be assured, dear Madame, of my deep affection and with a big kiss receive all the thanks of your little friend

Elizabeth of the Trinity

Please tell Adèle that I offered a lovely prayer for her while eating her delicious custard.

Please pass on my thanks to Marie-Louise and Framboise, whose good wishes really touched me; I saw them last week so I'm not writing to them, but my heart goes out to them, I love them both so much.

---

[1] For St. Elizabeth, the same day. Handwriting of 1902.
[2] An allusion to Mme. de Sourdon's husband, who died in 1895, and to Elizabeth's father.
[3] 1 Cor 1:9, for example.

L 147   To Madame Farrat   [before the end of 1902][1]
J. M. + J. T.

Very dear Madame,

The heart of your little friend needs to tell you that her prayer for your dear patient is very intense. My Communion today will be for him; we will have the Blessed Sacrament in the oratory then and, like Mary Magdalene at the feet of my Master, I am going to become wholly imploring and say to Him: "The one you love is sick."[2] Jesus gives His Cross to His true friends so He can come even closer to them; in His Heart, I see a very great love for you. Your dear little angel[3] is watching over you from Heaven, and I unite myself to her who loved me so much in order to touch the Heart of God.

I kiss you and remain very united with you in heart and prayer.
Your little friend

M. Elizabeth of the Trinity

[1] The original letter has disappeared. The copies indicate 1902 as the date. The absence of "r.c.i." after her signature indicates that Elizabeth was still a novice. The letter alludes to the illness of M. Farrat, who would die on February 13, 1904. The Farrats were neighbors of the Catezes.
[2] Jn 11:3.
[3] Her daughter Cécile Marie-Madeleine, who died on May 30, 1900, at the age of four.

L 148   To her mother   [around the end of 1902][1]
J. M. + J. T.

My very dear Mama,

Our Reverend Mother must have told you that because of recent events we are taking a few precautionary measures in case we should have to leave our dear cloister. I'd be very grateful if you'd give me your skirt pattern right away, the one that has one piece for the front and *one* piece for the sides, like Guite's grey dress, so a pleat can be placed on each side like I used to make for your skirts, then I could adapt it in several different ways. Would you also be kind enough to give me the man's hat[2] we bought in Paris, though this is less urgent. Thanks, my dear Mama. I'm waiting for the pattern; it will remind me of the times we used to work together. Do believe that He who took me all to Himself keeps me all for you.

Your Elizabeth

[1] Approximate date based on the handwriting and ink.
[2] Perhaps needed for the feast of the Holy Innocents, December 28. The novitiate traditionally prepared a "pious recreation" for that day.

L 149   To Madame Angles   [December 29, 1902]
     J.M. + J.T.   Dijon Carmel, December 29

Very dear Madame,

The Infant God kept a great joy in store for my soul, and on the feast of His Nativity He told me He was going to come as my Bridegroom:[1] on Epiphany[2] He will make me His queen and I will pronounce the vows that will unite me to Him forever! My joy is so profound, so divine! It cannot be put into words, but your soul has been in close enough communion with God to understand it. Help me, for I wish to be as He wants me to be, and on the day of my profession, I must console my Master and make Him forget everything. I feel my weakness, but He is within me to prepare me; so, wholly joyful and confident, I will dare to go before Him so He may consummate the union He has dreamed of in His infinite love. You will not be forgotten by your little friend on that day, I assure you. For your part, unite yourself to her on that morning, the most beautiful of her life, when she finally becomes the bride of Christ until death. Oh! thank Him for me, won't you, my part is so beautiful! A whole life to be spent in silence and adoration, a heart-to-heart with the Spouse! Pray that I may be faithful, that I may fulfill His plans for my soul right to the very end, that I may accomplish fully all that He wills, that I may make Him happy! Dear Madame, may our souls be united in consoling our Master! He is so offended in the world, for they want no more of Him; let us open ourselves to receive Him, and then let us not leave Him alone in that sanctuary of our soul; through everything let us remember that He is there and He needs to be loved. Tomorrow night I go into retreat to prepare for my profession. You can imagine how joyfully I look forward to those ten days of even more complete solitude and absolute separation; would you like to go away with your little friend?

Your good wishes really touched me. I did not write to you before Advent since I had written a short time before[3] and our holy Rule does not allow us to write so often, but our union is deep enough that we can communicate soul to soul.

A Dieu, dear Madame, please tell Marie-Louise and Monsieur le Chanoine about my happiness, if you tell him we write each other. All yours in Him,

Sr. M. Elizabeth of the Trinity

---

[1] On Christmas, Mother Germaine told Elizabeth that the community had accepted her for profession. It had been unanimous.
[2] Then celebrated on the Sunday after January 6, therefore January 11, 1903.
[3] L 138 of September 29, 1902. In principle, they wrote to friends only once every three months.

L 150   To Père Vallée   [December 31, 1902]
        J. M. + J. T.   Dijon Carmel, December 31

My Reverend Father,

The Master told you, didn't He, that your little one was going to become His bride, that His first word for her[1] was "Veni,"[2] and that on that beautiful feast of light and adoration, on that day of the Three, He was going to come before her to consummate the union of which He had dreamed in His infinite charity. Oh! my Father, how happy I am, with a happiness unlike any I have tasted up to now; it is less perceptible, it is in the depths of the soul; and then it is so calm, so tranquil! I am going into retreat this evening. Please pray, won't you, that I may be wholly surrendered, wholly vigilant, and that God may accomplish all He wills[3] for my soul. It seems to me that something so great is being prepared, and I feel wholly enveloped in the charity of Christ. Oh! Father, how good it is to give oneself in these times when He is so offended! On this beautiful day of my profession, I would like to console Him, to make Him forget everything, then too, I would like this to be the beginning of an endless act of adoration in my soul. You do want your little one to be

His adorer, don't you, like that Magdalene who was also quiet enough to hear the word that the Master was saying.

Dear Father, you have told me there is no distance for souls. Keep mine very close to yours then, *in* yours, and then offer me, so that I may be wholly taken by Christ, so that I may live no longer but that He may live in me.[4] Then from a wholly paternal heart, bless your little child.

Elizabeth of the Trinity.

[1] "At Christmas" is written in Mother Germaine's hand.
[2] "Come," to the profession.
[3] "The will of God": A Valléen expression; like "enveloped" in the next letter.
[4] Gal 2:20.

L 151   To Canon Angles   [December 31, 1902]
       J.M. + J.T.   Dijon Carmel, December 31

Dear Monsieur le Chanoine,

Since you have always been so good to me and have been so interested in my vocation, my soul is coming to yours tonight to confide its immense happiness.

The Bridegroom has said His "Veni" to me, and on the 11th of January, on that beautiful [feast] of the Epiphany, so full of light and adoration, I will pronounce the vows that will unite me to Christ forever. You who have kept an eye on me from my childhood and listened to my first secrets can understand the great happiness that is flooding my soul. Tonight I asked the prayers of my dear community and tomorrow I begin my ten-day retreat. That seems like a dream to me, I have waited so long for it, desired it so much. Would you remember me in a special way every morning at Holy Mass, for something so great is being prepared. I feel myself enveloped in the mystery of Christ's charity, and when I look back I see a divine pursuit of my soul; oh! what love, as if I were crushed beneath its weight, then I am silent and adore!

On that Epiphany morning, the most beautiful of my life, although the Master has already given me such divine days that quite resemble those spent in His paradise, on that day when all my wishes are fulfilled and when I finally become the "bride of Christ," would you, dear Monsieur le Chanoine, offer the Holy Sacrifice for your Carmelite; then offer her, that she may be wholly taken, wholly invaded, and that she may say with Saint Paul: "I live no longer I, but Christ lives in me."[1]

Do I need to tell you what my prayer for you will be, you know my soul and my heart well enough!...

I leave you to enter with the Bridegroom into profound recollection; pray, won't you, and bless your happy Carmelite.

Sr. Elizabeth of the Trinity

[1] Gal 2:20.

L 152   To Sister Marie of the Trinity   [January 10, 1903][1]

I have just seen Our Mother, who has admitted to me her uneasiness at seeing me pronounce my vows in such a state of soul. Pray for your little one, who is overwhelmed with anguish.

[1] The only source is the testimony of the recipient: "I affirm that I received this note from Sr. Elizabeth on the eve of (her) profession" (PO 167). In RB 8 (cf. PAT) she also speaks (without giving the text) of the "word *desperate* that I found on our chair on coming to Vespers on the eve of her profession." It was necessary to call P. Vergne in order to restore her peace of soul (cf. AL).

Elizabeth in monastery garden in early 1903. She is holding her profession crucifix (see L 156).

II

"To Live With ... Always With"
January 11, 1903 – November 20, 1904

In pure faith, after hours of great distress, Elizabeth pronounced her perpetual vows on January 11, 1903, the feast of the Epiphany. The public veiling ceremony took place on January 21.

Very quickly after her final commitment, peace returned entirely to her soul. Her sky was "all starry" (L 198). "During the night preceding the great day," she wrote on July 15, 1903, referring to her profession, "while I was in choir awaiting the Bridegroom, I understood that my Heaven was beginning on earth, Heaven in faith, with suffering and immolation for Him whom I love!" The same Letter 169 expresses other themes she lived by: her desires for infinite love, for giving unto death, for continual prayer, for joy in the presence of God: "I feel Him so alive in my soul. I have only to recollect myself to find Him within me, and that is my whole happiness." In silence and fidelity, she wished to "abide in Love" (L 170). She considered her life as a bride of Christ to be like "a heart-to-heart for one's whole life. It is to live with ... always with ... [and] to be fruitful, coredemptive, to bring souls forth into grace" (PN 13).

All of this, as well as her affectionate and prayerful attention to the needs of others, is manifest in the 62 letters and 4 poems of this period. It is evident again in her relationships with her Sisters in the community, for example in her new functions as second portress and second "habit Sister" (L 183, note 7). In 1903, she was the only "novice," but in 1904 she had as her companion Sr. Madeleine, who would eventually leave Carmel (cf. L 179, note 8). Her health was holding out. Her happiness acquired a new dimension with the birth of Guite's first child, Elizabeth, on March 11,

1904. On October 10, 1904, the Prioress and Sub-Prioress were both reelected for 3 years (cf. P 90).

Powerful Influences and Times

The direct and indirect influence of the Dominican P. Vallée (cf. Vol. I, 69–70), whom Elizabeth still quoted freely in her letters to a new correspondent, André Chevignard (all the more so since this seminarian belonged to the Dominican Third Order), becomes less visible than that of greater spiritual masters. Although Elizabeth had read less of her, St. Teresa of Avila strongly attracted her as a model of sanctity, as a "victim of love" (e.g., L 169 and 179); living her Carmelite life in the "mold" conceived by the Mother Foundress, Elizabeth shared her spirit of contemplation and apostolic fervor.

In the Dijon novitiate, this spirit was transmitted in particular through Thérèse of Lisieux, who had very quickly won the heart of Mother Germaine (cf. AL). The book she is opening before the postulant Elizabeth—a symbolic gesture—(see this photo in the present volume) is the *Story of a Soul.* Thérèse's name and influence often appear in the letters that follow (e.g., L 172 and 179), although Elizabeth of the Trinity kept her own special note of interiority. Mother Germaine went so far as to say that the "Mistress of Novices at Lisieux" was also that "of the Dijon Carmel, where her portrait presides" (cf. L 179, note 16).

Elizabeth was also nourished by the contemplative ideal proposed in the *Spiritual Canticle* and the *Living Flame of Love* by St. John of the Cross, whose works she had so desired (cf. L 106) and read with enthusiasm and spiritual affinity.

Letter 191 of January 25, 1904, reveals that she was in the process of extending her attention to Scripture, to the "magnificent letters" (the adjective is significant) of St. Paul. She had already condensed her ideal into desiring to become "the praise of glory" of God, an ideal and attitude that continued to deepen in the course of the three years of life that remained to her.

The autumn of 1904 was a powerful time for this Carmelite thirsting for God. Certainly she did benefit in 1903 and 1904 from the two "cenacle" times between Ascension and Pentecost, in which the community abstained from recreation but not from ordinary work, but only from September 26 to October 5, 1904, did she make her first personal retreat since her profession: ten days in "absolute solitude" with "several hours of additional prayer," enough to complete her happiness (L 211). Shortly afterward the daily recreations stopped for a new feast of silence: the community retreat, from the 12th to the morning of the 21st of November, preached by P. Fages, a Dominican (cf. PN 15, note 2.). At the end of this retreat, on the day of the renewal of vows, Elizabeth composed her celebrated prayer, "O My God, Trinity Whom I Adore" (PN 15), which is not simply a beautiful prayer but also a true offering of herself, marking a new stage.

Carmel in a Nation and a Diocese

Even if Elizabeth did not speak much about the situation of the church in France and in her diocese, she was not indifferent to it. But her "apostolate" was "union" with God, as she explained to P. Chevignard in the important L 191 already cited. Many things are hidden between these lines: "My soul loves to unite itself to yours in one and the same prayer for the Church, for the diocese."

In France, the July 2, 1901, Law of Associations was rigorously applied in 1902 and 1903 by the Combes government; numerous convents were closed, often with great local strife; this was a blow to tens of thousands of men and women religious, and many left their country (cf. L 160, note 5). A law of July 7, 1904, prohibited all congregations from teaching, which affected thousands of schools. Although unauthorized, the Dijon Carmel remained where it was; it only had to close the chapel to visitors, on April 16, 1903 (cf. L 165, note 6). In May 1903, Mother Germaine made a trip to Belgium where from then on a refuge awaited the Carmelites at Noiseux; soon afterward, part of their furniture was transferred there.

Elizabeth, immersed in God, kept her interior silence; she entrusted her Carmel, the church, and herself to the Lord. She no longer spoke in her letters about the matter of Bishop Le Nordez, which caused such a commotion throughout the diocese. A republican, lacking prudence but not ambition, the Bishop of Dijon was accused of being a Freemason (wrongly, in all probability). Elizabeth knew the Bishop well—he had presided at her clothing—but the Carmel was so little in favor of Bishop Le Nordez that, for Elizabeth's veiling, they chose a date on which the Bishop was absent from Dijon. The local newspapers grew more and more agitated. The clergy was divided. The seminarians refused in February 1904 to receive Orders from the hands of the Bishop, who sent some of them away. By common consent, all the seminarians went on strike and left the seminary. Threatened with immediate induction into the army, they returned several days later. On June 13, numerous parents refused to send their children to the Saint-Bénigne cathedral to receive the sacrament of confirmation. Summoned to Rome by Pius X (successor to Leo XIII, who died on July 20, 1903), Msgr. Le Nordez resigned as Bishop of Dijon on September 4, 1904. This call to Rome was one reason for the July 30 rupture in diplomatic relations between the French Republic and the Holy See.

Elizabeth certainly knew all this. In the parlor and inside Carmel, the subject could not have been entirely avoided. And one of the seminarians who had been on strike was the brother-in-law of her sister Guite, André Chevignard.

L 153   To Mother Germaine   [January 11, 1903][1]

My Mother, here is the Bridegroom!

He is inviting you to rest on His Heart.[2] There you will hear what is being sung in the soul of the bride and what is rising from her heart to [the heart] of the beloved Mother who prepared her for the day of union.

[1] On the day of her profession, Elizabeth expressed her gratitude on a holy card (see note 2). Text written in pencil.
[2] The holy card represents the Apostle John, his head leaning on the heart of Jesus. There is a chalice in front of them.

L 154   To her Rolland aunts   [January 12 (or a little after), 1903][1]
          J. M. + J. T.

My good little Aunts,

My first letter is for you. I'm in a hurry to tell you my happiness; in a hurry, too, to thank you for your beautiful remembrance. Your dear breviaries have arrived,[2] and from now on my soul and yours will be "one" when I sing the praises of God. I don't know how to express all my gratitude for the happiness you've brought me by giving me these beautiful breviaries that, coming from you, are doubly precious to me, and I ask my divine Bridegroom[3] to pay my heart's entire debt!... Oh! my little Aunts, how happy I am; here I am, the bride of Christ! I would like to speak to you about my profession, but, you see, it is something *so divine*, earthly language is powerless to repeat it. I had had very beautiful days before, but now I no longer even dare compare them with that day. It was a unique day, and I believe that if I found myself before God, I would not experience any emotion greater than what I felt; what happens between God and the soul at that time is so great! The ceremony is completely private, it takes place in chapter,[4] and the veiling doesn't take place on the same day; I did not explain that to you very well,[5] there are two ceremonies. I hope to receive the veil on the 21st for the feast of Saint Agnes, but it hasn't been decided yet for we don't know if his Excellency will be free that day.[6] Oh, if you knew how much your little Elizabeth prayed for her beloved aunts on that most beautiful day of her life! Dear Aunt Francine, if God has not restored your sight,[7] really believe that in His love, He has His own plans for you, and that if He asks so many sacrifices of you, it is in order to give you much; I prayed much for you, I assure you, and I do so every day. I would like to tell you much more still, but I want to finish my letter tonight; I am anxious for it to bring you all the thanks of your Elizabeth. Oh, thank God for me, won't you. I am so happy: profession is a day without twilight; it seems to me that it is already like the beginning of the day that will no longer end. A Dieu, I meet all three of you in the heart of my Bridegroom and I kiss you, thanking you again with all my heart.

Sr Eliz. of the Trinity[8]

I prayed fervently for your good Curé, tell him that, won't you?

I am sending you two little flowers, they were in the chapter room on the altar where I immolated myself.

---

[1] "My first letter" after January 11, 1903. The "21st" still seems far away.

[2] *Breviarium romanum cum propriis officiis ad usum sanctimonialium carmelitarum excalceatarum ordinis B. Mariae de monte Carmelo in Galliis erecti juxta primitivam observantiam* (Poitiers: Frères Oudin, 1876), six volumes. See also L 171, note 6.

[3] Before her profession, she usually called herself the betrothed of the divine Fiancé; now she will be the bride of the Bridegroom.

[4] See Plan 2, no. 19, in this volume.

[5] This may have been in a letter that has been lost in which she spoke about the breviaries, or through her mother.

[6] Msgr. Le Nordez, Bishop of Dijon. Cf. the Introduction to Section II of this volume.

[7] She had poor eyesight; Aunt Mathilde had poor hearing.

[8] Elizabeth was still not used to writing "r.c.i." (cf. L 155, note 5) after her name.

L 155   To Madame de Bobet   [February 4, 1903][1]
       J. M. + J. T.   Dijon Carmel, Wednesday

My dear Antoinette,

    I assure you that my soul has really responded to your appeal, I never stop praying for your dear little daughter;[2] I understand so well the agonies of your maternal heart, and Jesus, above all, understands them; so I fervently commend you to Him. He is so powerful, so good.

    He still lives who, at Mary's prayer, restored Lazarus to life. Like that much beloved saint, I come to the Master and say to Him: "Lord, the one you love is sick,[3] and my dear Antoinette is so unhappy." Take courage, remember that we are in His hands. He is the Master of life and death! Once, at His touch, the sick recovered their health; He is still there today, leaning over our angel and over you with an infinite love. He wept at the tomb of the friend He loved;[4] in the name of those divine tears, I am asking Him to wipe away those that flow from your eyes.

    Our Reverend Mother, whose soul is wholly maternal, is praying fervently for you, as well as my dear community. As for me, I am a very recent bride, since barely three weeks ago I had the happiness of making solemn vows that unite me to God forever; so I am using all my power over the Heart of my divine Bridegroom for my dear Antoinette. Your silence lets me assume that the news is better, but my heart needed to tell you that it is one with yours. A Dieu, I leave you in Him, and I remain your very affectionate little sister.

                 M. Elizabeth of the Trinity r.c.i.[5]

---

[1] The "Wednesday" "barely three weeks" after her profession.
[2] Presumably Simone, ten years old, or little Jeanne-Marie, two years old.
[3] Cf. Jn 11:3.
[4] Cf. Jn 11:35.
[5] Abbreviation for *"religieuse carmélite indigne"* (unworthy Carmelite religious), which was added to one's signature after profession.

L 156   To Madame Angles   [February 15, 1903]
         J. M. + J. T.   Dijon Carmel, February 15

Very dear Madame,

You were not forgotten during those two "divine" days, the 11th and 21st of January, for I assure you, if you pray for me, I, for my part, also feel strongly attracted to your soul, which I feel is so loved and so sought by the Master, who wants to possess us fully. I am very happy to think that you are consecrated to God, and it seems to me that you are better able to understand the happiness of your little Carmelite Sister. Who could describe the joy of my soul when, on contemplating the crucifix I received after my profession[1] that our Reverend Mother set "as a seal on my heart,"[2] I could say to myself: "At last He is all mine, and I am all His: now I have nothing else but Him, He is my All!"[3] And now I have only one desire, to love Him, *to love Him all the time,* to be zealous for His honor as a true bride,[4] to give Him joy, to make Him happy by preparing a dwelling and a refuge for Him in my soul, so that there He may forget, by the strength of my love, all the abominations of the wicked! Yes, dear Madame, let us console Him.

You ask me how I can endure the cold. Do believe that I am no more generous than you are, only you are ill, whereas I am in good health. I do not feel the cold. So you see, I have little merit, and I used to suffer much more from winter at home than I do in Carmel where I have no heat at all.[5] God gives the grace; besides, it is so good, when one feels these little things, to look at the Master who also endured all that because He "loved us exceedingly," as Saint Paul says;[6] then one thirsts to repay Him love for love! In Carmel we find many sacrifices of this kind, but they are so sweet when the heart is wholly taken by love. I will tell you what I do when I feel a little tired: I look at the Crucified, and when I see how *He* delivered Himself up for *me,* it seems to me that I can do no less for *Him* than spend myself, wear myself out[7] in order to repay Him a little of what He has given me! Dear Madame, in the morning at Holy Mass, let us share in His spirit of sacrifice: we are His brides, so we ought to be like Him. Then, after that, let us remain in Him during the day. Then, if we are faithful in living His life, if we identify ourselves with all the movements of the soul of the Crucified, quite simply, we no longer need to fear our weaknesses, for He will be our strength, and who can snatch us away from Him? I believe that He is very happy and that our sacrifices must console His Heart very much. During this Lent, I will keep a rendez-vous with you in the Infinity of God, in His Charity: would you like that to be the desert where, with our divine Bridegroom, we go to live in a profound solitude, since it is in this solitude that He speaks to the heart? [8]

A Dieu, Madame and dear sister, we are united, aren't we, and you do know my deep affection for you. Your little sister,

M. Elizabeth of the Trinity

I will tell you about my days the next time I write to you,[9] since that interests you.

---

[1] Elizabeth brought this crucifix when she entered Carmel; this is at least what tradition affirms (see also RB 8 in PAT). But Mlle. Isabelle Dromard declared, on May 25, 1945, in a manuscript note preserved in the ACD that "Marie Bourgoin, who had become Mme. de Laforest, gave her her profession crucifix." This large crucifix (8.75 inches x 4.5 inches, weighing 9.5 ounces), which she wore over her heart after her profession, is on black wood mounted on copper. Although mass-produced, the corpus is beautiful. At the foot of the crucifix, the date of her profession, January 11, 1903; on the back of the cross beam, an inscription engraved in the wood: *Amo Christum* (I love Christ), as was the custom in the Dijon Carmel. On the vertical beam, the religious could have the text of their choice inscribed; Elizabeth chose Galatians 2:20 (cf. L 99, note 3; L 107, note 3; L 150, note 4; L 151, note 1): *Vivo enim jam non ego, vivit vero in me Christus* (I live, no longer I, but Christ lives in me).

Where the two beams meet is a copper emblem representing a heart from which a flame emerges, pierced through by a dagger and surrounded by a crown. The Dijon Carmel was in fact dedicated to the suffering Heart of Jesus and the transpierced Heart of Mary. The initials M. T. (undoubtedly the Virgin Mary and Saint Teresa) always appeared on the back at the top and, on the bottom, E. T. (Elizabeth of the Trinity). Elizabeth is holding this crucifix in her hands in several of her photographs as a Carmelite.

[2] Cf. Song 8:6. The Bridegroom speaks in this verse from the Song of Songs: "Set me as a seal on your heart."

[3] The sentence that Elizabeth writes in quotation marks really seems to be a personal expression inspired by Song 2:16: "My Beloved is mine, and I am his."

[4] An allusion to the first antiphon for First Vespers of St. Teresa of Avila: "I am filled with zeal for the honor of my Bridegroom Jesus Christ, who said to me, like a true bride you will be zealous for my honor" (from *Spiritual Testimonies*, 31 of St. Teresa).

[5] Only the recreation room was heated, and then only at certain times.

[6] For the first time in her *Letters* (but already in P 75 from Christmas 1901), Elizabeth

quotes Ephesians 2:4 (in this translation); she will use this expression often. P. Vallée also used it freely: once in the 1902 retreat, in the seventh morning sermon; twice in the 1900 retreat; once in the address for Marie of the Trinity's veiling.

[7] Even before her profession, Elizabeth's health had caused concern. Perhaps the expression "wear myself out" alludes to a certain physical deterioration.

[8] Cf. Hos 2:16.

[9] In L 168.

L 157   To Madame de Sourdon   [February 21, 1903][1]

J. M. + J. T.   Carmel, Saturday evening

Dear Madame,

Before your letter I received a few lines from Madame de Maizières,[2] a cry from the heart my soul has really responded to, I assure you. When you write to her, would you tell her that we are praying fervently in Carmel and that I never once attend the Divine Office without commending to God the health of the dear patient[3] who causes so much concern to those who love him. I understand this distress so well, and God above all understands it!

You remember, dear Madame, the distressing hours I have known myself. I will never forget how good you were to the poor little one who thought she was about to lose her mother.[4] What painful memories—they are the bond, as it were, that unites our souls. Those are God's times. Père Didon says "any destiny that doesn't have its calvary is a punishment from God."[5] Oh, then, if we knew how to surrender ourselves totally into the hands of Him who is our Father.... I recommend your intentions to Him. Do not doubt Him, dear Madame, abandon *everything* to Him, as well as to your little friend.... She will be your advocate ... for her mission is to pray unceasingly, and you know how much that holds true for you! She is so HAPPY, with a happiness that God alone knows, for He is its sole Object, a happiness that closely resembles that of Heaven. During this Lent, so divine in Carmel, my soul will be especially united to yours. I am asking God to show you the sweetness of His presence and to make your soul a sanctuary where He can come to be consoled. Will you let me enter there and, with you, adore Him who dwells there?

I kiss my dear Françoise whom I love so much and your sweet Marie-Louise. I pray fervently for them, and I am always all yours; don't you feel that?

Your little friend,

Sr. M. Elizabeth of the Trinity r.c.i.

Would you tell my dear Mama that my soul is one with hers and that I love her with all my heart.

---

[1] After her profession ("r.c.i."), but before the new handwriting that begins around Easter (cf. General Introduction in Vol. I), on the "Saturday" before "this Lent," which seems imminent and begins February 25, 1903.

[2] Her sister who lived in Paris. Elizabeth must have written her a letter that has been lost.

[3] Probably Mme. de Maizières's husband, Joseph.

[4] Around the beginning of 1899. Cf. L 19-21, P 64-66, D 46.

[5] Elizabeth is quoting here from her notebook of quotations (cf. PAT). In 1901 (cf. L 49), she came across this phrase in the preface (p. XI) of the *Lettres du R. P. Didon à Mademoiselle Th. V.* (Paris: Plon, 1901). See also above, the Introduction to Section I of the *Letters from Carmel*, about this vision of suffering.

L 158   To Abbé Chevignard[1]   [February 24, 1903][2]
J. M. + J. T.   Dijon Carmel, February
Amo Christum

Monsieur l'Abbé,

Before entering into the great silence of Lent, I want to answer your kind letter. And my soul needs to tell you that it is wholly in communion with yours, letting itself be caught, carried away, invaded by Him whose charity envelops us and who wishes to consummate us into "one" with Him. I thought of you when I read these words of Père Vallée on contemplation: "The contemplative is a being who lives in the radiance of the Face of Christ, who enters into the mystery of God, not in the light that flows from human thought, but in that created by the word of the Incarnate Word."[3] Don't you have this passion to listen to Him?[3a] Sometimes it is so strong, this need to be silent, that one would like to know how to do nothing but remain like Magdalene, that beautiful model for the contemplative soul, at the feet of the Master, eager to hear everything, to penetrate ever deeper into this mystery of Charity that He came to reveal to us. Don't you find that in action, when we are in Martha's role,[4] the soul can still remain wholly adoring, buried like Magdalene in her contemplation, staying by this source like someone who is starving; and this is how I understand the Carmelite's apostolate as well as the priest's. Then both can radiate God, give Him to souls, if they constantly stay close to this divine source. It seems to me that we should draw so close to the Master, in such communion with His soul, to identify ourselves with all its movements, and then go out as He did, according to the will of His Father. Then it does not matter what happens to the soul, since it has faith in the One it loves who dwells within it. During this Lent I would like, as Saint Paul says, "to be buried in God with Christ,"[5] to be lost in this Trinity who will one day be our vision, and in this divine light penetrate into the depth of the Mystery. Would you pray that I may be wholly surrendered and that my Beloved Bridegroom may carry me away wherever He wishes. A Dieu, Monsieur l'Abbé, let us remain in His love;[6] is He not that infinity for which our souls so thirst?

Sr. M. Elizabeth of the Trinity, r.c.i.

Our Reverend Mother asks me to express her gratitude for the canticle; how good she is and how she gives God (to others), don't you agree? On Monday[7] I will offer Holy Communion for you; don't forget me either.

---

[1] The brother of Elizabeth's brother-in-law was then studying theology in the Dijon seminary. He received the tonsure on February 22, 1902, and would receive the four minor orders on March 28, 1903, from the hands of Bishop Le Nordez. He was ordained subdeacon on January 6, 1905, and deacon on April 8, 1905. His priestly ordination (by Msgr. Maillet, Bishop of Saint-Claude) was on July 29, 1905.

[2] The autograph has disappeared. The letter is placed after her profession and "before Lent." The copy in the ACD (Notebook 6), made from the autograph, indicates "February 24, 1903." Undoubtedly they repeated the date P. Chevignard himself inscribed *later* on several of the letters he received.

[3] "Address for the Veiling of Sister Marie of the Trinity" (described in L 133, note 4), pp. 7–8. The word "radiance" (like "clarity" and "light") appear frequently in P. Vallée. Elizabeth copies this faithfully. A note refers to 2 Corinthians 4:6 for "the Face of Christ."

[3a] "Passion for listening" (also in L 164): in the tenth sermon (on the Holy Trinity) of the 1900 retreat, P. Vallée speaks of the soul who "comes with the passion to listen; it is there wholly for listening."

[4] Cf. Lk 10:38–42.

[5] "Bury" (used twice in this letter) appeared already on August 13, 1901, in P 73. An image of the cloistered and hidden life, with Elizabeth it is not tied to the tomb but to the Resurrection. To die to oneself is to live in communication (cf. PN 13 of 1902: "It is a heart-to-heart for a lifetime. It is to live with ... always with ..."), as the quotation from St. Paul makes clear. It refers to Colossians 3:3: "You have died, and your life is hidden with Christ in God." It is in this sense that P. Vallée, who often used the word "bury," said in the third morning sermon of the 1902 retreat: "Thus you must ... live 'buried with Him in God,' as St. Paul says." Elizabeth is probably echoing P. Vallée. The word "buried" (instead of "hidden") in this quotation from St. Paul is connected with Romans 6:4. Paul expresses there how the Christian, united by baptism to the death of Jesus, dies to sin in order to be restored to a new life.

[6] Cf. Jn 15:9.

[7] Thus probably March 1st.

L 159   To her mother   [March 1903][1]
      J. M. + J. T.

My dear little Mama,

Our Reverend Mother, who is infinitely good, is letting me write to you, and you can guess how happy the heart of your daughter is to come and tell you that it is but *"one"* with yours. Oh! if you knew how true it is that I follow you everywhere and that there is no longer any distance between my dear Mama and me!...

I read many things between [your] lines.... If I were near you I would want to ease them; it used to cause me pain when I saw a cloud on your face, and I am still the same! I am asking the divine Bridegroom, for whom I left you, to be *"all"* for you; I am so happy you are going to Him like that! Darling Mama, if you feel ice[2] forming on your heart, go warm yourself near Him whose love is a consuming fire and who creates voids only so He can fill them completely!... Tell your good hosts[3] I'm delighted to think of you among them and that they are not forgotten in my prayers. Say that, too, to Mademoiselle Adeline, to Madame Massiet, I'm especially united to her (I am praying for her mother); may she pray a little for me and thank Him who chose the better part for me. You, too, my little Mama, thank Him for having a Carmelite daughter in spite of all the sacrifices and tears it has cost you. But if you saw this vocation in God's light, how you would bless Him! He is pleased with you, Mama, if you knew how He loves you, and how I, too, love you! Do you remember March 26th four years ago?[4] It was on that day that you said your "Fiat" to God and your Elizabeth. A Dieu, darling Mama. Offer Him all that wounds your heart, confide everything to Him, think that day and night you have someone in your soul who never leaves you alone. I love you my dear Mama, the best of mamas, and I kiss you very tenderly.

Elizabeth of the Trinity, r.c.i.

I feel wonderful.[5] Our Reverend Mother watches over her little child so well.

[1] New handwriting of 1903 (cf. General Introduction, Vol. 1); the change is nearly accomplished. The special "permission" to write presupposes that it is Lent (cf. note 4.).
[2] Her solitude since Guite's marriage.
[3] Cf. L 109 of the preceding year at the same time. Mme. Catez is thus staying at Lunéville, her native town, perhaps at Mme. Cosson's home.
[4] Cf. D 105 of March 26, 1899. Elizabeth made a mistake and wrote "three years ago."
[5] Undoubtedly intended to reassure her mother during this period of Lent, which is severe for Carmelites, especially for Elizabeth, whose state of health was weak. Mother Germaine repeats in a postscript: "Sister Elizabeth is feeling wonderful."

L 160   To Madame de Bobet   [April 27, 1903][1]
   J. M. + J. T.   Dijon Carmel, April 27

My very dear Antoinette,
    After the silence of Lent, my very first letter is for you. Ah, if you knew how true it is that my soul is in communion with yours and that I ask Him who is my One and All to take hold of you more and more. I share all your anxiety for the two darlings God has given you.[2] Through what anguish your maternal heart has passed.... All that, my dear Antoinette, is meant to bring you still closer to Him, it is to force us to abandon ourselves into the arms of the God who is our Father and who, in the most difficult hours, when He sometimes seems very far away, is in reality *so* close, so "within"[3] us. I understand your anguish so well, and I send you these words that the Divine Master addressed to Saint Catherine of Siena: "Think of me; I will think of you."[4] Go lose yourself in Him, dear Antoinette. He is

guarding your two treasures, and your little sister speaks to Him about it often!...

Yes, the future is very dark, and don't you feel the need to love much in order to make reparation …[5] in order to console this adored Master.... Let us make a solitary place for Him in the innermost part of our soul and remain there with Him; let us never leave Him, for it is His commandment: "Remain in me, and I in you."[6] Nothing will be able to rob us of this interior cell, no matter what trials we undergo: I carry my One Treasure "inside me," and all the rest is nothing![7] Oh! if you knew what happiness invades my soul when I think that it is really true that I am His, and I am persecuted like Him; thank Him, won't you, for your little sister, it is too good to be a Carmelite!... And then let us be united in loving Him. I would so like to live only by love, very high above this earth where everything leaves a void in the soul. Saint Paul says that we belong to "the City of the saints and the House of God."[8] Oh then, why not live there now, since in the depths of our soul we possess Him who will one day make our beatitude! There is the bell for Matins; I will take you with me. A Dieu, let us always be "wholly one" in Him. Share all my tender affection with your two darlings.

Sister M. Elizabeth of the Trinity r.c.i.

---

[1] "My very first letter" after "Lent." After her profession ("r.c.i."), this could only be in 1903, as the handwriting confirms.

[2] Cf. L 155, note 2.

[3] Probably an allusion to Lk 17:21, in the translation of Elizabeth's *Manual:* "The kingdom of God is within you." Elizabeth had already used the expression "within" in January 1900 (D 138).

[4] Cf. L 129, note 5.

[5] The Waldeck-Rousseau government was successful in the elections of April 27 and May 11, 1902, followed by Emile Combes as President of the Council of State. He pursued a very hard antireligious line. He closed 135 private schools by the decree of June 27, 1902, and, on July 15, all those of congregations that had not asked for authorization: around 3,000 schools at once. On March 18, 1903, the Chamber refused the authorization requested by the 25 teaching congregations of men, thus affecting 11,763 religious. On March 24, the same refusal was given to 28 congregations of preachers, affecting 2,942 religious. Eighty-one women's congregations met the same fate. Their goods were confiscated. Many of the communities went to regroup abroad. Others, like the Dijon Carmel, continued to wait.

[6] Jn 15:4.

[7] Perhaps an echo of the "All and Nothing" *[Todo y Nada]* of John of the Cross?

[8] Eph 2:19.

L 161   To Françoise de Sourdon   [April 28, 1903][1]
        J. M. + J. T.   Dijon Carmel, Tuesday night

My very dear Françoise,

Our Reverend Mother is so good, I told her about the misunderstanding between Mama and me,[2] and she let me come to tell you tonight how much I'm thinking of you, how much I'm praying for you, my darling whom I love so much. I really assure you that the grilles have not separated my heart from yours, they are so well fused together, aren't they, my Françoise? They will always be "one" in Heaven just as on earth!...

I had a very good Lent. Of everything I've seen in Carmel, Holy Week and Easter Day are the most beautiful, I would even say they are unique; I'll tell you about that when I see you. Oh, my darling, what happiness it is to live in intimacy with God, to make our life a heart-to-heart, an exchange of love, when we know how to find the Master in the depths of our soul. Then we are never alone anymore, and need solitude to enjoy the presence of this adored Guest. Do you see, my Framboise, you must give Him His place in your life, in your heart, which He has made so loving, so passionate. Oh! if you knew how good He is, how He is all Love! I am asking Him to reveal Himself to your soul, to be the Friend whom you always know how to find; then everything is illuminated and it is so good to be alive! This is not some sermon that I want to give you, it is the overflow from my soul, which brims over into yours so that together we can lose ourselves in Him who loves us, as Saint Paul says, "with an exceeding love"![3]

Good night, my Framboise, I love you a lot and kiss you with all my heart.

                        Sr. Elizabeth of the Trinity r.c.i.

Tell your good mother, whom I love so much, that I am not forgetting what I promised her. Affectionate thoughts to my dear Marie-Louise.

---

[1] New handwriting of 1903. "Easter" (April 12) is still near. The "Tuesday" after the "very first letter" since Easter (L 160) is April 28, 1903, which is the date, moreover, that the recipient indicated later.

[2] Probably on the subject of a visit by Françoise to the parlor (cf. "when I see you ...").
[3] Eph 2:4.

L 162   To her Rolland aunts   [April 28-30, 1903][1]
J. M. + J. T.   Dijon Carmel, April

My good little Aunts,

It seems to me that Carlipa and Dijon are very close, for my heart has quickly jumped the distance to go find yours! And my Divine Bridegroom gives me wings like this so I can fly off to you: these wings are prayer, and then this unity in faith and love creates the communion of saints!... I have many things to tell you, my little Aunts, but where to begin? Oh! if you knew how beautiful Holy Week is in Carmel! I wish you could have attended our beautiful Offices, and especially on our beautiful feast of Easter. On that day, we chant Matins at 3 o'clock in the morning, we enter the choir in procession, wearing our white mantles, each holding a candle and singing the Regina Coeli. At 5 o'clock, we have the Mass of the Resurrection, followed by a magnificent procession in our beautiful garden. Everything was so still, so mysterious, that it seemed our Master was going to appear to us along the solitary paths as He once did to Mary Magdalene, and if our eyes did not see Him, at least our souls met Him in faith. Faith is so good; it is Heaven in darkness, but one day the veil will be lifted and we will contemplate in His light Him whom we love; while awaiting the Bridegroom's "Veni" we must spend ourselves, suffer for Him, and, above all, love Him greatly. Thank Him for having called your little Elizabeth to Carmel for the persecution;[2] I do not know what awaits us, and this perspective of having to suffer because I am His delights my soul. I love my dear cloister so much, and sometimes I have wondered if I don't love this dear little cell too much,[3] where it is so good to be "alone with the Alone."[4] Perhaps one day He will ask me to sacrifice it. I am ready to follow Him everywhere, and my soul will say with Saint Paul: "Who will separate me from the love of Christ?"[5] I have within me a solitude where He dwells, and nothing can take that away from me!...

Guite had the good idea of passing your dear photographs on to me. I introduced you to our Reverend Mother, since she has

heard her little lamb,[6] who loves you so much, speak about you for
so long. I was also delighted to show her your dear house; what sweet
memories it brings back to me. I spent so many wonderful vacations,
certainly the best, there among you. And the Serre, is it still so beautiful? What fine prayers must be offered there! Would you tell Monsieur le Curé that I send him my soul to say the Office with him in
that dear little valley, pay him my respects and ask him to pray much
for me. He is so good, I am sure he would really want to remember
me at his Mass. My little Aunts, if you knew how I love your beautiful
breviaries! I can't say it enough, and each time I use them, I take
your souls with mine to enter into communion with all Heaven. I
assure you that you have made me *very happy;* they follow me everywhere, and day and night my prayer for you is my "thank you"!

I am leaving you to go to Matins "with you." I still have many
things to tell you, but there's the bell, so I only have time to kiss you,
as well as my good Aunt, from the best of my heart.

Your little Elizabeth of the Trinity r.c.i.

Pray for my dear Mama. Events have really saddened her, but
her courage edifies me and I thank Him who has given me such a
good one. Hello *to Anna.*

[1] Handwriting of 1903. In "April," but after the 27th (cf. L 160).
[2] Cf. L 160, note 5. The Dijon Carmel was preparing for the possibility of an exodus
(cf. L 148). On November 11, 1902, Mother Germaine had already gone to Switzerland, where she had been offered a house in Charmey. In May 1903, she went to
Noiseux in Belgium, where the schoolhouse would be prepared to receive the religious; from 1904 on, part of the furniture was in Noiseux. Despite the closing of the
chapel to the public (cf. L 165, note 6), the Dijon Carmelites were not anxious.
[3] Perhaps a scruple of 1902, during her painful novitiate (cf. AL).
[4] Teresa of Avila. Cf. L 109, note 5.
[5] Rom 8:35.
[6] "Lamb": a symbolic name for a novice. The Prioress was then the "Shepherdess."

L 163   To Madame Farrat   [May 16, 1903][1]
J. M. + J. T.   Carmel, Saturday night

Very dear Madame,

Your little friend could not remain silent, knowing how much
you are being tried; she needs to tell you how much she is praying

for the one who has gone to God[2] and also for those he has left behind! In the face of such trials, human language seems very trite and powerless. Only He who inflicts the wound can understand our heart and give the consolations it needs. So your little friend draws near to this God who strikes only because He loves, and with all her heart, all her soul, she speaks to Him of you. Dear Madame, through faith let us lift the veil and follow the one who has disappeared high above into those regions that are wholly of peace and light, where suffering is transformed into love. There our dear little Cécile already lives, and in union with her I am praying for you! Dear Madame, would you express to Madame Clerget-Vaucouleurs[3] my respectful and heart-felt sympathy and tell her that our Reverend Mother as well as the whole community in Carmel is praying with her for this soul who, in going to God, has not left her at all. For it is so true that we can live with those who are no longer here below....

A Dieu, dear Madame, I am not forgetting your dear little Olivier, and I ask him on the 17th[4] to remember his Carmelite friend.

I kiss you very affectionately, and Marie-Madeleine also.

Sr. M. Elizabeth of the Trinity r.c.i.

[1] Date deduced from notes 2 and 4.
[2] Her father, Claude Edmond Clerget-Vaucouleurs, died on May 13, 1903, at the age of 73.
[3] Her mother. Elizabeth spells it "Clergé."
[4] Olivier Farrat made his first Communion on May 17, 1903.

L 164   To Germaine de Gemeaux   [May 20, 1903]
J. M. + J. T.   Dijon Carmel, May 20

My dear Little Germaine,

After Mama told me that you were to have dinner next week at Marguerite's, I asked our Reverend Mother for permission to write and tell you that I truly think of you as my little sister. It seems to me that our two souls are one, that you are a Carmelite with me, for all that I do is with you; and when God looks at me among His beloved ones in Carmel, He also sees His little Germaine of the Trinity. On Sundays, I spend my day with you in honor of the Holy Trinity; oh, my little Germaine, how good God is to have given us an attraction to this mystery. May our life flow into His, as we were saying the other day,[1] may this truly be our dwelling on earth. There let us become silent so we may listen to Him who has so much to tell us, and since you too have this passion to listen to Him, we will meet close to Him so we may hear everything that is being sung in His soul!...[2] That is the life of the Carmelite: she is above all a contemplative, another Mary Magdalene whom nothing must distract from the One thing necessary.[3] She loves the Master so much that she wants to become one who is immolated like Him, and her life becomes a continual gift of herself, an exchange of love with Him who possesses her to the point of wanting to transform her into another Himself. There, in HIM, I feel quite close to you. Our motto must be these words of Saint Paul: "Our life is hidden with Christ in God."[4]

A Dieu, my little sister, tell your good, dear mama that I pray every day for her, that I love her with all my heart as well as Yvonne, who is also the little sister of my heart. We are going into retreat from Ascension to Pentecost,[5] and I will make it with you in the soul of the Master. Pray for your big sister, too.

M. Elizabeth of the Trinity

The little photograph is for Yvonne.[6]

[1] In a conversation in the parlor.
[2] In 1902, Elizabeth had copied this expression of P. Vallée: "They heard what was being sung in the soul of Christ" (fourteenth sermon of the 1897 retreat). She had heard during the 1902 retreat: "to overhear all that is being sung in the soul of Christ" (second morning sermon). The fourth morning sermon speaks of "the hymn ... that rises from the soul of Christ."
[3] Cf. Lk 10:42.
[4] Col 3:3.
[5] From the 22nd to the 30th of May. It was called the "cenacle" retreat and was not preached. They worked as usual, but there was no recreation.
[6] One of the four photos taken shortly after her veiling.

L 165   To Abbé Chevignard   [June 14, 1903][1]
         J. M. + J. T.   Dijon Carmel, June 14

"Having loved His own who were in the world,
He loved them to the end."[2]

Monsieur l'Abbé,
    It seems to me that nothing better expresses the love in God's Heart than the Eucharist: it is union, consummation, He in us, we in Him, and isn't that Heaven on earth? Heaven in faith while awaiting the face-to-face vision we so desire. Then "we will be satisfied when His glory appears,"[3] when we see Him in His light. Don't you find that the thought of this meeting refreshes the soul, this talk with Him whom it loves solely? Then everything disappears and it seems that one is already entering into the mystery of God!...
    This whole mystery is so much "ours," as you said to me in your letter. Oh! pray, won't you, that I may live fully my bridal dowry. That I may be wholly available, wholly vigilant in faith, so the Master can bear me wherever He wishes. I wish to stay always close to Him who knows the whole mystery, to hear everything from Him. "The language of the Word is the infusion of the gift,"[4] oh yes, it is really so, isn't it, that He speaks to our soul in silence. I find this dear silence a blessing. From Ascension to Pentecost, we were in retreat in the Cenacle, waiting for the Holy Spirit, and it was so good.[5] During that whole Octave[6] we have the Blessed Sacrament exposed in the oratory; those are divine hours spent in this little corner of Heaven where we possess the vision in substance under the humble Host. Yes, He whom the blessed contemplate in light and we adore in faith is really the same One. The other day someone wrote me such a beautiful thought, I send it on to you: "Faith is the face-to-face in darkness."[7] Why wouldn't it be so for us, since God is in us and since He asks only to take possession of us as He took possession of the saints? Only, they were always attentive, as Père Vallée says: "They are silent, recollected, and their only activity is to be the being who receives."[8] Let us unite ourselves, therefore, Father, in making happy Him who "has loved us exceedingly,"[9] as Saint Paul says. Let us make a dwelling for Him in our soul that is wholly at peace,[10] in

which the canticle of love, of thanksgiving, is always being sung; and then that great silence, the echo of the silence that is in God!... Then, as you said, let us approach the all-pure, all-luminous Virgin, that she may present us to Him whom she has penetrated so profoundly, and may our life be a continual communion, a wholly simple movement toward God. Pray to the Queen of Carmel for me; I, for my part, pray fervently for you, I assure you, and I remain with you in adoration and love!...

Sister Marie Elizabeth of the Trinity, r.c.i.

[1] In 1903 "June 14" fell "during ... [the] Octave" of Corpus Christi. Hence the eucharistic accent in this letter.
[2] Jn 13:1.
[3] Ps 16:15.
[4] Elizabeth had copied this text in her "personal notebook" (cf. PN 13, note l); we do not know its origin.
[5] Cf. L 164, note 5.
[6] During this Octave of Corpus Christi (from June 12 to 19), the Blessed Sacrament was exposed on the oratory side, because the chapel was closed to the public (cf. also L 198 of April 9, 1904; it would remain closed until the spring of 1906). A new government circular had ordered the closing of all unauthorized chapels. On April 16, during the Benediction sung by the Christian Brothers before they went into exile, and also the day of Marie of the Incarnation's golden jubilee (cf. P 87), Vicar General Marigny came in the name of Bishop Le Nordez to order the official closing of the chapel.
[7] We do not know who wrote this to her. The thought is obviously connected with 1 Cor 13:12–13.
[8] In the 1900 retreat, the tenth sermon on the Holy Trinity. But Vallée says "soul" instead of "being."
[9] Eph 2:4.
[10] Cf. John of the Cross, the poem "The Dark Night": "... my dwelling place was at peace."

L 166   To her sister   [June 15, 1903][1]

May a profound silence grow in the soul of my Guite, an echo of that being sung in the Trinity. May her prayer never cease, since she possesses what will one day be its Vision, its Beatitude!

St. Germaine, 1903
Elizabeth of the Trinity

[1] The original has disappeared. Two copies of the ACD and that of the Process indicate "St. Germaine 1903," thus June 15.

L 167   To Madame de Sourdon   [June 21(?), 1903]¹
        J. M. + J. T.   Dijon Carmel, Sunday

Dear Madame,

You can imagine how I will be thinking of you tomorrow and the following days;² besides, that is something my heart is quite inclined to do, as you well know. Françoise told me in one of her parlor visits that she hoped to take her examination, and it seemed to me that the time was drawing near, when your good letter came. I am full of confidence, and though I love my little Françoise with all my heart, I want her to do well on her examination even more for her dear mama's sake than for her own, for this mama has given herself so for her children! All the same, I am sorry that, as you say, the dear child has not worked harder, but the good God gave her so much aptitude. And then, He is so good that we must hope completely in His love.

And your sweet Marie-Louise? I see that I have not yet prayed enough for her since the person in question does not have all the qualifications.³ I am sorry he does not have another name, for I imagine this is what he lacks. It is a shame, I admit, it is so rare to find young men with his qualities, but all the same there was a sacrifice to be made! Believe me, I am praying fervently for you, dear Madame, and since the Sacred Heart⁴ attracts you so, I confide your maternal concerns to Him!...

As I write you, I am thinking of those summer evenings⁵ we used to spend together!... Now I am all alone in our little cell, alone with Him ... the "All...." If you knew what peace, what happiness floods my soul.... If you knew, too, how even "closer to you" I am and how true it is that I love you.

A Dieu, dear Madame, I am going down to Matins and carry all three of you in my heart.

                              Sr. Elizabeth of the Trinity r.c.i.

¹ After her profession ("r.c.i."). Handwriting of 1903. Notes 4 and 5 suggest June. Françoise de Sourdon, who had undoubtedly kept the date of her examination, noted later "June 21, 1903" (which was in fact a "Sunday").
² Days on which Françoise was taking the examinations to obtain her diploma.
³ A suitor, it seems.
⁴ The feast of the Sacred Heart was June 19th.
⁵ Summer begins June 21.

L 168   To Madame Angles   [June 29, 1903][1]
        J. M. + J. T.   Dijon Carmel, June 29

Madame and dear sister,

I see that you too are suffering persecution since your good
Capuchin Fathers have gone into exile,[2] and I understand what a
sacrifice this is for you. It is so good, isn't it, to meet a soul who knows
how to lead one to God. In the world, I had many sacrifices to make
in that respect,[3] but I saw that when God took away from me all that
seemed to be leading me to Him, it was only to give Himself even
more. Dear Madame, we must thank Him all the time, whatever happens, for God is Love, and He can create nothing but Love! In
Carmel, we have the calm, the peace of God: we are His, we are kept
by Him. On the eve of His death, Christ said to His Father: "Not one
of those you gave me has been lost,"[4] then what could we fear? They
could take away this dear cloister in which I have found so much
bliss, lead us to prison or to death: I must admit to you that I would
be very happy if such happiness were reserved for me!... You ask me[5]
what my work is in Carmel. I could answer that for the Carmelite
there is only one occupation: "to love, to pray." But since, while already living in Heaven, she still has a body on earth, she must, while
surrendering herself to love, keep busy in order to do the will of
Him who did all these things first to set us an example. We begin
our day with an hour of prayer at 5 o'clock in the morning, then we
spend another hour in choir to say the Divine Office ... then Mass.
At 2 P.M. we have Vespers; at 5 P.M., prayer until 6 P.M. At 7:45, Compline. Then we pray until Matins, which is said at 9 P.M., and it is only
around 11 P.M. that we leave the choir to go to take our rest. During
the day, we have two hours of recreation; then, after that, silence the
whole time. When I am not sweeping, I work in our little cell.[6] A
straw mattress, a little chair, a board for a desk,[7] and there you have
its furnishings, but it is filled with God and I spend such wonderful
hours there alone with the Bridegroom. For me, the cell is something sacred, it is His intimate sanctuary, just for Him and His little
bride. We are so much "together," I am silent, I listen to Him ... it is
so good to hear everything He has to say. And I love Him while I ply
my needle and work on this dear serge[8] that I have so longed to

wear. Dear Madame, you are enveloped in silence, there in your beautiful mountains, you have so much solitude, your health does not allow you to be busy. Oh! live with Him, make Him live through faith, think that He dwells in your soul and constantly keep Him company, won't you? Let us unite ourselves to make Him happy, and, for that, may our life be a continual communion!...

I saw Mama recently. I do wish she were going your way this summer,[9] you would do her some good. Since I have been in Carmel, God has taken her even more to Himself, and each time I have a visit with her, I am so thankful to see all He is doing in that beloved soul. Oh! How good He is! Let us love Him, and may the fruit of our love be surrender;[10] I leave you with that. Union more than ever in silence and adoration, in the soul of Him in whom I am your little sister.

Marie-Elizabeth of the Trinity r.c.i.

I am praying for your convert.

I found this letter[11] in our desk, and I am ashamed about it. You must have received my photograph as a Carmelite;[12] may it bring you all my soul!...

---

[1] Handwriting of 1903, the year confirmed by notes 2, 5, 9, 12.

[2] The Capuchins of Carcassonne. After the departure of most of the friars and novices, the last six religious were violently chased from their house on May 7, 1903, after a 10-day siege (cf. the *Semaine religieuse de Carcassonne*, May 8, 1903).

[3] Her mother opposed her changing confessor. Cf. D 5 and 145.

[4] Cf. Jn 17:12.

[5] In L 156 of February 15, 1903, Elizabeth had promised her that she would describe her day "the next time." See the horarium, slightly different during the winter, at the end of this volume. pp. 371–372.

[6] Elizabeth was "second habit Sister." When it was not necessary for her to work in the "habit room" (see Plan 2, no. 14), she worked in her cell (Plan 2, no. 15). This cell was small but harmonious: 10'6" long by 10'2.75" wide by 9'7.75" high.

[7] This "board" (20" x 13.25") was fixed to the wall in a corner at the left of the window and at a height of 25.5". Elizabeth kept several books there (cf. L 88 and 106); it could also serve as a little table. In another corner at the right of the window was affixed another round board (11.75" long and 4'4.5" high), where a jug of water, a rudimentary "lavabo" was placed. The "desk" was a little wooden box (17.25" x 2.75") where the Sister could put a few personal papers and that could be placed on her knees to write (cf. L 88).

[8] She was mending habits in particular.

[9] Which will be done, cf. below.

[10] Before entering, she copied the thought attributed to St. Augustine, "Surrender is

the sweet fruit of love," an introductory quotation for the poem "Abandon" [Abandonment Is the Sweet Fruit of Love] by Thérèse of Lisieux (HA 377).
[11] Of the unknown "convert"?
[12] Cf. L 164, note 6. Her mother must have sent it.

L 169   To Canon Angles   [July 15, 1903]
         J. M. + J. T.   Dijon Carmel, July 15

Monsieur le Chanoine,

My dear Mama, whom I saw last week, brought me your good letter, and I assure you that I can indeed sympathize with the suffering your eyes are causing you,[1] and I am praying fervently for you. I was wondering a little what had become of you, but you find your little Carmelite close to God, don't you? And that is where she finds you too; then no more distance, no more separation, but already, as in Heaven, the fusion of hearts and souls!... How many things have happened since my last letter! I heard the Church say "Veni sponsa Christi" [Come, bride of Christ]; she consecrated me, and now all is "consummated."[2] Rather, everything is beginning, for profession is only a dawn; and each day my "life as a bride"[3] seems to me more beautiful, more luminous, more enveloped in peace and love. During the night that preceded the great day, while I was in choir awaiting the Bridegroom, I understood that my Heaven was beginning on earth; Heaven in faith, with suffering and immolation for Him whom I love!... I so wish to love Him, to love Him as my seraphic Mother did, even to dying of it. We sing "O charitatis Victima" on her feast day, and that is my whole ambition: to be the prey of love![4] I think that in Carmel it is so simple to live by love; from morning to evening the Rule is there to express the will of God, moment by moment. If you knew how I love this Rule, which is the way He wants me to become holy. I do not know if I will have the happiness of giving my Bridegroom the witness of my blood [by martyrdom], but at least, if I fully live my Carmelite life, I have the consolation of wearing myself out for Him, for Him alone.[5] Then what difference does the work He wills for me make? Since He is always with me, prayer, the heart-to-heart, must never end! I feel Him so alive in my soul. I have only to recollect myself to find Him within me, and that is my whole happiness. He has placed in my heart a thirst for the infinite and such a great need for love that He alone can satisfy it. I go to Him like a little child to its mother so He may fill, invade, everything, and then take me and carry me away in His arms. I think we must be so simple with God! [6]

I am longing to send you my good Mama; you will see how God is working in this beloved soul. Sometimes I cry for happiness and gratitude; it is so good to be devoted to your mother,[7] to feel that she, too, is completely His, to be able to tell her about your soul and to be completely understood!… You really are the great attraction of the trip, I assure you; I love to remember those vacations at Saint-Hilaire, then at Carcassonne and Labastide, they were the best ones I had. With what fatherly goodness you received the confidences I so loved to make to you; I would be happy if one day they could be made once again through my dear grilles. Won't you come to bless your little Carmelite and, quite close to her, thank Him who "has loved her exceedingly,"[8] for, you see, my happiness can no longer be expressed. Listen to what is being sung in my soul and all that is rising from the heart of the bride to the Heart of the Bridegroom for you whose little child she will always be. Send her your best blessing; at Holy Mass, bathe her in the Blood of the Bridegroom; it is the purity of the bride, and she is so thirsting for it! A Dieu, monsieur le Chanoine, affectionately and respectfully yours,

Sr. Elizabeth of the Trinity r.c.i.

---

[1] We have the reply from Canon Angles dated July 22: "Thanks to you, my eyes are a little better," he writes. That this letter was not destroyed like the others is explained by the request made by the suffering Canon: "Please forward my letter … to Mama … she will excuse me from writing to her."

[2] Cf. Jn 19:30.

[3] Cf. her meditation in 1902 on her "life as a bride": PN 13.

[4] Elizabeth is associating here the two Teresas as representatives of the same ideal of total gift: "O victim of love" comes from the third stanza of the hymn for Vespers on the feast of Teresa of Avila. In her "Act of Oblation," Thérèse of Lisieux had also offered herself as "victim" and "martyr" of love. For the expression "prey of His love," cf. L 125, note 3 (also L 41, note 7, and L 54, note 5). A little farther on, note the expression "to live by love," the title of a very well-known poem by Thérèse of Lisieux. [Charitas, charitatis = caritas, caritatis; "Charitatis" appeared in the liturgical books Elizabeth used—TRANS.]

[5] Cf. L 156, note 7. This passage evokes a thought of Thérèse of Lisieux that Elizabeth had copied in 1902, as an introductory quotation for a poem composed by Sister Agnès (of the Dijon Carmel): "I want to win the palm of Saint Agnes; if not by my blood, it will be by Love" (cf. HA 255 [LT 54].

[6] On the child in the arms of its mother, cf. L 116, note 2. One can recognize here the movement of Thérèse of Lisieux's soul: to receive the infinite love of God. But this receptivity has a particular accent in Elizabeth: it is the fidelity to love by praying. A month later, Elizabeth revealed even more the presence of Thérèse in her life, cf. L 172.

[7] "To be devoted to your mother": Elizabeth took this expression from the *Letters of Father Didon,* p. 287 (cf. L 157, note 5). She who cherished her mother must have been very impressed (at the moment when she was going to leave her for Carmel) by P. Didon's confession of his ardent love for his mother; he went so far as to have her body exhumed because he arrived too late for the burial! (Cf. p. 292.)

[8] Eph 2:4.

L 170   To her mother   [around August 13, 1903][1]

        J. M. + J. T.   Dijon Carmel, August

"Let us remain in His love!..."[2]

My dear little Mama,

Remember how carefully your Elizabeth used to hide when your feast day drew near in order to prepare some pretty surprise for you? It was so nice to make you happy! I am making my little preparations this year, too, my "conspiracy" with my divine Bridegroom. He opens all His treasures to me, and I draw from them to offer you a wholly divine bouquet, a crown that will shine on your head for all eternity, and one day in Heaven your child will rejoice to think that she helped the Master prepare it, that she added beautiful rubies to it, blood from your heart and also from hers!...

I am overjoyed at thinking of you with our dear Guite, then with kind Madame Hallo and Marie-Louise;[3] do enjoy your daughter and all that dear affection. I'm writing to you before Matins, when our cell is filled with silence, filled above all with the presence of God. Mama, that doesn't bother you, does it? I am so happy in my Carmel. My thoughts are with you there in the midst of that dear group, I send each one very affectionate greetings, particularly Alice.[3a] Oh! if you knew how true it is that I have the better part; tonight I feel the need to say "thank you," for without your "fiat," you well know that I would never have left you, and He wanted me to sacrifice you for His Love.[4] Carmel is like Heaven, and we must part with all in order to possess Him who is All. It seems to me that I love

you as one loves in Heaven, that there can no longer be any separa-⎫
tion between my little Mama and me, since He whom I possess⎭
within me dwells in her, and thus we are quite close!

I had interrupted my letter and then received yours, which
made me very happy. I would have liked better news, but don't be
afraid of being sick: ask Him for strength, then abandon yourself;
your daughter who is praying for you is there. I am deeply touched
by Madame Hallo's goodness and ask God to repay my debt of gratitude. Benediction must have been very beautiful, and I rejoice that
God had so special a part in your vacation!...

I had a visit from Madame de Vathaire with Antoinette de
Bobet, who brought me her two little girls; our Reverend Mother
let me see[5] the children, and, to please their mother, she came to
see them too. The second one is ravishing. I so love these wholly
pure little creatures, and I really wish God would give one of them
to our Guite some day, do you want to tell her that when you give
her a kiss for me? Thanks for her kind letter; I'm united with her
not only in the morning, as she asks, but continually!

And now, my darling Mama, I have only enough room to tell
you one wish: that He who has taken me to Himself may always be
the Friend on whom you rely for everything. Live in His intimacy as
you would live with One you love, in a sweet heart-to-heart; it is your
daughter's secret of happiness, your daughter who kisses you with
all the love of her Carmelite heart, the heart that is all yours, for it is
all His, all the Trinity's.

I forgot to tell you that I'm feeling marvelous; if you knew how
good Our Mother is. She is a mother, doesn't that say everything?...
Until Monday!...[6]

---

[1] Letter written over a two-day period, a little before August 15, the "feast day" of her mother: 1903: Guite did not have any children yet.
[2] Cf. Jn 15:9.
[3] On vacation together, near Dijon (cf. L 171, note 4).
[3a] The wife of Commandant de la Ruelle.
[4] Cf. P 66 and D 105.
[5] "See": for this occasion they had opened the inner grille covered with a black curtain, a privilege usually reserved for the immediate family.
[6] August 17, before Madame Catez's departure for the South of France.

L 171   To her Rolland aunts   [August 15, 1903][1]
          J. M. + J. T.

My good little Aunts,

As my pen runs across the paper, my thoughts are with you there in that dear church where I so loved to pray between the two of you; I can see the pretty Virgin with her altar all decorated with flowers and lights by my beloved little Aunts![2] How many times I spent this beautiful feast of the Assumption with you.... This year I am there only in heart and soul, but that is already like it is in Heaven; there is no more distance, is there?...

In Carmel, too, we had our procession after Vespers, which we sing at 2 o'clock. We wore our white mantles: that is so beautiful in the midst of our cloisters, and I like to think of the procession of *Virgins who follow the Lamb wherever He goes.*[3] Already here on earth He has chosen your little Elizabeth to take part in the divine procession, among His brides in Carmel. Please thank Him for me every day, for my soul is overflowing with thanksgiving!...

If you knew how happy I am to send you my dear Mama; I commend her to you, my little Aunts: your kind affection, your care is so sweet to her heart. She would have been very happy to bring Marguerite along, but, you know, she knows how to make sacrifices, just as you do too. You shouldn't blame Georges for it. Guite is tired, and this year that long trip would perhaps not have been very sensible; she is resting in the country[4] and, as the village is close to Dijon, her husband spends Sundays with her. I assure you, the dear child would have been very happy to go see you; in this world, we must make sacrifices, my little Aunts, mustn't we? For Mama as for you, it is the same thing. Poor Mama, sacrifice has very often been her part in this world. I was the first; I really made her heart bleed by entering Carmel. Oh! if it were not for Him!... But you see, the soul cannot resist His call. He takes captive, enchains, you are no longer your own master but the prey of His love; the heart can be torn apart, but an ineffable peace reigns in the soul, a happiness that does not resemble any here below. When I left you three years ago,[5] I felt in the depths of my soul that it was the end, that I would never again return to Carlipa to be with those beloved aunts who were so good to me. Remember how the tears flowed when the carriage took us away? Well, now it is very simple to go to you, and I often make that journey: prayer, union in the One who is the Bond of all affection, that is my form of transportation. Don't forget it, my little Aunts, and come to me, too!... Before closing, let me say something more about your[6] beautiful breviaries; they would make Monsieur le Curé envious, only he would find them a little large and they would hardly be practical to take to the Serre, for they are 9" long and 6" wide; now you are really well-informed!... Tell your good Curé that I am infinitely grateful to him for remembering me at the Holy Sacrifice, I count completely on his prayers, and, for my part, I don't forget him either.

As for you, dear little Aunts, I send my most tender affection to you and to Aunt Catherine. Kiss Mama for me, love her for her Carmelite!...

Sr. M. E. of the Trinity r.c.i.

I told everyone about the procession from Saint-Roch[7] to Carlipa at recreation and they were very interested and edified.

Hello to Anna and Louise.[8]

[1] The evening of "this beautiful feast of the Assumption." 1903, based on the handwriting and notes 4 and 5.
[2] Cf. L 108, note 4. The Assumption was an important celebration at Carlipa; each year a procession of the Virgin passed through the streets of the village.
[3] Rev 14:4. Elizabeth wrote the words larger; we are placing them in italics.
[4] Guite is expecting her first child, who will be born seven months later. The village may be Sainte-Marie-sur-Ouche, as in 1906.
[5] At the beginning of September 1900. Cf. L 32.
[6] A present from the aunts, cf. L 154. The first of the six volumes weighs about 2.5 lbs.
[7] Cf. L 90, note 4.
[8] Louise, P. Tescou's maid.

L 172   To Germaine de Gemeaux   [August 20, 1903][1]
J. M. + J. T.
Carmel of the Suffering Heart of Jesus,[2] August 20

My dear little sister Germaine of the Trinity,[3]

Your kind letter and your confidences have made me very happy. I so love, when you lift the veil of your soul for me, to enter into that private sanctuary where you live completely alone with Him who wants you all for Himself and who creates a beloved solitude within you for Himself. Refresh Him there, my little Germaine, by resting in Him; listen to all that is being sung in His Soul, in His Heart; it is Love, Infinite Love that envelops us and wants us to share even here below in all His beatitudes. The entire Trinity rests within us, this whole mystery that will be our vision in Heaven: let this be your cloister. My little sister, it makes me so happy when you tell me that your life is spent there. Mine too: I am "Elizabeth of the Trinity," that is, Elizabeth disappearing, losing herself, letting herself be invaded by the Three; you can see that we are very close in Them, we are completely one, aren't we? From morning to night I do everything with you, and I think of you as the *true* sister of my soul. I commend you to all our saints, and very particularly to our holy Mother Teresa and to Sister Thérèse of the Child Jesus.[4] Yes, my little Germaine, let us live by love, let us be simple like she was, surrendered all the time, immolating ourselves minute by minute by doing God's will without seeking extraordinary things. And then let us make ourselves very little, letting ourselves be carried, like a child in the arms of her mother, by Him who is our All. Yes, my little sister, we are very weak, I would even say we are utterly nothing, but He knows that very well, He so loves to forgive us, to pick us up, then to carry us away in Him, in His purity, in His infinite holiness; that is how He will purify us, through His continual contact with us, through divine touches.[5] He wants us to be so pure, but He Himself will be our purity: we must let ourselves be transformed into one and the same image with Him, and that, quite simply, by loving all the time with the love that establishes unity between those who love each other!

I, too, Germaine, want to be holy, holy to make Him happy. Ask Him to let me live only by love, "it is my vocation."[6] And then let us join in making our days one continual communion: in the morning, let us wake in Love; all day let us surrender ourselves to Love by doing the will of God, in His presence, with Him, in Him, for Him alone. Let us give ourselves all the time in the way He wishes: you by devoting yourself to giving joy to your dear parents. And then when evening comes, after an endless dialogue in our heart, again let us sleep in Love. Perhaps we will see faults, infidelities; let us abandon them to Love: it is a consuming fire, so let us make our purgatory in His love.[7]

I am not saying anything to you on behalf of our Reverend Mother: she is so good, she wants to do it herself,[8] and that will be much better! Please kiss your dear mama for me and tell her that I love her like a true mama. Tell Yvonne that she is also my little sister, that I pray for her every day, as well as for Monsieur de Gemeaux. I am not leaving you, my little Germaine, I really believe that you are already a Carmelite with your big sister.

M. E. of the Trinity r.c.i.

Thanks for your pretty holy card, it made me so happy!… Thursday the 27th we celebrate the anniversary of the day when a seraphim transpierced the heart of our holy Mother Teresa;[9] let us ask him too for a wound of love!…

[1] 1903: cf. note 9.

[2] Cf. L 156, note 1.

[3] The young aspirant to religious life changed the name she had chosen ("Germaine of Jesus," L 133, note 6).

[4] The first explicit mention of Thérèse of Lisieux (cf. the Introduction to Section II of the *Letters from Carmel*). The following passage sums up very well a number of aspects of Thérèse's spirituality and its influence on Elizabeth ("let us be … as she was"), while bringing out, before and after, Elizabeth's particular charism of prayerful interiority.

[5] With the terms "divine touches," "transformed" and "image," which abound in the *Spiritual Canticle* and *Living Flame of Love*, Elizabeth reflects the doctrine of John of the Cross. The quotation "the love that establishes unity" (cf. L 121, note 4) confirms it.

[6] "To live by love" (HA 330–33) "is my vocation" (HA 208 [SS 194]): from now on the second formulation will often reappear next to the first, which has already been used often.

[7] We recognize here HA 144 [SS 181]: "I also know that the fire of love is more sanctifying than is the fire of purgatory." (Cf. also: "And I, for my purgatory / choose your burning love, O heart of my God!" Poem "Au Sacré-Coeur" [To the Sacred Heart] (HA 348) and "Vivre d'amour" [Living on Love], st. 6 (HA 331).

[8] Here is the text in a postscript: "Our Lady of Mount Carmel sends her blessing to her little child, and the Mother Prioress of Carmel recommends to her dear little postulant fidelity to Jesus in little things like Thérèse of the Child Jesus, for whose feast day on September 30 we cannot better prepare than by these acts of continual fidelity."

[9] Feast of the Transverberation of St. Teresa's heart (from the Carmelite Proper), August 27, which was a Thursday in 1903.

L 173   To Madame de Sourdon   [August 23, 1903][1]
          J. M. + J. T.   Dijon Carmel, Sunday

Very dear Madame,

I can assure you that I have indeed answered your appeal. After reading your letter, which our Reverend Mother delivered to me very quickly (she understands your feelings so well), I went to the oratory where we have the Blessed Sacrament and with all my heart, with all my soul, I prayed for your dear little patient.[2] There is a prayer that God does not resist: the prayer of Mary Magdalene. It seems to me that His Carmelites also have complete power over His Heart, and I am using all my rights in your favor. Dear Madame, what fatherly providence watches over you, and how evident it is to you in this trial, since if there had been even one day's delay, our dear Françoise would not have been treated in time. Oh! if you knew how I am praying for her! The dear child has such a big place in my heart, and I am so happy to think that from the depths of my beloved cloister I can do something for you, for I owe you such a big debt of gratitude! Believe that I am with you in heart and soul at the bedside of your dear patient and that my prayer envelops you.

I am going to ring the bell, and I am hurrying because I'm anxious for you to have this note from my heart to tell you how much I am praying.

Please remember me to Madame de Maizières and tell her I remember her in my prayers. And to you, dear Madame, I send the best of my heart.

                                   Sr. M. Elizabeth of the Trinity r.c.i.

If you tell Framboise that I have written to you, give her a big kiss for me, as well as Marie-Louise.

---

[1] An envelope preserved in the ACD addressed to Elizabeth by Marie-Louise Ambry was postmarked August 21, 1903, at Mas-Cabardès, the 22nd at Carcassonne, and arrived at Dijon at 6:45 on the 23rd ("yesterday," as L 175 says). Elizabeth returned this envelope and addressed it to the "Comtesse de Sourdon, c/o Mme. la Baronne de Maizières, 36 rue du Cherche-Midi, Paris." The letter was postmarked at Dijon on August 24 to arrive in Paris on August 25, 1903. Same handwriting as this letter written on "Sunday," thus August 23, 1903. The following letters confirm this.
[2] Her daughter Françoise, "gravely ill with appendicitis in Paris" (L 176).

L 174   To Françoise de Sourdon   [August 23(?), 1903][1]
          J. M. + J. T.

My good Françoise,

In the past, as soon as I knew you were tired I used to come very quickly to see you and keep you company. Now I can't take the train to go take care of you or even write to you as often as my heart desires, but you do feel, don't you, that I am quite present, right there beside you? We love each other too much, my little one, for there to be any distance, any obstacle between our hearts!

Poor Framboise, I am sorry to see you forced to rest in that Paris you love so much. But, you see, sacrifice is a sacrament that gives God to us; He sends it to those whom He loves and wants very close to Him! I know that you've offered it to Him with much generosity, and I am happy with my Françoise. If you knew how I am thinking about you, how I am praying for you, for that is one and the same for a Carmelite.... You see, I am happy, I am asking God to give you a taste, too, of the sweetness of His Love and His presence: that is what transforms, what illumines life, it is the secret of happiness!... My beloved Françoise, remember that if God has separated us, He wants to be the Friend you can always find. He is standing at the door of your heart.... He is waiting.... Open to Him.[2] Let that be the intimacy, the heart-to-heart, and since I am His bride and "the bride belongs to the Bridegroom,"[3] remember that I am there too; then we will never leave each other again, our hearts and our souls will be one!...

Kiss your good mother for me, and Marie-Louise, who must have many interesting things to tell you. Remember me to Madame de Maizières and give my greetings to your cousins. The best of my heart for you, my darling.

                                Sr. M. E. of the Trinity r.c.i.

[1] This letter probably accompanied the preceding one; or else it followed soon after.
[2] Cf. Rev 3:20.
[3] Cf. Jn 3:29.

L 175   To Marie-Louise Ambry (née Maurel)   [August 24, 1903][1]
     J. M. + J. T.   Dijon Carmel, August 24

My very dear Marie-Louise,
     I received your kind letter yesterday and am anxious tell you
of all the gratitude overflowing from my heart. How good you are,
each and every one of you, to my dear Mama. Oh! if you knew how
that touches me, I have tears in my eyes as I write to you, and I can
find no words to express what is flowing from my heart to yours;
please "listen" to it, dear Marie-Louise ... listen in silence close to
God, who will see to repaying His little Carmelite's debt of gratitude!
You tell me that my name comes up often in your conversations; I,
for my part, can tell you that in the intimacy and heart-to-heart with
my divine Bridegroom, "we are" often with you. For, you see, in
Carmel, like Heaven, there is no more distance, there is already a
fusion of souls. This consummation has really been the Master's
whole desire. Do you remember, on the evening of the Last Supper,
the prayer from His Heart overflowing with love for those whom "He
loved to the end": [2] "My Father, may they be one"! [3] I so love to make
this prayer with Him; then it seems to me that we are so close. My
dear Marie-Louise, you see, since I've been in Carmel (though out-
wardly I have scarcely given you any sign of life),[4] it seems to me I
am even closer to you, that I love you more deeply because He who
has taken me completely to Himself is all Love, and I am trying to
identify myself with all His movements; it is with His Heart that I love
you, with His Soul that I am praying for you. My dear Marie-Louise,
I rejoice in your hopes and about the arrival of the little angel.[5]
Don't be afraid, be completely in God's peace, He loves you, He is
watching over you like a mother over her little child. Remember
that you are in Him, that He makes Himself your dwelling here below; and then, that He is in you, that you possess Him in the most
intimate part of yourself, that at any hour of the day or night, in
every joy or trial, you can find Him there, quite near, entirely within
you. It is the secret of happiness; it is the secret of the saints; they
knew so well that they were the "temple of God"[6] and that in uniting ourselves to this God, we become "one spirit with Him,"[7] as Saint
Paul says; so they went forth to everything in His radiance. Dear

Marie-Louise, if He has permitted the trial, if your mother's heart has suffered so much, it is because He wanted you to share His Cross, as His well-beloved of whom He can ask everything, but He was there very close to help you. Now He wants you to be completely joyful in waiting for the little angel. Entrust yourself to His Love and to your Elizabeth, who is making herself your advocate with Him. She is so divinely happy, with a happiness that resembles what one tastes up above; thank God for her. And then, in closing this letter, let me tell you again of my gratitude to you, a true daughter to my dear Mama. Please kiss her for her Elizabeth, and be my interpreter to the dear visitors at Labastide. Tell your dear mama how I love her; I'll never forget her kindnesses. Remember me with much affection to your dear aunt Madame Angles and to Mademoiselle Victorine.[8] Tell your good papa and Monsieur Joseph they are not forgotten. And finally, remember me to everyone, and the best in my heart for you. Your little sister

> M. Elizabeth of the Trinity r.c.i.

What a delightful memory I have of your mountains and of our meeting…. I have given all that to Him!…

[1] Cf. L 173, note l.
[2] Jn 13:1.
[3] Jn 17:21.
[4] Two letters, L 134 and 142.
[5] Cf. L 186.
[6] 1 Cor 6:19 (or 1 Cor 3:16).
[7] 1 Cor 6:17.
[8] Mlle. Victorine Metge, Mme. Maurel's aunt and thus Marie-Louise's great aunt.

L 176   To her mother   [around August 27, 1903][1]
J. M. + J. T.

My darling little Mama,

I imagine you'll be very pleased to have a little note from your Elizabeth, so I can't resist the joy of making you happy. Our Reverend Mother did not wait for me to ask to write you.[2] She herself told me to do it, for she knows the heart of her little child and that of her dear Mama; then, you know, she is so good, she was very happy to give me such good news. As for me, I've told God of my joy and my thanks: what happiness to feel that you're pampered, cherished, surrounded by such affection; I knew very well it was necessary to send you to those good friends.

I followed you during your long trip. My soul was closely united with yours, the whole community prayed for you, and during Matins your child was so happy to envelop you with her prayer! [3] When I went to rest, I said to myself: "Tonight, my little Mama wouldn't be sorry to have our straw mattress!" and then I dreamed that I was with you ... as far as Tarascon!...[4] But it's not a dream, is it?... It is really true that we are quite close, that we love each other as in Heaven and no distance can separate us. Oh! don't you feel my prayer that is constantly rising up to Him and descending to you? Once you used to watch over me, and you looked after me so well; now it seems that I am looking after you with Him, and that is very sweet to me. Darling Mama, you don't mind, do you?

Did you know that Françoise de Sourdon is gravely ill with appendicitis in Paris? I wrote to her poor mother[5] who had sent me a cry for help!

Do really enjoy your stay with dear Monsieur le Chanoine, who must do you so much good, and then Madame Maurel, who is so good, and her sweet Marie-Louise. Tell them of all my gratitude and keep for yourself all the tender affection of your little

E. of the Trinity

I just received your good letter that makes me so happy. I'm following you everywhere and thank God who is giving you such a good vacation, so surrounded, so well cared for. Oh! how happy I am! Live with Him, won't you, Mama?

I had a visit from Madame de Cernon and her daughters;[6] she sends you her affectionate regards. I haven't seen Guite.

---

[1] Approximate date. Mme. Catez is still at Labastide, as in L 175.
[2] Because she had seen her mother on August 17 (cf. L 170, note 6). According to their custom, it was then necessary to wait a month before writing.
[3] "To envelop": again an expression dear to P. Vallée. But to "envelop with prayer(s)" is a familiar formula with Elizabeth; it is not her own invention, however; we find it already in a letter from Mother Germaine to Guite dated October 15, 1902.

[4] Probably one stage on her mother's "long trip."

[5] L 173.

[6] As a young girl, Mme. de Cernon lived on rue Saint-Lazare (cf. Plan 5, Vol. III) behind the monastery. In 1895, her house with its large garden was purchased by the Carmelites (cf. Plan 4, no. 4, Vol. III).

L 177   To Canon Angles   [around August 27, 1903][1]
J. M. + J. T.

Dear Monsieur le Chanoine,

I must send you my thanks as well! If you knew what a joy it is for me to think that my dear Mama is close to you! Isn't she good? And how much good you must be doing her, you have done so much good for her Carmelite! I still remember our conversations in the big room during those dear vacations in your beautiful mountains, and the moonlit strolls in the evenings.... Up above, near the church, it was so beautiful in the silence and calm of the night. Didn't you feel my whole soul carried away to Him?... And then Mass in the little chapel, that Mass you said ... what sweet memories that I'll never forget. Now, I'm with you in my soul and heart and feel so close to you. I so love to think that I have left everything for Him. It is so good to give when one loves, and I love Him so much, this God who is jealous of having me all for Himself. I feel so much love over my soul, it is like an Ocean I immerse and lose myself in: it is my vision on earth while waiting for the face-to-face vision in light. He is in me, I am in Him. I have only to love Him, to let myself be loved, all the time, through all things: to wake in Love, to move in Love, to sleep in Love, my soul in His Soul, my heart in His Heart, my eyes in His eyes, so that through His contact He may purify me, free me from my misery. If you knew how it fills me. I would love to tell you about it as I used to at Saint-Hilaire, then to bathe in the Blood of the Lamb.[2] My dear Mama almost makes me commit sins of envy. At least at Holy Mass, please place my soul in the chalice and then tell the Bridegroom to make me wholly pure, wholly virginal, wholly one with Him! I am going to ring the bell for Matins. I will say it with you, it is so sweet to repay a little of my debt of gratitude through prayer. I bring you my soul, bless it, then offer it to God; tell Him that I want to make Him happy!...

Sr. M. Elizabeth of the Trinity r.c.i.

[1] Written at the same time as L 176: "you ... as well...." L 176 and 177, moreover, are two halves of the same sheet.
[2] Allusion to the sacrament of penance.

L 178   To her mother   [September 6 (or 8), 1903][1]
         J. M. + J. T.

My dear little Mama,

I have just received your good letter, and you can guess how happy the good news about your health makes me. Never has that long journey been so well spent! You see, though your daughter can no longer take care of you as she used to, she really does much more, and it is such a joy for her heart to think she brings down on you all the love, all the blessings of God.

I am following you everywhere; you'll take my soul with yours to Notre-Dame de Marceille;[2] we so often went up there together, remember? Tell dear Madame Lignon[3] that her little friend still loves her very much, that she hasn't forgotten the pleasant vacations at Saint-Hilaire, the joyous evenings and the dancing.... I recall, darling Mama, that while I was dancing like the others and playing quadrilles downstairs in the large drawing room, I was haunted by this Carmel that attracted me so and where, one year later, I was to find so much happiness. What a mystery! Oh, do not regret having given me to Him, He willed it; and then, you well know that I am always all yours!

Cécile must be very pretty, I'll never forget her big blue eyes. Kiss her for me, and also Maria, her mother, Madame Sylvie Aiguesper,[4] I am not forgetting anyone!... Give my love to my good aunts, pray for me in that dear church I loved so much,[5] and remember that I am there ... that my soul is quite close to yours.... It is so true, my dear little Mama.

Guite came to see me when she got back with her husband,[6] and she had a fresh, rosy look that made me happy. They spoke with me about their hopes,[7] they looked so happy, they were so nice.... I thanked God for them, and then I thanked Him for myself. From an earthly standpoint, I seem to have made nothing but sacrifices,[8] but nevertheless, my little Mama, I have the better part; do believe it, and I think that despite the tears and sadness this imposes on a mother's heart, especially a mama like you, this mama must rejoice in having given God a Carmelite, for, next to a priest, I see nothing more divine on earth: a Carmelite, that implies such a divinized being!... Oh, ask our holy Mother Teresa, whom you taught me to love when I was very little,[9] ask her that I might be a holy Carmelite, and then rejoice in being loved by this little heart that belongs wholly to God. He has given it such a great power to love, and at times it has bled in thinking about you, but it is for Him. Darling Mama, if I love Him a little, it is you who directed the heart of your little one toward Him; you prepared me so well for the first encounter, that great day when we gave ourselves to each other completely!...[10] Thank you for all you have done. I would like to make Him loved, and, like you, give Him souls. I am praying so much for Monsieur Chapuis;[11] yesterday Guite came to say he was very low, and the whole community sang the *Salve* [12] for him. Georges told me he was going to try to prepare him to see a priest on the pretext of the novena for September 8th, and that he himself would receive Holy Communion with Guite, which made me happy. If you knew how well our Reverend Mother looks after me. You told her that hot weather made me tired; she has built me up so well that I've never had such a good summer; you will probably think I obey her better than you, my little Mama, for in that area I scarcely listened to you. We're going to begin the fast again on the 14th;[13] so ask God to continue to give me this grace of health!

A Dieu, my dear little Mama, I am so happy to think that you are so well surrounded. I don't see you, but I love you for yourself,[14] and I prefer your joy to mine. I am entrusting a kiss to my Christ so He can carry it to you on behalf of His bride, your beloved little
Elizabeth of the Trinity

Françoise is joyfully getting ready for her operation;[15] she has written me a priceless letter!... What a character....[16]

[1] Date deduced from note 12.

[2] A little sanctuary near Limoux (cf. L 17, note 2).

[3] To whom she will soon write: L 180.

[4] "Cécile" is Mme. Lignon's daughter. "Maria" (Resseguier), 33 years old, is their maid. Mme. "Sylvie Aiguesper" is actually Mme. Angèle Ayguesplus, Mme. Lignon's mother.

[5] Still the church of Saint-Hilaire.

[6] From her vacation near Dijon (cf. L 170, note 3).

[7] Guite is expecting her first child.

[8] Perhaps this is an echo of a sentence from P. Vallée that Elizabeth copied before she entered, "A Carmelite ... is a being who on this earthly side wishes to know only sacrifice...." *(Madame Louise de France,* Saint-Cloud: Impr. Belin, 1888, p. 6.)

[9] Mme. Catez loved Teresa of Avila very much and had copied out passages from her works as well as prayers addressed to the saint.

[10] April 19, 1891.

[11] Henri Chapuis, the owner of their house, 78 years old, for whose conversion Elizabeth had prayed very much (cf. her *Diary).*

[12] The solemn *Salve Regina* that they sang on Saturday nights and on the vigils of Marian feasts, in the present case on Saturday the 5th and also on the 7th, the vigil of the Birth of Mary. So "yesterday" indicates that Elizabeth is writing on September 6th (or the 8th, although the following sentence makes this less likely). Saturday, August 29 (vigil of the "novena"), is ruled out in view of the proximity of L 176 and the allusion to September "14th."

[13] The fast of the Order, from the 14th of September, the feast of the Exaltation of the Cross, until Easter.

[14] That is to say, with a true love, not a love that is selfish, not for myself. This may echo Thérèse of Lisieux explaining to her sister: "It is not our Mother whom you love, it is yourself." This passage occurs in *L'Histoire d'une Ame* on page 274; Elizabeth quotes from page 271 of that book in the following letter.

[15] Cf. L 173–74.

[16] The last two words are crossed out by a different hand (with different ink), probably by Mme. Catez, who used this black ink in 1907 (when she sent her daughter's letters to the Dijon Carmel).

L 179   To Germaine de Gemeaux   [September 20, 1903][1]
J. M. + J. T.
            Gloria Patri et Filio et Spiritui Sancto!...

My dear little sister Germaine of the Trinity,

    If you knew how I prayed for you on your fifteenth birthday! I offered Holy Communion for that intention, then I gave you to the Holy Trinity, and it seemed to me that this gift was even more true, more complete than it was last year. Yes, my little sister, you belong entirely to "Them," you are God's thing.[2] Oh! really surrender yourself to Him, to His Love!... Sister Thérèse of the Child Jesus says that "one is consumed by Love to the extent that one is surrendered to Love."[3] Since we aspire to be victims of His Charity[4] like our holy Mother Teresa, we must let ourselves be rooted in the Charity of Christ, as Saint Paul says in today's beautiful epistle.[5] And how? By always living, through all things, with Him who dwells within us and who is Charity.[6] He so thirsts to associate us with all that He is, to transform us into Himself. My little sister, let us awaken our faith, let us recall that He is there, within, and that He wants us to be very faithful. So, when you feel as if you are about to lose your patience or say something against charity, bring yourself back to Him, let go of this natural inclination in order to please Him. How many acts of self-denial can be offered to Him, known to Him alone! Let us not waste them, my little sister. It seems to me that saints are souls who forget themselves all the time, who so lose themselves in Him whom they love, without looking at self, without a glance at the creature, that they can say with Saint Paul: "It is no longer I who live, it is Jesus Christ who lives in me!"[7] Of course we must immolate ourselves to achieve this transformation, but, my little sister, you love sacrifice because you love the Crucified, isn't that so? Oh! look at Him attentively, lean on Him, and then bring your soul to Him, tell Him that you want only to love Him, that you want Him to do everything in you because you are too little. It is so good to be God's little child, to let yourself be carried by Him all the time, to rest in His Love! Let us really ask for this grace of simplicity and abandonment that belonged to Sister Thérèse of the Child Jesus; the novitiate[8] is preparing for her feast on the 30th[9] with a novena; if you would like to join us, we are saying the Magnificat, according to the desire that she herself had expressed to a Sister in one of our Carmels;[10] I am including you as a special intention in this novena.

Soon, in less than a month, we will have the great feast of our holy Mother Teresa,[11] I invite you to unite yourself to your big sister in Carmel; she is preparing for it by a sort of retreat;[12] her Cenacle is "Love," Love who dwells within us; and my only exercise[13] is to enter within once again, to lose myself in Those who are there!…

When I renew my holy vows, the vows that make me one who is "chained to Christ," to use Saint Paul's language,[14] I love to add your name to mine and thus give you along with myself! To give yourself, isn't that the need of your soul too, my little sister? Oh! it is the response to His Love. Let us also give Him souls, our holy Mother Teresa wants her daughters to be wholly apostolic; it is so simple, the divine Adorer is within us, so we have His prayer; let us offer it, let us share in it, let us pray with His Soul! A Dieu, my little sister, kiss your dear mama and nice little Yvonne for me. I entrust a kiss to my Crucifix for you, He will give it to you, "this kiss of the Bridegroom." [15] Union within, in silence and Love!

Your big sister

M. E. of the Trinity

I hope the waters will restore Madame de Gemeaux to complete health.[16]

[1] After September 17, 1903, Germaine's "fifteenth birthday." It was on September 20 that "today's beautiful epistle" was read, Eph 3:13–21 (the 16th Sunday after Pentecost in the liturgical calendar of that time).

[2] "Thing" is an expression already encountered in P 75 and one that recurs often in the speech of P. Vallée, who used it several times in his 1900 retreat (twice, for example, in the final sermon).

[3] HA 271.

[4] Cf. L 169, note 4.

[5] Eph 3:17. This text becomes very dear to Elizabeth.

[6] Cf. 1 Jn 4:16 (and 8).

[7] Gal 2:20.

[8] Elizabeth is still in the novitiate, where the professed remained for three years after their profession, without having the right to vote in chapter. The "we" here can refer only to the Mistress of Novices. We do not know who was in the novitiate at that time; perhaps the "Sister Madeleine" of whom the "Account Book" speaks between March 1904 and March 1905. The conventual books did not keep track of the postulants who entered during those years. Around 1920, in cutting the "minutes" of the "Book of Clothings" in order to paste them into a new book, someone also left out the accounts of the novices who left Carmel; one of the sheets that has been recovered gives witness to this (cf. L 327, note 5).

[9] Anniversary of her death six years previously; it was already a "feast" in the novitiate at Dijon. The Thérèsian atmosphere of the preceding passage is apparent.

[10] The reference here (perhaps in a private revelation?) is unknown at the Lisieux Carmel.

[11] October 15.

[12] Privately (as she does often), without any effect on community life. She had made her annual retreat before her profession. There was no preached retreat that year, undoubtedly because of the difficult situation religious found themselves in in France.

[13] "Exercise" [ejercicio] is an expression from John of the Cross (SC 309, 313 [K-RJ 28:2,

28:9]: "exercise of love") used to indicate the "office," the "occupation" of the soul. Cf. Thérèse of Lisieux: "My every act is love" (HA 140 [SS 178]).

[14] Cf. Eph 4:1 (prisoner); Eph 3:1 and Philemon 1 and 9 (prisoner). Cf. L 97, note 4.

[15] Perhaps an allusion to Song 1:2. Germaine de Gemeaux spoke of her visits to the parlor of Carmel: "One day, in the most delicate way, she had her crucifix passed to me for me to kiss, so He could transmit Elizabeth's kiss to me, and so I could see the dear Companion of her life in Carmel" (testimony of February 22, 1907, in PAT).

[16] Mother Germaine adds a postscript: "I am sending a relic of this little seraphim to Germaine of the Trinity, in honor of the feast of Sr. Thérèse of the Child Jesus. In kissing it, may the child entrusted by us to the angelic Novice Mistress of Lisieux and of the Dijon Carmel, where her portrait presides, [ask her for] the fidelity of the saints, the fidelity of love."

L 180   To Madame Lignon   [September 23, 1903][1]
J. M. + J. T.   Dijon Carmel, September 23

Very dear Madame,

How nice you are to remember your little Carmelite friend and send her a souvenir of your pilgrimage to Notre-Dame de Prouille.[2] Your pretty holy cards have made me very happy, please thank my dear little Cécile by giving her a kiss for me; we were such good friends at Saint-Hilaire, and her memory and that of her dear mama still live in my heart, neither will ever be forgotten!...

My good Mama came home yesterday morning, and in the afternoon she was at Carmel. You can imagine how we spoke of you! I am so touched by your care, your many kindnesses, that I do not know how to thank you. Tell Monsieur Lignon how grateful I am, that was just like him!...

I am praying fervently for you, dear Madame, for your Cécile and all your dear ones. If you knew how one's heart expands and grows larger in Carmel, and how the heart of your little friend remains always faithful to you. She has been in her dear solitude for two years now, and her happiness is ever new because God is its object. A Dieu, I love you always; thanks again, all of you share in the great affection I send you from the depth of my cloister.

                    Sr. M. Elizabeth of the Trinity r.c.i.

[1] 1903: "two years" in Carmel; see also the following note.

[2] The ACD still has a "holy card" sent to Elizabeth representing the basilica of Notre-Dame de Prouille, on the back of which is a printed prayer with these words in

pencil: "On pilgrimage to Prouille I thought of my dear little friend Elizabeth. September 20, 1903. Alice Lignon."

L 181   To Madame de Sourdon   [November 21, 1903][1]
J. M. + J. T.   Dijon Carmel, November 21

Very dear Madame,

A Carmelite's days are so filled minute to minute by prayer and work that I have not yet been able to find a moment to come to you. Today we renewed our holy vows, a holiday in Carmel,[2] and so I am taking advantage of my first free minute to tell you of all my gratitude. Your heart does not know how to forget: those who have entered it never leave, and you still remember your little friend faithfully, which has touched her deeply. If you knew how sweet it is in my dear solitude to receive such affectionate greetings,[3] which tell me that the grilles do not separate me from you! Thanks also for the delicious madeleines; the whole community celebrated Saint Elizabeth, and that reminded me of our joyful lunches. Here the great silence envelops our life and allows our souls to cross over into the infinite in order to lose ourselves, as in a foretaste of Heaven, in the love of Him who is our All. Dear Madame, you know that you are not forgotten in these divine intimacies. Then it is my heart that speaks ... and it addresses the One who loves you with such great love; so I have every chance of being heard.... Have confidence, dear Madame, God makes us wait sometimes,[4] but His fatherly Providence governs everything. "Think of me, I will think of you",[5] that is what He has His happy bride say to you today. She sends you the best of her heart, you know how much affection there is for you *there!*... I have prayed fervently for Madame de Maizières; I hope the operation went well.[6]

Sr. M. El. of the Trinity r.c.i.

Affectionate greetings to your kind Marie-Louise.

---

[1] First letter in full copper-colored ink. L 181 and 182 are two halves of the same sheet. "November 21" (L 181) and "Saturday" (L 182) coincide in 1903.
[2] Feast of the Presentation of Mary in the Temple. They did not work on that day.
[3] Greetings for her feast of November 19. The "madeleines" were for that.

[4] An allusion to the difficulties of her daughter Marie-Louise in finding a husband according to her wishes.
[5] St. Catherine of Siena (cf. L 129, note 5).
[6] She will have another operation in 1904 (cf. L 206) and will die in 1906, after a "cruel martyrdom" (L 312).

L 182   To Françoise de Sourdon   [November 21, 1903][1]
J. M. + J. T.   Dijon Carmel, Saturday

My dear Françoise,

Thanks for your letter and your good wishes. How many times we have celebrated Saint Elizabeth together; I can still see your radiant face when you used to appear with your beautiful bouquet and rush into my arms. Good Françoise, I still love you very much and assure you I prayed fervently for you during your illness,[2] all the same, if you had left your poor Sabeth, do you ever think of that, my darling?...

I am not at all surprised at what that Jesuit father said to you,[3] for I have always thought that, now more than ever. There is no reason to be frightened. Oh! if only you were willing, my Framboise.... All the same, hasn't your illness made you reflect? It seems to me it must be very good to see yourself so close to eternity. You are going to find this strange—I'm telling you this in confidence—I am already beginning my Heaven on earth, but sometimes I would like to see the other side so as to see Him, Him ... to love Him and lose myself in His Infinity. Oh, my Françoise, you have such an ardent heart; don't you understand what love is when it concerns Him who has so loved us? If only you knew how He loves you, and how I love you too!...

Our Reverend Mother asks me to send you these two series of raffle tickets; you have many friends and I am sure you'll sell them easily. It's to help one of our exiled Carmels; our Mothers from Belgium[4] who took them in have organized this raffle, and I'm sure you will really want to help with this good work. Our Reverend Mother wishes very much to send the series back to them for Christmas. So I'm counting on your great kindness, and while waiting to thank you in person, I am sending a thousand tokens of my love just for my little beloved Framboise.

                    Sr. M. E. o. t. Trinity r.c.i.

¹ Cf. L 181, note l.
² Of August/September, cf. L 174 and 178.
³ Unknown. He was undoubtedly talking with Françoise about her gifts, which were late in blossoming. Perhaps he intended to make her reflect on the possibility of a call from God.
⁴ Not identified.

L 183   To her sister   [November 22, 1903][1]
          J. M. + J. T.   Dijon Carmel, Sunday
              "The kingdom of God is within you." [2]

My good Guite,

If you knew what joy you gave my heart by celebrating my feast day like that…. Your kind note made me very happy and your beautiful photograph has done me so much good: Saint Elizabeth gave you the perfect inspiration, for it was just what I wanted; it increases my devotion in saying the Divine Office,[3] and I imagine, too, that we are both there close to Him! It is so true, my little one, that He is in our souls and we are quite close all the time, just like Martha and Mary; when you go about your activities, I keep you close to Him, and then, as you know, when we love Him, external things cannot distract us from the Master, and my Guite is both Martha and Mary!…[4] If you knew how close I feel to you, how I envelop you with prayers, you and your dear little creature who is already in the mind of God.[5] Oh! let yourself be wholly caught, wholly invaded by His divine life so you can give it to this dear little one who will arrive in this world showered with blessings! Think what must have been in the soul of the Virgin when, after the Incarnation, she possessed within her the Incarnate Word, the Gift of God….[5a] In what silence, what recollection, what adoration she must have been wrapped in the depth of her soul in order to embrace this God whose Mother she was. My little Guite, He is in us. Oh! let us keep very close to Him, in that silence, with that love of the Virgin; let us spend our Advent like that, shall we?

I didn't realize the other day that Advent was going to begin on Sunday and that this would be too close[6] for us to see each other again. Don't be upset about it, my little one, it's not very long, and you can come right after Christmas (on the third day, for we have the Blessed Sacrament), that will be hardly more than one month. You know our Reverend Mother loves you dearly, and if she could let you have a parlor visit she would, but this week there's going to be an overflow; I know something about that, since I'm portress.[7] We'll offer this sacrifice together for the little angel,[8] for I so love to see my Guite, who is the little sister of both my heart and my soul! A Dieu, let's be "one," let's stay close to each other in Him. Thank Georges for his good wishes; as for myself, I wish you a sweet little child, and I rejoice to think of all the happiness it will bring with it; I thank God for it, and I share your joy from the depth of my beloved solitude! Poor Monsieur Chapuis, I have wept over his soul;[9] God is very good, but He is a just Judge. He will repay you for all that Mama and your kind husband did to save him; it, too, is a blessing for the little angel. May God who is all Love envelop you ever more with His Charity; I rest on His Heart with you and I ask Him to consume in one divine embrace the two little sisters in Unity.

Sr. M. Elizabeth of the Trinity r.c.i.

I'm delighted to think you'll be at Benediction tomorrow[10] with Mama.

---

[1] The "Sunday" after her November 19th feast day. See also note 9.
[2] Lk 17:21.
[3] She kept the photograph in her breviary.
[4] Cf. Lk 10:38–42.
[5] Little Elizabeth will be born in four months.
[5a] Cf. Jn 4:10.
[6] Advent would begin November 29: so Guite had come less than a month before, which was the required interval of time between the visits of close relatives. There were no visits during Advent; hence the "overflow" during the preceding week.
[7] Second "Portress" or "Turn Sister," inside the enclosure (cf. Plan 1, no. 21), assistant to the Sub-Prioress, Marie of the Trinity, who was first portress. Elizabeth spent one hour at the turn in the morning and one hour in the afternoon. The rest of the time she continued to work in the habit room.
[8] The child who is going to be born.
[9] Cf. L 178, note 11. He died November 19, 1903, on Elizabeth's feast day. When she learned of his death, she said, "heaving a deep sigh: That unfortunate man!" (S 49). In the parish register of Saint-Michel, however, we read that on November 21, Henri Chapuis, "deceased two days before, fortified with the sacraments of the Church, has been buried by us, Curé de Saint-Michel." Perhaps Elizabeth did not know he had received the last rites of the church.
[10] November 23 is the vigil of the feast of St. John of the Cross.

L 184   To Madame Angles   [November 24, 1903]¹
     J. M. +J. T.   Dijon Carmel, November 24
          "My Beloved is all mine and I am all His!"²

Madame and dear sister,

I was very touched by your good wishes. I, for my part, celebrated your feast day, too, since Saint Elizabeth is your patron,³ for it does us much good to look into the soul of saints and then to follow them through faith right up to Heaven; there, they are all luminous with the light of God, whom they contemplate face to face for all eternity!... This Heaven of the saints is our homeland, the "Father's House"⁴ where we are awaited, where we are loved, where one day we too will be able to fly and rest in the bosom of Infinite Love!

When we consider the divine world that envelops us already here in our exile and in which we can move, oh, then things here below disappear: all of that doesn't exist, it is less than nothing. The saints, for their part, understood true knowledge so well, the knowledge that makes us leave everything, and especially ourselves, so we can fly to God and live solely with Him! Dear Madame, He is within us to sanctify us, so let us ask Him to be Himself our sanctity.⁵ When Our Lord was on earth, the Gospel says "a secret power went out from Him,"⁶ at His touch the sick recovered their health, the dead were restored to life. Well, He is still living! living in the tabernacle in His adorable Sacrament, living in our souls. He Himself said: "If anyone loves Me, he will keep My word, and My Father will love him and We will come to him and make Our home in him,"⁷ so since He is there, let us keep Him company as a friend does with the One he loves! The essence of our life in Carmel is this divine, wholly intimate union; it is what makes our solitude so precious, for, as our holy father John of the Cross, whose feast we are celebrating today, said, "Two hearts who love each other prefer solitude to anything else."⁸ On Saturday,⁹ the feast of the Presentation of the Blessed Virgin, we had the beautiful ceremony of the renewal of our vows. Oh! dear Madame, what a beautiful day, what joy to be bound to the service of so good a Master, to tell Him that one is His until death, "sponsa Christi." I am so happy to feel that you too are given to Him, and it seems to me that, from up in Heaven, our great Saint Elizabeth must bless and seal the union of our souls. Please tell your little Sister Imelda of Jesus[10] that I very happily grant her wish by remembering her each day before God; I ask her to pray for me too, especially to say "thank you" to Him who has chosen the better part for me! I was very happy to have news of you through Mama, who was so well received, so spoiled when she was with you,[11] I don't know how to express my gratitude to all of you for that. As for me, I will never go to your beautiful mountains again, but I will follow you there in soul and heart, asking Him who is our "rendez-vous" to draw us to those other mountains, those divine summits that are so far from earth they nearly touch Heaven; I remain wholly united with you there beneath the rays of the Sun of Love!...[12]

Sister M. Eliz. of the Trinity r.c.i.

[1] Cf. note 9.
[2] Song 2:16.
[3] Probably her patron as a Third Order Franciscan. Mme. Angles later became a religious with the name Marie-Elizabeth.
[4] Jn 14:2.
[5] Cf. PN 4 and 5 before her entrance, from the perspective of Thérèse of Lisieux's "Act of Oblation," which can be recognized here (HA 249 [SS 276]: "And I beg you, O my God, to be Yourself my Sanctity").
[6] Cf. Lk 6:19.
[7] Jn 14:23.
[8] SC 383 (st. 36; [cf K-RJ 36:1]), immediately preceded by the words "Love establishes unity," which Elizabeth has quoted twice: L 121 and 274.
[9] November 21, which was in fact a "Saturday" in 1903.
[10] Probably Sister Imelda of the Heart of Jesus, a Dominican nun of Prouille (Aude).
[11] In August (cf. L 175).
[12] On the influence of Thérèse of Lisieux in this image, see L 190, note 3.

L 185   To l'Abbé Chevignard   [November 28, 1903][1]
J. M. + J. T.   Dijon Carmel, November 28
"Ipsi sum desponsata cui Angeli serviunt."[2]

Monsieur l'Abbé,

Thank you for your good prayers, thank you for your letter.[3] What you tell me about my name does me much good; I love it so much, it expresses my entire vocation; when I think of it my soul is carried away in the great vision of the Mystery of mysteries, in the Trinity that even here below is our cloister, our dwelling, the Infinite within which we can pass through everything. At the moment I am reading some very beautiful pages in our blessed Father Saint John of the Cross on the transformation of the soul in the three Divine Persons. Monsieur l'Abbé, to what an abyss of glory we are called! [4] Oh! I understand the silence, the recollection of the saints who could no longer leave their contemplation; thus God could lead them to the divine summits where union is made perfect between Him and the soul who has become His bride, in the mystical sense of the word. Our blessed Father says that then the Holy Spirit raises it to so wonderful a height that He makes it capable of producing in God the same spiration of love that the Father produces in the Son and the Son in the Father, the spiration that is the Holy Spirit Himself! [5] To think that God calls us by our vocation to live in this holy light! What an adorable mystery of charity! I would like to respond to it by living on earth as the Blessed Virgin did, "keeping all these things in my heart," [6] burying myself, so to speak, in the depths of my soul to lose myself in the Trinity who dwells in it in order to transform me into itself. Then my motto, "my luminous ideal," as you said, will be accomplished: it will really be *Elizabeth of the Trinity!*... [6a]

I am very grateful to you for having sent me your instruction; it can apply to a Carmelite as well as to a priest, and I loved reading it on the 21st, the day we had the beautiful ceremony of the renewal of our holy vows. You see how perfectly it suited the occasion!

Monday I will say the Office of Saint Andrew for you, [7] and I will offer Holy Communion for that same intention. May you be submerged, invaded by the great river of Life, [8] may you feel the springs of living water [9] well up from the deepest part of your soul, so that God may be your All. I have entrusted this desire you formed in my soul into the hands of her [10] who was so completely God's "thing," [11] and she will speak to you in the silence of your soul. With you, I remain wholly adoring the Mystery.

                                        Sr. M. Eliz. of the Trinity r.c.i.

The death of Monsieur Chapuis [12] grieved me deeply: to think God has loved so much and that some souls close themselves off to the action of this love....

¹ Cf. notes 7 and 12.
² "I am the bride of Him whom the Angels serve" (ninth antiphon of Matins for the feast of St. Agnes, January 21).
³ On the feast of St. Elizabeth, November 19.
⁴ Elizabeth is thinking here particularly of st. 39 [K-RJ 39:4] of the *Spiritual Canticle*. The expression "abyss of glory" is found on p. 423 [in the French edition used by Elizabeth].
⁵ Beginning with "the Holy Spirit raises ...", an almost literal quotation from SC p. 421 [K-RJ 39:3].
⁶ Lk 2:19 and 51.
⁶ᵃ Words written larger by Elizabeth. We put them in italics.
⁷ The patron saint of André Chevignard, celebrated November 30; which was in fact "Monday" in 1903.
⁸ Cf. Rev 22:1: "the river of life-giving water"?
⁹ Cf. Jn 4:14 (according to the trans. of SC p. 122 [K-RJ 12:3]).
¹⁰ The Virgin Mary.
¹¹ Cf. L 179, note 2.
¹² Cf. L 183, note 9.

L 186   To Marie-Louise Ambry (née Maurel)

[December 15, 1903]¹

J. M. + J. T.   Dijon Carmel, December 15

My dear Marie-Louise,

Although we are in the holy season of Advent, when all correspondence stops in Carmel, our Reverend Mother, who knows the depth of my affection for you, is allowing me to make an exception for you, and I am very happy to tell you how I am praying for you and for the little angel who is on the way. It is already in the mind of God, and I love to envelop it with prayer so it will arrive in the world showered with blessings, and I am asking the Divine Master who dwells in your soul as in a little Host in the Tabernacle, to pass on to you a superabundance of His divine life so you can give it to the little angel whose mama you are going to be. Our good Mother is giving me this little heart for you.² Our Lord has promised the Sisters of our Order that all those who wear it will be protected, and it has worked real miracles. May it protect you, dear Marie-Louise, and bring you happiness. Abandon yourself, then, into the hands of God like a little child resting on the heart of its mother. If you knew how He loves you and wants you very close to Him, live in His intimacy…. He is the Friend who wants to be loved above everything;³ He so

loved us that He "came among us,"[4] and this year, see, He is confid-
ing a little angel to you so you can teach it to know Him and to love
Him…. That, dear little mama, is your mission…. Always stay united
to the God of the Host you love so much; He will teach you to suffer,
to immolate yourself, to pray, to love. He will tell you that your Elizabeth is praying fervently for you and is rejoicing at the coming of
the little angel; count on her prayers and those of her beloved
Carmel. She gives a kiss to you and your dear mama; I knew from
mine that she was close by you.

Sr. M. Eliz. of the Trinity r.c.i.

Please remember me to Monsieur Joseph, tell him I share in
your joy.

[1] Before the birth of little Jean Ambry, born December 27, 1903.
[2] Mother Germaine adds in a postscript: "The little heart was sent yesterday by Madame Catez. It contains, wrapped in a little gospel of the holy name of Jesus, a piece
of Agnus Dei, one of the Agnus Deis blessed by the Holy Father for young mothers,
thus having the mission of bestowing on them the blessings they need at difficult
times. We have obtained real miracles through these little hearts sent at times when
all seemed hopeless. They are sewn on the scapular." Marie-Louise had lost her first
child at birth, cf. L 134.
[3] A probable allusion to the *Imitation of Christ*, book 2, chap. 7: "How necessary it is to
love Jesus above all things." Elizabeth's *Manual* contained the *Imitation*, which seems
to have had little influence on her thought in Carmel. She received a copy of the
Imitation (Tournai: Desclée, Lefebvre et Cie, 1881), inscribed by Léonie Traxile, a
friend of her mother, on the day of her first Communion.
[4] Jn 1:14.

L 187   To her Rolland aunts

[December 30, 1903–January 3, 1904][1]

J. M. +J. T.   Dijon Carmel, December 30, 1903

My good little Aunts,
       I am writing you before Matins in our dear little cell, and I wish
I were a painter so I could make you a sketch of the scene that surrounds me. The sky is beautiful, all clear and starry; the moonlight
is flooding our cell through the frosted window panes, it's ravishing; our window looks out over the quadrangle, an interior garden
surrounded by our large cloisters; in the middle on a rock a large

cross stands out. All is calm and silent, and that makes me think of the night when the little Jesus was given to us. It seems I can hear the Angels singing their sweet canticle: "Rejoice, a Savior has been given to us."[2] Dear Aunts, did you have a nice Christmas? Mine was delightful, for you see, Christmas in Carmel is unique; in the evening, I settled down in choir, and there I spent my whole vigil with the Blessed Virgin awaiting the divine Little One, who this time was going to be born no longer in the crib, but in my soul, in our souls, for He is truly Emmanuel, "God with us."[3] At 10:15, we had Matins, sung entirely on two notes—we sing like that in Carmel;[4] I sang one lesson. Immediately after Matins, we had midnight Mass, after which we sang Lauds; and then thanksgiving. You were not forgotten that night, my little Aunts; I followed you into that dear little church I love so much. I had always dreamed of attending midnight Mass at Carlipa, and now that I'm a Carmelite and my Bridegroom gives me wings to fly away to you, it seems to me I can accomplish the dream that was never fulfilled before. How are Aunt Francine's eyes? When Mama returned, she gave me all the details about her eyesight, and I pray every day for that intention; what a sacrifice! My little Aunt, it is because the Master loves you and knows He can count on you; nevertheless, I am begging Him to illumine your soul with His divine light and to give your poor eyes that I love so much a complete healing. You can guess how happy I was to talk with Mama about you when she returned from the South.[5] She came back looking wonderful; and she continues to do well; I saw her at the beginning of the week,[6] for during Advent we don't go to the parlor. I also had a visit from Guite; she was fresh and rosy, in complete good health; I'm rejoicing over the coming of the little angel, who will bring so much happiness with it. From the depths of my cloister, I share in the joy of those I love so much, and then, gazing at the divine Little One in the crib, I tell Him with ineffable happiness: "You are my All." Yes, my little Aunts, the horizon looks very beautiful to me, for in my life, there is only Him! And isn't He all Heaven!… I love you always, I belong to Him who is "faithful,"[7] according to Saint Paul's expression, and He keeps the souls who belong to Him faithful. May the God of the crib, to whom I have confided my wishes for my little Aunts, bring them my whole heart.

These greetings will arrive late, for my letter, which I began four days ago, was left unfinished, but my heart went to you before it did. Please give my love to my Aunt. And please offer my respectful greetings to Monsieur le Curé and tell him that my little soul loves to be united with his in prayer! A Dieu, a good, happy, and holy New Year! Your little niece,

Sr. M. E. of the Trinity, r.c.i.

Hello to Louise, Anna, and the little ones.

¹ Letter begun "four days ago," December 30.
² Cf. Lk 2:10–11.
³ Mt 1:23.
⁴ On feast days and Sunday Vespers, they "sang" by lowering the pitch a half tone on the last accent before the pause and at the end of each verse. In all other cases, they chanted _recto tono_ [on one note].
⁵ She returned from her trip and her visit to Carmel on September 22 (cf. L 180).
⁶ At the earliest, Monday, December 28, "the third day" "after Christmas" (cf. L 183).
⁷ For example, 1 Cor 10:13.

L 188   To her mother   [December 31, 1903]¹
   J. M. + J. T.   Thursday evening, December 31

My dear little Mama,
      The Blessed Virgin wants to come back to you² to tell you all your Elizabeth's wishes. She brings her whole heart to you today!...
      I spent some delightful days with this dear statue in the intimacy of our little cell; she has told me so many things. You see how alive she is: may she come fill the emptiness of your solitude by telling you the secrets of union. Jesus and Mary loved each other so: the whole heart of one flowed into the heart of the other! I am in a good school, darling Mama! He is teaching me to love you as He loved, for He is the God who is all Love. But in order to do the will of His Father, He left that Mother whom He loved infinitely. For me, too, that's the reason I left you, but I am closer to you now, for I have but one heart, one soul³ with my little Mama! I'm confiding all my tender affection, all my wishes for you and for Guite to the Blessed

Virgin. Our Reverend Mother asks me to send you her best wishes.

Your Eliz. of the Trinity r.c.i.

I will spend my day with you, close to Him.

[1] "Thursday" and "December 31" coincide in 1903.
[2] The little statue of the Virgin of Lourdes that Elizabeth left to her mother when she entered. It is the "Janua Coeli" (Gate of Heaven), as she called it during her last illness. She was able to keep it in her cell during Advent, as this letter implies. Ordinarily a Carmelite did not have a statue in her cell.
[3] Cf. Acts 4:32.

L 189   To her mother   [January 1, 1904][1]

J.M. + J.T.   Friday, January 1

My darling little Mama,

I had already sent my little note when I received your beautiful New Year's gift, and our Reverend Mother is letting me come thank you. It's magnificent! [The Sisters in] the linen room are overjoyed, for it will be just perfect; you've really spoiled me, my little Mama, I assure you that I am really pleased and that you couldn't have given a more useful New Year's gift. Listen to my little heart, it is saying lots of "thank you's" to you!... Did the Blessed Virgin give you my message?... Poor Mama, I can understand how alone you feel during these days we used to celebrate with so much joy, but if you *knew* how much *He wants* to become your friend, your Confidant, how He wants to fill your life with His divine presence.... Today I too was thinking about the past, about all I left for Him, and, do you understand? don't be upset, it was so beautiful in my soul, there was so much peace, so much happiness.... I spent a heavenly day close to the Blessed Sacrament, and I took you with me, for you know very well I never leave [you]. I am so happy about the nice day you had. As I write, I am following you to good Madame de Sourdon's; please give her my best wishes and tell her I'm praying for her special intention.[2] Thank Madame d'Avout for her fine chocolate. A Dieu, darling Mama, I'm very talkative for a Carmelite, but when I am with you my heart doesn't want to be silent any more; I am becoming a very little child so you'll cuddle me; a mama's

affection is so good; it is not without suffering that one says goodbye
to a mama forever!

Your Eliz. r.c.i.

I am going to write to the Canon;[3] I am very happy for
Marie-Louise.[4] Soon your turn to be a grandmother. Thanks again
for your beautiful gift!...

[1] "Friday" and "January 1" coincide in 1904.
[2] A good match for Marie-Louise.
[3] L 190.
[4] Little Jean was born on December 27, 1903.

L 190   To Canon Angles   [January 4, 1904][1]
J. M. + J. T.   Dijon Carmel, January 4
"Deus meus et omnia"[2]

Monsieur le Chanoine,

Has the God of the crib whispered to you, in the silence of
your soul, the wishes that His Carmelite has confided to Him for
you? Since the divine Little One dwells in my soul, I have all His
prayer as well, and I love to make it come down on those my heart is
forever deeply grateful to, which is to tell you that you have a large
share of my poor little prayers!

The beautiful feast of Christmas, which I have always loved so
much, has a very special character in Carmel. Instead of spending
the holy vigil with Mama and Guite, this time it was in great silence,
in choir, quite close to Him, and I loved to say to myself: "He is my
All, my one and only All." What happiness, what peace that gives to
the soul. He is the only one, I have given Him all. If I look at it from
an earthly point of view, I see solitude and even emptiness, for I
cannot say my heart has not suffered; but if my gaze remains always
fixed on Him, my luminous Star,[3] oh, then all the rest disappears,
and I lose myself in Him like a drop of water in the Ocean.[4] It is all
calm, all peaceful, and the peace of God is so good; that is what Saint
Paul is speaking of when he says it "surpasses all understanding"![5]

I heard from Mama about the arrival of Marie-Louise's little angel, and I am sharing the joy of her heart; please tell her when you see her, I would be very grateful to you if you would; I had been praying fervently for her, that God might make her forget last year's trial. I saw Guite this week, overjoyed about becoming a mama soon; then I also saw my good Mama, who was impatiently waiting for Christmas, for we do not go to the parlor during Advent, and the time seemed long to her; I am happy, God is doing His work. Oh! how good it is to live by surrendering oneself and those one loves! Sunday[6] is the anniversary of the great day of my profession; I will be on retreat,[7] and I rejoice at spending the day close to my Bridegroom. I have such hunger for Him. He hollows out abysses in my soul, abysses He alone can fill, and to do that He leads me into deep silence that I never want to leave again. A Dieu, Monsieur le Chanoine, please pray for me, I need your help so much. At the Holy Sacrifice, at the altar of Him whom I love, remember your Carmelite, and tell God she wants to be His host so He may always dwell within her, so she may then give Him to others. My very best wishes are yours, and I ask your blessing.

Sr. M. Elizabeth of the Trinity r.c.i.[8]

[1] 1904: deduced from the contents as well as the handwriting in copper-colored ink.

[2] "My God and my all": the motto of St. Francis of Assisi.

[3] The image is again inspired by the end of an early edition of *Story of a Soul*. Even before entering Carmel (cf. L 41. note 7). Elizabeth spoke of the Eagle who carries the prey of its love very high. In March 1903, she compared Jesus to a "furnace of love" (L 159), like Thérèse (HA 214 [SS 200]: furnace of love); in November she called Him the "Sun of Love" (L 184) like Thérèse (HA 212 [SS 198]: "the divine sun of love"); here, she borrows from Thérèse the rather unusual vocabulary of the "Star" on which one's gaze "remains fixed" (HA 212 and 214 [SS 198-200]).

As with Thérèse, Jesus is both the eagle who is carrying and the star-sun-furnace (of the Trinity HA 213 [SS 198]) toward which He "carries [her] off" *[emporte]* (HA 214 [SS 200]). He is both the way and the goal at the same time, Jesus in both His glorified humanity and His divinity: "Savior" and "Word," as Thérèse says, placing them side by side (HA 213 [SS 199]), or "your only Son as my Savior and my spouse" ("Act of Oblation," HA 249 [SS 276]).

The image of the Star returns, for example, in PN 15; L 225, P 96 (with the star of Epiphany in P 86). Elizabeth again speaks of the divine "Sun" (for example, in L 193, or the Sun of Ps 18 in L 250, P 96, LR 19). Her life is "brightened by His ray of love" (L 315); "union (with God) is her brilliant sun" (L 209); "intimacy with Him ... the beautiful sun illuminating my life" (L 333). Above all, at the end of her life she speaks of the "Furnace *[Foyer]* of love" (L 330; HF 14; P 94, 100, 101, 106, 109), the "Furnace of light" (P 85), the "immense Furnace" (L 293), the "great Furnace" (L 316), the "burning furnace *[fournaise]* (P 98, 102, 117), "Furnace of His Heart" (L 289), the "Furnace of love" (L 287; P 94).

To complete her imagery, we should add the language of fire, light, brightness, radiance. See also the sun or the light in the "crystal" (L 131, note 4).

[4] Cf. L 110, note 3.

[5] Phil 4:7.

[6] Feast of the Epiphany (the first Sunday after January 6), in 1904, on January 10.

[7] For only a single day.

[8] A postscript from Mother Germaine alludes to the very difficult times: "She humbly recommends to his prayers and to the Holy Sacrifice her dear little flock around which the storm roars. To God's care!"

L 191   To Abbé Chevignard   [January 25, 1904][1]
J. M. + J. T.   "Amo Christum."

Monsieur l'Abbé,

Saint Paul says that "we are no longer guests or foreigners, but we belong to the City of saints and the House of God."[2] We already live in that supernatural, divine world by faith, and it is there that my soul feels quite close to yours, in the embrace of the God who is all Love! His charity, His "exceeding charity,"[3] to use the words of the great apostle once again, that is my vision on earth. Monsieur l'Abbé, will we ever understand how much we are loved? I think this is indeed the knowledge of the saints. In his magnificent epistles, Saint Paul preaches nothing but this mystery of the charity of Christ, so I borrow his words to express my wishes for you: "May the Father of O. L. Jesus Christ grant, according to the riches of His glory, that you might be strengthened inwardly through His Spirit, that Christ might dwell in your heart through faith, that you might be rooted and grounded in charity so you can comprehend, with all the saints, the breadth, the length, the height, and the depth of the charity of Christ that surpasses all knowledge, so you might be filled according to all the fullness of God" (Eph. C. III).[4]

My soul loves to unite with yours in one single prayer for the Church, for the diocese.[5] Since Our Lord dwells in our souls, His prayer belongs to us, and I wish to live in communion with it unceasingly, keeping myself like a little vase at the Source, at the Fountain of life,[6] so that later I can communicate it to souls by letting its floods of infinite charity overflow.[7] "I sanctify myself for them that they also may be sanctified in the truth."[8] Let us make these words of our adored Master all our own, yes, let us sanctify ourselves for souls, and since we are all members of one body,[8a] inasmuch as we have an abundance of divine life, we can communicate it in the great body of the Church. There are two words that sum up for me all holiness, all apostolate: "Union and Love." Ask that I may live that fully, and, for that purpose, dwell completely hidden away in the Holy Trinity; you could not wish anything more beautiful for me![9] A Dieu, Monsieur l'Abbé, I am praying very much for you so that, on the day of your subdiaconate,[10] God will find your soul just as He wishes it to be. Let us unite to make Him forget everything by the strength of our love, and let us be, as Saint Paul says, "the praise of His glory."[11]

Sr. M. Elizabeth of the Trinity r.c.i.

[1] Elizabeth did not date this very important letter in which for the first time she sums up her vocation as an effort to be "the praise of the glory" of God, after having quoted the Epistle to the Ephesians at length. Later, Abbé Chevignard, an orderly man who proved to be careful with dates, assigned the date January 25, 1904. P. Philipon later changed that date. He was [wrongly] convinced that the discovery of the "praise of God" dated only from the summer (or spring) of 1905 (cf. *The Spiritual Doctrine of Sister Elizabeth of the Trinity*, pp. 83–84, with this most unfortunate phrase: "For some time she had felt imprisoned within herself, unable to get free"; see also *Ecrits spirituels*, p. 18; *En présence de Dieu*, pp. 20, 30-31). In any case, he based his assumption on testimony given 30 years after the fact by Sr. Aimée of Jesus, then 78 years old—testimony that calls for a totally different interpretation (cf. AL). P. Philipon then wrote over the date given by Abbé Chevignard, making it "December"; he thus pushed the date of Elizabeth's letter up eleven months, still not enough to make it the spring or summer of 1905.

In reality, the letter is truly from *January 25, 1904*. The handwriting (Elizabeth's most beautiful calligraphy) and the copper-colored ink characteristic of these months completely rule out the 1905 hypothesis. Moreover, a piece of the following letter, L 192, belongs to the same sheet as this L 191, as can be seen in plate 1 of Vol. I: the two pieces of paper fit together, their torn edges coincide perfectly and the oblique lines of the paper pass from one sheet to the other (the thickness of the paper where it has been torn is equally significant). Letter 192 to Françoise de Sourdon is dated "January 27" (for her feast day on the 29th) and, moreover, contains the same quotation from Ephesians 3:16. Finally, the first page of L 192 is also from the same sheet of paper as L 193 from "February 11." So there is no doubt about the date, corroborated by the handwriting and ink.

[2] Eph 2:19.

[3] Eph 2:4.

[4] Eph 3:14, 16–19. Elizabeth quotes according to her *Manual* but puts the text in the singular. Elizabeth's expression "the knowledge of the saints" again echoes Paul's "to understand with all the saints."

[5] "The diocese" was already torn by the personality of its bishop, Msgr. Le Nordez. Submissive to the desires of the government, the bishop was suspected of being a member of the freemasons. The seminary was not very much in favor of him, which led several weeks later to the "seminarians' strike," among whom was André Chevignard (cf. AL).

[6] Cf. Rev 7:17; 21:6.

[7] Very probably reminiscent of Thérèse of Lisieux's "Act of Oblation"; "allowing the waves of infinite tenderness ... to overflow into my soul" (HA 251 [SS 277]). Here Elizabeth interprets the waves of grace in an apostolic perspective; two days later (L 192) she does so in a personal perspective (and also an apostolic one, since she wishes Françoise to be overwhelmed by the waves of infinite charity).

[8] Jn 17:19.

[8a] Cf. Eph 4:25 and 5:30; Rom 12:4-5 and especially 1 Cor 12.

[9] On the occasion of the new year and of the first anniversary of her profession.

[10] An important day, since it then included the (implicit) vow of celibacy. André Chevignard will receive the subdiaconate in one year, on January 6, 1905.

[11] Eph 1:12. The first appearance of this Pauline phrase in Elizabeth's writings. The many quotations from the Epistle to the Ephesians in this letter prove that the use of this expression is the fruit of a personal meditation on the "magnificent epistles" of Paul, as she says. P. Vallée does not use the expression "praise of glory" very frequently. We do come across it, however, in his discourse on Saint John of the Cross (Lille: Desclée de Brouwer, 1892), p. 183, which Elizabeth may have read. He uses it twice in the fourteenth sermon of the 1900 retreat (which she had most certainly read), but in a perspective that had more to do with the moral life than with praise: "In the measure in which we are in communion with his [God's] will, and the more we enter into it, the more we become 'the praise of glory' that his heart desired. In fact, the only 'praise of glory' for us is what we ourselves render." But very probably Elizabeth had read the expression on a holy card that she had kept since 1901 (cf. P 121, note 1).

L 192   To Françoise de Sourdon   [January 27, 1904][1]
J. M. + J. T.   Dijon Carmel, January 27

Happy feast day,[2] my Françoise, may the divine Master, to whom I have confided my wishes for you, make you understand all that is flowing from my heart to yours! Guess where I'll go to celebrate your feast? Quite simply, to Heaven, and I will meet you there, for, you see, this Heaven is quite close: "Wherever the King is, there is His court," as our holy Mother Teresa said,[3] and since He dwells in our souls, you can see that we don't have to go very far to enter the City of peace, in the Heaven of the saints; there I will unite with your holy patron in drawing God's sweetest blessings down upon my little Framboise, that He may fill her "according to all the riches of His glory," as Saint Paul says so well.[4] I entrusted a big kiss for you to my Mama through the grille, and I'm sure she will carry out my errand well; Friday morning, in a divine embrace on the Heart of the Master, I will ask that He fuse our two hearts together. I believe He did that a long time ago, but love is something infinite, and you can always go farther in infinity!

I saw your dear mama this morning. Please tell her I feel even closer to her after our parlor visit and I love her a lot…. Our Reverend Mother is very willing to let me see you before Lent[5] even though we saw each other two months ago; she is so good, and she knows how much we love each other, so she makes little exceptions for you!

A Dieu, my Françoise, I am one with your poor father,[6] who loved you so much; it seems to me he is up there in those regions of all peace, light, and love, where they contemplate God in an eternal face-to-face [vision]. Joining in prayer with Him who is all "Love" to overwhelm you, invade you with His waves of infinite charity; may He give you on January 29th all the best of His fatherly Providence; that is my wish, my dear little Framboise, and I am sending it to you through the Heart of the Bridegroom.

Your Elizabeth of the Trinity r.c.i.

Remember me with much love to Marie-Louise.

---

[1] Cf. preceding letter, note 1.
[2] Of "January 29th," the feast of St. Francis de Sales, her patron.
[3] *Le Chemin de la perfection* [The Way of Perfection], chap. 28 (Brouix trans., vol. 3 [1856], chap. 29, p. 199; [K-RT vol. 2, 28:2]).
[4] Eph 3:16.
[5] Lent began February 17. There normally had to be three months between parlor visits with friends.
[6] For the anniversary of his death, January 20, 1895.

L 193   To Abbé Jaillet[1]

[February 11, 1904][2]
Dijon Carmel, February 11
"Deus charitas est."[3]

J. M. + J. T.

Monsieur le Curé,

Our Reverend Mother, who has recovered from her bronchitis and whom we are happy to see once again in the midst of her dear community, will write to you herself, but she is letting me thank you for your letter and for your blessing, which made me very happy. Since our last parlor visit, I have been united with you especially, and my soul is brought to yours by a strong movement of prayer, especially during the Divine Office. I promise to offer a special intention for you every day at "Terce," so that the Spirit of Love, He who seals and consummates the "One" of the Trinity, may pour Himself out upon you in overflowing measure. May He lift you up in the light of faith to His heights, where one lives only by peace, love, union, made radiant by the rays of the divine Sun. Recently someone wrote this beautiful thought to me: "Faith is the face-to-face in darkness."[4] Oh, Monsieur le Curé, may that be true for our souls through all the stages God wishes to bring them through, and may nothing be able to distract us from the vision of His Charity. He had the Incarnate Word say to us: "Remain in my love."[5] May that be the divine rendez-vous for our souls on earth, while waiting for the rendez-vous in Heaven, where we will sing the Sanctus and the canticle of Love as we follow the Lamb![6]

I cannot tell you, Monsieur le Curé, how grateful I am for the remembrance you are willing to give me at the altar, and there I ask you to bless me.

Sr. M. Elizabeth of the Trinity r.c.i.

[1] Paul Jaillet, nearly 34 years old, Curé of Pontoux. He was in correspondence with Mother Germaine, who put him in contact with Elizabeth. She had already met him in the parlor before writing this letter.
[2] Cf. L 191, note 1.
[3] 1 Jn 4:16.
[4] Cf. L 165, note 7.
[5] Jn 15:9.
[6] Cf. Rev 4:8 and 14:3–4. "To sing the canticle of love" may once again be an expression borrowed from Ms. B of Thérèse (HA 210 [SS 196]).

L 194   To Madame Angles   [February 14–15, 1904][1]
J. M. + J. T.   Dijon Carmel, February 15

Madame and dear sister,

I have been very particularly united with you these past few days while reading the life of Saint Elizabeth, your mother and my patron in Heaven. I so love these words Our Lord addressed to her: "Elizabeth, if you want to be with me, I want very much to be with you, and nothing will be able to separate us."[2] Dear Madame, did the divine Bridegroom not whisper this to us in the silence of our soul when He invited us to follow Him more closely, to be one with Him by becoming His brides?... During these days of Forty Hours, we have the Blessed Sacrament exposed in our dear oratory. Today, Sunday, I spent nearly my whole day close to Him, and I so wished that, by means of my love, I could make Him forget all the evil being committed during these carnival days. You have not been forgotten during these long hours of silence, and I have also remembered your little Sister Imelda of Jesus, as I promised her.[3] I ask her to pray sometimes too for the little Carmelite and to say "thank you" to God for her. Wednesday we are going to begin Lent. Would [you] like to make a Lent of love together? "He loved me, He gave Himself up for me";[4] that, then, is the goal of love: to give ourselves, to empty ourselves entirely into Him we love. "Love makes the lover go out of himself in order to be transported by an ineffable ecstasy into the bosom of the Beloved."[5] Isn't that a beautiful thought?... May they let themselves be carried away by the Spirit of Love, and, in the light of faith, may they go even now to sing, with the blessed, the hymn of love that is sung eternally before the throne of the Lamb.[6] Yes, dear Madame, let us begin our Heaven on earth, our Heaven in love. He Himself is this love, as Saint John tells us: "Deus Charitas est."[7] Let us make that our rendez-vous, shall we?

I have not forgotten your dear Marie-Louise, and I am rejoicing over the happiness that has come to her with dear little Jean: soon it will be Guite's turn to become a mama. She came to me last week with her husband; you can imagine how much rejoicing there will be on the arrival of the little angel. Please pray, won't you, dear Madame, for the little mama. And now, à Dieu, I am very united to you in Him. Let us remain in His Love[8] and may His love remain in us. Your little sister,

M. Elizabeth of the Trinity

Thursday,[9] on the feast of Blessed Jeanne de Valois, I will be praying especially for you.

[1] 1904: little Jean was born (cf. L 189, note 4), and Guite is expecting her first child. "Today, Sunday," falls, however, on February 14. Either Elizabeth is mistaken in putting the 15th as the date, or she finished the following day and dated the letter at that time. See also note 9.

[2] Cf. Comte de Montalembert, *Histoire de Sainte Elisabeth de Hongrie, duchesse de Thuringe*, chap. 19 (Brussels ed., Société typographique belge, 1846, vol. 2).

[3] Cf. L 184.

[4] Gal 2:20.

[5] This is a rather free quotation (from memory) from a little treatise attributed to St. Albert the Great, *De l'Union avec Dieu [On Union with God]* chap. 12 (Fribourg: Oeuvre de Saint-Paul, 1895), pp. 71–72: "Because 'love is as strong as death,' it transports the lover outside himself, into the bosom of the beloved." According to M. Grabmann (*Benediktinische Monatschrift* 2 [1920]: p. 201), this treatise, attributed to St. Albert the Great, is in reality the work of the Benedictine monk Johannes von Kastl (cf. *Lexikon für Theologie und Kirche*, 5, col. 1049).

[6] Cf. Rev 5:6–9.

[7] 1 Jn 4:16.

[8] Cf. Jn 15:9.

[9] Normally the feast of Jeanne de Valois is on February 17, which would have been Wednesday. In any case, we are in 1904, since "Wednesday" (thus February 17) is in fact the beginning of Lent. There is no real explanation for why Elizabeth is "praying particularly" on that day for Mme. Angles. Perhaps it is because St. Jeanne de Valois had been married.

L 195   To Madame Farrat   [February 15, 1904][1]
      J. M. + J. T.   Dijon Carmel, February 15

Very dear Madame,

I learned just a moment ago that God has come to you with His Cross by asking you for the most painful of sacrifices, and I ask that He Himself will be your Strength, your Support, your divine Consoler! My whole soul, my whole heart are one with yours, for you know, dear Madame, what deep affection unites me to you. Today I share all your grief; you can read between these lines what my heart cannot say. In the face of such trials, God alone can speak, for He is the supreme Consoler! The Gospel says that at Lazarus's tomb, in seeing Mary's grief, "Christ was troubled and He wept...."[2] He is close to you, dear Madame, this Master whose Heart is so compassionate. He has received that dear soul in Heaven above, and you can be very sure he will have a share in our prayers and sacrifices every day. Live with him in that Beyond that is so close to us. It is so true that death is not a separation.... May your little angel,[3] who is in Heaven to receive the one for whom you are crying, obtain strength and courage for you. I am uniting myself to her, dear Madame, in asking God to be *"all that He has taken away from you"* and to wipe the tears from your eyes Himself, with His divine hand. The best of my heart is yours. Our Reverend Mother and all the community are praying very much for you. Your little friend,

Sr. M. E. of the Trinity r.c.i.

¹ On the occasion of the death of her husband, Dominique Farrat, on February 13, 1904.
² Jn 11:33, 35.
³ Little Cécile, who died on May 30, 1900.

L 196   To her mother   [March 11, 1904]¹
J. M. + J. T.

"How good God is!"²

Darling little Grandmother,

I am so very moved to call you by that sweet name, and this morning, when I learned of the arrival of little Elizabeth, big Elizabeth cried like a little baby. It's because she loves you so much: her heart is one with yours, and it is singing in unison with your three hearts close to that dear little cradle. Please tell that to Guite and Georges, tell them too of my great joy that the dear little one bears my name; it seems to me that God is giving her to me so I may be her angel, and I am adopting her completely. I prayed so much for her before she was born; and from now on my prayer and my sacrifices will be the two wings in whose shadow I will shelter her!³ What emotions, my darling little Mama, and how I thank God that everything went well. Tell dear little Guite my heart is so close to hers that it forgets the distance and that I am praying so much for her as well. I had a novena of Masses offered for her little Elizabeth so she might be washed in the Precious Blood; the novena ended this morning, on the feast of the "Five Wounds of the Savior,"⁴ and the little angel comes to us from the wound in His Heart, isn't that touching? I would be so grateful if you'd let me know the day of the baptism,⁵ for then I'll be able to accompany my beloved little niece to the baptismal font, while the Holy Trinity descends into her soul!

Darling Mama, your Carmelite would have loved to see you, but, you see, the sacrifice is so good, especially the sacrifice of one's heart, and we'll offer it to God for our dear little one: you have given Him one Elizabeth, He has sent you another, and we will compete with each other as to which one loves you the most!... Tell me now that you aren't spoiled by God and that He doesn't give you a hundred-fold in return even here on earth, as He promised.[6] I'm sending you a kiss, darling Mama, and one to my little Guite. Please make a little sign of the cross on little Sabeth's forehead for your

Elizabeth, r.c.i.

I hope you have the kind little Sister Thérèse with you.[7]

[1] The birthday of Elizabeth Chevignard, Guite's first daughter, a Carmelite at the Carmel of Dijon-Flavignerot, who died in 1991.
[2] Ps 72:1 *(Quam bonus est Deus)*.
[3] Ps 90:4. Psalm 90 will be quoted frequently from now on.
[4] At that time, one mystery of the Passion of the Lord was celebrated on each Friday of Lent.
[5] She was baptized privately the very day of her birth, and the subsequent baptismal ceremonies took place on the 4th of May.
[6] Cf. Mt 19:29.
[7] Sr. Thérèse-Agnès, 29 years old, a religious of the Sisters of Bon-Secours, who helped young mothers at home.

L 197   To her sister   [March 12(?), 1904][1]
         J. M. + J. T.

My darling Guite,
    We gave your little Sabeth a real ovation this morning at recreation.[2] Our Reverend Mother, who is so good, was overjoyed at showing us her photograph, and you can guess how hard Aunt Elizabeth's heart was beating!... Oh, my Guite, I think I love this little angel as much as her little mama, and that's saying a lot. And then, you know, I feel completely filled with reverence before this little temple of the Holy Trinity; her soul seems to me like a crystal that radiates God, and if I were near her, I would kneel down to adore Him who dwells within her. My Guite, would you kiss her for her Carmelite aunt, and then take my soul along with yours to recollect yourself close to your little Sabeth. If I were still with you, how

I would love to cuddle her, to rock her … goodness knows what else! But the good God has called me to the mountain[3] so I can be her angel and envelop her in prayer, and I very joyfully sacrifice everything else to Him for her sake; and then, there is no distance for my heart, and I am so close to you, you do feel that, don't you? I see that God does grant the prayers of His Carmelites since baby and mama are doing so well. Our Reverend Mother was very happy at the news my good Mama sent her today; I'm sure Saint Joseph will finish his work and you'll be able to nurse your little darling. I am praying fervently for that intention, for I can feel how important it is to you!

I'm delighted to send you these verses. You'll have no trouble guessing they aren't mine: our Reverend Mother let one of my Sisters lend me her muse[4] to sing by little Sabeth's cradle. That is where I'll meet you again, darling little mama. If you knew how moved I am to think you are a mother…. I'm entrusting you, you and your angel, to Him who is Love; with both of you, I adore Him and embrace you in His Heart.

Your Elizabeth of the Trinity r.c.i.

Tell your fine husband how I share his joy and how happy his photograph made me. And kiss the happy grandmother too for her other Elizabeth, who loves her with all her Carmelite heart and who is very happy to have her dear image so well engraved in my heart. I am very happy you have the kind Sister Thérèse.

[1] Georges Chevignard took and developed the photographs himself, so we can guess that the first "photograph" of his daughter did not take long to reach Carmel.
[2] "This morning." Actually, at noon during Lent.
[3] Of Carmel.
[4] Lost verses.

L 197a   To Madame d'Avout   [April 5, 1904][1]
J. M. + J. T.   Dijon Carmel, Tuesday

Very dear Madame,

With the singing of Alleluia, the great silence of Lent has ceased, and I come very quickly to tell you how I am praying for you and your dear little Bernard. I can read between [your] lines what you have not told me. Oh, if you knew how all that is taking place in your heart is echoing in mine; it's not surprising, for I love you so much, and it seems to me that, ever since I felt the Cross of the Master on you, I am even closer to you!... Each time I see Mama I ask her for news of Bernard; she can tell you how very often your names come up in our conversation. Dear Madame, I love to speak of you especially in the long hours of silence, in my heart-to-heart with God, for He "knows all, He can do all, and He loves us with so great a love; it is Infinite"!...[2] I am using all my rights as bride over His Heart for your benefit, you do know that, don't you? for you know your little friend. You have always been so good to her; that is how we repay our debts in Carmel!

This morning I saw the happy grandmother and asked her to pass on my thanks for your chocolate treats, and then too for all the clothes you sent us: we have done wonders with them, a thousand thanks! A Dieu, dear Madame, I am entrusting you to the Blessed Virgin, to her who was a martyr in her heart; I am asking her to make her sweet light shine in your heart, since she is the "Star," Stella matutina.... I send you all the best of my heart.

Sr. M. Elizabeth of the Trinity r.c.i.

[1] "Tuesday" after Easter. 1904: handwriting, ink, and the recent birth of Sabeth: cf. "happy grandmother," Mme. Catez.
[2] Up to "... loves us" is attributed to Teresa of Avila.

L 198   To her Rolland aunts   [April 9, 1904][1]
J. M. + J. T.   Dijon Carmel, April 9

My good little Aunts,

Now that we have sung Alleluia, my heart is coming once again to sing close to yours, listen closely ... the string that is vibrating is my affection! Yes, my little Aunts, this affection that nothing can overcome, for He has sealed it, and He is faithful!...

A big event has happened since my last letter: the arrival of little Elizabeth. Here I am, a respectable aunt; it seems like a dream to think that Guite is a mother! I have only seen my niece in a photograph so far; they are to bring her to me at the first ray of dawn, and it will be such a joy for me to adore the Holy Trinity in this little soul who has become His temple through baptism. What a mystery!...

Yesterday I saw the happy grandmother who was anxiously awaiting the end of Lent to tell me everything. Poor Mama, can you guess her happiness? An Elizabeth coming to replace the one she gave to God, it's like an answer from Him who promised the hundredfold here on earth! [2] Today I had a parlor visit with the religious[3] who is helping Guite; she told me how the dear child[4] edified her, and I'm delighted to think how well she will bring up her little daughter. Let's pray, dear Aunts, that this little flower may grow and blossom in God's sight, and that He may always dwell in her calyx!... One of my Sister poets lent me her muse[5] to sing by the dear little angel's cradle; I thought that would make you happy, especially Aunt Francine; so I asked our Reverend and very dear Mother for permission to send you these verses.

What is there to say about myself, dear little Aunts? My horizon is expanding ... my sky is all calm, all starry, and, in this "harmonious solitude," as my blessed Father Saint John of the Cross says in his *Canticle,*[6] I think God is very good to have taken me all for Himself and set me apart on the mountain of Carmel. That is the hymn of thanksgiving being sung in my soul while I wait to go sing in Heaven, following the Lamb!

I don't know if I told you how impressive Lent is here, especially Holy Week. We penetrate so deeply into the Mystery of the Crucified ... for He is the Bridegroom, our One and All. Although our chapel is closed,[7] we were able to have the Tomb[8] on Holy Thursday; you can imagine how I prayed for you, particularly at night. It was so divine, my dear Aunts; how good it was to keep watch with the Master in the great silence and calm of that night during which He loved us so much....[9] I could catch a glimpse of the little door of the Tabernacle through my dear grille, and I said to myself: It is really true, I am the prisoner of the divine Prisoner, we are each other's captives! And now I am leaving you to go sing His praises, for it will soon be time for Matins, and as I am in charge of the bells, I don't want to be late. I only have time to entrust all my tender affection for you to my divine Bridegroom and to tell you once again that I am always all yours.

Your little Elizabeth of the Trinity r.c.i.

(A big kiss for my Aunt.)

What hours I spend in choir with your beautiful breviaries in my hands, and your hearts in my heart!...

Please give my religious respect to your good Curé and tell him that I offer an intention for him every day. For my part, I count entirely on his good prayers and I am very grateful to him for his remembrance at Holy Mass.

Hello to Louise and Anna as well as to the little ones and all who remember me.

[1] 1904: little Sabeth is born. Easter is April 3.
[2] Cf. Mt 19:29.
[3] Sr. Thérèse, cf. L 196, note 7.
[4] The reference is to Guite.
[5] Cf. L 197.
[6] St. 15, SC 171 [K-RJ 15:25–26: "sounding solitude"].
[7] Closed to public worship. Cf. L 165, note 6.
[8] Solemn reposition of the Blessed Sacrament at the side altar of St. Joseph (cf. Plan 1, chapel, b). The Blessed Sacrament was reserved there from Mass on Holy Thursday (then in the morning) until Friday morning. The faithful (in normal years) came to venerate it.
[9] Cf. Jn 13:1.

L199   To Abbé Chevignard   [April 27, 1904][1]
J. M. + J. T.   Dijon Carmel, April 27
"Surrexit Dominus vere, alleluia." [2]

Monsieur l'Abbé,

"God is free from all save His love." This phrase, which I believe is by Msgr. Gay,[3] gives much to my soul, particularly at this time of the Resurrection, when Christ, the victor over death, wants to remain our captive. And it seems to me this is how we can rise with Him: by walking through life "free from all save our love," our soul and heart fixed on God, repeating those words that Saint Catherine of Siena loved to say in the silence of her soul: "I am sought, I am loved."[4] This is what is true, all the rest is not. Oh! how good it would be, as you say,[5] to live by this life of the Trinity that Jesus Christ came to bring us. He said so often that He was the Life, and that He came to give it to us in abundance.[6] "He has taken all in God to Himself to become the source for all," as Père Vallée said to us one day in his strong language; then he added that all those who came close to Him had an "awareness of the vision He carried in His soul."[7] Since He still lives, why shouldn't we ask Him for the definitive light, that light of faith that makes saints, that so shone in the soul of Saint Catherine of Siena, whose Office we will have on Saturday and to whom I will be praying very specially for you since you are a part of her great religious family.[8] In her *Dialogues,* she often repeats these words: "Open the eye of your soul in the light of faith."[9] Let us ask her, if you'd like, to draw our souls toward this God whom she so loved, so we too may be so well taken captive by Him that we might no longer leave His radiance. Is that not an anticipated Heaven? During this month of May I will be very united to you in the soul of the Virgin, for we will adore the Holy Trinity there. I very much like what you said to me about Mary in your letter, and since you live so close to her,[10] I would ask you to pray to her a little for me. I too see my Carmelite life as this twofold vocation: "virgin-mother."[11] Virgin: espoused in faith by Christ; mother: saving souls, increasing the number of the adopted children of the Father, the co-heirs of Jesus Christ.[12] Oh! how that magnifies the soul; it is like embracing the infinite!… I have prayed fervently for you and continue to do so every day, and I remain profoundly united to you in Him who is an immensity of love[13] and who fills us to overflowing on all sides.

Sr. M. Eliz. of the Trinity r.c.i.

[1] "Saturday," the feast of "Saint Catherine of Siena," and April 30 coincide in 1904.

[2] "The Lord is truly risen, alleluia": invitatory for Matins on Easter. Cf. Lk 24:34.

[3] The thought was well known in the Dijon Carmel. We come across it also in Mother Germaine's correspondence.

[4] In this form, it is rather an expression used by P. Vallée in his "Discourse for the Feast of Saint John of the Cross," November 24, 1901 (which Elizabeth heard and perhaps reread).

[5] In a letter.

[6] Cf. Jn 10:10.

[7] Elizabeth is quoting from memory the fifth morning sermon of the 1902 retreat: "Having taken to Himself the entire source, all of God that can be communicated to

the created being.... He is the indispensable source for the very reason that He has taken all to Himself.... And in the light, in the power of Him who is from all eternity within the vision, and through Him, we are brought into that same vision, we touch it and live in it by faith."

[8] André Chevignard was a Third Order Dominican.

[9] This is what P. Vallée affirms in the third morning sermon of the 1902 retreat. In fact, Catherine says several times: "Open the eye of your understanding" (cf. *Dialogue* [Paris: Poussielgue Rusand, 1855], 1:2, 53, 302, etc.), and she explains in chapter 45 (pp. 110–111) that faith is the pupil of this eye. The quotation from P. Vallée does not prove that Elizabeth had read the *Dialogue.*

[10] The seminary was at that time situated on rue Marey, close to the Cathedral and a few minutes away from the church of Notre-Dame, where the Virgin of Dijon, Our Lady of Good Hope, was venerated.

[11] Virgin and Mother, like Mary. "Too" indicates that the idea came from the letter of her correspondent. But one can detect a reminiscence of Thérèse of Lisieux: "I am a virgin, O Jesus! Yet, what a mystery! / When I unite myself to you, I am the mother of souls" (Poem, "Jésus, mon Bien-Aimé, rappelle-toi!" ["Jesus, My Beloved, Remember"] (HA 343).

[12] Cf. PN 13 and Gal 4:5-7.

[13] First appearance of "immensity" in her letters. The expression "immensity of love" (which returns in L 228), like "Ocean" (which overflows on all sides), is found in Thérèse of Lisieux (HA 198 [SS 254]).

L 200   To Abbé Chevignard   [April 27, 1904]
J. M. + J. T.   Wednesday, April 27

Monsieur l'Abbé,

I had just written to you when I learned of the painful sacrifice[1] God is asking of your heart, and my soul needs to tell yours how united it is to you in this trial. It seems to me that at such times, the Master alone can speak, He whose divinely loving Heart "was troubled" at the tomb of Lazarus.[2] So we can mix our tears with His and, leaning on Him, find strength and peace once again. I am praying fervently for your father's soul. He was really the just man of whom Scripture speaks,[3] what a consolation it must be for you, at the evening of his journey, to see such a full and beautiful life! For him, the veil has been lifted, the shadow of mystery has disappeared, he has seen.... Monsieur l'Abbé, let us follow him by faith into those regions of peace and love. Sursum corda, everything must end in God; one day He will say His "veni" to us too; then, like a little baby on the heart of its mother, we will fall asleep in Him, and "in His light we will see light"....[4]

A Dieu, Monsieur l'Abbé, let us live high above, very far away, in Him ... in us.... And since we are in contact with those who have left us through the communion of saints, let us envelop the soul of your dear father with one and the same prayer so that, if it has not already done so, it may soon go to enjoy the eternal face-to-face. I remain united to you in the radiance of the Face of God.

Sr. M. Elizabeth of the Trinity r.c.i.

[1] The death of his father, Alfred Chevignard, April 26, 1904.
[2] Jn 11:33.
[3] Cf., e.g., Wis 3:1–3.
[4] Ps 35:10.

L 201   To her sister

[April 27, 1904][1]

J. M. + J. T.

Dijon Carmel, Wednesday

My dear Guite,

Please tell Georges for me how much I share in the great suffering that has struck him. Human words seem so powerless in the face of such trials, but he can guess from these lines what my heart cannot express, for he knows very well that he has a little sister in Carmel who shares very intimately in his sufferings as well as his joys. Your dear father was truly the just man of whom Scripture speaks,[2] and the God of goodness and mercy has already given him a place in His Kingdom. And yet one must be so pure to enter it.... So I am praying *very much* for him, and very much, too, for those he left behind. Our Reverend Mother asks me to speak on her behalf and that of the community to your husband and to tell him how much we are praying for that soul who is so dear to you. God, who called him to Himself, wanted to give him one last joy: little Elizabeth came to blossom like the last bud of his crown. Dear little angel, already tears by her cradle!

Please express my respectful and sorrowful sympathy to Madame Chevignard.[3] In thinking back on what our poor Mama suffered when our dear Papa left us,[4] I think I can understand her grief even better; please tell her how much I am praying for her, that God may be her Support, her Protection. And now, my Guite, I give you a kiss as my darling little sister. I ask you again to give all my love to your fine husband; I am sure he knows that.

> Your little Sister Elizabeth of the Trinity r.c.i.

You were so pretty the other day[5] with your angel in your arms!... I can still see you.... Kiss her forehead for her Aunt Elizabeth.

[1] The day after Georges's father's death, cf. L 200, note 1.
[2] Cf. L 200, note 3.
[3] Georges's mother.
[4] October 2, 1887.
[5] In the parlor.

L 202   To Abbé Beaubis

J. M. + J. T.

[June 2, 1904][1]
Dijon Carmel, June 2

Monsieur l'Abbé,

My soul has been very profoundly united, I can assure you, with the divine joys that have flooded your soul during these two great days of your ordination and first Mass. I wish this little note could have arrived beforehand to tell you of my complete union with you, but that was not possible; yet for souls, there is no need of some set form of words; they penetrate the Infinity of God to meet again, to immerse themselves in one and the same adoration. It seems to me that adoration is the hymn that must be singing in your soul after the great mystery that has just taken place in it. During these days the seal of God has marked it with His divine impression, so you have truly become the "Lord's Anointed,"[2] and the All-Powerful whose immensity envelops the universe seems to need you in order to give Himself to souls! I beg you to remember me when you immolate the divine Lamb at the altar: place my soul in the chalice so that it may be baptized, purified, virginized in His Blood.[3] Since you have become the "dispenser of God's gifts,"[4] I will ask you a favor in His name. On June 15, the feast of Saint Germaine, we will celebrate in Carmel the feast of our Reverend Mother, and I would be so happy to offer her a Mass said by you as a feastday bouquet; I would be *deeply grateful* to you for it. A Dieu, Monsieur l'Abbé, I ask that you bless me with your consecrated hand and I remain united with you in Him who is Charity.

Sr. M. Elizabeth of the Trinity r.c.i.

[1] The "two great days" of his ordination and "first Mass" were May 28 and 29, 1904.
[2] That is to say, his priest. This expression, which was current in the spiritual language of the time, seems to derive from Lk 4:18, where Jesus quotes Is 61:1: "The Spirit of the Lord is upon me, because he has anointed me."
[3] Cf. L 126, note 2.
[4] 1 Cor 4:1.

L 203   To Canon Angles   [June 2, 1904][1]
J. M. + J. T.   Dijon Carmel, June 2
Deus Charitas est.[2]

Dear Monsieur le Chanoine,

Since you are the dispenser of God's graces,[3] your little Carmelite is coming to ask you for one in His Name. The little flock of Carmel will be delighted to celebrate the feast of its shepherdess on June 15th, the feast of Saint Germaine, and, for my part, I am dreaming of offering her a beautiful, wholly divine bouquet, tinged with the crimson Blood of the Lamb whom you would immolate for her at the altar! You are so much a father and so good to your little child that she dares to ask you for anything, just as she would her Father in Heaven, certain of being heard, and I would be delighted to offer our Reverend and dear Mother a Mass said by you! But I want to surprise her, so if you reply, I would ask that you write me in care of Mama, who would deliver your letter to me. If you knew how grateful I am to you…. But I won't try to tell you; it seems to me that for souls there is no need of set forms of words, they penetrate the Infinity of God, and there, in that silence and calm where He Himself is, they hear what flows from one to the other!… Dear Monsieur le Chanoine, that is how I love to meet you; there is no more distance since all is already "one" as in Heaven…. Heaven will come one day and we will see God in its light. Oh! the first encounter! It makes my soul tremble! Pray for me; the horizon is so beautiful, the divine Sun makes His great light shine; ask that the little butterfly might burn its wings in its rays!...[4]

I ask your best blessing and I am always your little child.

Sr. M. E. of the Trinity r.c.i.

[1] Same handwriting and ink as in L 202.
[2] 1 Jn 4:16.
[3] Cf. 1 Cor 4:1.
[4] The comparison of the soul with a butterfly is found in Teresa of Avila *(The Interior Castle,* V, chap. 2). But in its more developed form ("burn the wings" in a "light"), she would be indebted rather to P. Vallée (1900 retreat, tenth conference on the Holy Trinity) or more probably to Thérèse of Lisieux, where we also find the explicit mention of "Jesus, that divine fire" (HA 62 [SS 83]).

L 204   To her sister   [July 19, 1904][1]
    J. M. + J. T.   Tuesday evening, Carmel

"The eye of God is upon her,
His love surrounds her like a rampart."[2]

Dear little sister, "echo of my soul": this is what Thérèse of the Child Jesus called one of her sisters,[3] and tonight, on the vigil of your feast, on this day when I loved so much to spoil you, it makes me happy to give you that sweet name. My darling flower, beloved Marguerite, I am asking God to grant all the desires of your big "heart of gold" and to enflame you with the fires of His love, so that through the action of His divine rays you may grow and blossom, and in the shadow of your "great white petals"[4] another little flower, who is so very dear to my heart, may begin to open her tender leaves!...

How sweet your little Sabeth is! Yesterday, in the arms of her radiant grandmother, she put on all sorts of charming airs and sent me a big kiss from her little mama. After which she wanted to let me hear her beautiful voice by crying as much as she could, but her grandmother did such a good job of rocking her that she fell asleep. She was so cute, with her little eyes closed and her hands crossed over her heart... It made our Reverend Mother smile when I told her my niece was an "adoring" one.... That is her office: "House of

God."[5] My darling Guite, take your little angel in your arms, place her little hands around you in a hug and tell her to give you a kiss for this other Sabeth who feels the heart of a little mother for you. A Dieu, may He tell you all that is flowing from my soul to yours.

Your Eliz. of the Trinity r.c.i.

Give Georges my affectionate greetings and tell him that his daughter is the *living image* of him.

[1] "Vigil of her feast" (July 20). 1904, for Guite still has only one child. The copper-colored ink is no longer used, having been replaced for the first time by the blue-grey ink (cf. General Introduction, Vol. I).
[2] Free adaptation of Ps 31:8, 7. Sr. Geneviève had given this thought to Elizabeth in the little note referred to in L 206, note 7.
[3] HA 315 [LT 89], a letter from Thérèse to her sister Céline.
[4] The symbolic language of this passage, already used in P 78 and 82, was inspired by the name of the recipient. It may be an echo of Thérèse of Lisieux, in whom the image of the flower abounds (cf. P 78, note 2).
[5] Cf. L 107, note 2.

L 205   To her sister   [July 30 or 31, 1904][1]
         J. M. + J. T.

My darling little sister,
    I don't know how to thank you enough for your beautiful, hearty Russian salad. My Sister Agnès[2] and I admired Fanny's decorations[3]—she really outdid herself. You have the gratitude of our Reverend Mother and the impromptu Marthas.[4] You sent us such a large amount that we've had enough for two meals. Thanks, too, for the eggs, which were very fresh. We spent a thoroughly pleasant day in the kitchen, which seemed to me like another Bethany,[5] the only difference being that the divine Guest was to be found in the depths of our souls, where, little sister, I'm all one with you and your angel. Oh! how sweet she is! And the other day I would have liked to take her place so as to rest in your arms and say "Mama" to you. A Dieu; may He bless you and bring you my tender affection.

Your E. of the Trinity

A very warm thank you to Georges.

[1] The feast of St. Martha, July 29, is over. 1904, since Guite has only one child.

[2] Sr. Agnès of Jesus-Mary writes on January 17, 1907, to the Carmel of Angers (cf. PAT): "The feast of Saint Martha was a special delight.... We agreed that we were in Bethany, and we felt the Master so present!... My little Sister had the Provisor's office; I was the cook, for she was rather inexperienced at that kind of work—she was even full of extraordinary amazement at the sight of pots and vegetables, which really amused us! The sweet Laudem was the first to laugh about it."

[3] Guite's cook. Shortly after the death of his father, Alfred Chevignard (cf. L 200), Georges and Guite had taken up residence at the Chevignard Bank building on rue de la Prefecture.

[4] Cf. note 2. "Marthas" sometimes meant non-choir Sisters (or "white-veiled Sisters"), who were usually assigned to domestic work.

[5] Cf. Lk 10:38–42.

L 206   To Madame de Sourdon   [July 31, 1904][1]
   J. M. + J. T.   Dijon Carmel, Sunday

Dear Madame,

I have just received your second letter, and I thank God with you, asking Him to complete His work in your dear patient.[2] I admire her courage and calmness in the face of that serious operation! That is always so frightening.... But God is there, and He never fails those who trust in Him. Dear Madame, Carmel has heard your appeal, besides, that is our mission; here, "to pray is to breathe,"[3] and when it concerns those we love, how intense that prayer becomes.... I was very happy with Framboise at our last parlor visit. I missed Marie-Louise, who came during a community exercise; you can tell her how truly I think of her. I am as interested in her future[4] as if she were my little sister, and I am so full of confidence that the other day, when I saw your handwriting, I thought you were announcing some news to me, and I was already delighted about it, for you know my heart shares each one of your joys and hopes just as it shares your sorrows. We see in the Gospel that God sometimes wants to make us wait, but He refuses nothing to faith, to trust, to love.[5] As a little Carmelite who died in the odor of sanctity used to say, one must "take Him by the heart"!...[6] A Dieu, dear Madame, I leave you with these words of Saint Augustine: "He is there when we think we are alone. He listens when nothing answers us, He loves us when everything abandons us."[7] Please remember me to Madame D'Anthès[8] and keep the best of my heart for yourself, dear Madame.

Sr. M. E. of the Trinity r.c.i.

Our Reverend Mother asks me to tell you how much she shares in what you are feeling now and that she is very united with you in prayer.

[1] There is an envelope preserved in the ACD addressed by Elizabeth to the "Comtesse de Sourdon, c/o M. la Baronne d'Anthès, Avallon, Yonne," and postmarked Dijon, August 1, 1904. Now L 206, which has the same handwriting and blue-grey ink as this envelope, is folded in such a way that it alone of all the letters written to Mme. de Sourdon can fit into this little envelope of 4.4" x 2.3". "Sunday" thus indicates the day before it was mailed. Cf. also note 8.

[2] Her sister, Mme. de Maizières (cf. L 181, note 6).

[3] Cf. *Le Banquet sacré ou l'Idée de la parfaite carmélite* [The Sacred Banquet, or the Ideal of the Perfect Carmelite] (Albi: Rodière, 1844), p. 602: "The life of a Carmelite must be a continual prayer; it must be as natural for her to pray as to breathe." It is the first of a "collection of several maxims." Elizabeth's exact quotation was inscribed over the door of the chapter room (cf. Plan 2, no. 19).

[4] In her dreams of marriage.

[5] The Thérèsian atmosphere of this passage indicates HA 110–111 [SS 142] (MS A, 67 v°) as a probable background. There Thérèse of Lisieux recalls the resurrection of Lazarus (Jn 11) and the miracle at the wedding at Cana (Jn 2).

[6] Thérèse of Lisieux. Cf. HA 270 (LT 191).

[7] Elizabeth had read this thought, widely attributed to St. Augustine, in a note from Sr. Geneviève that she kept in her books (twelve days earlier she had herself drawn from it the quotation from Ps 31; cf. L 204, note 2.). The note also mentions St. Augustine.

[8] Cf. note 1. Mme. de Sourdon was at her mother's house.

L 207   To Madame Angles   [August 14-16, 1904][1]
        J. M. + J. T.

Very dear Madame,
    Tomorrow is your feast day,[2] and I am entrusting my best wishes to the Blessed Virgin. I am asking her, on the day of her glorious Assumption, to have Heaven's sweetest blessings descend on your soul and to reveal this divine secret to you: *"Dilectus meus mihi et ego illi,* my Beloved is all mine, and I am all His."[3] I see the Master is treating you like a "bride" and sharing His Cross with you. There is something so great, so divine in suffering! It seems to me that if the

blessed in Heaven could envy anything, it would be that treasure; it is so powerful a lever[4] on the heart of God! And then, don't you find it sweet to give to Him whom you love? The Cross is the heritage of Carmel: "Either to suffer or to die," cried our holy Mother Teresa,[5] and when Our Lord appeared to our Father Saint John of the Cross and asked him what he wanted in return for all the suffering he had endured for Him, John responded: "Lord, to suffer, to be despised for your love."[6] Dear Madame, would you ask that this passion for sacrifice be given to your little friend? For my part, I assure you, I am asking God to sustain you in your sufferings, which must be so painful to endure, for, in the long run, the soul feels the effects of it and grows weary; but then you have only to stay close to the Crucified, and your suffering is the best prayer. Before his death, Père Lacordaire, while so overwhelmed by suffering that he could no longer pray, asked for his crucifix and said, "I look at it."[7] Look at it too, and, close to the divine Victim, you will find strength and joy in your sufferings. Nevertheless, that does not keep you, dear Madame, from doing all you can to get well, or from seeking advice without hesitation, even while abandoning yourself into the hands of God, and I am asking Him to hasten your recovery, if that is His will.

Since you have Monsieur le Chanoine with you, would you deliver this little note to him?[8] I am delighted to think of you so well cared for. The arrival of Marie-Louise and her little Jean[9] must be a very sweet joy; please remember me with affection to the dear little mama. Mine left yesterday for Switzerland (for I have picked up this letter once again after having left it unfinished for two days) with Guite and her angel, and you can imagine her joy at leaving with those two treasures! A Dieu, dear Madame, our union is no less true for being silent; I beg you to keep me in your love and prayers; for my part, I am very united to you and I am asking God to make you more and more His.

Your little friend and sister.

M. Elizabeth of the Trinity r.c.i.

---

[1] Elizabeth begins her letter on August 14 (cf. note 2) and picks it up again "two days" later. 1904, because Guite has only one child.

[2] August 15. Mme. Angles's name is Marie.

[3] Song 2:16.

[4] "Lever": an image perhaps inspired by Thérèse, HA 200 [SS 258], although there it is prayer that raises the world (MS C, 36v°).
[5] *Life,* chap. 40 (Bouix trans., vol. 1, p. 622 [K-RT vol. 1, 40:20]).
[6] *Vie et oeuvres spirituelles de saint Jean de la Croix* [Life and Spiritual Works of Saint John of the Cross], vol. 1, op. cit., p. 216.
[7] An episode that was frequently related; cf., e.g., M. Foisset, *Vie du R. P. Lacordaire* [Life of the Rev. Fr. Lacordaire] (Lecoffre, 1870), vol. 2, p. 440.
[8] L 208.
[9] Marie-Louise Ambry and her child; all were together at Labastide-Esparbairenque, as follows from L 208 as well.

L 208   To Canon Angles   [August 14–16, 1904][1]
          J. M. + J. T.
          "Misericordias Domini in aeternum cantabo."[2]

Dear Monsieur le Chanoine,

A Carmelite must be silent, but if her pen is quiet, her soul and her heart defy space in going close to those she remains deeply united to. That is the way in which your little child has come to thank you warmly for the great joy you have given her by offering Holy Mass for her dear Mother;[3] it was so good to offer her this beautiful, wholly divine bouquet that came to her through you! Our Reverend Mother was very happy and deeply touched; she asks me to express all her gratitude to you. I am following you up there to your beautiful mountains that I loved so much. I will never forget our stay at Labastide, the trip we made with you.... What sweet memories! That was my last vacation; I celebrated my third anniversary of entering Carmel on the 2nd. Oh! how good God has been to me! It is like an abyss of love in which I lose myself while waiting to go and sing the mercies of the Lord in Heaven!...[4]

I saw my dear Mama last week with her granddaughter. I don't think I have ever seen her so radiant in three years, and I thank God for that. How good it is to surrender everything to Him with confidence, and then, like a little child in the arms of its mother, to rest in His love.[5] How I would love to meet you again in that unchanging dwelling place! A Dieu, dear Monsieur le Chanoine, please bless the one who still calls herself your little child.

                              Sr. M. Elizabeth of the Trinity r.c.i.

[1] Cf. L 207, note 8. In 1904 Elizabeth celebrated her "third anniversary of entering."
[2] "I will sing forever of the mercies of the Lord" (Ps 88:2).
[3] Mother Germaine. Cf. L 203.
[4] This perspective is also that of Thérèse of Lisieux. All the terms are found in HA 196-198 (formerly chap. 11; MS C, 34r°- 35r°) [SS 254]. Thérèse, moreover, had made the eternal song of the mercies of the Lord the central theme of her whole autobiography (HA 3 [SS 13]).
[5] On the Thérèsian origin of this image, cf. L 116, note 2., and L 129, note 4.

L 209   To her mother   [August 21, 1904][1]
     J. M. + J. T.   Dijon Carmel, Sunday

My darling little Mama,

It was truly a joy for me to read your nice long letter, and I am delighted to think of you so happy between your two darlings. How good God is to you! Three years ago that trip[2] was so sad, for you had just led your Elizabeth to Carmel, and this year you have a dear little angel in her place! I am following you there, in those mountains that carry you away toward God and where all three of us were so happy, so united.[3] Darling Mama, don't have any regrets about that time that was so sweet; the Master has done all things well.[4] He has chosen a very beautiful part for your daughter by calling her to Carmel. Know that she is happy, with a happiness no one can take away from her, for it is wholly divine. There is no doubt that she sacrificed what she loved most after God, but it's no longer a sacrifice now that the union between us is so intimate; what does it matter where the body lives so long as the souls and hearts are quite close, "knitted"[5] to each other? Haven't you felt the heart of your Sabeth beating when she recognized your dear handwriting; she loves her mother so much!... On the 15th, I entrusted my best wishes to the Blessed Virgin and asked her, in going up to Heaven, to draw the very best from God's treasures for my Mama. I also asked her to reveal that sweet secret of union with God that makes us remain with Him through everything: it's the intimacy of a child with its mother, of the bride with the Bridegroom; that is the life of your Carmelite; union is her brilliant sun, she sees infinite horizons unfold! When you go to that dear little church, say a prayer for me, remember the time when we came and knelt together before the poor Tabernacle, remember that I am the prisoner of the divine Prisoner and that, close to Him, there is no distance at all. One day in Heaven, we shall be even closer still, since we are separated now for love of Him! You ask what the temperature is. I'm not sure, but it seems to me that it's not so warm; the nights are cool, and last night after Matins when our Reverend Mother came to bless me in our cell,[6] she gave me permission to leave the window wide open. Oh, if you knew how good and how like a mother she is, if you saw the care with which she surrounds your daughter, it would make your heart melt; we speak of you, and Our Mother is also delighted that you feel so happy. Do enjoy your pretty Guite and her angel. Would you give them a kiss for me? When you see Monsieur le Curé, pay him my respects and tell him that I am praying for his parish, that I haven't forgotten I am his vicar.

A Dieu my little Mama whom I love with all my Carmelite heart, I entrust all sorts of tender affection for you to my little niece.

Your daughter Elizabeth of the Trinity r.c.i.

Say hello for me to that good fellow Koffman.[7] Remember me with love to Madame de Sourdon and the little ones.[8] Is there anything new for Marie-Louise? Tell her I am praying for her.

What happiness to see you looking well again. Let Guite take good care of you.

---

[1] The Sunday after "the 15th," the feast of Marie Rolland. 1904, since Mme. Catez has only one granddaughter.

[2] In August 1901 (cf. L 85–87).

[3] Mme. Catez had been with Guite and little Sabeth in Switzerland since August 16 (cf. L 207). Elizabeth's last stay in Switzerland went back to August-September 1899 (cf. L 24).

[4] Cf. Mk 7:37.

[5] An expression borrowed from the *Spiritual Canticle* 341 [K-RJ 31:2] (a translation of the Latin "conglutinata" [1 Kgs 18:1]) to describe the friendship between Jonathan and David. Other uses: L 238 (to Françoise de Sourdon), L 322 (to Mme. Gout de Bize) and P 119 (for Mother Germaine). Elizabeth also knows she is "wholly attached" to Guite's soul (L 243). Cf. Sr. Agnès: "There was such a great union of souls that, several days before her death, she said to me: 'We are united like Jonathan and David' " (PO 414); "We even used to say laughingly (in the past) that we were like an apartment with two connecting rooms" (PO 530).

[6] Every night after Matins the Sisters would kneel at the door of their cells to receive the Prioress's blessing.

[7] Cf. L 87. Most likely the proprietor of the Hôtel Beau-Site in Fleurier, cf. L 85, note 5.

[8] Probably the children of her sick sister, Mme. de Maizières.

L 210   To her sister   [August 21, 1904][1]
          J. M. + J. T.
                              God is Love![2]

My darling little sister,

      Yes, I meet you at the feet of Jesus; more than that, I never leave you; I share the joy of His Heart in finding a marguerite in which He can rest.[3] Be His paradise in this country where He is so little known, so little loved, open your heart wide to welcome Him, and then, there in your little cell, love, my Guite!... He thirsts for love....[4] Take your Sabeth with you, and then, let us both keep Him company.... I am pleased with you, my little one, and the Master loves His flower! And your angel? I hope her wretched teeth are leaving her in peace. How sweet she is! Our Reverend Mother, who came to bless her,[5] found her ravishing; I'll bet that makes the heart of her little mama happy. Sometimes I think I'm dreaming when I call you by that name, my little sister; and yet that time when we went climbing in the mountains seems very far away. I remember the pretty view from our room!... Don't you find that nature speaks of Him? The soul needs silence in order to adore.... I'm delighted to think of you with Mama, who is so happy, and I can understand what a sacrifice it is for you for Georges to be so far away from you. Nevertheless, do enjoy your stay in Switzerland and the sweet intimacy with our good Mama; it's a law here below: sacrifice and joy go side by side. God wants to remind us that we haven't reached our final happiness; but we are pointed in that direction and He Himself wants to carry us in His arms.[6] Up there in Heaven, my little sister, He will fill to overflowing all that is empty; while waiting, let us live in the Heaven of our soul, it is so good already! I'm uniting myself with you and your dear little angel to send you the best of my heart; I love you both so much and I'm enveloping you in prayer. Oh my Guite, there is no distance between two little sisters who live in Unchanging Love.

[1] 1904: Guite has only one child and is spending her vacation in Switzerland. L 209 and 210 were sent together, as proved by the fact that they do not contain any message for Mme. Catez or for Guite, as the case may be.
[2] 1 Jn 4:16.
[3] Cf. L 204, note 4. [A "marguerite" is a daisy—TRANS.]
[4] Perhaps reminiscent of HA 202 (chap. 11) [SS 189]: "He was thirsty!!! But when He said: *'Give me to drink,'* it was the love of His poor creature the Creator of the universe was seeking. He was thirsty for love."
[5] During the week of August 7th. Mme. Catez had come with little Sabeth (cf. L 208).
[6] Thérèse of Lisieux's idea of the "elevator." Cf. L 116, note 2.

L 211　To her sister　　　　　　　　[September 25, 1904][1]
J. M. + J. T.

My darling little sister,

There is so much happiness in my soul that I needed to come tell you about it while asking for your prayers as well. Our Reverend Mother is allowing me to begin retreat,[2] and tonight I am leaving for my great journey: ten days of complete silence, absolute solitude, with my veil lowered and several additional hours of prayer; it's a very enticing schedule, I'm taking you and your angel with me; please tell our dear Mama to pray for the *hermit* who, for her part, will not forget her.

Please recommend me to your brother-in-law, the Abbé, and to Marie-Louise.[3] A Dieu, little sister, I leave you, and I'm going to lose myself in Him, to let all this happiness I can no longer contain overflow. Union.

　　　　　　　　　　　　　　　　　　　　　　Your Sabeth r.c.i.

[1] This letter, written the "night" on which her retreat begins, can only be from 1904 (cf. note 2), which the handwriting confirms. (Her 1905 retreat would be preceded by another letter to Guite, L 245.) The retreat extended from September 26 to October 5, the dates indicated in her "retreat devotion" (cf. PN 16 note 1).
[2] Her first ten-day retreat since that of January 1903, which was in preparation for her profession (cf. L 216).
[3] Hallo.

L 212   To Yvonne Rostang   [October 6, 1904][1]
          J. M. + J. T.   Dijon Carmel, October 6

My very dear Yvonne,

I came out of retreat this morning and I am coming very quickly to tell you my heart is one with yours. I share your great sadness, I understand how totally heartbroken you are.... If you knew how I cried when I learned that God had taken your mother from you.... I loved her so much, and I know she really loved me too; what kindness and tenderness she showed me! Poor little Yvonne, I wish I could bring you words of consolation, but in the face of your grief I feel powerless, and I am asking God to be your Strength, your Support, for He is the supreme Consoler, and He is there quite close to you, His love surrounds you. He wants to be the Friend of all moments, and He will help you in the mission you have to fulfill for your father, your dear sisters and Raoul.[2] You must replace the one who has flown away to God; she too will watch over you; she loved her Yvonne so much! My little one, live with her.... You see, I feel her soul so alive close to mine, it seems we are so close to each other in Him who is Infinite Love.... He found her ripe, she was too beautiful to stay in the gardens here below. He plucked her for those of Heaven; she has seen the Unchanging beauty.... Let us follow her, my Yvonne, into those regions of peace and light where God wipes every tear from the eyes[3] of those He loves. He is counting on you, you have a great mission to fulfill. Your beloved mother watches over her darling daughter and is asking Him who took her to sustain her along the road.

A Dieu, you will be able to read between these lines what my heart cannot express, for, you see, I cannot think of you without crying. I am praying fervently for you, for good little Raoul, for your dear sisters. I cannot write to them individually; tell them, won't you, as well as Monsieur de Rostang, that I share in this great trial. Mama, whom I saw this morning, is sick about it. Courage, confidence, let us live with her. I loved her so much. She has not left us, for love lives in the soul, and the soul does not die.

                                              Sr. E. of the Trinity r.c.i.

[1] 1904: "came out of retreat this morning," October 6. Mme. de Rostang died on the 3rd.
[2] Mme. de Rostang had five children, of whom one was a son, Raoul, then 15 years old.
[3] Cf. Rev 7:17 and 21:4, referring back to Is 25:8.

L 213   To her sister   [November 12, 1904][1]
         J. M. + J. T.   Saturday night
              "Love is repaid by love alone."[2]

My dear Guite,
      Your brother-in-law the Abbé had our Carmel make some net squares that his sisters are going to embroider for an alb.[3] He was supposed to come by in two weeks for what was ready. Since he hasn't come and we already have eighty squares, our Reverend Mother thinks the best and quickest way to get them to him is through you; your sisters-in-law are perhaps waiting for them to begin their work, which will be a long and exacting job. So would you please deliver them to the Abbé? Thanks, my little sister. My soul is always close to yours. In our preparation for Advent and Christmas, I am keeping a special rendez-vous with you three times a day at the Angelus; we will ask the incarnate Word to establish His dwelling in our souls through love and that they *might never* leave Him again. A kiss to you and your angel, I will offer Holy Communion for her on the 19th;[4] have her say a prayer for Aunt

                                             Sabeth r.c.i.

      Kiss Mama.

[1] The "Saturday" before November 19 (cf. note 4). 1904, since Guite has only one child.
[2] Quotation from HA 209 [SS 195], which summarizes St. John of the Cross (SC 96 [K-RJ 9:7]). Elizabeth had read both.
[3] For his ordination to the subdiaconate on January 6, 1905.
[4] November 19th, the feast of St. Elizabeth.

Elizabeth in monastery garden in early 1903. She is holding her *Manual,* open at the New Testament.

III

"I Surrender Myself to You as Your Prey"
November 21, 1904 – March 1906

After having offered herself "as a prey" to the Trinity (PN 15) on November 21, 1904, Elizabeth immersed herself still deeper into her contemplative ideal, seeking God in interior silence and in the self-forgetfulness that she also lived by giving herself to others. A disciple of St. John of the Cross, she opened herself to the work of God, who made her ask: "Give peace to my soul; make it Your heaven, Your beloved dwelling and Your resting place. May I never leave You there alone but be wholly present" (PN 15).

The year 1905 began. She wrote: "May this be a year of love all for the glory of God" (L 218). St. Paul was now her great spiritual nourishment (cf. L 240, note 4). Elizabeth wished to become more and more a "praise" of the glory of the God of love (cf. Eph 1) and to arrive at the heights we are called to. The 52 letters return to the themes also found in the six poems of this period:

> ... do you really know your wealth?
> Have you ever sounded the abyss of Love? ...
> Truly, you are no longer you, you are becoming Him,
> At every instant the transformation is taking place....
> "Always believe in Love," whatever happens. (P 93)

Peace in the Storm

In the silence of her Carmelite life she was attentive to others. She shared in Guite's joy when her second daughter, Odette, was born on April 19, 1905, and in that of André Chevignard, who was ordained a priest on June 29 and celebrated his first Mass the following day at the Carmel.

There were other personal joys: the "cenacle" retreat (June 2–10, 1905); her own retreat (October 9–18, 1905); the community retreat preached by P. Rollin, S.J. (January 15–23, 1906).

Elizabeth should have left the novitiate at the beginning of 1906. She was kept there a little longer to help the three young ones who had entered during this period (cf. L 251, note 2). Elizabeth was "angel" for two of them.

During this time the situation in France remained tense. In November 1904, Emile Combes introduced the law of separation of church and state. After some harsh discussions, it was voted in during July 1905 and promulgated in December. State officials went on to take inventories of church property, which were often accompanied by great brawls with the people (cf. L 256, note 8 and 265, note 7). Pius X protested strenuously in his February 1906 encyclical, *Vehementer nos.* He consecrated fourteen new French bishops in St. Peter's Basilica in Rome. The diocese of Dijon, which had been without a pastor for a year and a half, received a new bishop, Pierre Dadolle, who was installed on March 15.

At the End of Her Strength

Without anyone in Carmel noticing, Elizabeth's health deteriorated greatly during this period. There was a very personal note in what she wrote in early January 1906 to Mme. Hallo: "Saint Paul said, 'I suffer in my body what is lacking in the passion of Christ.' You, too, are in a way another humanity for Him in which you permit Him to suffer, as it were, an extension of His passion.... You carry on the apostolate of suffering" (L 259).

Fatigue began to overwhelm her. In the spring of 1905, she was granted some exceptions to the observance of the Rule. In mid-August she was dispensed from her office of second portress. From then on, her health fluctuated.

At Christmas 1905, while preparing the crèche, a Sister heard her say: "Well! my little King of love, next year we shall have a closer look at each other." On January 1, 1906, the Carmelites drew a patron for the new year; St. Joseph fell to Elizabeth; she reacted in front of the community: "Saint Joseph is the patron of a happy death, he will come to lead me to the Father."

Because of her great courage, they had not noticed the seriousness of her condition, which she minimized when anyone spoke of it. But later she was to admit: "In the morning after the recitation of the little Hours, I already felt at the end of my strength and wondered how I would be able to make it through the day.... When you [the Prioress] gave me a rest, it did not make me feel any better; my whole being was so fatigued, I could not find a comfortable position or sound sleep, so in the end I could not have said whether the day or the night was more exhausting. Prayer was still the best remedy for my ills. I spent the time of the Grand Silence in a real agony that I united to that of the Divine Master, remaining at His side close to the choir grille. It was an hour of pure suffering, but gave me the strength for Matins, during which I had a certain facility for applying myself to God; afterward I again experienced my powerlessness and, without being noticed, thanks to the darkness, I somehow got back to our cell, often leaning against the wall" (S 172–73).

On February 28, 1906, Lent began. Around March 19, Elizabeth could no longer resist the illness that would lead to her death eight and a half months later.

L 214   To Abbé Chevignard   [November 29, 1904][1]
          J. M. + J. T.
          "Providebam Dominum in conspectu meo semper;
          quoniam a dextris est mihi, ne commovear."[2]

Monsieur l'Abbé,

I am very grateful to you for your feastday wishes, and I am very happy the Church has placed our saints so close to each other,[3] because that gives me the chance to offer you my best wishes today. Saint Augustine says that "love, forgetful of its own dignity, is eager to raise and magnify the beloved: it has only one measure, which is to be without measure."[4] I am asking God to fill you with that measure without measure, which is to say, according to the "riches of His glory,"[5] that the weight of His love may draw you[6] to the point of happy loss the Apostle spoke of when he wrote "Vivo enim jam non ego, vivit vero in me Christus."[7] That is the dream of my Carmelite soul and, I believe, also the dream of your priestly soul. Above all it is the dream of Christ, and I ask Him to accomplish it fully in our souls. Let us be for Him, in a way, another humanity in which He may renew His whole Mystery.[8] I have asked Him to make His home in me as Adorer, as Healer, and as Savior, and I cannot tell you what peace it gives my soul to think that He makes up for my weaknesses and, if I fall at every passing moment, He is there to help me up again[9] and carry me farther into Himself, into the depths of that divine essence where we already live by grace and where I would like to bury myself so deeply that nothing could make me leave. My soul meets yours there and, in unison with yours, I keep silent to adore Him who has loved us so divinely.

I unite myself to you in the emotions and profound joys of your soul as you await ordination[10] and beg you to let me share in this grace with you: each morning I am reciting the Hour of Terce *for you* so the Spirit of love and light may "come upon"[11] you to bring about all His creative work in you. If you would like, when you recite the Divine Office we could unite in the same prayer during this Hour that I have a particular devotion to. We will breathe in love[11a] and draw it down on our souls and on the whole Church.

You tell me to pray that you may be granted humility and the spirit of sacrifice. In the evening, while making the Way of the Cross before Matins, at every outpouring of the Precious Blood I used to ask for this grace for my own soul; from now on it will also be for yours. Don't you believe that, to achieve the annihilation, contempt of self, and love of suffering that were deep in the souls of the saints, we must gaze for a very long time at the God crucified by love, to receive an outflowing of His power[12] through continual contact with Him? Père Vallée once said to us that "martyrdom was the response of any lofty soul to the Crucified."[13] It seems to me that this could also be said for immolation. So let us be sacrificial souls, which is to say, *true* in our love: "He loved me, He gave Himself up for me!"[14]

A Dieu, Monsieur l'Abbé. Let us live by love, by adoration, by self-forgetfulness, in wholly joyful and confident peace, for "we are Christ's, and Christ is God's"!...[15]

Sister M. Elizabeth of the Trinity r.c.i.

On the 8th, we are going to give our Immaculate Mother and Queen a beautiful feast day in our souls; I will meet you under her virginal mantle.

[1] A little before December "8th" (1904, for the seminarian has not yet been ordained). Very probably November 29, "today," the vigil of St. Andrew (the 30th). That is the date indicated by Abbé Chevignard.

[2] "I set the Lord always in my presence, for with him at my right hand I cannot be shaken" (Ps 15:8, in the translation from the *Manual*).

[3] St. Elizabeth, the 19th, and St. Andrew, the 30th.

[4] Elizabeth is quoting verbatim from the fourth instruction of the retreat preached at Carmel by the Dominican P. Fages from the evening of November 12 to November 20, the text of which we have (cf. notes to PN 15, *O My God, Trinity Whom I Adore*, Vol. I, pp. 184–191). P. Fages refers frequently to letter 109 of St. Augustine (PL 33). This very Augustinian letter was in reality by Severus of Milevum. In *De diligendo Deo* (1:1), St. Bernard repeats the last phrase.

[5] Eph 3:16.

[6] An allusion to St. Augustine: "My love is my weight" (*Confessions*, 13:6). On November 19, P. Fages said: "Saint Augustine in particular said: 'I do not understand how any other weight could draw the human soul when it thus has a weight that shapes it'" (instruction 13). In her notebooks of quotations (cf. PAT), Elizabeth adds "(the weight) of divine love."

[7] Gal 2:20.

[8] In her prayer (PN 15) of November 21, 1904, Elizabeth has "asked" what immediately precedes and follows this. Later we will draw attention to the reflections of that celebrated PN 15. We have also pointed out in the annotations to that text the expressions found in the preceding letters that foreshadowed this prayer.

[9] Cf. "Living on Love": "But if I fall with each passing hour, / Picking me up, you come to my aid." (HA 332 [St. Thérèse of Lisieux, *Poetry*, tr. Donald Kinney OCD (Washington, DC: ICS Publications, 1995) Poem 17]). And HA 299 [LT 89]: "What does it matter if I fall at each moment!... My God, you see what I would do if you do not carry me in your arms...." In P 90, Elizabeth said: "At every passing moment."

[10] To the subdiaconate, January 6, 1905.

[11] Lk 1:35. Cf. PN 15, note 26.

[11a] Probably reminiscent of *Spiritual Canticle* 420-22 (quoted in L 185 [K-RJ 39:3]), where the Spirit breathes in the soul and penetrates it with love.

[12] Cf. Lk 6:19: "Power went out from him."

[13] The exact source of this thought is unknown. It is worth noting that in 1902, Elizabeth copied this text as an introductory quotation for a poem by Sr. Agnès (copy kept by ACD).

[14] Gal 2:20.

[15] 1 Cor 3:23.

L 215   To her sister   [November 29 or December 6, 1904][1]
      J. M. + J. T.   Tuesday night

My darling little sister,

For you there are always exceptions to the Rule! Our good Mother (who loves you very much) is granting my wish and is letting me write you a little note. Tonight at recreation she showed us some lovely palls[2] from which she had made her choice. I asked her to show them to you before sending them back: it might be useful to you for the Abbé; his sisters, who are already preparing their work, might like to profit from this good opportunity, for there seems to be nothing pretty here, and besides, everything is very expensive. These are very reasonable, and our Sister embroiderers, who are skilled in this, find them very well made. You could show them to Mama, who, I think, is intending to have her maid embroider something; she might do well to choose from among these pretty palls. My darlings, I think of you always and on every good occasion. I think of you especially when I am close to Him. Beloved little sister, my "little one" as I used to love so to call you and as I still call you in my heart, ah, if you knew how I cover you with prayer. I am keeping your secret,[3] I'm talking to Him about it! and I'm tell-

ing Him to make His home in you, to overwhelm you, invade you,
so that His Marguerite may be as it were a radiance of Himself,[4] and
so that little Sabeth, looking at her, may see a reflection of God. Kiss
your darling daughter for me, and on the *8th,* have her pray for me.[5]
We're preparing a beautiful feast for that great day. My Guite, I told
Our Reverend Mother you had found a raincoat for her poor
priest;[6] that good Mother was very pleased. I feel a bit silly seeing
nothing come. Was I being forward? *Tell me* plainly like I do with
you. A Dieu, little sister, let's have but one heart and one soul[7] to
love Him who is all Love.

Sr. E. of the Trinity r.c.i.

Little Sabeth, give your Grandmama a kiss for me!

---

[1] One of the two "Tuesdays" after the beginning of Advent (November 27th)—hence
the "exception to the Rule"—and before December 8th. 1904, since Guite has only
one child.
[2] In anticipation of Abbé Chevignard's ordination; probably before his priestly ordination the following summer.
[3] Guite is expecting her second child, who will be born in April.
[4] "To make one's home," or "establish oneself," "overwhelm," "invade," or "possess,"
"radiance": cf. PN 15.
[5] The 8th of December, the third anniversary of her clothing.
[6] Unidentified.
[7] Cf. Acts 4:32.

L 216   To her Rolland aunts   [December 31, 1904][1]
            J. M. + J. T.   Dijon Carmel, December 31

My dear little Aunts,

A Carmelite is one who is silent; that is why you haven't received anything from your little Elizabeth for so long. But today she
is taking her "large-size" paper that always seems too small when it's
going to you, her heart is so full!...

I am assuming the Blessed Virgin has not yet obtained the requested miracle,[2] or I'd know about it already, wouldn't I, my little
Aunt Francine? My whole dear community joined your important
Novena for December 8th, and you can guess how big a part I took
in it! I understand your great trial so well; what a sacrifice that makes

for you. I see God is treating you like a bride and wants to unite Himself to you through the cross. Suffering is something so great, and there are so few souls who consent to follow Our Lord that far.... I am praying fervently for you, and while waiting for Him to grant our prayers, I ask Him to make "the ray of love" shine in your soul!...

We had a beautiful feast for the Blessed Virgin on the 8th. Our cloisters were all lit up in the evening, and we had a magnificent procession: a large [statue of the] Immaculate Virgin was carried on a beautiful throne by four Sisters, and you can imagine how happy I was to be one of them; I wish God had given you wings so you could have flown to my Carmel, and that He had let you enter our cloister to share in the feast that, for our Sisters, was like an echo of the Heavenly feast. Since I last wrote you, I have had a very great happiness and a very great grace: a private ten-day retreat, my first since my profession.[3] During that time I had my veil lowered, and I had no contact with my Sisters; it was absolute solitude, "that solitude in which God speaks to the heart."[4] In order to hear Him better, I had several additional hours of prayer besides our regular ones, and I can say that these ten days of prayer and silence have been a foretaste of our Homeland. I'm sure it's not necessary to tell you I prayed for you, for you have a part in all my graces. On the night of the 24th, I placed all my wishes in the Heart of the Infant God and He must have brought them to you. My darling Aunts, may He fill you according to all the "riches of His glory,"[5] to use Saint Paul's language, and may His little divine hand caress you for His bride Elizabeth of the Trinity. Please give my very affectionate greetings to Aunt Catherine and tell her I think of her very often. Please pay my respects to Monsieur le Curé, too. I pray for [him] every day and count on his holy prayers. I dreamed recently that he came to see me in Carmel; will my dream ever come true? I hope so, and I would be very happy to speak with him of God. And you, my beloved little Aunts, I think if Sister portress ever came to announce your visit to me, my heart would beat *very hard* and it would take a moment for it to recover; I don't know if God will grant us this consolation, but I do know well that He opens wide His divine Heart to us so we can always meet each other there and forget the distance that separates our bodies but not our hearts or our souls! Last Thursday[6] I saw Mama, who was anxiously awaiting the end of Advent so she could see her Carmelite. Little Sabeth is so cute! Marguerite is to bring her to me some day soon; she is so happy with her angel in her arms!

A Dieu, my darling Aunts, I kiss you with the best of my heart, without forgetting Aunt Catherine. Your happy little niece,

Sr. M. Elizabeth of the Trinity r.c.i.

Aunt Francine can be reassured about her letters, which have been destroyed.[7] I did better than that, I sent my dear breviaries[8] to Mama's house, keeping only those that are necessary, and when I need any of them, she brings them to me. Give my best wishes to Louise and Anna, and don't forget the little ones.

[1] 1904: cf. note 3.
[2] The healing of Aunt Francine's eyes.
[3] From September 26 to October 5, 1904, cf. L 211, note 1.
[4] Hos 2:14 (in the Vulgate).
[5] Eph 3:16.
[6] December 29.
[7] Elizabeth was destroying all the letters she received except for a few she was supposed to send on to her mother. Aunt Francine may have requested this because of the poor handwriting caused by her eyesight.
[8] The six large, cumbersome volumes, cf. L 154, note 2.

L 217   To Marie-Louise[1]   [around 1905]

The soul who loves dwells in God, and God dwells in it. In this way, because of love and through love, the creature becomes the resting place of God, and God, the resting place of the creature.[2]

To my dear Marie-Louise.

Sr. M.E. of the Trinity r.c.i.

[1] This text is written in the margin of an "Act of consecration of the human race to the Heart of Jesus the Redeemer," representing a statue of the Sacred Heart supporting a cross. Marie-Louise Hallo is its most likely recipient, because of her devotion to the Sacred Heart. The handwriting allows us to date it approximately.
[2] This whole text, whose first phrase is borrowed from 1 John 4:16, is a quotation from Msgr. Gay, *Fleurs de doctrine et de piété* [Flowers of Doctrine and Piety], 2d ed. (Poitiers-Paris: Oudin, 1882), p. 54. Sister Agnès had given it to Elizabeth in a note that she kept in her books.

L 218   To Madame Hallo   [beginning of January 1905][1]
       J. M. + J. T.   God alone suffices.[2]

Very dear Madame,

I was very touched by your good wishes, and you can imagine how happy I was when I recognized your dear handwriting. My greetings for 1905 will reach you a bit late, but my heart at least, as you well know, is never late when it is a question of going to you, and, ever since you left Dijon, the capital seems so very close that I often fly there on the wings of prayer and love. Our Reverend Mother was very touched by your greetings and by the beautiful consecration to the Sacred Heart; she asks me to tell you this and to send you all her best wishes for this year now beginning. Dear Madame, may this be a year of love all for the glory of God. It would be so good to be able to say with our adored Master on the last day: "Father, I have glorified You on earth, I have finished the work You gave me to do!"[3] I see you are very busily engaged in this work,[4] and your letter was of much interest to me. What a consolation to give God to souls and souls to God! Isn't life completely different when you look at it from this point of view! From deep in my cell, I follow you everywhere; I commend to the Father of the family those "two" who are working so well on His house,[5] whereas I will be the little Moses on the mountain.[6] I had a visit from Charles several days before he left,[7] and on leaving the parlor, I thanked God for protecting him for you like that. I believe your sufferings have purchased that grace for him. How fortunate you are doing better; I am asking God that you may continue to improve; you have been the victim of His love for so long a time.[8] I saw my dear trio after Christmas; little Sabeth is very cute. Mama is delighted about seeing you in the spring,[9] and she is so touched by your kind invitation; I am too, I can assure you, and am certain the prayerful atmosphere you live in will be good for her soul. A Dieu, dear Madame, in the union of prayer, I kiss you with all my heart and I remain always your second daughter,[10]

                    M.E. of the Trinity r.c.i.

Please give my regards to Charles and tell him his sister in Carmel prays for him every day. I had a visit from Madame Mignard,

who recommends herself to you; she spoke to me about the
Desmoulins family, who are very interesting; I recommend them to
you, especially the son whom they would like to see convert.

[1] "My greetings for 1905," "this year now beginning." The Hallos had been living in
Paris since October 1904 (cf. RB 7 in PAT).
[2] A maxim of Teresa of Avila (cf. *Diary,* note 87).
[3] Jn 17:14.
[4] Lay apostolic activities.
[5] A probable allusion to their zeal for the construction of the basilica of the Sacred
Heart in Montmartre.
[6] Cf. Ex 17:8–13. *Le Banquet sacré ...* (see L 206, note 3) says of the Carmelite: "She is
a Moses on the mountain, holding her hands raised toward heaven so as to obtain
the victory for the leaders of the Lord's armies who are fighting on the plain" (p.
27). Elizabeth had also read the comparison of "Moses praying on the mountain" in
HA 307 [LT 135].
[7] Charles Hallo did his military service in Dijon (PA 795).
[8] Mme. Hallo suffered from rheumatism. From Elizabeth's perspective, suffering is
governed by the love of God. Cf. Introduction to the first section of *Letters from Carmel.*
[9] This will take place in May, cf. L 228.
[10] Elizabeth called Mme. Hallo her "second mama" (cf. L 228).

L 219   To Canon Angles   [beginning of January 1905][1]
    J. M. + J. T.   "Mihi vivere Christus est."[2]

Dear Monsieur le Chanoine,

    I am very late[3] in sending you my greetings for 1905, but you
know the heart of your little child well enough to know that it is
never late when it is a question of going to you. I have prayed fervently to my royal Bridegroom for you and have asked Him to give
you the very best of His treasures: and isn't that Jesus Himself, the
gift of God?[4] Every day He makes me experience more fully how
sweet it is to be His, His alone, and my vocation as a Carmelite moves
me to adoration, to thanksgiving. Yes, it is true what Saint Paul says,
"He has loved exceedingly,"[5] loved His little Elizabeth exceedingly.
But love calls forth love, and I ask nothing of God but to understand
that knowledge of charity that Saint Paul speaks of[6] and of which
my heart wishes to sound the very depths.[7] That will be Heaven,
won't it? But it seems to me that we can begin our Heaven even here
on earth, since we possess Him, and through everything, we can remain in His love.[8] This is what He made me understand during my

private retreat, which I had the happiness of making in October,[9] ten days of complete silence, absolute solitude: from Carcassonne you can see the happy hermit burying herself in her desert. Yes, I am happy, and it does me good to say so, especially to you, for I well know you still have quite a fatherly affection for me. I have seen Mama, Guite, little Elizabeth, and of course we spoke of you and the dear Maurels. I hope God has sent Monsieur Léon[10] that job he wanted so much and that I've prayed fervently for. Please remember me to them, particularly to Marie-Louise. Ah, if you knew how unchanged my heart is ... how it expands, enlarges in its contact with the God who is all Love. In Him I remain wholly yours, and I recollect myself beneath your dear blessing.

Sr. M. Elizabeth of the Trinity r.c.i.

[1] "Greetings for 1905." Cf. also note 3.
[2] Phil 1:21.
[3] The letter was actually written on January 5 at the latest (cf. the end of L 220 of that date).
[4] Cf. Jn 4:10.
[5] Eph 2:4.
[6] Cf. Eph 3:18–19.
[7] There is a notable similarity of thought between this passage and Thérèse of Lisieux, and perhaps an immediate influence in its formulation. Thérèse writes: "... I have never desired anything but to *love* You, and I am ambitious for no other glory. Your love has gone before me ... and now it is an abyss whose depths I cannot fathom. Love attracts love ..." (HA 198 [SS 256]). But we also note the Elizabethan accent: "My vocation as a Carmelite moves me to adoration...."
[8] Cf. Jn 15:9.
[9] Half in September, half in October. Cf. L 211, note 1.
[10] Léon Maurel, Marie-Louise's brother. Mme. Catez had already served as an intermediary in 1900 to secure a position for him (cf. L 34 and 35).

L 220   To Madame Angles   [January 5, 1905][1]
J. M. + J. T.   Dijon Carmel, January 5
God alone suffices.

Very dear Madame,

This letter will be a little late in bringing you my best wishes, but you surely know that my heart went ahead of my pen in going to find yours, passing through the heart of the Divine Master. I read some beautiful words in the epistles of Saint Peter that express the good wishes of your little Carmelite friend: "Sancify the Lord in your heart."[2] To do that, we must carry out those other words of Saint John the Baptist: "He must increase and I must decrease."[3] Dear Madame, in this New Year that God is giving us to sanctify us and to unite us more closely to Himself, let us make Him grow in our souls, let us keep Him alone and set apart;[4] may He be truly King. As for us, let us disappear, let us forget ourselves, let us be only the "praise of His glory,"[5] according to the Apostle's beautiful expression. I also wish you all the graces of health you need, since you've been so tried in that respect; remember what Saint Paul said: "I boast of my infirmities, for then the power of Jesus Christ dwells in me."[6] It is all in God's will, and rejoice, dear Madame, in your physical sufferings that affect your soul as well, and remember that if you bear this state of powerlessness with fidelity, with love, you can cover Him with glory.[7] Our holy Mother Teresa said: when we know how to unite ourselves to God and to His holy will, accepting everything He wishes, we are happy, we possess everything![8] So I wish you that profound peace in the divine good pleasure. I understand all the sacrifices your health imposes, but it is sweet to say to oneself: "It is He who wishes that." One day He said to one of His saints: "Drink, eat, sleep, do anything you like, as long as you love Me."[9] It is love that makes His burden so light and His yoke so sweet.[10] Let us ask the Divine Infant to consume us in that divine flame, in that fire He came to cast upon the earth.[11] I have seen Mama, who was anxiously awaiting the end of Advent to see me; I also had a visit from Marguerite and her dear little Elizabeth, who is very cute. These parlor visits are a great consolation to me and I am so thankful to see all God is doing in these two souls who are so dear to me. A Dieu, dear Madame, I am going to lose myself in Him to find you, since He is our Rendez-vous; say a little prayer for your little friend in Carmel, for she depends very much on it.

Sr. M. Elizabeth of the Trinity r.c.i.

Little Jean must be very cute. Kiss his dear little mama for me.[12] I am sure you won't mind doing me an act of poverty [a favor] by delivering this little note to Monsieur le Chanoine[13] when you have a chance; thanks in advance.

[1] 1905; Guite has only one child.
[2] 1 Pt 3:15.
[3] Jn 3:30.
[4] This expression *(séparé* = set apart or detached), seen again in L 278, is surely inspired by St. John of the Cross and is connected with formulations such as "the spirit in this contemplation is alone in regard to all things" (SC 170 [K-RJ 15:24]; "In this solitude, away from all things, the soul is alone with God" (SC 380 [K-RJ 35:5]); "her soul is detached and withdrawn from all things" (SC 438 [K-RJ 40:1] and cf. LF 506 [K-RJ 2:18]).
[5] Eph 1:12.
[6] 2 Cor 12:9.
[7] "To cover with glory": cf. PN 15, note 15a.
[8] Elizabeth does not use quotation marks. This is undoubtedly not a literal quotation but rather a conviction dear to St. Teresa of Avila that Teresa expresses, for example, in *The Interior Castle,* 5, chapter 3.
[9] Elizabeth is quoting Angela di Foligno rather freely (Ang 61): "Eat, drink, sleep; your whole life will please me as long as you love me!" [See note 3 to L 311.]
[10] Cf. Mt 11:30.
[11] Cf. Lk 12:49.
[12] Marie-Louise Ambry.
[13] L 219.

L 221   To her sister   (January 5, 1905) [1]
J. M. + J. T.   "May Jesus hold us firmly in His love." [2]

My darling little sister,

You insisted so sweetly the other day[3] that I ask you for anything I'd like that I don't think I'm being indiscreet in coming to you quite simply. It is the tradition in Carmel to celebrate the Kings on the day of Epiphany itself and not on Sunday. On that day, our Reverend Mother serves in the refectory, and it's our custom to have the traditional brioche. The person who usually sent it is not with us this year,[4] and since we don't know how to make it, Our Mother is a bit perplexed, for this little feast of the Kings is an old custom of the Order. She remembered the offer you made the other day, which she had refused because this wasn't needed then, and because this good Mother avoids anything contrary to the spirit of penance that governs everything in a Carmelite's life. So, my Guite, if you'd get us three couronnes[4a] for *twenty-one* people, order them to be as simple as possible, in keeping with our spirit of poverty. We will need them *tomorrow, Friday,* at 10 A.M. *at the latest.* You do understand, don't you, *tomorrow* and *not Sunday*, as in the world. Little Sabeth will offer them to Our Reverend and dear Mother, who in turn will be delighted to serve them to her daughters. Oh, how I love your angel, as much as you do, that says it all.... Just to see her in your arms draws me into prayer, for it makes me think this is how God treats me. Let us let ourselves be carried by Him, little sister, so He may fix us firmly in His Love. It is there that I leave you, or rather there that I remain, all silent, with you. A kiss to you and your angel, and I'm praying for the one I'll soon see in your arms. Your big sister,

E. of the Trinity r.c.i.

Don't forget to tell your dear brother-in-law that I am wholly in communion of soul with him.[5]

I'm ready to face Siberia with your pretty petticoat,[6] thanks again.

---

[1] "Tomorrow, Friday," "the day of Epiphany itself": January 6 falls on a Friday in 1905. Thus the letter dates from January 5. Guite is expecting her second child.
[2] Reminiscent of Jn 15:9 ("Remain in my love") or Eph 3:7 ("rooted and grounded in charity"), but also of "Living on Love," poem 17 of Thérèse of Lisieux, who says, in fact: "I make my home in your hearth" (HA 331). The expression appears again in L 227.
[3] During her visit to Carmel mentioned in L 220.
[4] Perhaps Mme. Hallo, who has left Dijon? Cf. L 218, note 1.
[4a] [Loaves in the shape of a crown—TRANS.]
[5] The next day, André Chevignard will be ordained subdeacon at the Cathedral Saint-Bénigne by Msgr. Maillet, Bishop of Saint-Claude (cf. SRD, 20, pp. 12–13). After the resignation of Bishop Le Nordez, the diocese was without a bishop until 1906.
[6] This may be an indication that Elizabeth's health has changed. She received permission to accept a warmer petticoat from her sister. We should recall that the Carmel was not heated. Elizabeth often had chilblains on her hands and face; we can see this in her photographs, and the Sisters who knew her often confirmed it.

L 222   To her sister   [January 6, 1905][1]
         J. M. + J. T.   *He is Love!*

Thanks, my little sister, for your superb brioches—there were more than enough. Our Reverend Mother asks me to express all her gratitude, and I don't have to be asked when it is a question of coming to my Guite! Our Mother got the bean,[2] she was happy the King had chosen her for His queen, and I was delighted with this reign of love. Thanks, my little sister, for spoiling us so. Thanks to little Sabeth, give her a kiss for her aunt and then let us keep silence close to her little soul to adore the God who dwells within her. He loves the little ones,[3] let's become His little child and let Him carry us in His arms. It is there that I am always yours. Thanks again.

Sr. E. of the Trinity r.c.i.

Give a kiss to our dear, good Mama for her Carmelite.

[1] She is thanking for the brioches spoken of in L 221.
[2] Hidden in the brioche. [Finding the bean or coin hidden in the Epiphany cake is considered a sign of favor or luck in countries where this custom is practiced— TRANS.]
[3] Cf. Mk 10:13–16. The comparison with the child in the arms of God (cf. L 116, note 2, and 129, note 4) indicates that Elizabeth is thinking of the "little way" of Thérèse of Lisieux, reserved for "little ones" (HA 148 [SS 208]).

L 223   To Madame de Sourdon [a little before January 20, 1905][1]
J. M. + J. T.

Very dear Madame,
Our Reverend Mother asks me to tell you she is very happy to grant[2] you the consolation of attending Mass on Friday in our chapel. As for me, dear Madame, I confess it will make me truly happy to pray so close to you: our souls will be even closer in Him who is "charity," according to the beautiful definition of the disciple of love.[3] I will join you in offering Holy Communion for the dear departed one, so that God who is rich in mercy may give him a share in the inheritance of the saints in light,[4] if He has not already brought him into that Kingdom. Yet it is into that Kingdom that my soul makes its way when I think of him, and I am moved to pray to him rather than for him; but I will do it all the same, for one must be so pure to appear before God. Yet even here below, He lets us live in His intimacy, and in some way we begin our eternity, living in communion[5] with the three Divine Persons. What a mystery! I lose

myself there in order to find you, dear Madame, asking God to seal the bond that unites your soul to that of your little

Elizabeth of the Trinity r.c.i.

I was delighted with my parlor visit with Françoise.

[1] An approximate date deduced from note 2.
[2] The chapel is still closed to the public. The Prioress "grants" her the special permission to attend Mass on "Friday," which will be celebrated for a "dear departed one." The same authorization for the same reason is mentioned in L 262, for January 20, 1906. Thus it refers to a Mass for the tenth anniversary of the death of Mr. Georges Huët de Sourdon, the husband of Mme. de Sourdon, deceased on January 20, 1895. That anniversary does in fact fall on "Friday" in 1905. The handwriting subsequently confirms these conclusions. Elizabeth had already thought about this anniversary in 1904 (cf. L 192).
[3] 1 Jn 4:16.
[4] Cf. Eph 2:4 ("God who is rich in mercy") and Col 1:12.
[5] 1 Jn 1:3. The first appearance in Elizabeth's writings of this expression *(société)*, which she comes to love.

L 224   To Madame Angles   [a little before March 8, 1905][1]
    J. M. + J. T.
    "Abandonment is the delicious fruit of love."[2]

Very dear Madame,

Before entering the great silence of Lent, our Reverend Mother is allowing me to tell you how much my dear community and I are praying for you. I can understand what apprehensions you must feel in facing an operation; I am asking God to ease them, to calm them Himself. The holy Apostle Paul says that "He works[3] all things according to the counsel of His will,"[4] thus we must receive everything as coming *directly* from that divine hand of our Father who loves us and who, through all trials, pursues His goal, "to unite us more closely to Himself."[5] Dear Madame, launch your soul on the waves of confidence and abandonment,[6] and remember that anything that troubles it or throws it into fear does not come from God, for He is the Prince of Peace[6a] and He promises that peace "to those of good will."[7] When you are afraid you have abused His graces, as you say, that is the time to redouble your confidence, for, as the Apostle says, "where sin abounds, grace abounds all the more,"[8] and farther on, "I boast of my weaknesses, for then the power of Jesus Christ dwells in me."[9] "Our God is rich in mercy because of His immense love."[10] So do not fear the hour we must all pass through. Death, dear Madame, is the sleep of the child resting on the heart of its mother. At last the night of exile will have fled forever, and we will enter into possession of the inheritance of the saints in light.[11] Saint John of the Cross says we will be judged in love.[12] That corresponds well with the thinking of Our Lord, who said to Mary Magdalene: "Many sins have been forgiven her because she has loved much."[13] I often think I will have a very long purgatory, for much will be asked of the one who has received much[14] and He has been so overwhelmingly generous to His little bride, but she abandons herself to His love and sings the hymn of His mercies while still on earth![15] Dear Madame, if we made God increase in our soul every day, think what confidence that would give us to appear one day before His infinite holiness! I think you have found the secret and that it is indeed that we arrive at this divine goal through renunciation: by that means we die to self in order to leave all the room to God. Do you remember that beautiful passage from the Gospel according to Saint John where Our Lord says to Nicodemus: "Truly I say to you, if one is not born anew, one cannot see the kingdom of God"?[16] Let us therefore renew ourselves in the interior of our soul, "let us strip off the old and clothe ourselves anew, in the image of Him who created him" (Saint Paul).[17] That is done gently and simply, by separating ourselves from all that is not God. Then the soul no longer has any fears or desires,[17a] its will is entirely lost in the will of God, and since this is what creates union, it can cry out: "I live no longer I, but Christ lives in me."[18] Let us pray much for each other during this holy time of Lent; let us retire to the desert with our Master[19] and ask Him to teach us to live by His life.

I saw Mama, Marguerite, and her dear little Sabeth; it was the last parlor visit until Easter, they find that very long. I know Marie-Louise is also expecting a little angel[20] and I recommend her particularly to God. Remember me to your dear ones. I am writing a little note in reply to Monsieur le Chanoine[21] and, as a poor Carmelite, I am being so bold as to entrust it to you to deliver to him whenever you have a chance; I hope that is not being indiscreet. A Dieu, dear Madame, courage and confidence, I kiss you as I love you.

Sr. M. E. of the Trinity r.c.i.

---

[1] "Before entering the great silence of Lent," which began on March 8 in 1905: Guite still has one child. Cf. also note 20.

[2] Elizabeth copied (and recopied) this thought attributed to St. Augustine in her notebook of quotations (cf. PAT); she found it in this form as an introductory quotation for a poem, "L'Abandon" ("Abandonment"), by Thérèse of Lisieux (HA 377, Poem 52).

[3] "He works" [in French, *Il opère]* alludes to the "operation" that Mme. Angles might have to undergo.

[4] Eph 1:11.

[5] The quotation marks do not necessarily indicate a quotation borrowed from someone else but sometimes, as seems to be the case here, a representative or concentrated formula. Elizabeth may possibly have been thinking of the very powerful pages from the *Living Flame* (st. 2, verse 5: LF 510–17 [K-RJ 2:23–30]) in which John of the Cross explains the necessity of suffering in order to arrive at profound union with God. One might also think of Rom 8:28: "We know that all works together for the good of those who love God" (trans. from her *Manual)*.

[6] An image from Thérèse of Lisieux: "He launched me full sail upon the waves of confidence and love" (HA 131; Ms A, 80v° [SS 174]).

[6a] Cf. Is 9:5.

[7] Cf. Lk 2:14 (translation of the period, inspired by the Vulgate).

[8] Rom 5:20.

[9] 2 Cor 12:9.

[10] Eph 2:4.

[11] Cf. Col 1:12.

[12] *Maxim* 70 [no. 60 of *Sayings of Light and Love* in 1991 edition of K-RJ].

[13] Lk 7:47.

[14] Cf. Lk 12:48.

[15] Cf L 208, notes 2 and 4.

[16] Jn 3:3.

[17] Col 3:9–10.

[17a] "Fears or desires": this expression calls to mind stanzas 20–21, 28 and 40 of the *Spiritual Canticle* on the "four passions" (cf. LR 26).

[18] Gal 2:20.

[19] Cf. Mk 1:12.

[20] Joseph Ambry, who will be born on July 9.

[21] L 225.

L 225   To Canon Angles   [a little before March 8, 1905][1]
J. M. + J. T.
"Deus meus es tu et confitebor tibi. Deus meus es tu et exaltabo te."[2]

Dear Monsieur le Chanoine,

Before I bury myself in the solitude of the desert, our Reverend Mother is letting me come tell you how happy your kind letter has made me. I knew from Mama that you were having trouble with your arm, and your dear letter makes me hope the rheumatism has disappeared. Poor Mama! As you can easily guess, she wishes the Alleluia had already been sung,[3] God will not overlook this long fast for her motherly heart. Yes, Monsieur le Chanoine, have a good Lent; as you say, there is much to expiate, much to ask for, and I think if we are to meet so many needs, we must become a "continual prayer"[4] and love much. The power of a soul surrendered to love is so great; Magdalene is a beautiful example of this: one word from her is enough to obtain the resurrection of Lazarus. We really need God to work resurrections in our dear France;[5] I love to place her beneath the outpouring of the Divine Blood. Saint Paul says that "in Him, we have the forgiveness of sins according to the riches of grace that have superabounded in us";[6] that thought does me so much good.... Oh, how good it is to go and be saved by Him at the times when we feel only our miseries; I am so full of them, but God has given me a Mother,[7] the image of His mercy, who, with a single word, can calm all the anguish in the soul of her little child and give her wings to fly away beneath the rays of the Creator Star. So I live in thanksgiving, uniting myself to the eternal praise that is being sung in the Heaven of the Saints; I am making my apprenticeship down here!... Our dear Mother asks me to tell you how very touched she was to be remembered by you so especially; she sends you her deep respect and recommends herself to your prayers at the holy altar during this holy season of Lent. Pray for your little child, too, consecrate her with the sacred Host so that nothing of poor Elizabeth remains but so that she may be wholly of the Trinity; then her prayer can become all-powerful, and you will profit by it since you have so large a part in her prayers, and by doing so, she would only be repaying a great debt of gratitude! A Dieu, dear Monsieur le

Chanoine, there is the bell calling me to Matins. I will not forget to "remember you" there; you will be the first.

Sr. M. E. of the Trinity r.c.i.

[1] Cf. L 224, notes 1 and 21. The style of handwriting in this letter clearly indicates 1905.
[2] In the translation of her *Manual:* "You are my God, and I will sing your praises: you are my God, and I will exalt your greatness" (Ps 117:28).
[3] After Lent, in order to visit her daughter.
[4] Cf. L 206, note 3.
[5] In November 1904, Emile Combes set forth a plan for the separation of church and state. The law of separation would be passed in July 1905. Discussions were about to begin in Parliament at the time of this letter. The climate was tense.
[6] Eph 1:7–8.
[7] Mother Germaine, as L 271 clearly reveals. The apposition "image of [God's] mercy" was inspired by Thérèse of Lisieux, who writes to her sister Agnès: "You are for me the image of divine mercy," in contrast to another Sister who is "the image of God's severity" (HA 225–26 [LT 230]).

L 226   To Abbé Chevignard   [April 7, 1905][1]
J. M. + J. T.   Friday evening
"Misericordias Domini in aeternum cantabo."[2]

Monsieur l'Abbé,

Because our Reverend Mother is not free this evening, she asks me to come to you so you will receive a little note from Carmel telling you how united with you we are on this great day. As for me, I am withdrawing in recollection into the depths of my soul where the Holy Spirit dwells. I am asking Him, that Spirit of love "who searches everything, even the depths of God,"[3] to give Himself superabundantly to you and to send forth His rays into your soul so that, beneath this great light, it might receive the "anointing of the Holy One"[4] of which the disciple of love speaks. With you, I am singing the hymn of thanksgiving and keeping silent to adore the Mystery that is enveloping your whole being: the entire Trinity is leaning down and bending over you to make the "glory of His grace"[5] blaze forth.

Our Reverend Mother asks me to tell you she is very happy you have chosen our chapel in which to celebrate your first Mass and that on Friday[6] at 8 A.M., we will be with you at the altar of the God of love. As for me, I can assure you my happiness will be great and my union profound.

A Dieu, Monsieur l'Abbé. On the evening of this feast of the Precious Blood[7] I place myself with you beneath the divine outpouring so that our Christ may keep us "holy and spotless in His presence in love."[8] As the Apostle tells us, this is God's great desire, so may it be fulfilled in us.

Sr. M. Elizabeth of the Trinity r.c.i.

[1] "Friday evening," "evening of this feast of the Precious Blood," then celebrated on the Friday after the fourth Sunday of Lent. Thus, April 7, 1905. By means of her letter (which will arrive the following day), Elizabeth will be present "on this great day" of his ordination to the diaconate, on April 8 (by Bishop Maillet, in the chapel of the major Seminary, cf. SRD, 20, p. 217). There is nothing to stop them from thinking already of his first Mass (cf. note 6) three months later. She will write another letter for his ordination to the priesthood.
[2] Cf. L 208, note 2.
[3] 1 Cor 2:10.
[4] 1 Jn 2:20.
[5] Eph 1:6.
[6] Friday, June 30, 1905, the day after his priestly ordination.
[7] Cf. note 1.
[8] Eph 1:4.

L 227   To her sister   [April 22, 1905][1]
J. M. + J. T.   Alleluia.

My darling Guite,

We have sung the Alleluia, so our Reverend Mother is letting me come tell you right away how united I am with you in your joys of motherhood. I'm so happy to be an aunt once again, and especially of a little girl, for, you see, I think the union that existed between us is going to live on in your sweet home, and I'm delighted that Sabeth has an Odette just as Aunt Elizabeth had a Marguerite. Our dear Mother, who takes such an interest in you, was overjoyed at announcing the big news to me, and she asks me to tell you so. Sabeth was born on the feast of the Five Wounds of Jesus,[2] and here is Odette arriving on the day when the Master was sold[3] to redeem her little soul. Isn't that touching?...

I hope you can have dear Sister Thérèse;[4] I have certainly been asking that of God. And then I hope too that you can nurse her like last time. Mama will tell me all that on Wednesday.[5] We have so much to tell each other. Kiss that dear grandmother for me, tell her I share her happiness and thank her for her kind letter.

I've carried your soul with mine everywhere during this great week, especially during the night of Holy Thursday, and since you could not go to Him, I told Him to come to you. In the silence of prayer, I whispered to my Guite those words that Père Lacordaire addressed to Mary Magdalene when she was searching for her Master on the morning of the Resurrection: "No longer ask anyone on earth or anyone in Heaven for Him, for *He* is your soul; and your soul *is He!*"[6] Oh, little sister, how He is blessing your little nest, how He loves you in entrusting these two little souls "whom He chose in Him before creation that they might be holy and spotless in His presence in love" (Saint Paul).[7] You are the one who must guide them to Him and keep them all His.

Please tell Georges, my Guite, how all your joys echo in my heart, for which I give thanks to "God, from whom every perfect gift comes."[8]

A Dieu. In Him, little mama, I recollect myself with you close to the little ones; each has her own beautiful angel beside her who sees the Face of God.[9] Ask Him to carry us away in Him and hold us firmly in His Love. I'm surrounding you as well as your two treasures with all my tender affection and prayer. I'm delighted to see Sabeth. Tell her to give a kiss to her grandmother for her aunt.

I'm sending Odette a medal that has touched the miraculous Infant Jesus of Beaune;[10] it's of copper, for I'm a poor Carmelite; you can put it on her cradle, so that God, who so loves little ones, may bless and protect her.

                                                    Sr. M. E. of the Trinity

Please remember me to Sister Thérèse.

---

[1] For the birth of Odette Chevignard, Guite's second daughter (cf. note 3). "We have sung the Alleluia," at that time sung on Saturday morning, the vigil of Easter (which falls on April 23 in 1905).
[2] Cf. L 196, with note 4.

³ April 19, 1905, the Wednesday of Holy Week, the day on which the Carmel of Dijon meditated on Judas' betrayal in selling Jesus.
⁴ As a help to the household following the birth. Cf. L 196, note 7.
⁵ April 26, in the parlor.
⁶ *Sainte Marie-Madeleine,* a text already quoted more precisely in L 75, note 4.
⁷ Eph 1:4.
⁸ James 1:17.
⁹ Cf. Mt 18:10.
¹⁰ A statue venerated in the Carmel of Beaune.

L 228   To Madame Hallo   [around April 30, 1905]¹
    J. M. + J. T.   "Lord, stay with us."²

Very dear Madame,

I am overjoyed at the thought of the good visit my dear Mama is going to have with you. She came to see me a few days ago and spoke to me about her trip to Paris, which she is very delighted about. She told me of your kindness and consideration. I know Marie-Louise is giving her her room, and that touches me deeply. But nothing surprises me, for I know the heart of my second mama! With what joy will I listen to the account of your life there, all the details of your house; when she gets back there will be so many things to tell me.... You can be sure I will be a part of your life there at home, my train will reach you before Mama's, for distance is quickly crossed by souls and hearts. You will take me with you on all your pilgrimages. How many times I have prayed next to you; that was very sweet for me, and what God has united, no one can divide;³ He is an immensity of love that overflows us on all sides, and our embrace in Him is even stronger and truer. I know, with your inexhaustible devotion, you work for His greater glory. In one form or another, that is how our life must be spent, it is our "predestination," according to Saint Paul's language.⁴ Thursday I met my niece Odette; she had a charming bonnet, which I admired, and they told me where it came from; I see you are always spoiling [us]. A Dieu, dear Madame, thank you for all your goodness to Mama; I am always your second daughter, and I kiss you as I love you. Please remember me with much affection to Charles.

Sr. M. E. of the Trinity r.c.i.

[1] Soon after the birth of Odette, whom she has seen for the first time: "I met [her] Thursday"; she has also seen Mme. Catez "a few days ago" (Wednesday, April 26, cf. L 227, note 5). We again see the required one-month interval before the visits at the end of May, of which L 230 speaks.
[2] Lk 24:29.
[3] Cf. Mt 19:6.
[4] Cf. Eph 1:11; Rom 8:29–30.

L 229   To her mother   [May 1905][1]
         J. M. + J. T.

My dear little Mama,
        Our dear and Reverend Mother has given me a message for you. I'm passing it on with pleasure, for it's always sweet to come to my little Mama, and then, it's a question of appealing to her self-sacrifice, and I know that's inexhaustible. Last year, Our Mother got you interested in a poor family, for whom you found some clothes for the marriage of one of their children. This time, if you could find something at the d'Avouts or Sourdons to set them up for summer and spring, you would be doing a very good work. They are so special and in such need. It's so sad, this hidden poverty; the poor mother suffers from it so much, and our good Mother, whose heart overflows with charity, is so happy to come to her aid…. So I'm counting on you, dear Mama, for it can be said of you just as it's said of God: "Ask and you shall receive,"[2] and I'll be delighted to see dresses and blouses arrive for our dear Mother's dependents. Perhaps Georges would have something for the young men?
        I'm sending Odette a pretty Agnus Dei.[3] Thanks to our good Mother, I have the joy of giving her this present. Give a kiss to the dear little ones for their aunt, and don't forget my Guite! And your heart? Take good care of it…. If I were near you, with what happiness I would *"pamper"* this Mama whom I love so much and whom I commend to God with so much love. It's the month of May…. What sweet memories! Let's unite ourselves close to the Blessed Virgin in the same prayer; I'll ask this divine Mother to give all my tender affection to my darling Mama.
        Remember me to Sister Thérèse.

[1] "It's the month of May" after Odette's birth.
[2] Mt 7:7.
[3] "Agnus Dei": a white wax medallion made with the wax from the Paschal candles from the churches of Rome, imprinted with the head of the Paschal lamb and blessed by the pope.

L 230   To Canon Angles   [June 1, 1905][1]
J.M. + J.T.

Dear Monsieur le Chanoine,

My dear Mama told me you have just been very ill, so I asked leave from our Reverend Mother to come pay you a little visit. Today is the day when the Master returns to His Father, who is our Father,[2] and goes to prepare a place for us[3] in His glorious heritage.[4] I am asking Him to make captive all your captivities[5] and to set you very quickly on your feet again. Tell me if He listens to His Carmelite! We had our last recreation this morning, and we are going into retreat[6] in the Cenacle until Pentecost. I feel I will be even closer to you during these ten days since I will be more in Him. Saint Paul, whose beautiful letters I am studying with much enjoyment, says that "No one knows what is in God except the Spirit of God."[7] The plan of my retreat will therefore be to hold myself by faith and love beneath the "anointing of the Holy One" of whom Saint John speaks,[8] since He is the only one who "penetrates the depths of God."[9] Oh, pray that I will not sadden this Spirit of love[10] but will allow Him to work all the creations of His grace within my soul. Pray too for my dear community and especially for Our Mother and all her intentions; please help me repay my whole debt of gratitude to her. If you only knew what she is to your little child.... At every moment "power from God"[11] flows from her soul into mine. If, on her feast day, June 15th, you could offer her the beautiful bouquet tinged red with the Blood of the Lamb that pleased her so much last year, I can assure you my happiness would be great; I thank you in advance, certain that my desire will be granted if it is possible. How simply I act with you! But are you not the father of my little soul? Everyone is fine, I saw Mama yesterday with her little Sabeth, and last week Guite with her two little angels. I give thanks

for them to Him from whom every perfect gift comes.[12] It is so sweet
to see their happiness! A Dieu, dear Monsieur le Chanoine, bless me
and give me to the Spirit of love and light.

Sr. M. E. of the Trinity r.c.i.

[1] Ascension Day (cf. note 6).
[2] Jn 20:17.
[3] Cf. Jn 14:2–3.
[4] Cf. Eph 1:18.
[5] Cf. Eph 4:8, which cites Psalm 67:19, a verse read that day during the Eucharist before the Gospel. Elizabeth alludes to the Canon's physical ailments.
[6] The annual retreat from the evening of the Ascension (June 1) until Pentecost (June 11); there was no recreation during those days.
[7] 1 Cor 2:11.
[8] 1 Jn 2:20.
[9] 1 Cor 2:10.
[10] Cf. Eph 4:30.
[11] Lk 6:19.
[12] James 1:17.

L 231   To Abbé Chevignard   [the beginning of June 1905][1]
J. M. + J. T.   "Si scires donum Dei."[2]

Monsieur l'Abbé,

God, who "works all things according to the counsel of His
will,"[3] willed the meeting of our souls, as you say, to receive thereby
more love, adoration, and praise. So we must help each other by
prayer, and I cannot tell you how strong is the movement that carries me toward you as you prepare for your first Mass.[4] In fact, I am
on retreat, "hidden with Christ in God,"[5] and I am asking Him
whom Saint Catherine of Siena called her "sweet Truth"[6] to accomplish in your soul the desire that He expressed to His Father in
His supreme prayer: "Sanctify them in the truth.... Your word is
truth...."[7]

Saint Paul says in his Epistle to the Romans that "those whom
He foreknew, God also predestined to be conformed to the image
of His Son."[8] It seems to me you are really the one he speaks of here:
aren't you the predestined one whom the Eternal One has chosen
to be His priest? I believe that in His work of love, the Father is bending over your soul, shaping it with His divine hand, with His deli-

cate touch, so that resemblance to the Divine Ideal may always increase until that great day when the Church will say to you: "Tu es sacerdos in aeternum."[9] Then everything in you will be a copy of Jesus Christ, the High Priest, and you will be able to reproduce Him unceasingly in the sight of His Father and before souls. What grandeur! The "supereminent power of God"[10] is flowing into your soul to transform and divinize it. What recollection, what loving attention[11] to God is called for by this sublime work! Saint John of the Cross says "that the soul must hold itself in silence and absolute solitude so the Most High may accomplish His desires in it; then He carries it like a mother who takes her child in her arms, and, assuming charge of its interior direction Himself, He reigns in it through the abundance of tranquility and peace that He bestows within it."[12]

I congratulate you for having Our Lady of Good Counsel on your vestment. It seems to me it is truly the priestly Virgin whom the priest must invoke and look to always. May she obtain for you the "knowledge of the glory of God shining on the face of Christ"[13] that the Apostle speaks of. Let us beg for this close to her in the silence of prayer.

A Dieu, Monsieur l'Abbé, may He make us *true to His truth*,[14] so that even here on earth we may be the "praise of His glory."[15]

Sr. M. El. of the Trinity r.c.i

[1] She is "on retreat" (cf. L 230, note 6) while Abbé Chevignard is "preparing for his first Mass."

[2] "If you knew the gift of God," Jn 4:10.

[3] Eph 1:11.

[4] June 30, cf. L 232, note 12. At that time the ordination Mass was not usually considered to be the "first Mass."

[5] Col 3:3.

[6] *Dialogue*, 3 and 4 (Cartier trans., Lib. Poussielgue-Rusand, 1855), Vol. 1, pp. 5 and 7. Elizabeth could have read the expression and its source in P. Vallée's 1900 retreat, the 17th instruction on the sacrament of the Eucharist.

[7] Jn 17:17.

[8] Rom 8:29. This is the first time Elizabeth quotes this verse, which will reappear frequently.

[9] "You are a priest forever": Heb 5:6 and 7:17, quoting Ps 109:4.

[10] Eph 1:19.

[11] The expression "loving attention" occurs twice in the *Living Flame* 564–66 [K-RJ 3:33–34]), where St. John of the Cross describes the attitude to be assumed in infused contemplation. See also the following note.

[12] Elizabeth closes the quotes (which she had never opened). She is referring again to the third stanza of the *Living Flame* from which she freely quotes this passage (LF

586 [K-RJ 3:54]): "… having introduced them into this solitude and emptiness … so that he [God] might speak to their hearts, which is what he always desires. Since it is he who now reigns in the soul with an abundance of peace and calm…." The comparison to the child in the arms of God occurs a little farther on in John of the Cross, *Living Flame* 603–4 [K-RJ 3:66].
[13] 2 Cor 4:6.
[14] A Valléen expression. It occurs four times, for example in the last two instructions of P. Vallée's 1900 retreat.
[15] Eph 1:12.

L 232   To Abbé Chevignard   [around June 25, 1905][1]
      J. M. + J. T.   "Sacerdos alter Christus"[2]

Monsieur l'Abbé,

I had asked our Reverend Mother for permission to write and tell you how completely one my soul was with yours during these last days before your ordination; but now that I draw near you, before the great mystery that is being prepared, I can only be silent … and adore the exceeding love of our God!

With the Virgin, you can sing your "Magnificat" and leap with joy in God your Savior, for the Almighty is doing great things in you,[3] and His mercy is eternal….[4] Then, like Mary, "keep all that in your heart,"[5] draw your heart very close to hers, for this priestly Virgin is also the "Mother of Divine Grace,"[6] and in her love she wants to prepare you to become "that faithful priest who is entirely according to God's heart"[7] of whom He speaks in Holy Scripture.

Like that high priest, "without father, without mother, without genealogy, without beginning of days, without end of life, the image of the Son of God," of whom Saint Paul speaks in the Epistle[8] to the Hebrews, you too will become, by this holy anointing, that being who no longer belongs to earth, that mediator between God and souls called to make "the glory of His grace blaze forth,"[9] participating in the "supereminent greatness of His power."[10] When He entered the world, Jesus, the Eternal Priest, said to the Father, "Here I am, O God, to do your will."[11] It seems to me that at this solemn hour when you enter into the priesthood, this ought to be your prayer, too, and I love to make it with you!… On Friday[12] at the holy Altar, when Jesus, the Holy One of God, will for the first time become incarnate in the humble host in your consecrated hands, do not forget the one He led to Carmel so she might be the praise of His glory; ask Him to bury her in the depths of His mystery and to consume her in the fires of His love; then offer her to the Father along with the divine Lamb.

A Dieu, Monsieur l'Abbé, if you knew how I am praying for you. "May the grace of Our Lord Jesus Christ, the love of God and the fellowship of the Holy Spirit be with you."[13]

Sr. Elizabeth of the Trinity r.c.i.

[1] "During these last days before your ordination": June 29, 1905, on the feast of Sts. Peter and Paul, by Bishop Maillet, in the Cathedral of Dijon (RSD, 20, p. 391).
[2] "The priest is another Christ." A maxim popular at that time.
[3] Cf. Lk 1:49.
[4] Cf. Ps 135:1.
[5] Cf. Lk 2:19 and 51.
[6] From the Litany of Loreto.
[7] 1 Sam 2:35.
[8] Heb 7:3. Elizabeth writes "his epistles."
[9] Eph 1:6.
[10] Eph 1:19.
[11] Heb 10:7, quoting Ps 39:8–9.
[12] On Friday, June 30, feast of the Sacred Heart, André Chevignard would celebrate the Eucharist in the Carmelite chapel at 7 A.M., as follows from Mother Germaine's postscript to this letter. Mother Germaine reveals some of the background of Sister Elizabeth's life when she asks the new priest "to consecrate the Carmelites as hosts of the priests."
[13] 2 Cor 13:13.

L 233   To her sister
J. M. + J. T.

[July 3, 1905][1]
Monday evening

My dear little sister,

Your brother-in-law, the Abbé, chose a large-sized vestment, and since he's very thin, the neckline is a little big for him; he mentioned this to our Reverend Mother and, because her sweetest joy is to make others happy, she asked my Sister Marie-Xavier[2] if she couldn't fix it. Charity doubts nothing, it can do all things,[3] and the dear Sister is waiting for the vestment. So if you would have the kindness to ask your mother-in-law to send the vestment, the work could be done during the Abbé's trip so he'll be surprised when he returns. I'm counting on you, my Guite, to get that vestment as soon as possible.

What a fine, beautiful day last Friday was.[4] I've truly been sharing in the shower of graces along with your brother-in-law; I saw him for a few moments, and he told me he would say the Mass for me tomorrow at Notre-Dame-des-Victoires;[5] you can imagine how happy I am, and I am immersing you as well as the little ones into the chalice so you can be bathed in the Blood of the Lamb. A Dieu, little sister, let us remain at the center of our soul, there where He dwells; then it will be a heart-to-heart through all things. Oh! if you knew how He loves you and how, through you, He wants to be loved by your little angels! I'm entrusting my good Angel[6] with a kiss for each one, including their visible angel, who is their little mama, my own little child. Her big Carmelite sister,

Sr. M. E. of the Trinity

Be sure to have Sabeth pray for Tata.[7] Our Reverend Mother has a beautiful little niece[8] who weighs 8 pounds.

[1] The "Monday" after June 30, 1905 (cf. notes 4 and 8).
[2] Her death circular describes her as "very gifted at all artistic works.... Her magical little needle never ceased to enrich her office as sacristan with magnificent vestments...."
[3] An allusion to 1 Cor 13:7.
[4] The day of his first Mass at Carmel (cf. L 232).
[5] In Paris.
[6] Her guardian angel.
[7] Her Carmelite aunt *(tante)*.
[8] Mother Germaine explains in a postscript: "Marie-Chantal. She is eight days old and was baptized on the feast of the Sacred Heart." This refers to Marie-Chantal Favier, born June 26, 1905, in Paris.

L 234   To Abbé Chevignard   [July 21, 1905][1]
         J.M. + J.T.

Monsieur l'Abbé,

Tomorrow is the feast of Saint Mary Magdalene, she of whom Truth said: "She has loved much,"[2] and it is also a feast for my soul, for I celebrate the anniversary of my baptism. And since you are the priest of Love, I am coming to ask you, with our Reverend Mother's permission, to please *consecrate me* to Him tomorrow at Holy Mass. Baptize me in the Blood of the Lamb so that, pure of all that is not Him, I may live only to love with an ever-growing passion,[3] until I reach that happy *unity* to which God has predestined us in His eternal and unchanging will. Thank you, Monsieur l'Abbé, I recollect myself beneath your blessing.

Sr. M. E. of the Trinity r.c.i.

[1] "Tomorrow is the feast of Saint Mary Magdalene" (July 22).

[2] Lk 7:47.

[3] About this time (to judge from the handwriting), Elizabeth writes on the back of a holy card (ACD) representing the Blessed Virgin, "Queen conceived without sin," the following text: "The virgins set apart for love, virgins through love and for love, have only love to satisfy their passion." We do not know if this is a personal thought.

L 235   To her Rolland aunts [August 1, 1905][1]

J. M. + J. T.   Our life is in heaven[2] (Saint Paul).

My good little Aunts,

I know today is the special feast day, and I am coming with the many other guests to pay a little visit to Carlipa. In the silence fitting for a Carmelite, I make my way toward the little church I loved so much, and there, in the chapel you have decorated in its loveliest adornments,[3] I imagine I am right next to you, as I was five years ago, for when you are close to the Tabernacle in which Love incarnate dwells, there is no distance. I'm sorry that Mama, Guite, and her little ones are not with you this summer; those two little darlings would have made you happy. Odette is the best daughter in the world, sweet and quiet like her mother; the parlor visits are so enjoyable when she's along, for she is happy just to look at us with her big eyes without moving. Sabeth is something else; she has to be the center of attention or she is not satisfied. But, on the other hand, when I speak to her about Jesus, she sends Him big kisses that must delight His Heart, for He so loves little ones; she is really very charming, and I believe I have a weakness for her: she is mine!

We celebrated the feast of Saint Martha for our dear white-veil Sisters.[4] In honor of their patron saint, they have a special holiday from their duties so, with Magdalene, they can be occupied in the sweet repose of contemplation; the novices replace them and do the cooking. I am still in the novitiate—we stay there for three years after our profession—and so I spent a whole day at the stove. I didn't go into ecstacy while holding the handle of the frying pan like my holy Mother Teresa, but I believed in the divine presence of the Master who was in the midst of us, and my soul, at its center, adored Him whom Magdalene was able to recognize under the veil of humanity![5] We also sang in honor of our good Sisters. As for me, I tried to profit from the good lessons of my little poet Aunt, and I wrote some verses about love;[6] I tried to stammer something about what it is to love. I do believe this is the knowledge of the saints, and I want to know no other.[6a]

And you, dear Aunts, how are you getting on, how are those eyes I loved to look at so much? With these long, clear days, Aunt Francine must have fewer sacrifices to make in this regard; let us persevere in prayer, for perseverance wounds the Heart of God. And how is Aunt Mathilde doing? My heart often flies to hers. I hope that Aunt[7] doesn't still need all her sedatives and is having entirely good nights. There are so many things I recommend to God, who wanted us to call Him "our Father."[8] On her holy mountain, your little Elizabeth tastes this joy, this love of the children of God, of those who believe in the "love He has had for them,"[9] to use Saint John's expression. A Dieu, my good Aunts. Here it is, the month of August; what memories it brings back to me…. I must say they are among the sweetest, among those engraved so deeply in the depths of my heart that they will never be erased from it; you were so good to me…. So I am asking God to repay my debt of gratitude to you: may He fill you with His sweetest blessings and make your hearts a sanctuary where He may rest and a Heaven on earth. There, beneath the gaze of the Master, I kiss you as I love you.

Sr. M. Elizabeth of the Trinity

Every night before going to sleep, why don't you send me your soul to go to Matins with me? The Divine Office is so good; I love it with a passion.

Hello to Louise and Anne; how are her little ones?

How beautiful the meadow must be.... It seems to me I would pray so well there, as well as on the Serre.

Please remember me to Monsieur le Curé; I count *very much* on his prayer, especially at Holy Mass, and I share with him all my Carmelite life.

[1] "Today is the special feast day" (at Carlipa): the feast of St. Pierre-aux-Liens, the patron of the parish church, August 1. (This feast is now set on the preceding or following Sunday.) "Here it is, the month of August," Elizabeth says. See also note 4. 1905, since it is after Odette's birth.
[2] Phil 3:20.
[3] Cf. L 108, note 4.
[4] July 29th. Cf. L 205, note 2.
[5] An allusion to Lk 10:38–42.
[6] P 94.
[6a] Echoes Eph 3:18–19 and 1 Cor 2:2.
[7] Aunt Catherine, their mother.
[8] Cf. Mt 6:9.
[9] 1 Jn 4:16.

L 236   To her mother   [August 11 or 12, 1905][1]
    J. M. + J. T.

My dear little Mama,

You can guess the joy in my heart when I received your nice long letter. I'm delighted to think of you in the calm and tranquility of that beautiful Switzerland with its magnificent horizons. It's better, you know, to be without Guite and her little angels, for at least you are going to be able to get a complete rest. Marguerite wrote and told me about the concern Sabeth has given her; if you had had her there with you, I'm sure you would really have been worried and your little stay in Sombernon would have been very gloomy. Fortunately she is well now, and I *forbid* you, my darling Mama, to worry as much about the little mother as about the babies. Take good advantage of your stay in Switzerland. Your little nest seems so pretty.... Our Reverend Mother admired the sketch printed on your letter, and as for me, I'm there with you, for you well know that distance is no longer an obstacle between us. How that beautiful nature would transport my soul and move it to thanksgiving to the Creator; to think that He has made all that for us!... Our good Mother, who looks after your Sabeth with a truly maternal heart, insists that I spend time out in the fresh air,[2] so, instead of working in our little cell, I'm settled like a hermit in the most deserted part of our big garden, and I spend delightful hours there. All nature seems so full of God to me: the wind blowing in the tall trees, the little birds singing, the beautiful blue sky, everything speaks to me of Him. Oh! Mama, I want you to know my happiness keeps on growing, it takes on infinite proportions, like God Himself, and it is such a calm, sweet happiness; I would like to share my secret with you! Saint Peter, in his first epistle, says: "Because you *believe,* you will be filled with an unshakable joy."[3] I think the Carmelite actually draws her happiness from this divine source: faith. She believes, as Saint John says, "in the love God has for her."[4] She believes that this same love drew Him to earth ... and into her soul, for He who is called Truth has said in the Gospel "Remain in me, and I in you."[5] Then, quite simply, she obeys this most sweet commandment and lives in intimacy with the God who dwells within her, who is more present to her than she is to herself.[6] All that is not just sentiment or imagination, darling Mama, it is pure faith, and yours is so strong that God could repeat to you what He once said: "O woman, your faith is great."[7] Yes, it was great when you led your Isaac to sacrifice him on the mountain.[8] God has recorded this heroic act carried out by your mother's heart in the great book of life;[8a] I believe your page will be very full and that you can await the day of divine revelation in sweet confidence!

My darling little Mama, Tuesday is your feast day and, although in Carmel it is not the custom to write on such occasions, for we must be sacrificial offerings and the sacrifice of the heart is the greatest sacrifice of all, our good Mother has let me make my letter coincide with this date that is so dear to me. She asks me to offer you her best feastday wishes, for you know she loves you very much. As for me, I don't have to tell you I am sending you all that is most tender in my heart. Do you remember the joy it used to give me to prepare my surprises for this day? I have sacrificed all that on the altar of my heart to Him who is a Spouse of blood.[9] It would be very far from the truth to say this cost me nothing, and sometimes I wonder how I was able to leave so good a Mama. The more one gives to God, the more He too gives Himself; I understand this better every day. So happy feast, my dear Mama; it would make me so happy if the Blessed Virgin would on the day of her Assumption carry away all your cares, present, past, and future, for you worry too much, you know, and your Sabeth can't stand to see a shadow cross your beloved face. *Take good care of yourself* so your stomach can recover completely, and if your stay goes well, you should prolong it; don't let the expense stop you, *think a little more about yourself.* I have some good news from our dear Guite: the little ones are well, she seems happy where she is,[10] don't make her worry. A Dieu, my good Mama, I kiss you as I love you, and that says everything.

Sr. M. E. of the Trinity r.c.i.

Our good Mother of the Heart of Jesus[11] asks me to tell Mademoiselle Surgand that she is still praying fervently for her and hopes her health is better. I am very happy you have these ladies with you. I had a visit from Madame d'Avout with Anne-Marie; yesterday, from Madame Hallo's Marguerite.[12]

Once again, happy feast, I will offer Holy Communion for you, and you can guess how fervent my prayer will be. May the Virgin carry all my tender affection to you; I love you so much, little *Mama.*

Our Reverend Mother gave my letter back to me so I could offer you her most devoted and affectionate wishes; she will pray fervently for you. I received a note from Françoise announcing the death of her grandmother de Sourdon; I'm going to write them.

---

[1] "I've received a note from Françoise ..." (cf. above, the end of the letter). The death certificate indicates that Rose Capelin died on August 10, 1905, at 9:00 P.M., in her house on rue Charrue. Françoise and her mother were not there (cf. L 237 and 238). Françoise's letter could therefore have only been written on August 11 and could only have arrived on the 12th (or on the evening of the 11th). The envelope of L 237, on which Mme. de Sourdon has noted "August 12, 1905," is preserved in the ACD. L 237 and L 238 are two halves of the same sheet.

[2] Her health has changed, which will be confirmed by L 239: on the 13th she is still (assistant) portress, but on the 14th, she must take a "little vacation from the turn ... for a month."

[3] 1 Pt 1:8.

[4] 1 Jn 4:16.

[5] Jn 15:9.

[6] We can recognize the thought of St. Augustine's *Confessions* in this: "Deus intimior intimo meo."

[7] Mt 15:28.
[8] Cf. Gen 22.
[8a] Cf. Rev 21:27. The same expression occurs in L 238.
[9] Cf. Ex 4:26, but Elizabeth probably borrowed the expression from Thérèse of Lisieux (HA 297 [LT 82]).
[10] On vacation; at Sombernon (Côte-d'Or), cf. L 239, note 15.
[11] Mother Marie of the Heart of Jesus, the former Prioress of Dijon. (She will be Prioress again from 1907 to 1913.)
[12] Marguerite Cherillon, who worked for Mme. Hallo, whom she had followed to Paris.

L 237   To Madame de Sourdon   [August (11 or) 12, 1905][1]
       J. M. + J. T.

Very dear Madame,

I see God has marked you with the seal of the predestined and the Cross is often found along your pilgrimage here on earth! For someone in Madame de Sourdon's condition, death is actually more a release, but the circumstances accompanying it were particularly sad, and I can understand, after you lavished so much care and devotion on your mother-in-law, how painful it must have been for you not have been with her at the final hour, when she needed you. Now she sees everything in God's light, and she understands that this sacrifice was the will of the Lord who, at this moment of the divine rendez-vous, wanted in His love to enrich her crown. Dear Madame, I am praying very much for her whom God has called from this world, and I am asking in the name of His mercy that He admit her into His glorious heritage.[2] There, I am confident that her prayer will be all-powerful over the Heart of God for those two dear granddaughters[3] who were her joy and her happiness. Sursum corda, dear Madame, let us lift the veil through faith and rest in those regions of peace and light. Saint Paul says that "we are no longer guests or foreigners, but we belong to the City of saints and the House of God."[4] Yes, He has predestined us for such greatness: "We know that we are God's children now,"[5] said the apostle of love, and "one day we will know Him as we are known."[6] Courage, dear Madame, your little Carmelite is praying and begs you to believe in her wholehearted devotion and respectful but very tender affection.

                 Sr. M. E. of the Trinity r.c.i.

[1] Cf. L 236, note 1.
[2] Cf. Eph 1:18.
[3] Marie-Louise and Françoise.
[4] Eph 2:19.
[5] 1 Jn 3:2.
[6] Cf. 1 Cor 13:12.

L 238   **To Françoise de Sourdon**   [August (11 or) 12, 1905][1]
         J. M. + J. T.

I can understand your grief, my dear Framboise, at not having been present at your poor grandmother's last moments: it is a sacrifice God has recorded in the great book of life. Death is such an unfathomable mystery and, at the same time, such a simple act for the soul that has lived by faith, for those who, according to Saint Paul's words, "have not sought what is visible, for it is passing, but what is invisible, which is eternal."[2] Saint John, whose very pure soul had been wholly illuminated by divine light, gives in very few words what to me is a lovely definition of death: "Jesus, knowing that His hour had come to pass from this world to His Father"....[3] Don't you find that touching in its simplicity?... Darling Framboise, when the *decisive* hour (since we will remain for all eternity in the state in which God finds us and since our degree of grace will be our measure of glory) comes for us too, we need not think that God will come to *meet*[4] us in order to judge us; rather, our soul, once released from our body, will be able to see Him without the veil *within itself,* just as it *possessed Him during its entire life,* but without having been able to contemplate Him face to face; this is entirely true, it is theology. It is very consoling, isn't it, to think that He who is to judge us lives within us all the time to save us from our misery and to pardon us. Saint Paul actually said: "He has justified us as a gift, through faith in His blood."[5] Oh, Framboise, how God has enriched us with His gifts; He has predestined us to divine adoption and thus to be heirs of His glorious heritage![5a] "From all eternity, He chose us in Him that we might be holy in His presence in love,"[6] this is what we are called to be through a "divine decree,"[7] says the great Apostle. A Dieu, my darling. I have offered Holy Communion for your dear grandmother, and if you'd like to join me, I am going to make a novena of Stations of the Cross for her. I leave you without leaving you, for my soul and yours are "knitted"[8] to each other.

I won't forget Marie-Louise's two feast days, the 15th and the 25th.[9] Give her all my love.

[1] Cf. L 236, note 1.
[2] 2 Cor 4:18.
[3] Jn 13:1.
[4] We have italicized this word and put parentheses around a subordinate phrase above to make the text easier to understand. Elizabeth wants to stress that the same eternal God who will judge us is already, *even now, within us.*
[5] Cf. Rom 3:24–25.
[5a] Cf. Eph 1:5 and 1:14, 18.
[6] Eph 1:4.
[7] Eph 1:5.
[8] Cf. L 209, note 5.
[9] August 15th for Marie and August 25th, the feast of St. Louis, for Louise. ·

L 239   To her sister [August 13 (and the following days), 1905][1]
J. M. + J. T.
"He who is united to the Lord
becomes one spirit with Him"[2] (Saint Paul).

My dear little sister,
Today is Sunday,the most blessed of days, because I spend it before the Blessed Sacrament exposed in the oratory, except for the time when I'm at the turn. While carrying out my duties as Portress, I'm coming to have a chat with you in the sight of Him we love. I have taken a large sheet of paper, for when I am with my Guite, there are so many things to say....

First of all, thanks for your nice long letter; you can imagine my joy when I recognized your handwriting, and that joy doubled when I felt how thick it was. I said to myself: "In all that, surely she will speak to me a little bit about her soul," for you know I love it so much when you allow me to enter your Heaven that the Holy Spirit creates in you.

Dear little mama,[3] how worried you must have been about Sabeth! But a beautiful Angel was watching over her, and he was guarding her from all evil for you.[4] I hope she won't cause you any more of that anxiety. We must see all that in the light of God and say "thank you" to Him just the same and always. I know from one of Mama's letters that you are tired, and I beg you to be very wise and *sleep well*, you need that so much. Do you remember how I knew how to take care of you?... I think I've always been a little like a mother with you, and I hope your two angels may be as united as we; it would be impossible for them to be more so, wouldn't it? I have just been reading in Saint Paul some splendid things on the mystery of the divine adoption. Naturally, I thought of you—it would have been quite extraordinary if I hadn't, for you are a mother and know what depths of love God has placed in your heart for your children, so you can grasp the grandeur of this mystery: to be children of God, my Guite, doesn't that thrill you? Listen to what my dear Saint Paul says: "God chose us in Him, before creation. He predestined us to the adoption of children in order to make the glory of His grace blaze forth,"[5] which means that in His omnipotence He seems to have been able to do nothing greater. And then listen again: "If we are children, we are heirs as well."[6] And what is that inheritance? "God has made us worthy of having a share in the inheritance of the saints in light."[7] And then, as if to tell us that this is not off in some distant future, the Apostle adds: "You are therefore no longer guests or strangers, but you belong to the city of saints and the House of God"....[8] And again: "Our life is in Heaven"....[9] Oh! my Guite, this Heaven, this house of our Father, is in "the center of our soul"! As you will see in Saint John of the Cross, when we are in our deepest center, we are in God.[10] Isn't that simple, isn't it consoling? Through everything, in the midst of your cares as a mother, while you give yourself to your little angels, you can withdraw into this solitude to surrender yourself to the Holy Spirit so He can transform you in God and imprint on your soul the Image of the divine Beauty, so the Father, bending over you lovingly, will see only His Christ and say: "This is my beloved daughter, in whom I am well pleased."[11] Oh, little sister, in Heaven I will rejoice to see my most beautiful Christ in your soul; I won't be jealous, but with a mother's pride I will say to Him: It is I, poor wretch, who have brought forth this soul to your life. This is how Saint Paul spoke of his followers,[12] and I am quite presumptuous enough to want to imitate him; what do you think?

Faith

While waiting, "let us believe in love" with Saint John,[13] and, since we possess Him within us, what does it matter if nights obscure our heaven: if Jesus seems to be asleep, oh, let us rest near Him;[14] let us be very calm and silent; let us not wake Him but wait in faith. When Sabeth and Odette are in their dear mama's arms, I doubt if they worry much about whether there is sunshine or rain; let us imitate the dear little ones and live in the arms of God with the same simplicity.

I received a letter from Mama when she arrived. She seems very happy about her stay, but she tells me her stomach is bothering her; I hope she is doing better. You are really going to miss her, but I agree with you that she will rest better there, and I wrote to her that she shouldn't have any second thoughts. And you, my Guite, your big park[15] attracts me; solitude is so good, and I know your dear little soul can appreciate it. Would you like to join me on a month-long retreat until September 14th? Our Mother is giving me this little vacation from the turn; I won't have to talk or think any more, and I am going to bury myself in the depths of my soul, that is, in God. Do you want to follow me in this very simple movement? When you're distracted by your many duties, I will try to compensate; and, if you like, in order to recollect yourself, every hour when you think of it (and if you forget, it doesn't matter), you can enter into the center of your soul where the Divine Guest dwells; you could think of those beautiful words I told you: "Your body is the temple of the Holy Spirit who dwells within you"[16] ... and of those from the Master: "Remain in me, and I in you"....[17] It is said that Saint Catherine of Siena always lived in a cell, even though in the midst of the world:[18] that was because she lived in that inner dwelling place where my Guite too knows how to live! A Dieu, little sister, I can't stop myself, what a journal! I've written it at several sittings, which explains my delay. I'm sending a kiss for all three of you, as I love you. Your big sister and little mother,

Sr. E. of the Trinity r.c.i.

If Georges is nearby, please remember me to him with much affection. My kind regards to your mother-in-law. (My letter is only for the two of us.)

Summer, 1905. Elizabeth's sister Marguerite (Guite) with her husband Georges Chevignard and their daughters Sabeth and Odette.

Did you know Madame de Sourdon, the mother, died?

I am very pleased you love Saint John of the Cross; I was sure you would, for I know *my child.*

[1] "Madame de Sourdon, the mother, has died." "Today is Sunday," therefore August 13. But the long letter, written "at several sittings," admits a "delay." It may not have been sent before August 17 (cf. L 241, postscript).

[2] 1 Cor 6:17.

[3] Guite.

[4] Cf. Ps 90:10–11.

[5] Eph 1:4, 5, 6.

[6] Rom 8:17.

[7] Col 1:12.

[8] Eph 2:19.

[9] Phil 3:20.

[10] Cf. LF 465 [K-RJ 1:12] (st. 1, verse 3). Elizabeth had lent her book to Guite.

[11] Cf. Mt 3:17.

[12] 1 Cor 4:15.

[13] 1 Jn 4:16.

[14] This thought as well as the following are a faithful echo of Thérèse of Lisieux, HA 127 [SS 165] (Ms A, 75v°).

[15] At Sombernon (cf. L 236 and 243), where she was spending her vacation with her two children and other members of the Chevignard family (cf. the end of the letter and L 243). It is also evident from the end of the letter that her husband Georges was staying in Dijon for the most part because of his work but joined her regularly (as in 1903, cf. L 171). The "big park" of about 2 acres (the only one in this town of 700 inhabitants in 1905) and the buildings seen in the photos spoken of in L 243 reveal that this refers to the Château Pétolat, a Dijon family friend of the Chevignards (to-day the "Le Pourpris" estate). From the end of the park there is a magnificent view of the valley called little Switzerland.

[16] 1 Cor 6:19.

[17] Jn 15:4.

[18] This is the advice Catherine herself often gave to Blessed Raymond of Capua, cf. L 89, note 10.

L 240   To her nieces Elizabeth and Odette Chevignard

[around August 15, 1905][1]

J. M. + J. T.

My dear little nieces, my two beautiful, pure, white lilies, whose calixes contain Jesus, if you knew how I pray to Him for you, that His shadow might cover you and guard you from all evil.[2]

To those who gaze on you in your mama's arms you may seem very small, but your little aunt, who looks at you in the light of faith, sees in you a nature of infinite grandeur: for from all eternity you were "in the mind of God; He has predestined you[3] to be conformed to the image of His Son Jesus, and by holy baptism He has clothed you with Himself, thus making you His children, and at the same time His living temple"[4] (Saint Paul). O dear little sanctuaries of Love, when I see the splendor that radiates in you and yet is only the dawn, I fall silent and adore Him who creates such marvels!...

Don't forget to pray every day for your Tata[5] and also for her good Mother Germaine of Jesus.

[1] This letter is preserved in a little envelope that Elizabeth made herself and that carries her manuscript inscription: "Mesdemoiselles Elizabeth and Odette Chevignard." Marguerite has written on the envelope: "August 1905." The same handwriting and ink as L 239, which L 240 must have accompanied.

[2] Cf. Ps 90:4:10.

[3] Elizabeth writes "v^s" (for "vous"). This is the first time she abbreviates this word in her correspondence. She will use more and more abbreviations because of fatigue: "v^s" *(vous* [you]), "n^s" *(nous* [we]), "qqs" *(quelques* [some, a few]), "touj." *(toujours* [always]).

[4] Cf. Rom 8:29; Gal 3:27, 26, and 2 Cor 6:16. We note that Elizabeth was already thoroughly permeated with the doctrine of the New Testament, especially the epistles of St. Paul, but also the last chapters of the Gospel of St. John and his first epistle. She writes on June 1, 1905, to P. Angles: "Saint Paul, whose beautiful letters I am studying with much enjoyment" (L 230). "My dear Saint Paul," she said on August 13th (L 239), adding that he writes "splendid things." Three months later she would say "the great Saint Paul" (L 249), who has "words that are so simple and at the same time so profound" (L 250). He has a "large, great heart" (L 264). In short, his letters are "magnificent" (L 191, 299), he is "the great Saint Paul" (L 304, cf. L 191), "my dear saint" (L 306), "the father of my soul" (S 176). In 1905, Elizabeth made indexes of Saint Paul's letters, demonstrating that she was studying them seriously.

[5] ["Tata," the French equivalent of "Auntie"—TRANS.]

L 241 To Madame de Bobet		[August 17, 1905][1]
     J. M. + J. T.		Dijon Carmel, August 17

My dear Antoinette,

Our Reverend Mother is so kind and sensitive, and she knows the deep affection that unites us; when she delivered your kind letter to me, she told me to write you a little note *at once.* I thank God for giving me the joy of telling you how much *everyone here* will be praying for the dear little blind one so that she who is called the Health of the sick[2] may grant the miracle of opening her eyes to the light. I will be spending the *18th and 19th* at Lourdes, and I will do everything for this intention. Dear Antoinette, my prayer is quite powerless, but I possess within me the Holy One of God,[3] the Great Supplicant, and that is the prayer I am offering for the dear little blind one.

I am asking God to make you well again, my dear Antoinette. He is marking you with the seal of the elect, that of His Cross. Oh! if you knew how He loves you, how at every passing moment He wants to give Himself to you more! I am *praying very much* to Him, that He may carry out fully the dream of His love in you. Since our wonderful parlor visit, it seems to me He has tied the knot of our union, and I can no longer leave you; I hold you in the center of my soul, right where the Divine Guest dwells, and I am exposing you to all the sweet rays of His love, saying to Him: Master, Antoinette is there![4] I am asking Him to imprint Himself on you so you can say with the Apostle: "I live no longer I, but Jesus Christ lives in me"[5] and so you may be His sacrament in which your two dear little daughters may always see Him! A Dieu, may He guard you in the shadow of His wings,[6] may He root you in His love,[7] may your soul be His sanctuary, His resting place on this earth where He is so offended;[8] pray to Him a bit for your little friend who feels her powerlessness to thank Him for His graces. My soul embraces yours, dear Antoinette, in His Heart, without forgetting Simone and Baby.[9]

Sr. M. E. of the Trinity r.c.i.

If you knew how I too would like to have a rosary from you; it will be *our chain* in truth. Thank you. How good you are, and how you spoil me! Your volume of Saint John of the Cross is the whole nourishment of my soul.[10]

Dear friend, I act in all simplicity with you by asking you to help me do an act of poverty by being kind enough to stamp and mail the letter that accompanies mine. *Thank you.*

[1] The style of writing is characteristic of 1905. She will thank her for the rosary received in L 261.
[2] From the Litany of Loreto.
[3] Cf. Mk 1:24.
[4] Cf. Jn 11:28, where Martha informs her sister Mary that Jesus is there. Elizabeth reverses the perspective.
[5] Gal 2:20.

[6] Cf. Ps 90:4.
[7] Cf. Eph 3:17.
[8] Elizabeth undoubtedly feels the weight of the law about the separation of church and state, enacted the preceding month.
[9] Her two children.
[10] It was Antoinette who had given her this gift (cf. L 106).

L 242   To Yvonne de Rostang

[August 18, 1905][1]
Dijon Carmel, August 18

My dear Yvonne,

Today is a date very dear to your heart, and I have chosen it to come to you with the dear departed one; in union with her, I share in the joy of your engagement, and I pray to the God from whom every perfect gift descends,[2] that He may pour out the dew of His graces all along this new path opening before your steps. The Psalmist sang one day, under the inspiraiton of the Holy Spirit: "The Lord will cover you with His shadow and you will hope under the protection of His wings; no evil will come near your dwelling; for He has commanded His Angels to take care of you and to guard you in all your ways."[3] Yes, my dear Yvonne, may they carry you in their hands,[4] while she whose joy and crown you were watches over you. Oh, how intense her prayer must be for her darling daughter, and I love to unite myself with her in drawing down a superabundance of graces on you. If you knew how I live with her, how alive she is for me;[5] it seems to me that death has brought us closer together, because now she lives only in that God in whom alone we live in Carmel! Dear little Yvonne, on the day your mother flew away to Heaven I understood the depths of your grief, and today I am asking God, in the name of that sacrifice, to pour out over you His best graces. Marriage is also a vocation; how many saints have glorified God in it, particularly my dear Saint Elizabeth. I will give you some words from Holy Scripture to help you be equal to your mission: "Look and act according to the model that has been shown to you."[6] Yes, remember your dear mother: self-forgetfulness, self-sacrifice seemed to be her motto; you are truly her daughter, and before leaving this earth she was able to see that you bore her imprint. So, when Mama announced that you were engaged, I said to myself and even said aloud that your fiancé is truly blessed, for I know all the treasures enclosed in the heart of my Yvonne! A Dieu, time and distance will never separate us, will they? Another bond unites us; when you think of your dear departed one you can say to yourself: "Elizabeth is very close to me!" May God grant you a share of happiness as big as mine; may His love be a shadow that accompanies you everywhere and always. I send you a big kiss, and every day my prayer for you goes up to Him who will be our Bond and our Rendez-vous.

Sr. M. Eliz. of the Trinity r.c.i.

Remember me to your father, dear Raoul and each one of your sisters. You can guess how happy I was to have news of you through Mama when she returned from Paris. Do you remember those fine months we spent at Tarbes?[7] Tell your sisters that those sweet family memories remain in my heart.

[1] On August 24, 1905, Yvonne will marry Joseph Tassin de Saint-Péreuse (L 260 is written on the back of their wedding announcement). We still need to find an explanation for why Elizabeth speaks twice, one week before the ceremony, of Yvonne's "engagement." The most probable is the assumption that she did not really understand "when Mama announced" the news to her. In any case, we are in 1905, after the death of Yvonne's mother (cf. L 212), who "flew away to Heaven." This August 18, a "date very dear" (Elizabeth writes "datte") to Yvonne, was Mme. de Rostang's birthday, born in 1855.
[2] James 1:17.
[3] Ps 90:4, 10, 11.
[4] Cf. Ps 90:12.
[5] Before Elizabeth's entrance, Mme. de Rostang and Yvonne, old and dear friends of hers (cf. L 11, 14, 16, 30), had come to see her from Dieppe (cf. L 69). Mme. de Rostang had offered her (and inscribed, but without a date) volume 3 of *Vie et Oeuvres ... de saint Jean de la Croix* [Life and Works ... of Saint John of the Cross], 3d ed. (Paris-Poitiers: Oudin, 1893) (which contains book 3 of the *Ascent of Mount Carmel* and the *Dark Night*). There is nothing to indicate that Elizabeth ever read it.
[6] Ex 25:40.
[7] Cf. L 11 and 14–16.

L 243   To her mother   [September 17(?), 1905][1]
        J. M. + J. T.   Dijon Carmel, Sunday evening

My dear little Mama,

What joy you have given me by sending me these dear photographs![2] Your image is engraved on my heart, but, all the same, I was very happy to see it on paper. The group photograph is charming, and I recognized you with no trouble at all. The little Chevignards are charming; the second is surely Georges's sister. Sabeth looks something like her; she is so sweet and natural with her dolls, and with her hand in her mouth; she has inherited her dear mama's habit! The group picture of the little ones is very charming. Sabeth has a protective little air for Odette that reminds me of her Carmelite aunt, who so loved to play big sister with her little Guite. On seeing how she has filled out, I can hardly believe that this is that thin little girl whose blouses I had to pad; tell her I am very happy to have it. My thanks, too (to Georges),[3] for the last two photographs.

How I thank God knowing you're so well over there. I can't tell you what a joy it is for my heart, for you see I love you more than I do myself, and to feel you are happy is so sweet for me. This little note is also for Guite; tell her I am thinking of her, that my soul is *wholly attached* to hers. God must love her very much to have given her those two little angels; if she knew how I love them, how I pray for them…. You must feel perfectly free to enjoy them and I unite myself to the joys of this dear grandmother. I will never kiss them, for my Master has made me His prisoner, but behind my dear grilles, my prayer will never cease to rise up for these little, wholly pure creatures whom I love with a true mother's heart. We'll be seeing each other soon; I think I'm going to find the little ones changed, for they are growing up before our eyes. While waiting, you are all in our *Manual*;[4] better than that, my darlings, you are in my soul, in that inner sanctuary where I live night and day with Him who is my Friend at every moment. How good it is to live in this sweet intimacy! He knows His little spouse…. He knows how her heart needs to love, and He wants to be that love; in Him I feel so close to you, I know you are very close to me, I envelop you with prayers so that "His Angels may cover you with their wings and guard you all along the path of life," as holy King David sang.[5] A Dieu, darling Mama, a Dieu, my Guite and my two little angels, may He fill you according to the riches of His grace,[6] "may Jesus dwell through faith in your hearts and may you be rooted and grounded in love"…![7] What Saint Paul wished for his followers also breaks forth from my heart for you: no more separation or distance between us, my darlings; I remain with you and embrace you on the Heart of the God who is all Love. He alone knows the depth of my love for you.

Sr. M. E. of the Trinity r.c.i.

Thanks, Mama, for the pretty card; I had no idea that Sombernon was so pretty a spot.

I'm happy Sabeth feels better. Odette is more precocious with those teeth; she's following in the footsteps of her little mama, and I congratulate her. The little group is truly charming. I'm so very proud of *my nieces.*

[1] After her stay in Switzerland, Mme. Catez is again (cf. L 236) at Sombernon, close to Guite and her children. The letter is also for Guite. "We'll be seeing each other soon," writes Elizabeth, a meeting that would occur on October 2 (cf. L 245, note 2). "Soon": this letter written on a "Sunday evening" could well be placed on September 17, after the regular one-month interval since L 236 and 239, after the end of her "month-long retreat until September 14" (L 239). The Sundays of September 10 and 24 seem a little less probable.

[2] According to the description, there were at least six photos. But the two photographs of which the letter speaks in detail have been preserved: Sabeth with her hand in her mouth, and Sabeth leaning against the chair where Odette is sitting.

[3] Who took and developed the photos himself.

[4] They were still there in 1979. Elizabeth used her *Manual* every day.

[5] Cf. Ps 90:4, 11.

[6] Cf. Eph 3:16.

[7] Eph 3:17.

L 244   To Abbé Chevignard
J. M. + J. T.
"Our life is in Heaven." [2]

[October 8, 1905] [1]
Dijon Carmel, October 8

Monsieur l'Abbé,

I am setting out this evening on a long journey, nothing less than my private retreat. For ten days, I am going to be in even more absolute solitude, with several extra hours of prayer and our veil lowered whenever I go about the monastery. So you see, your soul sister is going to lead the life of a hermit in the desert; and before burying herself in her Thebaid, she feels a great need to ask for the help of your good prayers, above all for a special intention at the Holy Sacrifice of the Mass. When you consecrate the host in which

Jesus, "who alone is the Holy One,"[3] is about to become incarnate, would you consecrate me with Him, "as a *sacrifice of praise to His glory*,"[4] so all my aspirations, all my impulses, all my actions may be a homage rendered to His Holiness. "Be holy for I am holy"; these are the words I will keep in mind as I enter into recollection;[5] they are the light in whose rays I am going to walk during my divine journey. Saint Paul provides the explanation and commentary for me when he says: "From all eternity, God chose us in Christ, that we might be immaculate, holy before Him in love."[6] This, then, is the secret of virginal purity: to remain in Love,[7] that is, in God, "Deus Charitas est."[8] So pray fervently for me during these ten days; I am counting on that entirely. I will even say it seems quite simple to me; God has united our souls so we can help each other; hasn't He said that "he who is helped by his brother would be like a fortified city."[9] That is the mission I entrust to you; for my part, I don't say I will pray for you; for that goes without saying, and particularly since *June 30th*[10] my soul is quite simply inclined to it. Would you, Monsieur l'Abbé, offer for me the prayer that rose to God from the great heart of the Apostle for his dear Ephesians: "May the Father, according to the riches of His glory, strengthen you with power through His Spirit, so that Christ might dwell through faith in your heart and so that you might be rooted and grounded in love; that you might comprehend the height, the depth of this mystery, know the love of Christ that surpasses all other knowledge, to be filled according to the fullness of God."[11]

A Dieu, Monsieur l'Abbé, I would be happy to have some details about your new life;[12] you know how interested I am in your ministry. "Let us sanctify Christ in our hearts,"[13] so as to carry out what David sang under the inspiration of the Holy Spirit: "Upon him my sanctification will shine."[14] I enter into recollection, Monsieur l'Abbé, in order to receive through you the blessing of the Holy Trinity.

Sr. M. Elizabeth of the Trinity r.c.i.

---

[1] 1905, because André Chevignard is already a priest. "This evening" Elizabeth's private retreat begins, lasting ten days, from the 9th to the 18th of October (cf. PN 16, her "retreat devotion," where the dates are indicated).
[2] Phil 3:20.
[3] From the Gloria of the Mass.

[4] "Sacrifice of praise": Ps 115:17 and Heb 13:15, but Elizabeth combines it with the expression "praise of glory" (Eph 1:12). Thirteen months before her death, she here formulates explicitly for the first time her ideal of praise within the perspective of holocaust. [Elizabeth uses the word *hostie,* with its multiple sense of victim, host, sacrifice—TRANS.]

[5] Lev 11:44–45 and 19:2. But more probably (cf. note 13), Elizabeth was inspired by 1 Pt 1:16, which cites Lev 11:45. She did not read the Old Testament much except in the liturgy and in the refectory. "These are the words I will keep in mind as I enter into recollection," Elizabeth writes; it is in fact on these words that she bases the "devotion" she composed at the end of her retreat, cf. PN 16.

[6] Eph 1:4.

[7] Cf. Jn 15:9.

[8] 1 Jn 4:16.

[9] Prov 18:19. Elizabeth could have read this verse in Thérèse of Lisieux (HA 176 [SS 236]).

[10] The date of his first Mass at Carmel (cf. L 232, with note 12).

[11] Eph 3:16–19 (with slight adaptations).

[12] André Chevignard had been named Vicar of Meursault (cf. SRD, 20, p. 434).

[13] Cf. 1 Pt 3:15.

[14] Ps 131:18 (v. 19 in her *Manual*).

L 245   To her sister   [October 8, 1905][1]

My dear little sister,

Monday,[2] when you asked me when I was going to make my retreat, I didn't know that God and our Reverend Mother were preparing it for this evening. So I am coming to ask you for Saint John of the Cross[3] for my long journey; I will return it to you afterward, for as long as you like; I am so happy he does you some good.... I'm taking your little soul along with mine. Pray fervently for your Sabeth and be sure to make your angel pray for her little Tata, so she responds fully to the graces of her Master. Let us be holy, little sister, for "He is holy"[4] and so let us never cease to love. I send you all, mama and babies, the very best in my heart.

Thanks for the inkwell.

[1] 1905, for Guite has two children. "Retreat," "this evening": cf. L 244, note 1.

[2] Monday, October 2.

[3] Her book, which she had lent to Guite (cf. L 239, note 10).

[4] Cf. 1 Pt 1:16 (cf. L 244, note 5).

L 246   To Madame de Sourdon   [November 12(?), 1905][1]
     J. M. + J. T.   Carmel, Sunday

Very dear Madame,

I am sure my dear Mama has faithfully delivered my message to you; but that is still not enough for me and, with the permission of our Reverend Mother, I am coming to express my great gratitude for the magnificent engraving[2] you sent me. I so love this mystery, called by one pious author the "descent of love,"[3] and I think it must have been in contemplating this mystery that Saint Paul said: "God has loved us exceedingly."[4]

In the solitude of our little cell, which I call my "little paradise" because it is entirely filled with Him for whom all live in Heaven, I will look very often at this precious picture and will unite myself to the soul of the Virgin at the time when the Father was overshadowing her, while the Word was becoming incarnate within her, and the Holy Spirit was coming upon her[5] to bring about the great mystery. It is the whole Trinity in action, surrendering themselves, giving themselves; and the life of the Carmelite must be lived within this divine embrace.... You can tell, dear Madame, how appropriate your dear engraving is for our cell, and I can assure you it is *doubly precious* to me coming from you!...

If you knew how I am praying for *our intention*.[6] I am interesting the Blessed Virgin in our cause so we will be certain of victory. The Gospel says "there was a marriage at Cana and the Mother of Jesus was there,"[7] and this was the occasion when Our Lord performed His first miracle at the request of the Virgin: this is recounted to show us how interested God is in all our needs, even the most material ones. So let us have confidence in His love! A Dieu, dear Madame, and thanks again. Please remember me respectfully to Madame d'Anthès and tell her that her requests have been made to the One who is All-Powerful. Don't forget to greet Marie-Louise and Framboise for me, and know that you have my deep and respectful affection.

Sr. Eliz. of the Trinity r.c.i.

[1] The gift spoken of in the letter (the handwriting suggests the period) fits in well with Elizabeth's feast day, Sunday, November 19. The envelope, which has been pre-

served (and could only belong to this letter), is dated "November 12, 1905," written by Mme. de Sourdon. She would have "sent" the gift several days before the feast day (she was probably away on a trip, and seems to be, along with her daughters, at the home of her mother, Mme. d'Anthès).

² "Magnificent" according to the taste of that era, this engraving depicts the Annunciation. Elizabeth would hang it on the wall over the head of her bed. In the spring of 1906, she was photographed in bed in the infirmary with this engraving behind her. In the context of PN 15 (cf. note 26), it is understandable that this mystery had great meaning for her.

³ We do not know which "pious author" Elizabeth refers to here.

⁴ Eph 2:4.

⁵ "Overshadowing," "coming upon": cf. Lk 1:35.

⁶ The marriage of Marie-Louise; hence the allusion to the wedding at Cana.

⁷ Jn 2:1.

L 247   To Marie-Louise de Sourdon   [November 18, 1905]¹
J. M. + J. T.   Saturday evening

My dear Marie-Louise,

I am coming to give you an award for your talents at making candy² and my thanks for the beautiful box you sent me; it is so pretty to look at that it's really a shame to touch it. Our Reverend Mother has already let me sample your good chocolates, which will be served with solemnity in the refectory, and I am asking our holy Mother Teresa, whose great soul was so filled with gratitude, for very special protection and *urgent help* for the kind confectioner who is spoiling her daughters in Carmel like this. Although, in our deep solitude, we can say with Saint Paul: "Our life is in Heaven," ³ we are still interested in those on earth, and you know what a large share you have in the prayers of your Carmelite friend. I hope God will grant them and that, as a feastday bouquet, He will obtain for me, through the intercession of my dear saint, a *grace* that you can guess and that, in union with your dear mother, I am asking for you.⁴

A Dieu, my dear Marie-Louise, "may He overshadow you with His wings, may His Angels guard you in all your ways." ⁵ I am asking Him on my holy mountain; from there I send you a warm thank you and the best of my heart. Your old friend,

                                                    Eliz. of the Trinity r.c.i.

¹ L 246 and 247 are written out on a new kind of writing paper, light but solid and ruled in small rectangles, which we will encounter often in the following months. The

handwriting indicates 1905. The content confirms the date: Marie-Louise (away on a trip, cf. L 246, note 1) had sent Elizabeth some chocolates for her feast day. Elizabeth thanks her on "Saturday evening," November 18; the chocolates "will be" served the next day; she will ask St. Elizabeth of Hungary ("my dear saint") as a "feastday bouquet" for a grace for Marie-Louise. The allusion to St. Teresa, whose feast was celebrated on the same Sunday that year, does not indicate a chronological error; Elizabeth was in her long retreat at that time (cf. L 244, note 1) and would not have written for that reason.

[2] There are similar compliments in L 272.
[3] Phil 3:20.
[4] Cf. L 246, note 6.
[5] Ps 90:4, 11.

L 248   To Sister Marie of the Trinity   [November 24, 1905][1]

Charitas numquam excidit!...[2]
November 24, 1905

[1] This was the feast of St. John of the Cross. The thought is written on the back of a holy card representing the saint, with one of his maxims printed on it: "In the evening of life, we shall be examined in love." Elizabeth gave the holy card to Marie of the Trinity (PO 135).
[2] "Love never ends": 1 Cor 13:8 (trans. from the *Manual*).

L 249   To Madame Angles   [November 26(?), 1905][1]
J. M. + J. T.   God alone suffices.[2]

Madame and very dear sister,

I was very touched by your feastday greetings, and thank you for the prayers you are offering for your little friend in Carmel. For her part, I assure you she remembers you very faithfully in Him who is our indissoluble bond. If you knew how attached my soul is to yours, I would even say how "ambitious" I am for it! I would like it to be wholly surrendered, wholly adhering to that God who loves it with so great a love! Yes, dear Madame, I believe that the secret of peace and happiness is to forget oneself, not be preoccupied with oneself. That doesn't mean not feeling one's physical or mental sufferings; the saints themselves passed through these crucifying states. But they did not dwell on them; they continually left these things behind them; when they felt themselves affected by them, they were not surprised, for they knew "they were but dust,"[3] as the Psalmist sings; but he also adds: "With God's help, I will be unblemished, and I will guard myself from the depths of sinfulness within me."[4] Dear Madame, since you allow me to speak to you like a beloved sister, it seems to me that God is asking you for abandonment and unlimited trust during the painful times when you feel those terrible voids. Believe that at those times He is hollowing out in your soul greater capacities to receive Him, capacities that are, in a way, as infinite as He Himself. Try then to will to be wholly joyful under the hand that crucifies you; I would even say that you should look at each suffering, each trial, "as a proof of love" that comes to you directly from God in order to unite you to Him.

Forgetting yourself with respect to your health does not mean neglecting to take care of yourself, for that is your duty and the best of penances, but do it with great abandonment, saying "thank you" to God no matter what happens. When your soul is burdened and fatigued by the weight of your body, do not be discouraged, rather go by faith and love to Him who said: "Come to me and I will refresh you."[5] As for your spirit, never let yourself be depressed by the thought of your sufferings. The great Saint Paul says: "Where sin abounds, grace abounds all the more."[6] It seems to me the weakest, even the guiltiest, soul is the one that has the most reason for hope; and the act of forgetting self and throwing oneself into the arms of God glorifies Him and gives Him more joy than all the turning inward and all the self-examinations that make one live with one's own infirmities, though the soul possesses at its very center a Savior who wants at every moment to purify it.

Do you remember that beautiful passage where Jesus says to His Father "that He has given Him power over all flesh so that He might give eternal life to it"?[7] That is what He wants to do in you: at every moment, He wants you to go out of yourself, to leave all preoccupations, in order to withdraw into the solitude He has chosen for Himself in the depths of your heart. *He* is always there, although you don't feel it; He is waiting for you and wants to establish a "wonderful communion"[8] with you, as we sing in the beautiful liturgy, an intimacy between bride and Bridegroom; He, through this continual contact, can deliver you from your weaknesses, your faults, from all that troubles you. Didn't He say: "I have come not to judge but to save."[9] *Nothing* should keep you from going to Him. Don't pay too much attention to whether you are fervent or discouraged; it is the law of our exile to pass from one state to the other like that. Believe that *He* never changes, that in His goodness He is always bending over you to carry you away and keep you safe in Him. If, despite everything, emptiness and sadness overwhelm you, unite this agony with that of the Master in the Garden of Olives, when He said to the Father: "If it is possible, let this cup pass me by."[10] Dear Madame, it may perhaps seem difficult to forget yourself. Do not worry about it; if you knew how simple it is…. I am going to give you my "secret": think about this God who dwells within you, whose temple you are;[11] Saint Paul speaks like this and we can believe him. Little by little, the soul gets used to living in His sweet company, it understands that it is carrying within it a little Heaven where the God of love has fixed His home. Then it is as if it breathes a divine atmosphere; I would even say that only its body still lives on earth, while the soul lives beyond the clouds and veils, in Him who is the Unchanging One. Do not say that this is not for you, that you are too wretched; on the contrary, that is only one more reason for going to Him who saves. We will be purified, not by looking at this wretchedness, but by looking at Him who is all purity and holiness. Saint Paul says that "He has predestined us to be conformed to His image."[12] In the saddest times, think that the divine artist is using a chisel[13] to make His work more beautiful, and remain at peace beneath the hand that is working on you. This great apostle I speak of, after being carried off to the third Heaven,[14] felt his infirmity and complained about it to God, who answered: "My grace is enough for you, for power is made perfect in weakness."[15] That is very consoling, isn't it?…

So, courage, Madame and dear sister, I am entrusting you very especially to a little Carmelite named Thérèse of the Child Jesus, who died at the age of twenty-two[16] in the odor of sanctity. Before her death, she said she would spend her heaven doing good on earth;[17] her grace is to expand souls, to launch them on the waves of love, confidence, and abandonment.[18] She said she found happiness

<u>when she began to forget herself.</u>[19] Will you invoke her every day with me, so she can obtain for you the knowledge that makes saints and gives the soul so much peace and happiness!

A Dieu, dear Madame; since this is the last week before the solitude of Advent, I will be seeing Mama, Marguerite, and her little family; I won't fail to offer them your regards. My little nieces are very cute and give much happiness to their dear grandmother. Marie-Louise's babies must be as much of a joy for you. Please tell Marie-Louise I'm praying for her and haven't forgotten the nice reunion at Labastide.[20] Please remember me to Madame Maurel, too. As for you, dear Madame, you may trust in my deep affection and my union in Him of whom Saint John says: "He is Love."[21]

Your little Sister and friend,

M. Elizabeth of the Trinity r.c.i.

[1] "Since this is the last week before the solitude of Advent, I will be seeing...." The letter seems to have been written on Sunday, November 26 (in any case at the beginning of that week). Advent began on December 3. The year is 1905, because Guite has two children.

[2] Teresa of Avila. Cf. *Diary*, note 87.

[3] Cf. Ps 102:14.

[4] Ps 17:23 (17:26 in the *Manual*).

[5] Mt 11:28.

[6] Rom 5:20.

[7] Jn 17:2.

[8] First antiphon from First Vespers of the feast of the Circumcision (January 1).

[9] Jn 12:47.

[10] Mt 26:39.

[11] Cf. 1 Cor 3:16.

[12] Rom 8:29.

[13] Recent readings of John of the Cross had perhaps sharpened Elizabeth's conviction of the necessity of suffering. The image of the artist who puts the finishing touches on a statue with a chisel is perhaps borrowed from LF 590 [K-RJ 3:57], although this text does not refer directly to God.

[14] Cf. 2 Cor 12:2.

[15] 2 Cor 12:9.

[16] Thérèse was actually 24 years and 9 months old at the time of her death.

[17] Cf. HA 235 [LC, p. 102].

[18] Cf. HA 131 [SS 174]. Elizabeth had already quoted this sentence for Mme. Angles in L 224.

[19] Cf. HA 73 [SS 99].

[20] In 1900, cf. L 32–33.

[21] 1 Jn 4:16.

L 250   To Abbé Chevignard   [around November 29, 1905][1]
J. M. + J. T.

Monsieur l'Abbé,

A few minutes ago I was reading[2] in Saint Paul these words that are so simple and at the same time so profound: "Nostra autem conversatio in coelis est [but our conversation is in heaven],"[3] and I was thinking that my soul should go precisely there to meet yours!... Don't you experience daily the truth of this thought: "You are no longer guests or strangers, but you already belong to the City of saints and the House of God."[4] But to live beyond the veil like that, how necessary it is to be closed to everything below! The Master is urging me to *detach*[5] myself from all that is not Him—that word says so many things to me—and that is how I am preparing for the feast of the Immaculate One, the anniversary of my clothing. May I ask you for a very special intention that day, so that Christ, through the outpouring of His Blood, may clothe me with the purity, the virginity that allows the soul to be irradiated with the very light of God. The holy time of Advent is here; it seems to me that it is very especially the season of interior souls, those who live unceasingly and through everything wholly "hidden with Christ in God"[6] at the center of themselves. In expectation of the great mystery, I love to go deeply into that beautiful psalm XVIII, which we often say at Matins, and particularly these verses: "There he has placed his tent in the sun, and this star comes forth like a bridegroom coming from his bed, rejoices like a champion to run its course. At the end of the sky is the rising of the sun; to the furthest end of the sky is its course; nothing is *concealed* from its burning heat."[7] Let us empty our soul so He can come forth in it and communicate the eternal life[8] that is its own; the Father has given Him "power over all flesh"[9] for that purpose, as we are told in the Gospel. And then, in the silence of prayer, let us listen to Him, for He is the "Source"[10] who speaks within us and who has said: "He who sent me is true, and I tell all I have heard from Him."[11] Let us ask Him to make us true in our love, to make us sacrificial beings, for it seems to me that sacrifice is only love put into action: "He loved me, He gave Himself for me."[12] I love this thought, that the life of the priest (and of the Carmelite) is an Advent that prepares for the Incarnation in souls. In one psalm,

David sings that "fire goes before the Lord."[13] Isn't fire love? And isn't our mission also to prepare the way of the Lord through our union with Him whom the Apostle calls a "consuming fire"?[14] At His touch our soul will become like a flame of love spreading into all the members of the body of Christ, the Church;[14a] then we will console the Heart of our Master, who, showing us to the Father, will be able to say: "I am already glorified in them."[15] Help me, Monsieur l'Abbé, I have great need of it, for the more light there is, the more I feel my powerlessness. On December 8th (since you are a high priest), would you consecrate me to the *power of His love* so I may in truth be "Laudem Gloriae";[16] I read that in Saint Paul and I understood that it was my vocation[17] even now in exile while awaiting the eternal Sanctus.[18]

A Dieu, Monsieur l'Abbé, I have not forgotten that I am the vicar of the Vicar of Meursault,[19] which should tell you how much I am praying for him. Please bless me and make the light of the Father, of the Word, and of the Spirit descend into my soul. As for you, may the anointing you received from the Holy One[20] remain in you and teach you all things.

Sr. M.E. of the Trinity r.c.i.

---

[1] 1905: cf. note 19. "The holy time of Advent is here": written a little before December 3, the beginning of Advent, this letter probably dates from the 29th of November, so as to arrive on the 30th, Abbé Chevignard's feast day.

[2] On her assiduous reading of St. Paul, cf. L 240, note 4.

[3] Phil 3:20.

[4] Eph 2:19.

[5] We are missing the autograph copy of this letter. The copy in Notebook 6 (ACD) underlines the word *detach.* "This word [which] says so many things [to her]" has the same resonance with Elizabeth as in John of the Cross: cf. L 220, note 4.

[6] Col 3:3.

[7] Ps 18:5–7.

[8] Cf. Jn 17:2.

[9] Jn 17:2.

[10] Jn 8:25.

[11] Jn 8:26.

[12] Gal 2:20.

[13] Ps 96:3.

[14] Heb 12:29, repeating Dt 4:24.

[14a] Cf. Col 1:24.

[15] Jn 17:10.

[16] "Praise of Glory": Eph 1:12. This is the first time Elizabeth quotes the *Latin* expression (cf. AL); a little later she will say that it is her name (cf. L 260). In using this

name, Elizabeth should have used the nominative instead of the accusative from the Vulgate: *"Laus* Gloriae". Cf. the pious reflection of P. Vergne in S 115: "Happy the souls who have only grammatical errors to regret."

[17] Elizabeth describes the same "vocation" in L 256. This shows a deeper understanding of an ideal that is no longer new: she has been saying "let us be" this praise of glory for 22 months (cf. L 191 and also L 220). Someone seems even to have proposed this ideal to her before she entered Carmel (cf. P 121, note 1). The word "vocation" may indicate an internal link with Thérèse of Lisieux, who found her own in love (cf. HA 208 [SS 194]; Ms B, 3v°). *Praise* is only an accent of Elizabeth's within the same vocation of *love,* the Thérèsian expression she quotes repeatedly and makes her own in 1906.

[18] Cf. Rev 4:8. Also in L 256, 307, 331 and HF 43; cf. LR 20.

[19] Cf. L 244, note 12. Elizabeth is the "vicar" of the priest (as in L 209) through prayer and the gift of self.

[20] Cf. 1 Jn 2:20.

L 251   To Françoise de Sourdon   [December 28, 1905][1]

My dear little Framboise,

Today, in honor of the Holy Innocents, is a feast for the novices[2] in Carmel. Tonight at recreation we are going to act out the martyrdom of Saint Cecilia, and since we have no instrument for the celestial melodies, I would be very grateful to you if you could lend me your little Swiss music box; I think it would do perfectly. In case you're not there to give it to the extern Sister,[3] would you have the great kindness to have it brought to us around 6 or 6:30? Thanks in advance, my Framboise; you see how simply I behave with you. I kiss you as I love you.

Sr. E. of the Trinity r.c.i.

We are praying fervently for Madame de Maizières.[4]

[1] The feast of the Holy Innocents. The year is 1905; although the copper-colored ink is unusual for this time (and thus drawn from another inkwell), the style of writing on this note as well as that on the extant fragments of the pious recreation on "the martyrdom of Saint Cecilia" (cf. Vol. III) leave no doubt as to the period.

[2] Along with Elizabeth, who was still in the novitiate because she had not completed the three years following her profession, there were at this time at least two young ones in the novitiate: Sister Marie-Joseph (a lay sister, cf. L 327, note 5) and Sister Thérèse of Jesus (cf. L 255, note 1), who had entered thirteen days before. And probably Clémence Blanc as well (cf. L 293, note 1).

[3] Who would come to get the instrument.

[4] Her sick aunt (cf. L 257, note 2).

L 252   To Germaine de Gemeaux   [end of December, 1905][1]
J. M. + J. T.
"Our life is hidden with Christ in God."[2]

My dear Germaine,

My heart has had a large share in the sorrow with which your family has just been afflicted, and I beg you please to pass this on to your dear mother at this painful time; I am praying for your dear deceased so "that God who is rich in mercy may lead him as soon as possible into the inheritance of the saints in light."[3] I also pray for those who remain behind, for they have the sad part. Yes, my little Germaine, life is a succession of sufferings, and I believe the happy ones of this world are those who have chosen the Cross as their share and their inheritance, out of love for Him of whom Saint Paul has said: "He loved me, He gave Himself for me."[4] It seems to me that the whole doctrine of love, which is true and strong, is contained in those few words. Our Lord, during His mortal life, said: "Because I love my Father, I always do what pleases Him";[5] and He adds, "He has not left me alone, He is always with me."[6] Germaine, let us, too, tell Him of our love through all our actions by always doing what pleases Him, and He will not leave us alone, but will remain at the center of our soul in order to be Himself our fidelity; by ourselves we are only nothingness and sin, but He, He alone is Holy,[7] and He dwells in us to save us, to purify us, and transform us in Himself. Do you remember that beautiful challenge made by the Apostle: "Who will separate me from the love of Christ?"[8] Ah! since he had sounded the Heart of his Master, he knew what treasures of mercy were contained there, and in a burst of trust, he cried out: "I boast of my infirmities, for when I am weak, the power of Jesus Christ dwells in me."[9] Always love prayer, dear little Germaine, and when I say prayer, I don't mean so much imposing on yourself a lot of vocal prayers to be recited every day as that elevation of the soul toward God through all things that establishes us in a kind of continual communion with the Holy Trinity by quite simply doing everything in Their presence. I think you still have as much devotion to this great Mystery, and if you would like, my dear little friend, this will be the Rendez-vous of our souls; we will enter into the most interior part of ourselves, where the Father, Son, and Holy Spirit dwell, and in Them we will be *wholly one.* I will make a very special rendez-vous with you at 5 o'clock in the evening, during our prayer, if you would like? I won't speak to you of my happiness, despite the joy I would have to see you share it some day, for I do not want to influence your dear little soul, and, besides, our vocation is so beautiful, so divine, God alone can give it: "It is not we who have chosen Him, but He who has chosen us."[10] I am asking Him to make you always more His; since, according to the words of Saint Paul, "He dwells in your heart through faith so you might be rooted in His love."[11] Then nothing will be able to separate you from Him, His little Germaine will be the joy of His heart, her soul will become a little Heaven where God, whom some want to banish, will come to find His refuge, to console Himself; she will be the joy of her dear parents, for a soul united to Jesus is a living smile that radiates Him and gives Him!

A Dieu, my very dear Germaine, I love you like a sister, and Yvonne, too, has a large share in my heart. I am united with you and your dear mama, for whom I have a very special affection, please tell her; I give all three of you a big kiss. Please remember me to Monsieur de Gemeaux; I can still hear his beautiful voice; I so loved our long music sessions;[12] I'm sure you have made a lot of progress since I entered Carmel!

Your big and *true* friend and sister,

M. Elizabeth of the Trinity r.c.i.

Please remember me to Mademoiselle Pauline, if she is with you.

---

[1] Condolences after the death of a "dear deceased" on Germaine's mother's side of the family. This was Mme. de Gemeaux's brother, Jean-François-Paul Pinet des Ecots, who died on December 26, 1905, at La Machine.
[2] Col 3:3.
[3] Cf. Eph 2:4 and Col 1:12.
[4] Gal 2:20.
[5] Cf. Jn 8:29.
[6] Ibid.
[7] From the Gloria of the Mass.
[8] Rom 8:35.
[9] Cf. 2 Cor 12:9 and 10.
[10] Cf. Jn 15:16.

[11] Eph 3:17.
[12] In 1893, Elizabeth spent two weeks with the Gemeaux and often went to the chateau to play the piano (cf. L 6). Elizabeth's photograph was taken at the piano there; she had just won her first prize at the Conservatory. She was also regularly at the chateau for the Corpus Christi procession (cf. the testimony of Germaine de Gemeaux on February 22, 1907, in PAT).

L 253   To Sister Louise de Gonzague

[August 1905–March 1906][1]

+

I have not done the work I expected to and, since I will be getting up late tomorrow[2] and will have to make up my prayer and Office, don't come to prepare the lower part for me.[3] I will be able to try it on, and if I can't, I will let you know in the evening. Thanks, dear Habit Sister; I am taking advantage of you....

[1] In pencil. Sister Louise was the Sister in charge (the "Habit Sister," or "Officer," as Elizabeth called her) of the habit room. Elizabeth was not yet in the infirmary but was already getting weaker.
[2] For Mass at 8 o'clock.
[3] The lower part of the habit to be mended.

L 254   To Sister Louise de Gonzague   [August 1905–March 1906][1]

Sr. Louise de Gonzague. Before Mass. *In a hurry.*

+

My dear sister,

I'm a little confused as to where to place the patch[2] you just gave me. I left the two sides unsewn until I could be more sure, and I would be very grateful if you could come by after Mass. Please come in and mark the place, and then look at what I've devised for the front,[3] which was too tight. If you don't like the idea, give me a better one. You will find pencil and paper on the table in case you have some explanation to give your little assistant, who loves you and prays for you.

[1] Like L 253, a message about work, written in haste on a scrap of very poor paper. The same handwriting in pencil.
[2] On the habit being mended.
[3] The "front" of the habit.

L 255   To Sister Thérèse of Jesus [December 1905–March 1906][1]

"May He live and give me His life! May He reign, and may I be His captive! My soul no longer wants any other liberty!"[2]

Sister Elizabeth of the Trinity to her dear little Sister Thérèse of Jesus, with the permission of our Reverend Mother.

[1] Sister Thérèse of Jesus (this was her name as a postulant) stayed "nine months in the Carmel of Dijon, from December 15, 1905, to September 1906" (cf. PA 860). Then she went to the Carmel of Bordeaux (then in exile at Zarauz in Spain; later transferred to Saint-Sever); she received the habit with the name Sister Elizabeth of the Trinity. She recalled: "I remember that one day I had been captivated at recreation by this exclamation of our Mother St. Teresa [the quotation from L 255 follows]. In the evening, when going to bed, I found on our bed a very simple holy card of our Mother St. Teresa with the Child Jesus. Beneath was written the passage I so loved, with a little note at the side (text of L 255). I have kept this holy card a very long time! I had been so touched by this delicate attention" (cf. PA 860). Elizabeth was thus not yet in the infirmary.

[2] Teresa of Avila, *Le Livre des exclamations,* excl. 17 (Bouix trans., vol: 2, p. 609 [cf. K-RT vol. 1, p. 462: Soliloquies 17:3]).

L 256   To Canon Angles   [end of December 1905][1]
       J. M. + J. T.   "Instaurare omnia in Christo."[2]

Dear Monsieur le Chanoine,

I believe I can truly say to you that remark made by the Apostle: "Our conversation is in Heaven,"[3] for it has been a very long time since I have communicated otherwise with you; but if the holy Rule of Carmel imposes silence on my pen, I can assure you my soul and my heart are not prevented from going to you; they often break enclosure ... but I think the Master forgives me, for it is with Him ... *in Him* ... that the journey is made! Our Reverend and very dear Mother is granting me the joy of coming to offer you my very best wishes on the occasion of this new year that will soon begin. We will have the Blessed Sacrament exposed inside our dear oratory on January lst; I will spend the day there, and there your little Carmelite will confide her wishes for you. Pray for her also, that this year may be full of fidelity and love,[4] I would so like to console my Master by remaining constantly united with Him. I am going to tell you a very personal secret: my dream is to be "the praise of His glory,"[5] I read that in Saint Paul and my Bridegroom made me understand that this was to be my vocation while in exile, waiting to go sing the eternal Sanctus in the City of the saints. But that requires great fidelity, for in order to be a praise of glory, one must be dead to all that is not He, so as to be moved only by His touch, and the worthless Elizabeth does such foolish things to her Master; but like a tender Father, He forgives her, His divine glance purifies her[6] and, like Saint Paul, she tries "to forget what lies behind and press on toward what is ahead."[7] How we feel the need to be sanctified, to forget ourselves in order to belong wholly to the interests of the Church.... Poor France![8] I love to cover her with the blood of the Just One, "of Him who is always living to intercede and to ask mercy."[9] What a sublime mission the Carmelite has; she is to be mediatrix with Jesus Christ, to be another humanity for Him[10] in which He can perpetuate His life of reparation, sacrifice, praise, and adoration. Oh, ask Him that I may be equal to my vocation and not abuse the graces He lavishes on me; if you knew how fearful that makes me sometimes....[11] Then I cast myself on Him whom Saint John calls "the Faithful and True,"[12] and I beg Him to be Himself my fidelity![13]

I have seen my dear Mama, Guite, and little Sabeth; Odette was not feeling well because of her vaccination, so they did not bring her to me at all. How I thank God for all the happiness He is sowing in that little family.... It is so good to share those joys and then say to yourself: "And I, I am His and He is mine."[14] As I went back up to our cell Christmas night to get a little rest after Mass, what sweet joy inundated my soul when, thinking of those sweet memories of the past, I said to myself like the Apostle: "For love of Him I have forfeited everything"![15] Ask Him that I might lose myself in order to bury myself in Him. The Sunday of Epiphany will be the third anniversary of my nuptials with the Lamb; at Mass, when you consecrate the host in which Jesus becomes incarnate, would you also consecrate your little child to *All-Powerful Love,* so that He may transform her "into a praise of glory." It does me so much good to think that I am going to be given, surrendered, through you!...

A Dieu, dear Monsieur le Chanoine, with all my best wishes,

please be assured of my respect and affection. I beg your fatherly blessing.

Sr. M. Elizabeth of the Trinity r.c.i

Our good and Reverend Mother has asked to be remembered to you; I think that if you knew her, your soul would be at home with hers.

---

[1] 1905: Guite has two children. The end of December, because Elizabeth refers to "this year that will soon begin."

[2] "To restore all things in Christ": Eph 1:10 (trans. from the *Manual*). It was the theme of the first encyclical of Pius X (cf. P 89, note 1).

[3] Phil 3:20.

[4] This will be the year of her death.

[5] Eph 1:12.

[6] Cf. the "Act of Oblation" of Thérèse of Lisieux: "If through weakness I sometimes fall, may your Divine Glance cleanse my soul immediately."

[7] Phil 3:13.

[8] The law of separation, passed in July 1905, was promulgated on December 9 by the President of the Republic and published in the *Official Record* on December 11. A decree of public administration concerning the inventories of church property was published on December 29.

[9] Cf. Heb 7:25, with an echo of Heb 4:16.

[10] Cf. PN 15.

[11] Cf. AL on her feelings of weakness and unworthiness during this period.

[12] Rev 19:11.

[13] We can see her recourse to the attitude of Thérèse of Lisieux with respect to her weakness, already expressed in [Elizabeth's] PN 4, 5, 15, but experienced with greater intensity.

[14] Reminiscent of Song 2:16.

[15] Phil 3:8.

L 257　　To Madame d'Anthès

[around the beginning of January 1906][1]

J. M. + J. T.

Very dear Madame,

Our good and Reverend Mother anticipated my desire by telling me to write to your dear patient,[2] and I am entrusting this little note to you so it will reach her through one of your letters. The letter you were kind enough to forward to me truly grieved me deeply, and I thought of the sword of sorrow that must have pierced[3] your motherly heart at this distressing account. But, dear Madame, faith tells us to ascend higher, to God, "who works all things according to the council of His will,"[4] as the Apostle Saint Paul tells us, and this will, at times so crucifying, never ceases to be all love, since love is the very essence of God. Saint John defines Him that way: "Deus Charitas est."[5]

I join my feeble prayer to yours, dear Madame, or rather, I offer the prayer that Christ, the great Adorer who lives in our souls, Himself makes within us. United to Him, we can be all-powerful. Oh, let us repeat that prayer of Mary Magdalene: "Lord, the one you love is sick."[6] Didn't she obtain a miracle in her naive and touching confidence? Courage, dear Madame, let us redouble our prayers in the peace and abandonment of the children of God; please remember me to my dear Madame de Sourdon, and also to my two beloved little friends, and keep for yourself, dear Madame, the assurance of my deep respect and affection.

Sr. E. of the Trinity r.c.i.

---

[1] The handwriting is a good justification for this approximate date. This is confirmed by note 2 and Mme. de Sourdon's information on the autograph copy: "January 1906."
[2] Her daughter, Mme. de Maizières, who was ill in Paris and would die within eight months after a "cruel martyrdom" (L 312). L 251 has already alluded to this illness.
[3] Cf. Lk 2:35.
[4] Eph 1:11.
[5] 1 Jn 4:16.
[6] Cf. Jn 11:3.

L 258   To her Rolland aunts   [beginning of January 1906][1]
         J. M. + J. T.

My dear little Aunts,

It has been a sacrifice thinking that my best wishes would not reach you until after the 1st of January, but I've not been able to find a moment since Christmas to put them down on this paper; fortunately I have made up for it close to the divine Master, and I hope He has Himself brought into the innermost secrecy of your hearts all that His little bride confided to His Love for her dear Aunts, who always have such a big part in her affection. I saw Mama recently and we spoke of you, of course; Guite also came, and if you knew how cute the little ones are, you can guess all the happiness they find in their sweet home; it radiates to the home of their dear grandmother and even behind the grilles of the monastery, for the Carmelite aunt is not indifferent to the joys of those she loves! Has Mama told you that our very dear and Reverend Mother, who is so good, let one of our Sisters dress up a beautiful doll as a Carmelite for Sabeth? It's truly a little masterpiece: nothing is lacking, from head to toe she is completely like us; what a shame you couldn't see her, it would have given you an idea of how your little niece is dressed. As regards clothes, did I tell you that I was habit sister, which means I am responsible for mending the habits of the community under the direction of the Sister in charge of that office;[2] she furnishes me with work and explains it to me, and I do it in the solitude of our dear cell. You would be edified to see the poverty of our clothes. After twenty or thirty years, you can guess they have a few patches.... I love to work on this dear serge, which I so desired to wear and in which it is so good to live in Carmel.

I will be happy to have news of you, especially about Aunt Francine's eyes; I imagine she has many sacrifices to make at this time of year when the days are so short; that is all being counted by her good Angel and recorded in the great book of life. God so needs sacrifices in order to compensate for all the evil that is done ... and this is so little understood in the world. So, when the divine Master finds a soul generous enough to share His Cross, He takes her as a partner in His suffering, and that soul must accept it as a proof of the love of Him who wants her to be like Him. Nevertheless, dear little Aunts, I didn't come to wish you crosses today; on the contrary, I would be tempted to divert any that might be along your path in order to place them on mine. The daughters of Saint Teresa are not afraid of the cross, for it is their heritage, their treasure! Sunday I am going to celebrate the third anniversary of my wedding to the Lamb;[3] I will be on retreat that day, which means that I won't go to recreation, but will spend that time close to my divine Bridegroom. It seems to me I understand my happiness even better and that it is deeper than on the beautiful day of my profession; oh, little Aunts, how sweet it is to belong wholly to God; I see nothing more beautiful than Carmel except Heaven itself. But don't think that memories of the past have been erased from my heart; if you knew how your names have been engraved there in indelible letters by the hand of Jesus Himself.... A Dieu, my good, beloved Aunts; may He fill you with His graces; may His Angels guard you from all evil[4] and on their wings bring you, as well as Aunt, the best wishes and tender affection of your little niece.

Sr. M. E. of the Trinity r.c.i.

I hope Monsieur le Curé is better. Please give him my respectful best wishes. Hello to Louise and Anna and to all those who remember me.

[1] Cf. note 3. The letter will not arrive until "after the 1st of January."
[2] Cf. L 253–54.
[3] They celebrated Epiphany (January 6) the following Sunday: on January 7 in 1906 (it was on January 11 in 1903, the day Elizabeth pronounced her vows).
[4] Cf. Ps 90:10–11.

L 259   To Madame Hallo

L 259   To Madame Hallo   [beginning of January 1906][1]
         J. M. + J. T.   "Adveniat regnum tuum." [2]

Dear Madame and second mother,[3]

I was very touched by your good wishes, and it has been a sacrifice not to come to you sooner to offer you my own; that has been impossible for me to do, but I have made up for it close to God. On January 1st, we had the Blessed Sacrament exposed in our dear oratory; I spent my day at His feet; you can well believe that you were not forgotten between the Bridegroom and bride: I confided all my wishes for my second mama to Him. I see that the Master keeps you constantly nailed to the cross with your neuralgia. Saint Paul said: "I suffer in my body what is lacking in the passion of Christ."[4] You, too, are in a way another humanity[5] for Him in which you permit Him to suffer an extension of His passion, for your pain is truly supernatural. But how many souls you can save like that.... You carry on the apostolate of suffering as well as that of action, and I believe the first must draw many graces down on the second. May God bless your zeal and your self-sacrifice for His glory and His reign in souls. He is truly giving you a very special grace to do all you are doing in your state of suffering: I listened with such interest to Marguerite[6] when she came to see me this summer and told me all the details of your life…. Would you please say hello to her for me? You are so kind to think of my dear Mama like that; I won't fail to give her your message when I see her. She still has such pleasant memories of her stay with you; I would be very happy to send her to you again, for the supernatural atmosphere in which you live did her so much good…. Did she tell you about the beautiful doll our Reverend Mother let one of our Sisters dress up like a Carmelite for little Sabeth? Nothing is missing in her costume, from head to foot.[7] Madame de Sourdon, whom I saw today, told me it was a marvel. The dear little child apparently pressed it to her heart, calling it "Tata." I'll be happy to have news of you from Alice.[8] Marguerite told me in fact that her mother was expecting her. I am praying for Charles, that God may keep him completely pure for you in the midst of this evil world;[9] I believe you are winning many graces for him through your sufferings! A Dieu, my second mama, when will you be coming to visit Carmel? While waiting, I will meet you in Him who has united us so completely that nothing can separate us; may He bring you all my tender affection. Your second daughter,

Sr. M. Elizabeth of the Trinity r.c.i.

An affectionate hello to Charles.

---

[1] A little after January 1. 1906: cf. notes 6 and 7.
[2] "May your kingdom come": Mt 6:10. Mme. Hallo led a very apostolic life, as the letter gives witness.
[3] A title Elizabeth gave her; she thus calls herself "your second daughter."
[4] Col 1:24.
[5] Cf. PN 15.
[6] Her servant Marguerite Cherillon, who came in August 1905 (cf. L 236, note 12).
[7] Cf. the preceding letter.
[8] Undoubtedly Alice, the wife of Commandant de la Ruelle.
[9] Charles Hallo was a soldier. Cf. L 342, Elizabeth's last letter.

L 260   To her sister   [beginning of January 1906][1]
            J. M. + J. T.

My dear little sister,
        You were so tactful in offering me the Kings' brioches that I
gave your message to our dear Mother. Since it's not likely that
they'll be given to us on Saturday, our good Mother gratefully ac-
cepts your kindness in indulging us so; you will be keeping up an
ancient custom of Carmel, and our holy Mother Teresa as well as
the little angels will bless you from on high. If you can have the
brioches sent early, for *10 o'clock*, it would be good, for my Sister
Agnès[2] is always afraid of being late. Your excellent chocolate has
been kept for the occasion: you can see you're bearing the expense
of this little feast in the refectory; it is *Saturday,* not Sunday. May the
Master nourish your soul at His banquet of love, may He overwhelm
and invade you, dear little one, so that you may be no longer you,
but *Him!* On January 1st, I spent my day close to God; I confided to
Him all my wishes for my Guite and her whole little nest; may He
pour out over you His sweetest blessings. I kiss you, little mama, with
your two treasures, of whom I'm so proud in my rather maternal
love as an aunt. Your big sister,

                                        "Laudem Gloriae."[3]

        That is what we'll both be called in Heaven!...

[1] 1906: Guite has two children. "The Kings' brioches" (cf. L 221) are for "Saturday,"
January 6th.
[2] The "provisor," in charge of the food.
[3] Cf. L 250, note 16.

L 261   To Madame de Bobet   [January 4, 1906(?)][1]
            J. M. + J. T.   Carmel, Thursday evening

My very dear Antoinette,
        This morning, your dear aunt brought me your *magnificent*
rosary,[2] which she was anxious to give me herself. She will be able to

describe the joy she felt coming through the grille. How can I express my gratitude to you? That would be impossible for me, dear Antoinette, for it is one of those things that cannot be conveyed; so I have said my thank you to *Him,* so He can tell you about it in the depths of your heart. Oh, if you knew what sweet perfume I breathed when I opened the precious box; it was like an emanation from your heart, for I felt your heart had gone completely into this dear rosary. But how you do spoil me! I never could have imagined a rosary so beautiful; and yet it is so religious. It is already on our cincture.[3] If you could see how well it goes with our dear serge: it is so devotional with its large, spaced beads; the medal is lovely; as for the cross, it is so expressive ... and *your soul* chose it to do mine good; I love to contemplate it, for it reveals to me the exceeding love of my Master and tells me that love is repaid only by love![4] Dear Antoinette, I am offering a prayer for you that Saint Paul made for his followers: he asked that "Jesus dwell through faith in their hearts so they might be rooted in love."[5] That thought is so profound, so mysterious.... Oh yes, may the God who is all love be your unchanging dwelling place, your cell, and your cloister in the midst of the world; remember that He dwells in the deepest center of your soul as if in a sanctuary where He wants always to be loved to the point of adoration. He remains there to fill you to overflowing with His graces, to transform you in Himself. Oh, when you sense your weakness, go to Him; He is the Strong One, the One who gives victory through the holiness at His right hand, as the Psalmist sings.[6] He covers you with His shadow.[7] Trust in His love completely, for that is where I will leave you to go to Matins. But, what am I saying, I am not leaving you: there is no separation for those who abide in love. Thanks again, dear Antoinette, I don't know how to express it to you. I brought our rosary quite triumphantly to our Reverend Mother, who found it magnificent, as did my Sisters, and I find that I am a Carmelite who is very spoiled by my good Antoinette. I kissed the cross with love; I will do it often; I am sure you have done that as well, and I *meet* you in this embrace.

Sr. M. E. of the Trinity r.c.i.

I am offering my first rosary every day for you.[8]

[1] Although the "rosary" in question was requested as early as August 17, 1905 (cf. L 241), it was late in reaching Elizabeth. The fainter handwriting and the paper ruled in small rectangles suggest that we place the letter around this period. The rosary was not sent by post; Mme. de Vathaire, Antoinette's aunt, "brought" it, undoubtedly from Paris, where Antoinette was living. Perhaps Antoinette entrusted the rosary to her during a New Year's visit. This "Thursday" might therefore have been January 4.
[2] From Lourdes, cf. L 241.
[3] Carmelites often wear, hidden under their scapulars, a second rosary that is easier to use than the large one on their cinctures.
[4] Thérèse of Lisieux, summing up John of the Cross (cf. L 213, note 2).
[5] Eph 3:17.
[6] Cf. Ps 43:4–5.
[7] Cf. Ps 90:4.
[8] "First" rosary: this implies that Elizabeth said three "chaplets," the complete rosary of fifteen decades, undoubtedly while working. But perhaps only after August 1905, a period of greater rest.

L 262   To Madame de Sourdon   [January 13(?) 1906][1]
J. M. + J. T.

Very dear Madame,

I cannot tell you the sorrow[2] your letter has caused me and, with the permission of our good and Reverend Mother, I am coming to beg you not to lose confidence. Oh, if you knew how, behind the grilles of Carmel, you have a heart profoundly devoted to you that pleads your cause! Remember, dear Madame, that beautiful passage of the Gospel where a woman pursued Our Lord in the ardor of her prayer. He who is so good seemed to become unfeeling and pushed her away, but in the end, in the face of her faith and trust, He could no longer resist her, and He says to her: "O woman, your faith is great!"[3] That, dear Madame, is what we must give Him: to hope against all hope[4] and never doubt His goodness; I am begging Him in the name of His love to soothe your maternal heart and to leave the balm of peace and patience there. Believe that my disappointment was great when I received your letter, but I think God wants to draw many graces down on our dear Marie-Louise, and prayer and sacrifice are still needed! We will meet again close to the altar on the 20th,[5] for our Reverend Mother was pleased to grant you this consolation. We will pray with him who has gone before us to the Abode of light and peace, where God wipes every tear from the eyes of His elect,[6] that He may give you strength and courage, dear Madame. Know that my prayer as a bride is very intense for you.

Sr. E. of the Trinity r.c.i.

I hope your pain from neuralgia is completely gone. If you knew what good your beautiful Annunciation[7] does in our cell....

[1] The letter was surely written after L 246 of November 1905 (cf. note 7) and shortly before January "20th" (cf. note 5). The original folds of the letter would make it fit into a small 4" x 2.5" envelope addressed to the "Comtesse de Sourdon, rue Chabot-Charny," on the back of which the recipient noted: "January 13, 1906."
[2] The "sorrow" still concerns Marie-Louise and her desires for marriage. This explains Elizabeth's "disappointment."
[3] Mt 15:28.
[4] Cf. Rom 4:18.
[5] Mass for Mme. de Sourdon's husband, on the anniversary of his death (cf. L 223, note 2).
[6] Cf. Rev 7:17.
[7] The engraving mentioned in L 246.

L 263   To Madame de Sourdon

J. M. + J. T.

[January 26, 1906][1]

Dijon Carmel, January 26

Very dear Madame,

Your touching letter reached me during our retreat, which just ended,[2] and our Reverend Mother, who has such a tender and sensitive heart, has given me leave once again[3] to come pay you a little visit. Dear Madame, there is no distance between souls, and my heart is so close to yours that it seems to me Paris and Dijon are completely one. I am right beside your bed of pain, and every night I wish I had wings to replace your nurse and give you consolation from a heart that is deeply devoted to you. But at least my prayer surrounds you, and I say Mary Magdalene's prayer to the Master: "Lord, the one you love is sick."[4] Oh yes, you are loved by Him, dear Madame, and I beg you on His behalf to cast all your anguish and concerns into His Heart. You can unite your agonies to His; He wanted to suffer first so that in crucifying hours we might be able to say, while looking at Him: "He has suffered even more than I, and did so in order to tell me of His love and to lay claim to mine." The

Psalmist says, speaking of Him, "that His suffering was as immense as the sea."[5] And Saint Paul said after him: "We do not have a high priest who is unable to sympathize with our weaknesses, for He was tested in all things like we are."[6] Surrender yourself to Love, dear Madame. You tell me you must make atonement, but our God is called a "consuming Fire"[7] and also "rich in mercy because of His exceeding love."[8] What cause for confidence for the soul who says with Saint John: "I believe in His love"![9] I am asking this God who is so good not to agree to *the thing* of which you spoke to me; I am begging Him to have pity on you and to place the peace and confidence of the children of God in your heart. It seems to me that if I saw death, even despite all my infidelities, I would abandon myself into the arms of my God like a child who falls asleep on its mother's heart: it is really the same thing, and He who is to be our Judge dwells within us, He has made Himself our companion on our pilgrimage to help us cross the painful passage. Oh, may His love keep you for your beloved children, how I am asking [that] of Him! I know you have lost your little medal, and our good Mother is attaching one[10] to this letter; may it bring you a ray of peace in your very dark sky. I kiss you very affectionately and your dear daughters, too.

Sr. M.E. o. the Trinity r.c.i.

I was very happy Our Mother let me listen[11] to Monsieur Joseph[12] and to speak to him about you.

Dear Madame, would you tell Framboise I'm not forgetting the 29th?[13] But in Carmel we have the law of love and, consequently, the law of sacrifice.... We do not have the joy of sending feastday greetings to those we love; we make a very intimate feastday for them in our hearts. Please excuse this writing, but we have no heat, and I cannot hold my pen....[14]

---

[1] The handwriting and the paper ruled in small rectangles attest to the period; the day and the month were specified by Elizabeth.
[2] Preached by P. Rollin, a Jesuit, from January 15 to 23. The text of this retreat is almost completely preserved in the ACD. For the general outline of this retreat and Elizabeth's personal notes, cf. PAT.
[3] She had written very recently: L 262.
[4] Cf. Jn 11:3.
[5] Lm 2:13. It is therefore a prophet, not a "Psalmist."

[6] Heb 4:15.

[7] Heb 12:29, repeating Dt 4:24.

[8] Eph 2:4.

[9] Cf. 1 Jn 4:16.

[10] The "miraculous medal" of St. Catherine Labouré, attached to this letter.

[11] "Listen": they did not open the parlor curtain except for close relatives (cf. L 112, note 4).

[12] Cf. L 313, note 2. Joseph de Maizières, Mme. de Sourdon's brother-in-law.

[13] January 29th, the feast of St. Francis de Sales. Elizabeth did write to Françoise, however, in 1902 (L 105) and 1904 (L 192). She confirms in L 236 that it is "not the custom to write on such occasions."

[14] In this letter (rediscovered in 1979 in an envelope in which it did not belong) are still two small printed notes, bearing the emblem of the Sacred Heart, with the words: "Sacred Heart of Jesus, I trust in You."

L 264　　To Madame Angles　　　　　　　[end of January 1906][1]

　　　　J. M. + J. T.

　　　　　　"Love is the fulfillment of the law."[2]

Very dear Madame,

　　I do not want to let this first month of the year pass without coming to thank you for your good wishes and to offer you mine, which have long been placed in the Heart of God. May 1906 be for your soul a chain of fidelity in which each link, soldered by love, unites you more closely to the Master and makes you truly His captive, His one "in chains,"[3] as Saint Paul says. In his great, generous heart, he wished for his followers "that Jesus Christ might live by faith in their hearts, so that they might be rooted and grounded in love."[4] This is also the wish I express for you, dear Madame. May the reign of love then be fully established in your interior kingdom, and may the weight of that love draw you[5] to complete self-forgetfulness, to that mystical death of which the Apostle spoke when he exclaimed: "I live no longer I, but Jesus Christ lives in me."[6] In that beautiful discourse after the Last Supper, which is like a last love song of the soul of the Divine Master, He says these beautiful words to His Father: "I have glorified You on earth, I have finished the work You gave me to do."[7] It seems to me that we who belong to Him as brides, dear Madame, and who consequently ought to be completely identified with Him, should be able to repeat these words at the close of each day. You will perhaps say to me: How are we to glorify Him? It is very simple. Our Lord gives us the secret to it when He says to us: "My food is to do the will of Him who sent me."[8] Be devoted, then, dear Madame, to the will of this adorable Master; look at every suffering as well as every joy as coming directly from Him, and then your life will be a continual communion, since everything will be like a sacrament that will give God to you. And that is very real, for God does not divide Himself, His will is His whole Being. He is completely in all things, and these things are in a way nothing but an emanation of His love. You see how you can glorify Him in these states of suffering and listlessness that are so difficult to bear. Forget yourself as much as you can, for it is the secret of peace and happiness. Saint Francis Xavier exclaimed: "What concerns me does not concern me, but what concerns Him concerns me powerfully."[8a] Happy the soul who has attained this total detachment, for it loves indeed!...[9]

I saw Marguerite today; the little ones had the flu, so she did not bring them along, for the temperature in the parlors of Carmel would hardly be good for colds.[10] The little darlings are so cute, and the second is the image of her mother, sweet and pleasant like her. You can imagine the joy these little angels radiate in their sweet home. Their dear grandmother enjoys them very much as well, and their aunt, in the depths of her cloister, is united with the happiness of these dear hearts. When you see Marie-Louise,[11] please tell her I am not forgetting her good mother, either; how cute the babies must be and how they must give joy to all....

A Dieu, dear Madame, may He grow greater in your soul every day of this year; that is the wish of your little friend who kisses you.

Sr. M. Elizabeth of the Trinity r.c.i.

[1] Cf. the beginning of the letter.

Forget yourself.

[2] Rom 13:10.
[3] Cf. L 179, note 14.
[4] Eph 3:17.
[5] Reminiscent of St. Augustine, cf. L 214, note 6.
[6] Gal 2:20.
[7] Jn 17:4.
[8] Jn 4:34.
[8a] We do not know Elizabeth's source.
[9] Probably based on Teresa of Avila, *Life,* chap. 40 (Bouix trans., vol. 1, p. 610 [K-RT vol. 1, 40:1]), where the Lord says to her: "Do you know what it is to love me truth-

fully? It is to understand that everything that is displeasing to me is a lie."
[10] The parlors were not heated.
[11] Marie-Louise Ambry.

L 265   To her mother   [March 14, 1906][1]
   J. M. + J. T.   Carmel, *Wednesday*

My darling little Mama,
  You know how good our Reverend Mother is; her heart is truly
a mother's heart, which says everything, doesn't it? So, with her permission, I am coming to pay a little visit to my dear patient, who I
thought was already off to Lorraine![2] My whole heart is close to you,
to that bedside over which I have bent so often, and you can tell
yourself at every moment: My Carmelite is praying for me. I've been
dreaming of you all the time lately, spending my nights with you.
Surely God is doing that so my prayer for you will be even more intense when I wake up. There is a proverb that says: "Out of sight,
out of mind"; in our dear country of Carmel, it is just the opposite,
and I can even say that when I was with you, I didn't know *I loved you
so much*. It seems to me my heart, which God made so loving, has
expanded since it was enclosed behind the grilles in continual contact with Him whom Saint John calls "Charitas,"[3] Love. Ah, if you
knew how sweet it is to live in "communion"[4] with Him, according
to the expression of that same saint, you wouldn't ever leave that
divine company again, for He is close to you. He would be so happy
if you would make Him a Friend, a Confidant; the more one lives
with this Divine Guest, little Mama, the happier one is, and the more
strength one has to go to the sacrifice. I am sending Him to you at
every moment, I am entrusting to Him all the love He has placed in
my heart for this good mother He has given me. I am not surprised
at the kindnesses of the wonderful Madame de Sourdon. What a
friend! It relieves me to know she is close to you. Tell her I am praying very much to Saint Joseph; I was hoping something might hap-
pen on his feast day;[5] I am full of hope! And our dear Guite, how
lucky you are to have her near you[6] with her little angels. Tell her
how united I am with her. I love my little sister so much.... How
sweet it is for me to think of you in the midst of so many loved ones.

Here below, everything ends in sacrifice, for it's a law; I am offering to God the sacrifice you made to Him by giving Him your naughty Sabeth, who knew very well, however, how to take care of her Mama. I won't say anything more about sacrifice, since I understand so well that there is no distance between my heart and yours. I kiss you as I love you. Your daughter,

E. of the Trinity r.c.i.

I don't understand what you mean when you speak to me of Our Mother's worries with the government;[7] we are completely at peace, set your mind at rest about that.

How happy I am about the Commandant de la Ruelle's nomination. Tell that to Alice and her mother. I had prayed fervently for Nicole.[8]

---

[1] Proximity of March 19th, the feast of "Saint Joseph." 1906, since Guite has two children. RB 2 (cf. PAT) indicates that Mme. Catez was sick "for nearly a month" until April 9. On "Wednesday," March 21, Elizabeth herself had already been confined to bed in the infirmary, which leaves Wednesday, March 14, as the date. (The expression "I was hoping" does not indicate that the feast of St. Joseph had already passed, but only that she had begun to hope ever since the beginning of the preparatory novena; "I am full of hope" indicates that the feast is therefore not yet past.) The "permission" of the Prioress indicates that it is in Lent.

[2] For Lunéville, her hometown, as during the Lent of 1902 (L 109) and that of 1903 (L 159).

[3] 1 Jn 4:16.

[4] 1 Jn 1:3.

[5] Another allusion to Marie-Louise's future. She seems to have had much difficulty finding a husband. They are invoking St. Joseph, the patron of families.

[6] Perhaps Mme. Catez is at Guite's home, on the rue de la Prefecture. It is less likely that Guite would bring her little daughters to the rue Prieur-de-la-Côte-d'Or.

[7] An allusion to the difficulties that arose nearly everywhere when the police tried to make inventories of church property (cf. L 256, note 8). On March 6, a man was killed in Boeschèpe (Nord) in the course of taking these inventories, which led to the fall of the Rouvier government.

[8] The daughter of Alice Bertrand, the wife of the commandant.

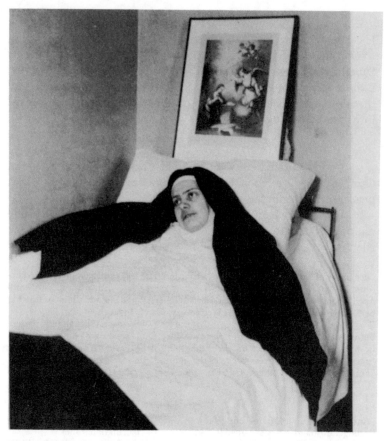

Elizabeth in infirmary in April, 1906. Above her head is placed the print of the Annunciation given to her by Mme. de Sourdon (see L 246).

IV

"I Am Going to Light, to Love, to Life"
End of March – November 9, 1906

Before the end of March 1906, Elizabeth entered Carmel's infirmary. The progressive weakening of the last few months ended in a total loss of strength. She ate with more and more difficulty. On the evening of April 8, Palm Sunday, a fainting spell suddenly made her weak state worse. Abbé Donin gave her Extreme Unction (the sacrament of the sick, at that time reserved for those in real danger of death) and Viaticum (cf. L 266, note 3). All of Holy Week remained very difficult, and her condition was particularly alarming on Good Friday. The next day a noticeable improvement took place. The Sisters no longer had any illusions, however, about her chances of recovery, except through the miracle they were seeking.

Solitude and Communication

We have 78 letters and 27 poems from this period in the infirmary. That is a great deal. In her increased solitude, Elizabeth wanted to be present through this correspondence to her Prioress and her Sisters, to her family and friends, and to express to them her affectionate gratitude for their care and attention, to speak to them of God, to console them, to share in their joys and their concerns. No longer able to work except for brief moments, she now had more time at her disposal.

Life in the infirmary would have been extremely monotonous if not for God and the love of her Sisters, which made her exclaim: "What a Carmel!" (L 268 and 308). The "events" can be mentioned quickly! Mother Germaine's feast day, June 15, took on a particular prominence that year in the intimacy of the infirmary. Incapable until then of standing for any length of time, on the 8th or 9th of July, after having invoked Thérèse of Lisieux, the young patient suddenly received just enough strength in her legs to allow her from then on to return to the terrace or the corridor along the cells, but above all to the little tribune that looked out on the chapel and from which she attended Mass and Office.

From the evening of the 15th until the 31st of August, Elizabeth made a long retreat, her "novitiate for Heaven" (L 307). At the request of Mother Germaine,[1] she wrote her *Last Retreat,* a spiritual treatise full of autobiographical resonances.[2] Just before, she had composed *Heaven in Faith* for Guite. In September and October, she wrote her two other little treatises for Françoise de Sourdon and Mother Germaine. The triduum from October 13 to 15 in honor of the sixteen recently beatified Carmelite martyrs of Compiègne (cf. L 324, note 7) was another event.

We should also mention the visits of Mme. Catez to the infirmary parlor, about every two weeks from May on. And those of the doctors, who were powerless in the face of the illness that consumed her relentlessly.

"A True Ascent of Calvary"

This is what Mother Germaine called the eight and one-half months of Elizabeth's terrible illness (Circ. 8). It is impossible for us to retrace here in detail the evolution of this illness or all the spiritual richness that accompanied it; for that, we refer the reader to our work, *Elisabeth ou l'Amour est là [Elizabeth, or Love Is There].*

Probably following tuberculosis, Elizabeth was attacked by Addison's disease, a then-incurable chronic disease of the adrenal glands, which no longer produce the substances necessary for metabolism. This results in the characteristic debility, gastrointestinal troubles, nausea, arterial hypotension, virtual inability to eat, emaciation, all of which lead to total physical exhaustion and death. Elizabeth also had other complications, such as internal ulcerations, severe headaches, and insomnia. The closer she got to death, the more violently all these symptoms manifested themselves. There were also more acute crises, like that of May 13, when she narrowly escaped death.

Around the beginning of May, three doctors considered on two occasions the possibility of surgical intervention, then rejected it. During this entire period, nourishment remained a question of life and death. Elizabeth ate ices, milk, or cottage cheese; they tried several kinds of cake; all in minuscule portions. She also sucked chocolate or candy, seeking those that would make her the least sick and not burn her stomach. "You can see that I'm attentive to my stomach," she wrote, "and, for the love of God, I do what I can not to let it die of hunger" (L 309). It was a real torture for her to drink (cf. the key letter of Mother Germaine of May 17, quoted in L 271, note 1) She used her voice less and less. In the last weeks, her palate and tongue were on fire, and she suffered great interior inflammation (cf. L 327, note 2). The last eight days, she ate and drank absolutely nothing. One day she said to her Prioress: "My Mother, it is very bad, but I believe the first thing I will do when I get to Heaven is drink."

By comparing the photographs taken during her illness (on her bed, in April or May; seated, at the beginning of October) and on her deathbed, the "work of destruction ... throughout her whole being" can be ascertained (L 294). Sometimes she let an admission escape: there were beasts devouring her inside, it was as if they were tearing out her intestines. She was never given morphine or pain-killers. Elizabeth knew that God and faith kept her from suicide (cf. L 329, note 2). Often she was burning up internally, but she said: "God is a consuming Fire, it is to His action that I submit" (S 241). Mother Germaine speaks of her body as being "like a skeleton," "literally burned to death" (S 240–41). Françoise de Sourdon, recalling the sight of her close friend's body after her death, said: "She was frightening. You had the sense of a creature who had been ravaged, consumed."

"So I May Be That Victim of Love" (L 299)

But the Sisters who lived closer to this long agony recognized in this emaciated body a spiritualized being, burned by the fire of love. They also remembered the inexhaustible energy of this officer's daughter. Elizabeth never retreated. She knew that the

Bridegroom was calling her. "Never," writes her mother, "did she give [me] one word of hope for a cure."[3]

The letters, poetry, and treatises of this period show the spiritual supports of her rapid progress:

- her desire for Heaven (e.g., L 266);
- the presence of the "Three," which, after the feast of the Ascension (May 24), became even more intense;
- the certitude of being loved by the God who is all Love (cf., e.g., L 275, 280);
- the presence of Mary, Queen of martyrs and Gate of Heaven;
- the desire for union with God on earth as in Heaven, a desire revived again by reading Ruysbroeck during the summer;
- the desire to live in a profound recollection in God, by means of interior silence and detachment from everything;
- the desire to be a "praise of glory" throughout everything, singing "nothing but the glory of the Eternal" (LR 17);
- above all, the thirst for conformity to Christ crucified, the ideal taken from St. Paul and, in September and October, developed by reading Angela di Foligno: "She has buried herself in the Man of sorrows" (P 112);
- the growing awareness of having a "mission" to accomplish in Heaven.[4]

In these last months, a sacrificial and eucharistic spirituality also deepened within her (cf. L 294, note 6). Her Prioress assumed a quasi-sacerdotal mediation (cf. L 320, note 3). The gift of self, with Christ and for the Church, constituted her happiness (cf., e.g., GV 7)—this happiness overcame the agony (L 320).

Attention to Others

The letters that follow contain many expressions of her joy. Her correspondents knew the gravity of her condition (but not in detail); Elizabeth therefore speaks of it, but she never complains. In order not to increase Mme. Catez's suffering, Elizabeth and Mother Germaine (cf. L 271, note 1) even hide certain distressing details from her. Elizabeth always stresses that she is well cared for and what a good Mother is replacing Mme. Catez.

She insisted that she was receiving good care because outside the monastery it was rumored that the dying young woman was not receiving all the care she should. Guite's husband assuredly shared that opinion. His sister Madeleine recalled "Georges's anger on the subject of the last illness of the Servant of God. 'One does not allow a 26-year-old girl to die without caring for her'; he meant that she should have left her convent to receive more adequate care." Thus when Elizabeth speaks of the "wise and zealous" care that was "lavished [on her] by everyone around [her]" (L 308), we are correct in detecting behind these words a delicate rectification and a way of calming her mother.

The letters and poems of this period confirm all the affectionate attention she gave to others up to her last days. A very spiritual letter to Guite, with a last sublime flight on Love, ends in this charming unexpected sentence: "What happiness that Sabeth's finger is getting better" (L 298). And what a profusion of gratitude for the candy received! She is concerned about the health of her mother, the future of Marie-Louise de Sourdon; she plans a marriage for Mother Germaine's brother with a girl whom she used to know and whose youth is fading....

"Love Alone Remains"

On October 30, 1906, Elizabeth pressed her profession crucifix to her heart and said, "We have loved each other so much." Her exhausted body resisted no longer. She was permanently confined to her bed. In the evening, a great trembling shook her.

The next day she received Extreme Unction and Viaticum for the second time.

On All Saints Day she received Communion for the last time. Around ten o'clock in the morning, they thought the hour of her death had arrived. The community gathered around her and recited the prayers for the dying. Elizabeth regained enough strength to ask pardon of her Sisters in moving words. Invited by them to say more, she replied: "Everything passes away! At the evening of life, love alone remains.... We must do everything by love; we must forget ourselves at all times. The good God so loves us to forget ourselves.... Ah! if I had always done so!..."

She remained lucid in the days that followed, but her eyes, which were bloodshot, were nearly always closed. She suffered greatly. Sometimes she spoke again, to make others happy or give last testimonies of her union with God and her desire to offer Him everything. She could no longer receive Communion but said: "I find Him on the Cross; it is there He gives me His life."

After a violent attack, she cried out: "O love, Love! You know if I love you, if I desire to contemplate you; you know, too, if I suffer; yet, thirty, forty years more if you wish, I am ready. Consume my substance for your glory; let it distill drop by drop for your Church."

On the 7th and 8th of November, she kept almost constant silence. Yet these words could still be heard: "I am going to Light, to Love, to Life!..."

The night of the 8th to the 9th of November was very painful. Asphyxiation was added to her other sufferings. Toward morning, her acute pains abated. The alteration of her features showed she was on the point of dying. The community was called. Elizabeth's eyes were now wide open and luminous. Almost without anyone noticing, she stopped breathing. It was around 6:15 in the morning.

Prophet of God, Elizabeth of the Trinity belonged henceforth to the entire Church.

[1] Cf. Vol. I, p. 131.
[2] Ibid., pp. 133ff.
[3] RB 2 in PAT.
[4] Cf. Vol. I, pp. 28–32.

L 266   To her mother   [April 15, 1906][1]

+

My darling little Mama,

Never have I felt so close to you! My heart does not leave you; I have never felt so much your daughter. Your letter[2] was a joy for my heart, a rest for my soul; I kissed it like one of your relics, thanking God for having given me such an incomparable Mama. If I had gone to Heaven, how I would have spent my life with you! I would never have left you; I would have made you feel the presence of your little Sabeth. As I'm sure you will understand me, I'll confess in a whisper my great disappointment at not going to Him whom I love so much. Think what an Easter Day your daughter would have had in Heaven! But that was still selfish, and now I'm entirely given to obedience, which makes me ask to be cured, and I do so in union of prayer with you, my Guite, and my dear little angels, whom I would have so loved to protect if I had flown away. If you knew how good Our Mother is! A true mama for your daughter; and I assure you, I needed to hear her voice and to feel my hands in hers on the night I had the attack,[3] in spite of my joy at going to God, for that is a very solemn moment even so, and you feel so little and empty-handed.[4] I hope to see you soon, dear Mama, along with my darling Guite, but right now I send you my thanks for your letter, which I'm keeping with love, as well as the one from my little sister that was also so delightful. And then thanks again for your treats, those ices[5] that are my only consolation; if you could see with what happiness Our Mother brings them to me and how she herself has me take them like a little child…. Let's thank God for these days, however painful they are to your heart; I have a real sense that they are passing over us, dear Mama, like a wave of love; let's not waste any of it and let's thank Him who knows only how to love us. I kiss you both, my two darlings whom I love more than ever. Thanks to my dear Georges for his touching solicitude for his little Carmelite sister. I will never forget it.

[1] This letter, dictated by Elizabeth and written by Mother Germaine, dates from that "Easter Day," April 15, after the "great change for the better" that occurred on Holy Saturday (Circ. 8).

[2] Cf. RB 2, in PAT: "She wrote to her Elizabeth that she was resigned to the Will of God and that she agreed to drink the cup. This letter, which the patient was to re-read often, was an immense consolation for her." Mme. Catez's letter dated from April 9 or the following days; in any case during Holy Week.

[3] On April 8, "Palm Sunday, during Compline, a fainting spell occurred that made us obtain the grace of Extreme Unction for her" (Circ. 8). S 177–78 adds: "The crisis was over by the time the priest entered the infirmary.... How beautiful she was at that time, her eyes ablaze, hands joined, clasping her profession crucifix, and repeating over and over again in transports of devotion: O Love! Love! Love!" See, in PAT, the letter from the priest Maurice Donin, then vicar of Saint Pierre (the parish the Carmel was located in). Cf. Elizabeth's own account, in L 278.

[4] Cf. Thérèse of Lisieux's "Act of Oblation," HA 151 [SS 277]: "In the evening of this life, I shall appear before You with empty hands...."

[5] Her family obtained these for her (cf. L 285). Circ. 8 says about the period preceding the first crisis: "The illness was progressing, nourishment became more and more difficult, her strength was declining...."

L 267   To her mother   [(after) April (19), 1906][1]

+ God is Love![2]

Dear little Mama,

Your little patient wants to send you a little note from her heart, from that heart so full of love for her mother who is so close to her. I know you're ill,[3] and my good Mother here, who is constantly at the bedside of her little child, keeps me posted about *your dear health*. You can't imagine the care she lavishes on me, with all the tenderness and delicacy of a mother's heart! If you knew how happy I am in the solitude of my little infirmary; my Master is here with me, and we live night and day in a sweet heart-to-heart. I appreciate the happiness of being a Carmelite even more, and I pray to God for the little Mama who gave me to Him. I've been drawn still closer to Heaven since this illness; I'll tell you all about it one day.[4] Oh, little Mama, let us prepare for our eternity, let us live with Him, for He alone can accompany and help us on this great journey. He is a God of love; we cannot comprehend the extent to which He loves us, *above all when He sends us trials.*

I cover you with tender caresses, dear, beloved Mama, as well as my Guite and the little angels.

Sabeth.

See you soon.

---

[1] Letter written in pencil with smaller and weaker handwriting. Elizabeth was confined to bed until the 8th or 9th of July (cf. L 295), which made writing letters more difficult. All her letters, except those to the Prioress, are written in pencil from then on. The contents of this letter, as well as S 183, place it before the first meeting in the infirmary parlor at the beginning of May. An envelope addressed by Elizabeth to "Madame Catez" is preserved in the ACD; inside is the postmark "April 19, 1906." But this might be the envelope for L 273.
[2] 1 Jn 4:16.
[3] Cf. RB 2, in PAT.
[4] Mother Germaine must have already planned a visit to the parlor "soon."

L 268   To Madame de Sourdon

[about the end of April (27?), 1906][1]

+ I feel surrounded by your very motherly affection, dear Madame, during these days that will remain with me as an ineffable memory, for they have drawn me still closer to God, to the invisible world. I feel as if I'm coming out of a beautiful, luminous dream, but Saint Paul tells me that in my soul, through faith, I possess in substance these splendors, these divine riches that I thought I was going to contemplate in the great brightness of God.[2] Dear Madame, God has made me understand in His light what a treasure suffering is, and we will never understand enough the extent to which He loves us when He gives us trials; the cross is a token of His love! I am keeping your special intention very much in mind in my illness;[3] *I have taken it very much to heart,* and if I had gone close to my God, have no doubt what a good advocate you would have had; I am *full of hope.* I am much better, though I still feel very weak. If you knew what a Mother I have at my side: a true mama, her heart has the tenderness, the delicacy known only to the hearts of mothers. As for my infirmarians,[4] they rival each other in charity. What a

Carmel! I wish you could have seen it. Thank you, dear Madame, for your goodness to my wonderful Mama; it puts my heart at rest. Ah! may He who is infinite Love reward you. I fully expect to see you again here on earth; in any case, if I do go to Him, I will be your little protectress and I will always love you like a mother.

S. E. o. the Trinity

[1] Letters 268–70 say "I am much better," which gives us an approximate date. Mme. de Sourdon notes on the autograph copy: "April 27, 1906."
[2] Cf. Heb 11:1; perhaps also 1 Cor 13:12.
[3] Still Marie-Louise's marriage.
[4] Anne of Jesus (cf. P 104, note 1), helped by Marie of the Holy Spirit and Martha of Jesus (cf. L 281, note 1).

L 269   To her sister   [around the end of April 1906][1]
+ "Having loved those who were His own in the world,
He loved them to the end."[2]

Darling little sister,

I don't know if the hour has come to pass from this world to my Father, for I am much better and the little saint of Beaune seems to want to cure me.[3] But, you see, at times it seems to me that the Divine Eagle wants to swoop down on His little prey and carry her off to where He is:[4] into dazzling light! You have always put your Sabeth's happiness before your own, and I am sure that if I fly away, you will rejoice over my first meeting with Divine Beauty. When the veil is lifted, how happy I will be to disappear into the secret of His Face,[5] and that is where I will spend my eternity, in the bosom of the Trinity that was already my dwelling place here below. Just think, my Guite! to contemplate in His light the splendors of the Divine Being, to search into all the depths of His mystery, to become one with Him whom we love, to sing unceasingly of His glory and His love, to be like Him because we see Him as He is!...[6]

Little sister, I would be happy to go up above to be your Angel. How jealous I would be for the beauty of your soul that I have loved so much already here on earth! I leave you my devotion for the Three, to "Love."[7] Live within with Them in the heaven of your soul; the Father will overshadow you,[8] placing something like a cloud[9] between you and the things of this earth to keep you all His, He will communicate His power to you so you can love Him with a love as strong as death;[10] the Word will imprint in your soul, as in a crystal, the image of His own beauty,[11] so you may be pure with His purity, luminous with His light; the Holy Spirit will transform you into a mysterious lyre,[12] which, in silence, beneath His divine touch, will produce a magnificent canticle to Love; then you will be "the praise of His glory" I dreamed of being on earth. You will take my place; I will be "Laudem Gloriae" before the throne of the Lamb, and you, "Laudem Gloriae" in the center of your soul; we will always be united, little sister. Always believe in Love.[13] If you have to suffer, think that you are even *more loved,* and always sing in thanksgiving. He is so jealous for the beauty of your soul.... That is all He has in view. Teach the little ones to live in the sight of the Master. I would love for Sabeth to have my devotion to the Three. I will be at their first Communions, I will help you prepare them. Pray for me; I have offended my Master more than you think; but above all thank Him; say a Gloria every day. Forgive me for having often given you a bad example.

A Dieu, little sister, how I love you.... Perhaps I will go soon to be lost in the Furnace of love;[14] whether in Heaven or on earth, we must live in Love to glorify Love!

---

[1] Cf. L 268, note 1. Almost 30 years later, Guité said this letter dates from "April 1906." It was a "letter-testament; we did not expect to see each other again" (PS in PAT).
[2] Jn 13:1.
[3] The Venerable Marguerite of the Blessed Sacrament, a Carmelite of Beaune (1619–1648). Cf. her biography by L. de Cissey (Paris: Bray, 1862). A bulletin from SRD, in 1905 (20, p. 392), reveals that they were working on her cause of beatification. Circ. 8 says: "Together with several of our Carmels, the dear Carmel of Beaune in particular, we undertook a true crusade of prayers to bring glory to Venerable Marguerite of the Blessed Sacrament through the healing of our dear little sister."
[4] Cf. HA 214 [SS 199–200]. Even before she entered Carmel, Elizabeth had spoken in a Thérèsian context of the Eagle and His prey (cf. L 41, note 7). The image of the prey is seen often in her writings from Carmel (cf. L 125, note 3). The image of the Eagle is found again in L 270, and previously in P 77 and 83.
[5] The expression "the secret of His Face" is found also in P 97 (which very probably accompanied this letter); it is undoubtedly drawn from John of the Cross, LF 505 [K-RJ 2:17]. The image of the "veil" (in LF 476–87 [K-RJ 1:29–36]) seems to confirm this. The saint, in turn, seems to have been inspired by Ps 30:21, which Elizabeth's *Manual* (v. 25) translates as: "You will hide them in the secret of your face against the mischief of people." Elizabeth's perspective brings her closer to John of the Cross.

[6] Cf. 1 Jn 3:2.

[7] 1 Jn 4:16.

[8] Cf. Mt 17:5 (cf. the following note); also Lk 1:35.

[9] An allusion to Mt 17:5, the scene of the Transfiguration (cf. PN 15, notes 30 and 31) in which the "cloud" "overshadows [the disciples]."

[10] Cf. Song 8:6.

[11] The image of the crystal, which reflects with great purity what it receives, is undoubtedly drawn from Teresa of Avila (cf. L 131, note 4), but also from John of the Cross speaking of the transformed soul: LF 466 [K-RJ 1:13], 615 [K-RJ 3:77], and SC 294 [K-RJ 26:17] (cf. also SC 122 [K-RJ 12:3]). The comparison is seen rather often in Elizabeth: P 82, 95; L 131, 136, 197; HF 24, 43; LR 8.

[12] The comparison with the "lyre," which had already appeared in Elizabeth's P 59, undoubtedly owes its power to Thérèse of Lisieux, who uses it several times in her poetry: cf. HA 334 (where the Face of Jesus is the lyre), and above all 372, 402, 451 (where the human heart is the lyre) and 317 (Céline, "the lyre of Jesus"). Recall (cf. L 97, note 4) that Elizabeth kept in her breviary a picture of Thérèse with her hand on a little harp. *Spiritual Canticle*, st. 21, also speaks of "lyres," but there it refers to the sweetness and favors the soul *receives* from God. The image occurs often in Elizabeth the musician during this period: P 100; L 306, 307; HF 43; LR 3, 35, 42.

[13] Cf. 1 Jn 4:16

[14] Cf. L 190, note 3.

L 270   To Françoise de Sourdon [around the end of April 1906][1]
    + J. M. J. T.   God is Love.

My darling Framboise,

What a beautiful dream I've just had! I don't have any secrets from you, I have a feeling you understand me, and I'll admit to you that it cost me something to return to earth. Heaven would only have made the fusion of our souls more true. You've often said I was like a little mother to you, and I do in fact feel that my heart holds a maternal affection for you; just think what it would be like if I were in the great Furnace of love.... Oh, Framboise, what divine days I've spent in the anticipation of the great vision of God; it seemed to me as if the Divine Eagle were going to swoop down on me and carry me away into His dazzling clarity, and you can guess the joy in my soul at the thought of this first face-to-face with Divine Beauty. Oh, if I had gone to lose myself in it, how I would have watched over my Framboise: I'm so ambitious for your soul.... You see, it is good[2] for me to suffer in order to draw down superabundant grace on you. Your letter made me immensely happy; I feel God is at work in you and that you are drawing close to Him; that is an ineffable joy to me;

it is so good to be His.... The two of us are so happy together here in the solitude of my little infirmary; it is a heart-to-heart that lasts night and day,[3] and it's delightful!

A Dieu, Framboise, I am much better, I expect to see you again here on earth; in any case, in Heaven or on earth, our souls will always be ONE.

Sabeth.

[1] Cf. L 268, note 1. Françoise notes on the autograph copy: "April 1906." This letter must not have accompanied the one to Mme. de Sourdon; writing to Mme. Catez on June 20th (cf. PAT), Mother Germaine says: "Two letters [a day] would tire her."
[2] In the first draft this read "it did me good." Elizabeth brings it up to date: the suffering continues.
[3] Taken word-for-word from "Vivre d'amour" ["Living on Love"] poem 17 by Thérèse of Lisieux: "A heart-to-heart lasting night and day." Even Thérèse's preceding verse finds an echo here: "Lovers [Elizabeth: "The two of us are so happy together"] must have solitude [Elizabeth: "in the solitude of my little infirmary"]" (HA 331).

L 271   To Canon Angles

J. M. + J. T.

[May 9, 1906][1]
Amo Christum
"In His light, we will see light."[2]

Dear Monsieur le Chanoine,

I am sending you a little note from my heart, which is so touched by your kind prayers. I do not know if the hour has come for me "to pass from this world to my Father,"[3] but He is drawing me very strongly! To you, who have always been my confidant, I know I can tell everything: the prospect of going to see Him whom I love in His ineffable beauty, and of being immersed in the Trinity that was already my Heaven here below, fills my soul with immense joy. Oh! what it costs me[4] to return to earth; it seems so ugly to me, coming out of my beautiful dream. Only in God is everything pure, beautiful, and holy; fortunately we can dwell in Him even in our exile! But my Master's happiness is mine, and I surrender myself to Him so He can do whatever He wants in me. Since you are His priest, oh, consecrate me to Him like a little sacrifice of praise[5] who wants to give glory to Him in Heaven, or on earth as much suffering as He wishes. And then, if I go, you will help me get out of purgatory. Oh, if you knew how deeply I feel that everything within me is soiled, everything is miserable, I really need my good Mother to help free me of it. Oh! what a Mother! For the body, a true mama; for the soul, the image of the God of mercy, peace, and love.[6] Every morning, she comes to make her thanksgiving beside my little bed; so I communicate in her soul, and the same Love flows in the souls of the mother and her child. This morning, they brought me Holy Communion for the fifth time,[7] for my Mother spoils me as much as she can! Mama and Guite are wonderful, I have never loved them so much. The other day[8] Our Mother had me carried on a little bed to the grate; you can guess the joy of that meeting.

I tell Our Mother, who is praying so hard for my healing, to let me go and I will be her Angel in Heaven; I will pray so much for you, too; it will be such a delight to do something in return for my good, dear Monsieur le Chanoine. A Dieu. Oh! how sweet it is to live in expectation of the Bridegroom! Pray that I might give Him *everything* in the sufferings He sends me and that I might already live by love alone.

Bless your little child *for eternity*.[9]

M. E. of the Trinity, praise of His glory.

Tell everyone that the little Carmelite does not forget them, particularly Marie-Louise.

[1] The date is deduced from the beginning of a letter of "May 17, 1906," addressed by Mother Germaine (cf. PAT) to Canon Angles: "You should have had this little angelic letter eight days ago, but I was reluctant to send it without a few lines, and I have not had time." A week, plus one day for the trip, make May 9th, or a day very close to it. Let us quote a few lines from this very enlightening letter: "This morning I am writing to you beside our little saint whom we have just put in a bed in front of the parlor grille to give one last consolation to her dear family. It is probably the last time these beautiful, deserving souls will see each other on earth.... The dear little one has been much more ill since Sunday [May 13], when we thought we would lose her in an attack that lasted from 4 in the morning until 2 in the afternoon. Since then, what sufferings throughout this poor body! Her mother does not know the whole truth of her crucifying condition; her heart is broken enough already, I tell her only what is necessary to keep her in her present admirable disposition of abandonment and submission to God's will. But to you, dear Monsieur le Chanoine, I can confide that our Elizabeth reminds us of the Divine Master on the Cross. She is in a lot of pain from little afflictions added to her general condition—the sense of a fire consuming her inside, and thus a scorching thirst that cannot be quenched because the least drop of water causes very acute suffering in that poor stomach, which is in-

capable of receiving any nourishment and *very* painful, etc., etc. But in the midst of all that, what peace, what beautiful serenity! She suffers as she has lived, like a saint. We are in the middle of our sixth novena to our dear little Venerable of Beaune.... I know Sr. Elizabeth would be truly happy to hear from you once more, she loves you so much!... She has loved [God] alone and has surrendered everything to Him.... I feel as though I have a priesthood to exercise with the Divine Master over this holy little victim of Love."

[2] "Amo Christum": cf. L 91, note 2. "In His light...": Ps 35:10.

[3] Jn 13:1.

[4] Someone else, probably Mother Germaine, has corrected this by putting "would cost." But Elizabeth writes in the indicative.

[5] Cf. L 244, note 4.

[6] Cf. L 225, note 7.

[7] Daily Communion had only been authorized since December 20, 1905, following the decree of Pius X (published in SRD of April 21, 1906, pp. 248–54). It was still not the custom to have the priest enter the enclosure to bring the Eucharist to the sick (except for the Viaticum of April 8). So Elizabeth had to be strong enough to be carried to the Communion grille of the infirmary (cf. Plan 3, letter B, the corner of the infirmary's inner parlor; the priest went up the staircase beside the sacristy and, passing through the "outer room," came to the Communion grille). Marie of the Holy Spirit (who was strong) testifies: "For a long time I carried her to receive Communion in the morning; I took her in my arms and she clasped me to her heart, telling me that O. L. was imprinted in me, so grateful she was to me" (PO 470).

[8] According to RB 2 (cf. PAT), this first meeting took place "a few weeks" before the "new attack" of May 13: probably on one of the last days in April or the first in May. A second meeting would take place on May 17 (cf. note 1).

[9] First draft: "in aeternum."

L 272   To Marie-Louise de Sourdon   [May 10, 1906][1]
J. M. + J. T.

My dear Marie-Louise,

Your delicious cake seemed to bring your whole heart to me, and I am sending all mine to tell you how touched I am by your tender care. I tasted your appetizing masterpiece; it was delicious, but my wretched stomach won't agree to anything, it's very bad-tempered; but I am grateful to it all the same for giving me the happiness of suffering for love of my Master and also for those I love. If you knew how much I think of you in my sufferings and in my even more profound solitude. I talk over your concerns[2] with the Virgin, and she has inspired me to send you a little statue[3] that I used to carry around with me and that I call my lucky charm: she wants to sow some of that in my little Marie-Louise. We often speak of you to

Our Reverend Mother, who looks after me and cares for me like a true mama; she is also praying for you and has her daughters pray too. A Dieu. My little Virgin will tell you everything that comes from my heart to yours, and if my Master carries me away, I will look after you as if you were a little sister.

Sabeth r.c.i.

[1] The handwriting of L 271 and 272 is already clearly larger and firmer than that of the first letters of April. Mme. de Sourdon has noted on the autograph copy: "May 10, 1906." See also note 3.
[2] Still the concerns about marriage.
[3] A small piece of paper in which this little unidentified statue was wrapped has been preserved in the ACD. Elizabeth writes on it: "My lucky charm for M. Louise." Mme. de Sourdon has noted: "May 10, 1906." They have also preserved a note with these words from Elizabeth: "Medal that was on my rosary which I take the liberty of sending to my 2nd Mother." Mme. de Sourdon also indicates the date as "May 10, 1906."

L 273   To her mother   [around May 27, 1906][1]
J. M. + J. T.

"If anyone loves Me he will keep My word,
and My Father will love him and
We will come to him and make our home in him."[2]

My darling little Mama,

I am beginning my letter with a declaration. Oh, you see, I loved you so much already, but since our last meeting[3] that has even doubled. It was so good to pour my soul into my mother's and to feel them vibrate in unison; you see, it seems to me that my love for you is not only that of a child for the best of mothers, but also that of a mother for her child. I am *the little mama of your soul;* that's all right, isn't it?

We are on retreat for Pentecost, I even more so in my dear little cenacle.[4] Separated from everything, I am asking the Holy Spirit to show you this presence of God within you that I spoke to you about. I have looked over some books for you that discuss this, but I would rather see you again before giving them to you. You can believe my doctrine, for it is not mine; if you read the Gospel of John, you will see over and over again that the Master insists on this commandment: "Remain in me, and I in you,"[5] and also that beautiful thought at the beginning of my letter, in which He speaks of making His home in us. Saint John, in his epistles, wants us to have "fellowship"[6] with the Holy Trinity; that word is so sweet, and it is so simple. It is enough—Saint Paul says this—it is enough to believe: God is spirit, and we approach Him through faith.[7] Realize that your soul is the temple of God, it is again Saint Paul who says this;[8] at every moment of the day and night the three Divine Persons are living within you. You do not possess the Sacred Humanity as you do when you receive Communion; but the Divinity, that essence the blessed adore in Heaven, is in your soul; there is a wholly adorable intimacy when you realize that; you are never alone again! If you'd prefer to think that God is close to you rather than within you, follow your attraction, as long as you live with Him. Don't forget to use my little chaplet,[9] I made it especially for you *with so much love;* and then I hope you are making your *three* prayers, *five* minutes each, in my little sanctuary. Think that you are with Him, and act as you would with Someone you love; it's so simple, there is no need for beautiful thoughts, only an outpouring of your heart.[10]

Thank you for the nice cake you sent, it so touched my heart, but you see it's too fine for my wretched stomach, which prefers lowly cottage cheese. Our good Mother is always close to me with little attentions; we speak of you very often, she loves you very much; oh, what a mother for your Sabeth! She is going to find me very talkative, and I think I'd better bring this little chat to an end. A Dieu, darling Mama, I send my most loving affection to you and that dear trio. Tell my Guite how closely united I am with her, I'm not far from any of you. Have Sabeth pray for Tata so she may profit from the graces of her illness. Remember me to Madame de Sourdon; tell her I feel like her third daughter and I'm praying for her intentions for her dear Marie-Louise. A Dieu again, let us live with Him. Oh! the earth and the things here below are nothing in comparison with eternity!

Your Sabeth

[1] "We are on retreat for Pentecost," a retreat (cf. L 230, note 6) that must have begun the evening of the feast of the Ascension, May 24, and ended on Pentecost morning, June 3. The letter is perhaps from *Sunday*, the 27th. The handwriting, after the new

attack of May 13, is again much less firm than that of the two preceding letters.
[2] Jn 14:23.
[3] May 17th (cf. L 271, note 1).
[4] Her more isolated infirmary cell.
[5] Jn 15:4.
[6] 1 Jn 1:3.
[7] Cf. Heb 11:6.
[8] Cf. 1 Cor 3:16–17 and 2 Cor 6:16.
[9] A little chaplet of movable beads for counting acts, in this case, of attention to God.
[10] Cf. the description of the prayer of Thérèse of Lisieux, in HA 182 (Ms C, 25r°) [SS 242]: not a "beautiful formula" or "beautiful prayers," but "an aspiration of the heart."

L 274   To Mother Jeanne of the Blessed Sacrament[1]

J. M. + J. T.   [June 3, 1906][2]
                                      "My vocation is love."[3]

My Reverend and very dear Mother,

I am sure the Master has already whispered to you in the silence of your soul how much His little bride appreciated your delicate attention; the dear rose[4] rests on the Heart of the Crucified; I never stop looking at it, it says so much to me!... My wretched, recalcitrant stomach enjoyed His Majesty the Bonbon[5] completely; I think it acquired a particular power for comforting the little patient simply by passing through your motherly hands. How she has prayed, in union with you, to draw down superabundant grace in Turin for a soul very dear to yours!

I know from our good Mother that you are about to go into retreat, and I am delighted to immolate myself to Love for you, so that this God whom Saint Paul calls "a consuming Fire"[6] might transform and divinize your whole being. I also know from Our Mother that your vocation is love, and, in reading Saint John of the Cross, the great doctor of love, I thought of you; he says that "God is pleased only by love. We can give Him nothing nor satisfy His one desire, which is to raise the dignity of our soul. The only thing that pleases Him is the exaltation of the soul; now nothing can elevate it as much as becoming in some way the equal of God; that is why He demands of it the tribute of its love, since the property of love is to make the lover equal to the one loved. The soul in possession of this love takes the name of the bride of the Son of God and appears on equal footing with Him, because their reciprocal affection makes everything common between them. Love establishes unity."[7]

In this unchanging dwelling place, dear Reverend Mother, my soul will be united to yours; I will ask the Holy Spirit, He who alone knows what is in God,[8] according to the words of the Apostle, to allow you to penetrate the unfathomable depths of the Divine Being. Ah, how happy I would be if He wanted to remove the veil so my soul might fly to Him and contemplate His Beauty in an eternal face-to-face. While waiting, I live in the heaven of faith in the center of my soul, and I strive to make my Master happy by being "the praise of His glory" already here on earth. Would you please ask this of Him, my Reverend Mother, and believe in the very respectful affection of this little Carmelite who sends you all the gratitude of her heart and asks you to bless her like one of your daughters.

Sr. M. E. of the Trinity r.c.i.

Please tell the little community that its little sister in Carmel is praying for it.

[1] This is the "Mother de Sambuy" of L 69, the Prioress of the Dominican Sisters, nurses of the poor, on rue Saumaise in Dijon.

[2] In a letter to Mother Germaine, Mother Jeanne of the Blessed Sacrament writes: "This was surely in May, since we were going to leave for the retreat in Beaune that took place that year during the Octave of Pentecost, and my dear Father ["a very dear soul," as Elizabeth says] had been so sick after Easter. The rose must have been one of those blessed for Pentecost." "You are about to go into retreat," Elizabeth says. But Pentecost was on the 3rd of June in 1906. The indication of "May 1906," made on the autograph by a different hand, is therefore incorrect.

[3] HA 208 [SS 194]; the quotation is repeated in the course of the letter.

[4] Cf. note 2.

[5] Candy she received from the Dominican Sisters. Her "wretched stomach" (an expression already encountered in L 272 and 273) can tolerate hardly any nourishment (cf. L 271, note 1). To take in as much nourishment as possible, Elizabeth ate ices and sometimes sucked on candy and chocolates, as we see in the following letters and in other documents (in PAT) from that period.

[6] Heb 12:29, quoting Dt 4:24.

[7] SC 307–8 [cf. K-RJ 28:1] (with some omissions). "Love establishes unity" is found in SC 383 [cf. K-RJ 36:1] (cf. L 121, note 4).

[8] Cf. 1 Cor 2:10; also the words "to penetrate the depths (of God)."

L 275   To Canon Angles   [beginning of June 1906][1]
           J. M. + J. T.   Deus ignis consumens.[2]

Dear Monsieur le Chanoine,

We are getting close to the feast of Saint Germaine, and this time I am coming to pay you a rather selfish visit; but you can imagine how happy I am to take advantage of this good excuse to come to you, although I am so often there in soul and heart. Yes, I need your chalice[3] to celebrate my Mother's feast day. You know that gratitude is the law of my heart, and it so overflows with it toward this good Mother! I was whispering to myself: "Quid retribuam?"[4] And then I thought of you and I had the answer. Oh! thank you for the happiness you give me!

Since I wrote you last, Heaven seemed to open again, and you prayed so hard that I am still captive; but a happy captive who, in the depths of her soul, sings night and day of the love of her Master. He is so good.... You would think He had only me to love and think about from the way He gives Himself to my soul, but this is so I, in return, might surrender myself to Him for His Church and all His interests, so I might care for His honor like my holy Mother Teresa.[5] Oh! ask that her daughter might also be "Charitatis victima"![6]

A Dieu, dear Monsieur le Chanoine, I send you all the respectful affection and thanks of my heart. Your wonderful letter[7] brought me so much happiness. Please bless your little child,

                                        Sr. E. of the Trinity r.c.i.

---

[1] "We are getting close to the feast of Saint Germaine [June 15]," hence this approximate date. We may also note that in 1904 and 1905, she writes *right at the beginning* of the month for this same reason (cf. note 3). Cf. also note 7.
[2] "God is a consuming Fire": Heb 12:29, quoting Dt 4:24.
[3] She is asking for a Mass as she has done the preceding years (cf. L 203 and 230).
[4] "What shall I give in return?" Ps 115:12 (115:3 in the *Manual*).
[5] Cf. L 156, note 4.
[6] "Victim of Love," cf. L 169, note 4.
[7] Of May 19. The letter has been preserved, cf. PAT.

L 276   To Madame Hallo   [around June 7, 1906][1]
       J. M. + J. T.   God alone suffices![2]

Dear second Mama,[3]

With what happiness I am sending you my dear little Mama, who has just gone through such an emotional time. I am so glad to think of all the affection her heart is going to find among you; she passed your kind letter on to me, and I surely recognized the heart of my second mama in Paris. Think how much a part I will be of your good, sweet family; it is so true that there is no distance between souls who have God as their center. I had another attack[4] that seemed like it would carry me away, but your good prayers assailed Heaven, and I am much better. Every morning I have the happiness of being carried to my Communion grille next to our cell,[5] and I come back with my Master to make my thanksgiving in my little bed. This morning I even attended Mass[6] on a chaise longue. I am so well cared for by our good Mother…. Mama will tell you all about that; you will see how suffering has done God's work in her soul, and I am filled with thanksgiving and gratitude. What mercy, what love the Master shows His little bride by sending her this illness; sometimes I say to myself that He acts as if He had no one but me to love! And you too, you are always working for His glory; you know I want to help you; as a true daughter of Saint Teresa, I desire to be an apostle so I can give every glory to Him whom I love, and, like my holy Mother, I think He has left me on earth so I might be zealous for His honor just like a true bride.[7] A Dieu, may He reveal to you all the tender affection for you in the heart of your second daughter, who is so grateful for everything you are doing for her poor Mama.

                                                        Elizabeth

---

[1] This and the following letter, of which we have only copies, seem to have been brought by Mme. Catez on her visit to Paris ("I am sending you my dear Mama"). She is already at the Hallos's when Mother Germaine writes to her on June 9 (cf. PAT). Mme. Catez perhaps left on the 8th, after having made her third visit to the sick Elizabeth, which Elizabeth had expected after Pentecost. Elizabeth must have entrusted these letters to her then, on the 7th (or 6th or 5th?) of June.

[2] Teresa of Avila. Cf. *Diary*, note 87.

[3] A title she also gave Mme. de Sourdon; in her overflowing affection she also called Sister Marthe of Jesus "Mama" (L 281 and 283), Sister Marie of the Incarnation

"Grandmama" (P 87), and said she had "the heart of a child" toward Sister Anne of Jesus (P 104).
[4] May 13, cf. L 271, note 1.
[5] Cf. L 271, note 7. Communion had therefore become daily.
[6] Still in the little oratory on the infirmary floor spoken of in L 271, note 7. A grille looked out on the chapel, cf. Plan 3, chapel, B.
[7] Cf. L 156, note 4.

L 277   To Marie-Louise Hallo   [around June 7, 1906][1]

+ Darling Sister,

I am coming to ask you to grant me the *same happiness* as last year by having a Mass said for Our Mother at Montmartre. It will be an *immense joy* for me to offer this to her on *your behalf* for her feast day![2] I am also entrusting a project to you: I *was dreaming* of giving Our Mother a symbolic picture;[3] you be the judge if Charles can do it, I give it entirely over to you. It should represent the Holy Trinity and three souls holding a harp on which to sing His glory; one of these souls should be more beautiful, for it is to represent Our Mother, the other is a little Sister of my soul[4] in this Carmel, and I am the third. Could you write on this picture with your lovely little writing: "Deus predestinavit nos ut essemus laudem gloriae ejus" (which means: God has predestined us to be the praise of His glory)? I did the translating, Charles will be able to correct my Latin.[5] Don't worry about it; I put it all in your hands; I know you'll be happy to take part in the little private feast day I am preparing for so good a Mother. Could you make me a regular-size chalice out of gold cardboard? I can't do that on my bed. Oh, how grateful I am to you, my little sister.

[1] Cf. note 1 of the preceding letter.
[2] June 15.
[3] Neither this nor the "chalice out of gold cardboard" has been found.
[4] Sister Anne-Marie of the Child Jesus (whom Elizabeth calls "my Sister of the Child Jesus"), a lay sister then 33 and a half years old. As her health deteriorated, she spent more time in the infirmary (but does not seem to have been sleeping there at this time). Although giving the impression that she would soon die, she lived to the age of 71. Childlike and joyous by nature, with an easy and easily influenced piety, she proved to have a fertile and "enlightened" imagination and to be a bit of a pseudomystic not exempt from jealousy. Her death circular would say of her (while stressing her good sides): "A rich, overflowing imagination made her slip quite na-

ively into many little illusions with respect to the supernatural ..." (there are other details in AL). In her great love for her Sisters, Elizabeth would draw this Sister with her. Cf. also P 101–3 of the following days.
⁵ This would be necessary. Elizabeth should have written "laus" (cf. L 250, note 16).

L 278 To Germaine de Gemeaux [(around?) June 10, 1906]¹
J. M. + J. T.

> The Father is love, the Son is grace,
> the Spirit is communion (Saint Paul).²

My dear little sister Germaine,

Thanks for your nice letter; it gave joy to my heart by drawing it even more intimately to yours, and I need to tell you how much I think about you in the even more profound solitude in which God has placed me. Since the end of March, I have been in the infirmary, keeping to my bed, with nothing to do but love.³

On the evening of Palm Sunday, I had a very severe attack, and I thought the hour had finally arrived when I was going to fly away into the infinite realms to contemplate unveiled this Trinity that has already been my dwelling place here below. In the calm and silence of that night, I received Extreme Unction and the visit of my Master. It seemed to me He was awaiting that moment to break my bonds. Oh! my little sister, what ineffable days I spent expecting the great vision! Our good and Reverend Mother was constantly at my bedside, preparing me to meet the Bridegroom and, in my desire to go to Him, I felt He was very slow in coming. How sweet and gentle death is⁴ for souls who have loved only Him, who, according to Saint Paul's expression, have not sought what is visible, because it is passing, but what is invisible, because it lasts eternally.⁵ I was so happy to die a Carmelite that I think in Heaven I would have asked the Holy Trinity to let my little Germaine come replace me in this Carmel. Her dear mama will forgive me, and now that God seems to want to leave me once more on earth, she needn't be anxious any more.

Dear little Germaine, the advice you have been given is very good; be faithful to your resolutions, practice the way of sacrifice and renunciation, for this must be the great law for all Christian life, and with even more reason for a soul who, like yours, aspires to follow the Master very closely, whatever His plans for her might be. Live always with Him within; that requires great mortification, for to unite oneself to Him constantly like that, one must be able to give Him everything. When a soul is faithful to all the least desires of His Heart, Jesus, in return, is faithful in protecting it, and He establishes between them so sweet an intimacy…. I am asking Him always to be the Master who instructs you in the secret depths of your soul. Little Germaine, be wholly attentive to His voice and remember that when He has thus found a place in a heart, it is to live there *"alone and set apart."*[6] You understand in what sense I mean this: I am not speaking of religious life, which is a great separation from the world, but of the detachment, the purity that places a veil over all that is not God and allows us to adhere constantly to Him through faith. May the Father overshadow you, and may that shadow be like a cloud that envelops you and separates you; may the Word imprint His beauty within you, in order to contemplate Himself in your soul as if in another Himself; may the Holy Spirit, who is Love, make your heart a little hearth that rejoices the Three Divine Persons through the ardor of its flames;[7] but do not forget that love, to be true, must be sacrificed: "He loved me, He gave Himself for me,"[8] there is the culmination of love. To prove to Jesus how much you love Him, learn how to forget yourself always in order to make your dear ones happy, and be very faithful to your duties and all your resolutions. Live more by will than by imagination. If you feel your weakness, my dear little Germaine, God wants you to use it to make acts of the will that you offer Him like so many acts of love rising up to His Heart to move it with delight. He loves you so much, little sister, He so wants you to be *His,* whatever might be the way you are to follow here below. Oh! how our soul needs to draw strength in prayer, doesn't it, especially in that intimate heart-to-heart in which the soul flows into God and God flows into it to transform it into Himself; this is my only occupation in my little cell, which is a true paradise. What a shame you can't come pay me a little visit; nevertheless, our souls meet and are "but one" through the Heart of Jesus, in the Holy Trinity.

Please kiss your dear mama for me, she is a little like my own, since you are my little sister, as well as Yvonne, to whom I also send a very loving kiss. Albert is very much in my thoughts, and I will be happy to learn the results of his examinations. How is Monsieur de Gemeaux? Tell him how often I think of him; I love to recall our happy reunions at the Gemeaux! A Dieu, my dear little Germaine, "may our life be hidden with Christ in God."[9] I leave you that thought from Saint Paul that says so much to my soul, and I am for all eternity your sister

E. of the Trinity r.c.i.

[1] This excerpt (note 2) is borrowed from the liturgy of the feast of the Trinity, June 10, which suggests the date (Elizabeth was continuing to say her breviary as much as she could, cf. Circ. 11). The "letter" received from Germaine was perhaps inspired by Elizabeth's second feast (the Trinity). Germaine's brother Albert's "examinations" are approaching.
[2] Cf. 2 Cor 13:13, but formulated in this way, the reference is to the seventh antiphon of Matins for the feast of the Holy Trinity.
[3] Cf. SC 313 [cf. K-RJ 28:9]: "All this work is directed to the practice of love...."
[4] Probably reminiscent of the "gentleness" and "sweetness" of the "death (of love)" described in LF 478 [K-RJ 1:30].
[5] Cf. 2 Cor 4:18.
[6] John of the Cross. Cf. L 220, note 4.
[7] Note the similarities (and differences) between these eight lines and L 269 (where the biblical references are indicated).
[8] Gal 2:20.
[9] Col 3:3.

L 279   To Sister Marie of the Trinity   [(June 10, 1906)][1]

Love is as strong as death.[2]

[1] Written on the back of a little holy card (not preserved), according to the recipient (PO 144). This quotation, which is found for the first time in L 269, very probably dates from this last illness. This was perhaps a holy card for the feast of Marie of the Trinity, June 10, which accompanied P 99.
[2] Song 8:6.

L 280   To her mother   [June 12, 1906][1]

My darling little Mama,

It's my fault if you haven't had any news. Yesterday Our Mother told me to write you and I didn't understand, but I'm sure you learned from Guite that you can be very much at peace about me and take full advantage of your stay with *such good friends*. Tell my other little mama how much I thank her for her letter, for her *kindnesses* to me and to you, for I love you more than myself, and all her attentiveness to you moves me to the depths of my heart; what a joy to think of you close to her, to my dear little sister and to Charles. I am with you, too, I'm sure you have no doubt about that, for wasn't that sweet home mine, too, in the past?[2] I feel like one of their children!

It seems to me the soul of your Carmelite is participating along with yours in the Triduum in honor of our blessed martyrs.[3] Oh! what happiness if your daughter could also give her God the witness of her blood! That would be worth the pain of staying on earth and seeing her dream of Heaven vanish. But she has found that Heaven on earth; I said that to our good Mother this morning, too. Oh, you see, there is a phrase from Saint Paul that is like a summary of my life and could be written on every one of its moments: "Propter nimiam charitatem." Yes, all these floods[4] of graces are because He has loved me exceedingly.[5] Darling Mama, let us love Him, let us live with Him as with a loved one from whom we cannot be separated. Tell me if you're making progress in the path of recollection in the presence of God, and if your little beads are being used faithfully;[6] you know I'm the little mother of your soul, so I'm full of solicitude for it. Remember these words of the Gospel: "The kingdom of God is within you."[7] Enter into this little kingdom to adore the Sovereign who resides there as in His own palace; He loves you so much, and He has given you so many signs of it by asking you often, on your path of life, to help Him carry His Cross. Marguerite is coming today; I'm delighted, for I think she will show me what you sent her.[8] I'll be glad to have more news of you through her, and to think that she'll be able to give some to you. Be very much at peace, you know what a Mother I have at my bedside, how well she cares for me. She makes me eat in front of her to encourage me to take more. She hasn't been able to have me carried onto the terrace[9] lately because the strong wind would have been too much for me, and she's regretted this, for she really insists that I get fresh air, and so does the doctor.

A Dieu, darling Mama, I am joining that dear little group on rue Vavin[10] to send all the best in my heart. Thank them on my behalf for you.

S. M. E. of the Trinity r.c.i.

Hello to Marguerite.[11] I am praying for her.

[1] "Marguerite is to come today." And on June 16 she will write: "I saw Guite Tuesday." The date is therefore Tuesday, June 12. Cf. also note 3.
[2] Rue Saint-Lazare in Dijon. "We saw each other nearly every day," says Charles Hallo (PA 793).
[3] The sixteen Carmelites of Compiègne, beatified by Pius X on May 27, 1906. The *Bulletin paroissial de Saint-Sulpice* from Paris (no. 9 from June 25) gives us ample information about this triduum from June 11 to 13 in the Church of Saint-Sulpice, the family parish of Blessed Teresa of Saint Augustine, the Prioress of the Carmelites of Compiègne.
[4] Written over the first draft: "this whole series."
[5] Eph 2:4.
[6] About her little "chaplet," cf. L 273, note 9.
[7] Lk 17:21.
[8] For the feast of St. Germaine on June 15.
[9] Cf. Plan 2, no. 3, or Plan 3 (where the last photograph of Elizabeth alive would be taken). The expression "lately" implies that there have already been other times spent on the terrace.
[10] The Hallos lived at 5 rue Vavin.
[11] The Hallos' servant, Marguerite Cherillon.

L 281   To Sister Marthe of Jesus[1]   [(Spring?) 1906][2]

+ Little Mama whom I love,[3]

You fill the dishes of your little child so full that you don't need to send her any cheese after Mass, for there is enough left from last night, and it's still cold. I like this way better, I will tell you why. I am praying for you, little Mama, and my Master asks me to tell you to live very close to Him, very much *in Him.* Then the outside activities, the noises within, will no longer be an obstacle; He will deliver you. Look at Him, love Him, little Mama whom I love.

+

[1] A lay sister, then 44 years old. She was the cook, carried the meals to the sick, and also helped a little in the infirmary. Elizabeth addressed P 105 and 114 to her. She

would testify: "[Elizabeth] was so affectionate and delicate in her gratitude for the least service one gave her that it was a joy to go to her" (PO 217).
[2] This note and the two that follow, written in pencil, date with certainty from her last illness. They may have been written in the spring. In her letter of June 9 to Mme. Hallo, Mother Germaine says: "We are still just having cottage cheese, but in a bigger quantity," and she also speaks of "Swiss chocolate" (cf. L 282, note 1).
[3] Cf. L 276, note 3.

L 282   To Sister Marthe of Jesus   [(Spring?) 1906][1]

If you knew the gift of God and Who it is who is crucifying you:[2] He is LOVE.

[1] Cf. preceding letter, note 1. Written on a piece of "Milka Suchard" chocolate wrapper.
[2] Cf. Jn 4:10. Elizabeth changes the word "speaking" to "crucifying."

L 283   To Sister Marthe of Jesus   [(on or after June 15) 1906][1]
+

Darling little Mama,
How happy the Bridegroom was to see that a maternal hand has made His bride's little bed all pure and white. He, in turn, wants to make you all pure and beautiful by His divine touch, an adorable embrace. Little Mama, look at Him: "Whoever looks at Him is radiant,"[2] as the Psalmist sings.

[1] An approximate date deduced from note 2.
[2] Ps 33:6, but according to the Eyragues translation (Ps 34:6). This very probably refers to the "book" Elizabeth gave Mother Germaine on June 15 (cf. L 288, note 5).

L 284   To Mother Germaine   [June 15, 1906][1]

The riches of our poverty.[2]
It is from His fullness that we have received all.[3]
+

PROPTER NIMIAM CHARITATEM[4]

Impelled by His immense love for our venerated Mother, the adored Master has made His two praises of glory[5] enter into His depths to make them His accomplices in enriching her with ineffable graces, and from this day on they will not cease to pray and immerse themselves in the heaven of their soul to be faithful to the mission entrusted to them.

MYSTICAL FLOWERS
gathered with the Bridegroom in His enclosed garden by His two "Praises of Glory" for their dearly beloved Mother.

THIRTY-THREE COMMUNIONS
in which we have asked the Master, through the fullness of the years of His life, to fill any emptiness that might have been found in those of our venerated Mother, and also so He might enclose her ever more deeply in the *"holy fortress of holy recollection"*[6] where His love jealously wishes to bury her so He can fill her with His infinite riches.

FOR THIS SAME INTENTION
our Master has asked us to offer all the Masses said every day as well as all the acts of the will (like so many acts of love) through which we return to the holy fortress.

ALSO EVERY DAY
the hour of Prime, so that the Holy Trinity may penetrate ever more completely the heaven of our beloved Mother, where we so love to adore Him.

SEVENTY-TWO MAGNIFICATS
to the Most Holy Virgin, God's most beautiful Praise of Glory, and also the one who penetrated most deeply into the holy fortress of holy recollection.

ALL THIS
placed in the bottom of the chalice where the Blood of the Lamb will be offered four times on the feast of Saint Germaine for our Shepherdess and our Queen.

And now, what will the two Praises of Glory give the Lord in return for the gift He has made them of so good a Mother who has willingly consented to be but *"one"* with them in the image of

GOD, THREE AND ONE?

[1] For the feast of "Saint Germaine." These are the "spiritual bouquets" spoken of in L 288.
[2] Written on four pages (one leaf folded in quarters) in *violet* ink, an ink not otherwise used by Elizabeth. She wanted to stress its festive character by doing so.
[3] Jn 1:16 (Elizabeth writes "tout" instead of "tous": "we have received all" instead of "we have all received").
[4] "Because of His exceeding love": Eph 2:4.
[5] Elizabeth and Anne-Marie. Cf. L 277, note 4 .
[6] The image also occurs for the first time on the same day in P 101. She is referring to John of the Cross, who describes the soul who has reached spiritual marriage and has henceforth taken refuge "in the fortress, the impregnable citadel of holy recollection with the Bridegroom" (SC 439–40 [cf. K-RJ 40:3]). The image will be repeated often: for example, L 316, note 8; P 101, 111, 113; HF 11; LR 14, 31, 43, 44; see also the inscription of the little banner of L 307, note 2.

L 285   To her mother   [June 16, 1906][1]
          J. M. + J. T.

My dear little Mama,

I'm so glad you're extending your stay…. It does me good to think of you close to dear Madame Hallo; your nice letter, the excellent news of your health made me very happy. I saw Guite on Tuesday[2] with the little ones; two true loves; my good infirmarian[3] saw them when she came to open the grille for me, which gave her true joy, for she has a very tender heart, and everything that touches me interests her. Sabeth was so good, kneeling down to say her prayer; these little angels are so pure; it seems to me that the Master must look on them with happiness, just as His bride does!

Our good Mother was really touched by your letter and delighted with the medal; she told me it was too beautiful. That dear Mother is so touched by heartfelt attention, and she loves you very much! I gave her your remembrance with such pleasure…. My little private feast day was last night;[4] I'm going to tell my other mama about it,[5] she made so much of it possible; she'll tell you about it. You were all there with us; you must have felt all the gratitude of the

two[6] little Sisters, who were so happy to celebrate the feast of a
Mother who can never be loved enough! The great Octave of Corpus Christi has begun. We have the Blessed Sacrament in the chapel
this year.[7] I used to love spending hours and entire days there.... But
I love the will of my adored Master even more, and there are no
more sacrifices for me; if I cannot go to Him, He comes to me to
embrace my soul with the tenderness of a mother.[8] Your daughter is
truly a happy creature, a child spoiled by God. Close to Him, oh,
how she thinks of her little Mama whom she loves ever more and
more! You wouldn't be satisfied if I didn't speak of my health. You
can be at peace on that account. I'm still eating cottage cheese and
Bruges bread,[9] by taking it all the time like this, my stomach is less
tired out; Guite is always sending me ices, and I suck on her chocolates; I give all these treats to my Master, I don't have any more
scruples like that. Lately the weather hasn't allowed me to go out
on the terrace, and I have not left my little sanctuary, except to go
sing to our Mother Thursday evening[10] in chapter, which is close to
the infirmary.[11] I was carried there for a few minutes on a chaise
longue. It was the first time in nearly three months that I had seen
my dear community again;[12] if you knew how happy my Sisters were
and how they looked after me.... It is touching to see how one is
loved here! A Dieu, I'm hurrying, for Our Mother is coming to get
my letter. I kiss you as I love you.

Your happy Carmelite Sabeth.

[1] Date deduced from note 4.

[2] June 12.

[3] Sister Anne of Jesus. "Open the [inner] grille": cf. L 112, note 4.

[4] June 15. Cf. L 286 and 288 for the "little feast day."

[5] Mme. Hallo, in the following letter.

[6] Elizabeth and Anne-Marie.

[7] Closed since the spring of 1903 (cf. L 165, note 6), the chapel was again open to the
public for several days. Mother Germaine writes on June 14 (the feast of Corpus
Christi) to Mme. Catez (who she assumes does not yet know the news) about "the
Blessed Sacrament, whose special feast it is today. Our chapel is no longer closed; I
hope that O. L. will have fervent adorers." After the law of separation was promulgated on December 9, 1905, private worship was not restricted. SRD of May 12, 1906,
mentions reopening for the first time.

[8] God as "mother": one can understand how Mother Germaine could be a transparent image of God for Elizabeth.

[9] A kind of cake, a little like brioche. Mother Germaine speaks of it in her June 9
letter to Mme. Catez: "The soups have been replaced by Bruges bread, which is

greatly appreciated, and which allows her to take some eggs. Sr. Elizabeth would not want them yet in any other form, and the Doctor does not want to force her, saying that nothing can be better for her than what her stomach digests best. Ices are better; Sr. Elizabeth says that it is Swiss chocolate, very sweet and nourishing."
[10] June 14th, the vigil of the feast of St. Germaine.
[11] Cf. Plan 2, no. 19, and Plan 3.
[12] That is, all the Sisters at once. She was too weak, ordinarily, to bear the presence of a whole group (cf. L 287).

L 286   To Madame and Marie-Louise Hallo   [June 16, 1906][1]
          J. M. + J. T.

My dear little Mama and my little sister,

How I thank you for the immense joy you have given to the heart of this little patient! I don't know how to express my gratitude to you for all your goodness, and I feel that only my Master can repay all my debts. Thanks to what you sent, my little feast day was complete. The dear chalice,[2] which surpassed all my hopes, arrived in perfect condition; I received it yesterday morning with the pretty stole ribbons, which touched me deeply; I could feel your whole heart in that package. Our Mother's little private feast day took place in the evening, in our little cell, just between her and her two Benjamins.[3] My dear little Sister, who is a true seraph, will repay you before God for the joy you have given her. She had arranged a small table with flowers and quite an exhibition: your beautiful chalice was in the place of honor along with the beautiful picture of the Holy Trinity, for which I owe you a very large thank you; the ribbons streamed on each side; the medal from Mama and the little gift from Guite were there too; then the little pieces of handwork;[4] finally the spiritual bouquets,[5] of which your Mass was the most beautiful flower. We were so happy to celebrate the feast of our good Mother.... She asks me to express all her gratitude to you. A Dieu, I'm leaving you, for my hand is very lazy, but my heart is not, and it is near you, forgetting the distance between Dijon and Paris. Thanks again, I gather your dear trio[6] together to send it all my heart. Your daughter and sister,

                                        M. E. of the Trinity, r.c.i.

Thanks for your kindnesses on behalf of my dear Mama.

¹ "Yesterday" the "little private feast day" of June 15. This letter undoubtedly accompanied L 285 in the same envelope.
² Cf. L 277.
³ Elizabeth and Anne-Marie.
⁴ Of needlework and embroidery. The Dijon Carmel still has several small pieces of work done by Elizabeth during her last illness; two small frames of fabric carry a text written by an unknown hand beneath Elizabeth's inscription: "The Virgin remaining in complete adoration of the gift of God" (cf. Jn 4:10) and "Deus Charitas est" (1 Jn 4:16).
⁵ This refers to L 284.
⁶ Mme. Hallo, Marie-Louise, and Charles.

L 287   To her mother   [June 19, 1906]¹
     J. M. + J. T.

My good little Mama,

Our good Mother, who understands your mother's heart so well, just came to tell me to write you and was sorry you did not have any news yesterday; but you know the proverb: "No news is good news." Today I'm coming myself to tell my dear Mama that her little patient still feels better, has more strength for sitting up in bed, and her head is fairly sound; it's her legs that don't want to hold her up; if it weren't for that I think she could do some of the little things for herself that her infirmarians² are so eager to do with so much love and affection. This morning Our Mother granted me the great joy of hearing Mass from the little tribune and of staying there for a good hour afterward before the Blessed Sacrament.³ They put me in the chaise longue, on the same level and quite close to the Blessed Sacrament, like a queen at the right hand of her Spouse.⁴ I exercised all my rights over His heart in favor of the little group on rue Vavin so He might pour all the riches of His grace over it in great abundance.

Yesterday I spent an hour and a half on the terrace in the morning, and that much again in the evening; since it has windows that open onto the choir, I heard them singing Benediction. It was our good Mother *herself* who set up my chaise longue. Oh, it is touching to see her motherly goodness to your little one; sometimes I tell her she has kept me from going to Heaven. Your letter was very interesting. How beautiful the ceremony of our Blesseds must have been, and how you must have given thanks to God, who led me onto this mountain of Carmel, in this Order made famous by so many saints and martyrs. Oh! how happy I would be if my Master also wanted me to pour out my blood for Him! But what I ask of Him especially is that martyrdom of love that consumed my holy Mother Teresa, whom the Church proclaims a "victim of charity"; and since the Truth has said that the greatest proof of love is to give one's life for one's beloved,[5] I am giving Him mine; it has been His for a long time, so He can do with it whatever He wishes, and if I am not a martyr by blood, I want to be one by love![6]

I'm delighted to read the little book[7] from Madame Hallo; please thank her for this new treat as well as for everything she sent me for Our Mother. That made me immensely happy, I couldn't have hoped for such a beautiful chalice, and her good Angel has counted up all the trouble I've put her to. I'm very glad your stay has been extended like that and you're in such good health; it's thanks to Madame Hallo's good care; how right you were to go to her to recover from the fright I gave you.... Madame de Vathaire came, saying you had given her complete permission to *see me*, which surprised me. Our Mother, who so loves to give joy to your heart, makes an exception for you, but it is against our Rules to carry sick Sisters to receive visits like that[8] (Madame de Vathaire). Our Mother said she would rather do that as a favor to Madame de Sourdon, who was so good to me this summer before she left Dijon. Besides, I wouldn't have the strength to carry on a parlor visit with the grille closed;[9] when I go to confession, it is all I can do to tell my sins; I don't see my Sisters at all except for the other evening, as I told you,[10] which would in any case be less tiring. I'll write a little note to Madame de Vathaire[11] to explain this to her.

Tell Madame Hallo I'm praying for her dear tourist,[12] that the Blessed Virgin might send all her Angels to guard him; and tell Marie-Louise that on Friday[13] I'll celebrate her feast day *solemnly* in the Heart of Jesus and I'll keep a rendez-vous with her in that ardent Furnace of love. A Dieu, Mama whom I love, remember that He dwells in your soul and that He wants you to withdraw there to love and adore Him. He will bring you all the tender affection of your darling daughter there.

Sr. M. E. of the Trinity r.c.i.

Kiss my other mama and my sister, thank them again for you and for me.

(Friday on the train, don't forget to pray, it's the perfect time for it, as I remember.)

---

[1] Mme. Catez is still in Paris. The exact date is determined by a process of elimination. A letter dated June 21 would arrive on Friday the 22nd, the day of departure from Paris (cf. note 13 and postscript) and is therefore excluded. The 20th is also excluded, since Mother Germaine writes on that day to Mme. Catez: "Sr. Elizabeth is writing to Mme. de Vathaire, which is why I am taking her place in writing to you, for two letters would tire her." Elizabeth has already written on the 16th (L 285), so Mme. Catez received some "news" on the 17th; the "yesterday" without any news is therefore the 18th, and the 19th is the "today" of the letter.

[2] Cf. L 268, note 4.

[3] Exposed because of the octave of Corpus Christi, during which they sang "Benediction" in the afternoon.

[4] Cf. Ps 44:10. During solemn exposition, the Blessed Sacrament was at the top of the neo-Gothic altar.

[5] Cf. Jn 15:13.

[6] A thought from Thérèse of Lisieux, cf. HA 255 (LT 54).

[7] On the basis of L 289, we can deduce that this refers to a "little book" on the sixteen martyred Carmelites of Compiègne.

[8] That is, with the interior grille open so the visitor can see Elizabeth, something reserved for the closest family members (cf. L 112, note 4).

[9] Cf. the preceding note. Her voice had become much weaker.

[10] In L 285.

[11] The letter has been lost. The visit would take place later just the same, cf. L 302.

[12] Charles on a trip.

[13] June 22, the feast of the Sacred Heart. Marie-Louise had tried religious life at Sacré Coeur (cf. L 27 and 30). Mother Germaine's June 20 letter to Mme. Catez tells her that her fourth visit to her sick daughter would take place on Saturday, June 23.

L 288   To her sister   [June 24, 1906][1]
+   From the little heaven of my soul.

Dear little sacrifice of praise,

Since I didn't see you yesterday with Mama, I asked "our" good Mother if I could tell you about our little private feast day, in which my three little victims[2] took part. My Sister of the Child Jesus (the other sacrifice of praise, who declared to me that she loved my Guite as much as I do) had brought a beautiful bouquet that formed the background of our display; in the middle was the dear little group,[3] and I can assure you that, of all our presents, this was what Our Mother looked at most; the chalice, which was truly magnificent, contained three little hosts, representing you with the little angels, one for her, and one for me.[4] Marie-Louise also sent some ribbons like we used to put on the stoles in the sewing room; they streamed all around; your dear book,[5] with your bookmark on it, was in front; both things really touched Our Mother, and I am very grateful to you for the book. How quickly you ran to satisfy my desire! The holy card of the Holy Trinity, the medal, and my little pieces of work, made with so much happiness for my Mother whom I love so much, decorated the rest of the little table; your letter was there with our spiritual bouquets and obviously pleased Our Mother, who is *entirely your Mother.* Then we sang the verses that my Sister of the Child Jesus and I had composed;[6] we were so happy to be able to pour out in this secret intimacy our love for the Mother who gives us so much of God!

Our Mother betrayed her child's desire by writing to Mama to bring back with her a book titled *L'Admirable* [The Admirable One], and which is so in fact! When I opened it just now, I came across these few lines, which I'm sending to nourish your soul: "The one who is holiest is the one who is most loving, the one who gazes the most toward God and most fully satisfies the desires of His gaze."[7] Isn't that beautiful, little praise of glory? And we are so united in sensing that this is what our Master is asking of us.... Oh, you see, I have so many desires for your soul, or rather I have only one, that you love, that you be all love, that you move only in love, that you give happiness to Love; that He might hollow out His abyss in your soul and that you might always be present to Him there: "Nothing can prevent the one who seeks and tastes God in everything from being solitary in the midst of a whole multitude; he is invincible to things that change the simple gaze and unalterable in the face of changing images; for he transcends them, seeking God alone."[8]

That is what I've just read for you in my beautiful book. Little praise of glory, let us sing our hymn to Love together day and night;

with David let us say: "I want to awake the dawn!,"[9] that is: before the dawn appears, I am already loving…. It is so simple to love, it is surrendering yourself to all His desires, just as He surrendered Himself to those of the Father; it is abiding in Him, for the heart that loves lives no longer in itself but in the one who is the object of that love;[10] it is suffering for Him, gathering up with joy each sacrifice, each immolation that permits us to give joy to His Heart. May He Himself teach you the science of love[11] in your interior solitude; I keep you in mine and it seems to me you are *quite close* to me there, "within me,"[12] in my heaven. I am writing you from there, and I ask my Trinity for a blessing for my three dear little sacrifices of praise.

M.E. of the Trinity, praise of His glory.

[1] "Yesterday" was June 23 (cf. L 287, note 13). Cf. also note 7.

[2] Guite and her two children. [Throughout this letter, Elizabeth again uses the word *"hostie"* with its varied nuances: sacrifice, host, victim.—TRANS.]

[3] Unidentified photograph.

[4] The three "hosts" should not be confused with the three "souls" of whom L 277 speaks and of whom Mother Germaine is one. In the context of the "hosts," Mother Germaine is the "priest"; cf. P 100 of this June 15, in which Germaine's "sacerdotal" mediation is well developed in stanzas 2, 3, and 5. For the development of this symbolism, cf. L 294, note 6, and L 320, note 3.

[5] In all probability, this refers to *Psaumes, traduits de l'Hébreu* [Psalms, translated from the Hebrew] by M.B. d'Eyragues (Paris: Lecoffre, 1904), LXIV + 427 pp. In any case, it has always been said in the Carmel of Dijon that Elizabeth used this book, as we will clearly see in the months to come. The book does not bear the library stamp of the monastery or any inscription, which can be explained by the "bookmark" that accompanied it: "How quickly you ran to satisfy my desire." Elizabeth had therefore suggested the choice of this book during her June 12th parlor visit (cf. L 285). Mother Germaine would have allowed this gift for the use of her patient.

[6] Cf. L 277 note 4.

[7] *Rusbrock l'Admirable (Oeuvres choisies)*, [Ruysbroeck the Admirable (Selected Works)] trans. Ernest Hello (Paris: Perrin et Cie, new ed., 1902), LXIV + 253 pp. (we abbreviate: Ru). The text quoted is found in Ru 113. In her letter of June 20, 1906, to Mme. Catez (cf. PAT), Mother Germaine writes: "I wanted to suggest an idea to you in case you would like to bring her a memento of your trip. Along with prayer, what makes her happy are books that speak of God in the movement of her soul; these fill her solitary days. Now among these books one captivates her, but I cannot let her have it because it is the only one in the Community and has many friends. It is *Rusbrock…*" (the description follows).

[8] The first phrase: Ru 115. The second (Elizabeth omits "and naked, plunged in divine contemplation" after "simple"): Ru 117. This passage is actually from G. van Wevel (cf. Vol. I, p. 69).

[9] Ps 56:9 (Eyragues trans.).

[10] Cf. L 299, note 11.

[11] Cf. HA 142 [SS 187]: "the science of love," Christ's words to St. Margaret Mary.
[12] Lk 17:21 (trans. from her *Manual*).

L 289   To Madame Hallo   [June 25 (or a little after), 1906][1]
          J. M. + J. T.

I have been longing, very dear Madame, to come tell you of my gratitude for all your goodness to my dear Mama, whom you have returned to me looking wonderfully healthy. She told me[2] about all your care, your thoughtfulness and what delightful days she had spent with you! You can guess with what interest your second daughter listened to the account of these things, as also to the details of your life, your works, etc. What a consolation for your souls to be able to spend yourselves like that for the glory of God in the midst of Paris where He is so offended. I was very interested in the details of the beautiful ceremony for our blessed martyrs as well as in the little book;[3] thanks too for the *Maxims* of our Father Saint John of the Cross,[4] which is a delight to my soul. What a treasure you have sent me, and how happy I am to have it to use, to be able to draw from it in all my needs. Union in suffering: it seems to me this sickness brings me even closer to you, for, like yours, it seems a little mysterious to me, and I call it the sickness of love,[5] for is it not He, my little Mama, who is working on us, who is consuming us! I am still on my little bed, wholly abandoned to my Master, wholly joyful beforehand for all that He will do. I know from Mama how you hurried to satisfy my desires, and I send you all the thanks of my heart, reuniting you with my dear Marie-Louise so I can keep my rendez-vous with you in His embrace, in the furnace of His Heart. Your second daughter,

S.M.E. of the Trinity r.c.i.

[1] Presuming that Elizabeth is still observing the regulation of a single letter a day (cf. L 287, note l), this one cannot be from the 24th, the date of L 288. It must be from shortly after June 23 (cf. the following note).
[2] During her visit on Saturday, June 23 (cf. L 288, note l).
[3] The Carmel of Dijon still has two "little books": Ph. Mazoyer, *Les seize Carmélites de Compiègne martyrisées le 17 juillet 1794, béatifées le 27 mai 1906* [(The Sixteen Carmelites of Compiègne martyred on July 17, 1794, beatified on May 27, 1906) (Paris: Lethielleux, 1906), 32 pp.; and Raphaël of the Immaculate Conception, *Les seize*

Carmélites de Compiègne. Le triomphe de la charité. 1794–1906 (The Sixteen Carmelites of Compiègne. The Triumph of Love. 1794–1906) (Lethielleux, 1906), 57 pp.

[4] *Maximes et avis spirituels de notre bienheureux Père Saint Jean de la Croix. Publié par les Carmélites de Paris* (Maxims and Spiritual Counsels of Our Blessed Father Saint John of the Cross. Published by the Carmelites of Paris) (Paris-Poitiers: Oudin, 1895), 107 pp.

[5] Elizabeth was perhaps inspired by John of the Cross, who develops this theme in stanzas 9–11 of the *Spiritual Canticle*. The expression "sickness of love" is in SC 119 [K-RJ 11:13] and also in a summary in SC 98 [K-RJ 10:1].

L 290   To Cécile Lignon   [end of June 1906][1]
J. M. + J. T.

My dear little Cécile,

I cannot tell you how touched I was by your kind letter; it seemed to bring your whole heart to me. It came to visit me in the solitude of the infirmary where I have been for three months. I really thought I was going to fly away to Heaven. Death is so sweet for a Carmelite that its perspective gave me only joy, and I knew it would not take me away from those I love any more than the dear grilles that hide me have separated me from them. You know that in my heart I am always your little mama, and if I had gone to Heaven, I would have been so even more. Sometimes people think that those inside the cloister are no longer able to love,[2] but it is just the contrary, and for my part I have never had more affection. It seems to me that my heart has expanded, and my dear Cécile holds a very big place there, as well as her little mama by whom I have always felt so loved! Oh, how I think of those nice vacations at Saint-Hilaire; I have not forgotten anything, not even the "four-step" danced by my Cécile! I am writing to you on my little bed, for I no longer have the strength to get up. If you saw how well I am cared for…. Our Reverend Mother is a true mama to me, she showers me with kindness just as a mother would shower her little child. Oh, my little Cécile, how happy I am in my Carmel; it seems to me one cannot have more happiness except in Heaven, and this happiness is like a prelude, since God alone is already the Object of it. But, just as in Heaven, they do not forget those on earth; your Elizabeth thinks of those she has left and prays for them. I kiss you as well as your darling little mama and your grandmother; remember me too to your kind father, for I love his big heart so much; greetings too to Antoine. Your little mama,

                                      Sr. Elizabeth of the Trinity r.c.i.

---

[1] "For three months" in the infirmary, still "on her little bed." The approximate date is based on this. Cécile Lignon is 15 years old, her brother "Antoine," 21.
[2] Possible allusion to Teresa of Avila, *The Way of Perfection*, chap. 8, a text already quoted by Elizabeth in her *Diary* (D 15).

L 291   To Louise Demoulin   [end of June 1906][1]
     J. M. + J. T.   "God alone suffices."[2]

It has been a long time since I have seen you, my little Louise, and I don't know if I will see you again here below, so I asked our Reverend Mother for permission to write you this little note on my little bed where it has pleased God to keep me for three months. I don't know if He will take me soon into His Heaven that I so desire, but before leaving I was anxious to tell you that in paradise as on earth, and even more so, I will always look on you as my little child. I am asking Our Lord Himself to be your Master, your Friend, your Confidant, your Strength; may He make your soul into a little heaven where He can rest with happiness, and remove from it anything that might offend His divine gaze. He loves brave and generous hearts, and He said to one of His saints: "Your measure will be my measure."[3] So make Him a very large measure: He so desires to fill His little Louise.... And then remember that love must end in sacrifice. Saint Paul tells us when speaking of the Master: "He loved me, He gave Himself up for me."[4] May His holy will be the two-edged sword that immolates you at every moment; go learn this science near Jesus in the agony of the garden, when His crushed soul cried out: "May Your will be done and not mine."[5] My little Louise, live with Him wherever you are, whatever you are doing; He never leaves you, so remain unceasingly with Him; enter into the depths of your soul, for you will always find Him there desirous of your well-being. A Dieu, my little child; will you help me thank Him: He has fulfilled all my desires, and I hope I will soon go to see Him in His light, in His beauty, to sing the canticle of the Lamb with the procession of virgins.[6]

Sr. M. Elizabeth of the Trinity r.c.i.

[1] An approximate date. Same reason as in L 290, note 1. Louise is 19 years old. Her chronological information: "one month before leaving this earth" (testimony of February 10, 1907, cf. PAT) is surely wrong, unless it refers to a letter that has been lost.

[2] Teresa of Avila. Cf. *Diary*, note 87.

[3] A sentence from P. Vallée. It is found in the 1897 retreat, fifth conference ("Remember Our Lord's words to Saint Catherine of Siena: Your measure will be my measure"); in the 1900 retreat, ninth conference; in the third morning conference and the fifth evening conference of the 1902 retreat.

[4] Gal 2:20.

[5] Mk 14:36.

[6] Combination of Rev 14:4 and 15:3.

L 292   To her sister   [beginning of July 1906][1]
        J. M. + J. T.

Darling little sister,

I'm really in a hurry, for it's time for prayer and Our Mother will come to take my letter, but I want you to have a little note from my heart. I hope to receive a few lines from your soul. I will, won't I, my little one?

I'm reading magnificent things in the book from Mama (tell her that); it always speaks of that interior "abyss" in which we must immerse and lose ourselves, that abyss of love we possess within us where beatitude awaits us if we are faithful in returning there. Little sister, union in that very simple movement, in that descent toward our interior abyss.[2] Our Mother wonders if it would be possible for you, little Guite, to give orders for the Infant Jesus of Prague[3] to be returned to us for July 16th. We are putting the statues back in the chapel; the Bishop[4] will undoubtedly come for Benediction[5] and I would be grateful to you if you could have the little Jesus sent to us; our Sisters could even go get it if you don't have anyone; thanks in advance. A Dieu, little sister, how fortunate you are to care for our darling Mama;[6] it's for both of us, isn't it? I'm sending all my heart to you as well as to the angels, passing through that of the Three, the immense sea: may it engulf you....

Sabeth, Laudem gloriae.

[1] "July 16th" is not yet very close; the Bishop's presence at Benediction is not yet certain (cf. note 5).

[2] Elizabeth is thinking particularly of Ru 52–53: "The descent to simple, immense love produces pleasure in us; now love is an abyss, and there is no bottom to the abyss. Now abyss calls to abyss; the abyss of God calls to the elect for unity.... United in the spirit of God ... we will possess with Him and in Him salvation and beatitude."

In the following months, this image will be above all an echo of Ruysbroeck. Yet for Elizabeth, it has several much earlier and rather inextricable layers: the word "abyss" springs up spontaneously in Elizabeth, who so loves to recollect herself in the depths of her soul to encounter there the depth of the mystery of the God who is present; she writes even *before* entering Carmel: "I so love the mystery of the Holy Trinity, it is an abyss in which I lose myself!..." (L 62).

The image, moreover, is a familiar one in the piety of that time. Elizabeth was still reading regularly in the Office, in Ps 41:8: "Abyss calls to abyss." She has also encountered (and taken up, cf. L 115) this image in the *Prayer to the Holy Trinity* of Catherine of Siena, who often used the expression "abyss of love"; in Thérèse of Lisieux, in the former ending of the *Story of a Soul,* which she often echoes (HA 198, Ms C, 35r° [SS 256], and HA 214, Ms B, 5v° [SS 199–200]); in John of the Cross (SC 129, 299 and 423 [cf. K-RJ 12:9, 27:1, 39:5]: "abyss of glory," quoted in L 185 and HF 31; LF 609 [K-RJ 3:71]); finally, in the very last months, in Angela di Foligno, who used the image very often: noting in particular the "double abyss" (cf. P 118, with note 7, and GV 5).

In Elizabeth's writings the image of the abyss is found, for example, in L 62, 125, 185, 190, 208, 288, 292, 298, 316; P 93, 101, 106, 109, 115, 118, 120; HF 4, 7, 21, 32, 35, 36, 37, 40, 43; GV 2, 5; LR 1, 7, 21, 44. "To immerse oneself *(s'abimer),"* for example in L 202, 271; P 93, 106; HF 25. Compare this also with the image of "being lost" (which is often present in Elizabeth) in "the ocean," cf. L 110, note 3.

[3] During the time when the chapel was closed (cf. L 165, note 6) and the nuns felt the threat of having to flee to Belgium, the Carmel had placed the statues from the chapel in private homes. The Infant Jesus of Prague was in Guite's. She had "to give orders" to have it returned because she was not in Dijon but on vacation (cf. note 6). Mother Germaine explains in a postscript to this letter: "The iron rods that support this statue look bad in the chapel without it, but that doesn't matter."

[4] After Bishop Le Nordez resigned, the episcopal seat of Dijon was vacant for more than 17 months. On February 25, 1906, Pius X ordained 14 new French bishops at the same time at Saint Peter's in Rome. Among them was Pierre Dadolle, 49 years of age, named Bishop of Dijon. He took office on March 15, 1906.

[5] In the afternoon. It was the feast of Our Lady of Mt. Carmel (cf. SRD, 21, p. 462).

[6] Mother Germaine's postscript confirms that Guite was away from Dijon. Mme. Catez is at home (cf. RB 2). Elizabeth sends her letter of July 11 to her at "Sainte-Marie-sur-Ouche," a town situated a little over 13 miles west of Dijon.

L 293   To Clémence Blanc

[(around the beginning of?) July 1906][1]

J.M. + J.T.   "My vocation is love."[2]

My dear little Tobias,[3]

My Angel's heart has been delightfully moved by your kind letter. I am happy you feel how true it is that I am not leaving you; it seems to me that my prayer and my sufferings are the wings I cover you with to "guard you in all your ways."[4] If you knew with what joy I would endure the greatest sufferings to obtain ever more fidelity and love for you.... You are the darling child of my soul, and I *want* to help you, to be your Angel who is invisible but always present to give you help. Yes, little sister, I believe love does not allow us to pause for long here on earth, and besides Saint John of the Cross says so definitively; he has a wonderful chapter in which he describes the death of souls who are victims of love, the last assaults He gives them, then all the rivers of the soul, which are so immense they already resemble seas, go to lose themselves in the Ocean of divine love.[5] Little sister, Saint Paul says that "our God is a consuming Fire."[6] If we remain always united to Him by a simple, loving gaze of faith; if, like our adored Master, we can say at the end of every day: "Because I love my Father, I always do what pleases Him,"[7] He will really be able to consume us, and like two little sparks we will lose ourselves in the immense Furnace, free to burn there for all eternity. You tell me to ask God for a sign so you will know if we will see each other again and if you will come take your place close to your little Angel; but, despite my intense desire to make you happy, I cannot do it, for that is not my grace, and it seems to me that it would mean putting aside abandonment. What I can tell you, darling sister, is that you are loved, very much loved by *our* Master and that He wants you for *His own*. He is divinely jealous for your soul, with the jealousy of a Bridegroom. Keep Him in your heart "alone and set apart";[8] may love be your cloister; you will carry it everywhere and thus you will find solitude among whole multitudes. I have read that "the one who is holiest is the one who is most loving, who gazes the most toward God and most fully satisfies the desires of His gaze."[9] May this be our plan. A Dieu, beloved sister, everything speaks to me of my departure for the Father's House; if you knew with what serene joy I await the face-to-face. In the midst of dazzling light, I will always be leaning over my darling child to keep her for her Master like a beautiful lily so He may pick her with happiness for His flower bed of virgins and rest His consuming gaze on this flower He has cultivated with so much love. I kiss you in Him. Your little Angel,

Sr. E. of the Trinity

[1] Clémence Blanc had been a postulant, perhaps a novice, in the Carmel (cf. note 3). Having left recently (we do not know exactly when), she is the "little ex-Carmelite" who is referred to on July 16 (L 298) and August 2 (L 302); from these letters we can deduce that she stayed temporarily with Guite at Sainte-Marie-sur-Ouche. The tone of this letter, which may have accompanied L 292, situates it shortly after Clémence's departure.
[2] HA 208 [SS 194].
[3] Cf. L 102, note 2.
[4] Ps 90:11 (Eyragues trans.).
[5] Cf. *Living Flame,* stanza 1, in particular p. 478 [K-RJ 1:30]: nearly all the words of this last sentence are taken from him.
[6] Heb 12:29, quoting Dt 4:24.
[7] Cf. Jn 8:29.
[8] John of the Cross. Cf. L 220, note 4.
[9] Ru 113.

L 294   To Canon Angles   [July 8 or 9, 1906][1]
          J. M. + J. T.   "Deus ignis consumens."[2]

Dear Monsieur le Chanoine,

I am sure the Master has given you all the messages of His little bride and that you already know all the gratitude I would like to try to express to you today. You can guess with what joy I offered your divine bouquet[3] to my beloved Mother, who asks me to express all her gratitude to you; thank you for the happiness you have given my heart! Your dear letter made me very happy. Oh, how I love the thought by Saint Paul you sent me! It seems to me it is being realized in me, on this little bed that is the altar[4] on which I am being immolated to Love. Oh, ask that my likeness to the adored Image might be more perfect each day: "Configuratus morti ejus."[5] That is what haunts me, what gives strength to my soul in suffering. If you knew what a work of destruction I feel throughout my whole being; the road to Calvary has opened, and I am quite joyful to walk it like a bride beside the divine Crucified. I will be twenty-six on the 18th; I do not know if this year will end in time or eternity, and I ask you, like a child of her father, to please consecrate me at Holy Mass as a sacrifice of praise to the glory[6] of God. Oh, consecrate me so completely that I may be no longer *myself but Him,*[7] so the Father, in looking at me, may recognize Him; so "I might be like Him in His death,"[8] so I may suffer in myself what is wanting in His passion for His body, the Church,[9] and then bathe me in the Blood of Christ so I may be strong with His strength; I feel so little, so weak.... A Dieu, dear Monsieur le Chanoine. I saw my good Mama last week;[10] she seems very tired; she worries; the doctor told Guite she is getting much weaker. I am sharing all this with you so you might bear it with God, and I ask you to bless me in the name of the Trinity to which I am especially consecrated. Would you also please consecrate me to the Blessed Virgin, for she, the Immaculate One, gave me the habit of Carmel[11] and I am asking her to clothe me again in that "fine linen robe" in which the bride is dressed to present herself at the marriage feast of the Lamb.[12] Be assured, dear Monsieur le Chanoine, of the respectful affection of the little Carmelite who will call herself your child in Heaven as on earth.

Sr. M. Elizabeth of the Trinity r.c.i.

On August 2nd, I will have been in religious life five years!

[1] July 1906: "I will be twenty-six on the 18th." We can be even more specific (with a 1906 calendar before us) because of the unexpected improvement that allowed the patient to get out of bed and walk.

On July 15th, a Sunday, Elizabeth affirmed that this sudden improvement took place "one fine day last week" (L 296), therefore between July 8th and 14th. Letter 295 (July 11) relates this event as having happened "the other day" (which eliminates the 10th, for Elizabeth would have written "yesterday"). The only possibility left is *July 8 or 9.* The letter to Canon Angles implies that Elizabeth is still "on this little bed"; moreover, she would surely have told about this sudden improvement thanks to the intercession of Thérèse of Lisieux if the letter had been written *after* the 8th or 9th. It cannot be dated *before* the 8th or 9th either, for Elizabeth says she saw her mother "last week." That cannot be an allusion to the visit on Saturday, June 23 (cf. L 287, note 13), for Elizabeth could not say "last week" if she were writing in *July.* Now Mme. Catez's visits during this illness took place "every two weeks" (RB 2 in PAT), which L 315 confirms; between the visit of Saturday, June 23, and that of Saturday, July 21 (cf.

L 300), there was this fifth visit of Saturday, July 7 (or one or two days before, if the interval was not completely regular).

[2] "God is a consuming Fire": Heb 12:29, quoting Dt 4:24.

[3] The Mass requested for the feast of June 15 (cf. L 275).

[4] The comparison of her "bed" of suffering with an "altar" is found again in Elizabeth's words quoted by Mother Marie of Jesus (cf. L 306, note 1).

[5] Phil 3:10. Elizabeth writes "mortis."

[6] "Sacrifice of praise": Ps 115:17 and Heb 13:15. The expression is for the first time united with "praise of glory" in L 244. Elizabeth thus sees herself as a "sacrifice of praise" in the chalice of the Mass (cf. L 288) on "the altar" of her "bed" of suffering (cf. the following lines). The comparison is developed in L 309.

[7] Cf. Gal 2:20.

[8] Phil 3:10, cf. note 5.

[9] Cf. Col 1:24.

[10] July 7? Cf. note 1.

[11] An allusion to her clothing, *December 8, 1901.*

[12] Cf. Rev 19:8–9.

L 295   To her mother   [July 11, 1906][1]
J. M. + J. T.

Darling Mama,

I've just read your nice letter and I'm answering very quickly. What happiness to feel you surrounded by Guite during this crisis in your health…. How I wish God would give me all your illnesses…. But I love you too much, and I want to let Him have you share His Cross too. My stomach is still recalcitrant when it comes to food, but imagine, I'm starting to walk; I can't get over it, for I'm no stronger than before, when I couldn't even sit up. The other day,[2] when Our Mother came, I felt very tired and told her I was going; she replied that instead of talking like that I would do much better to try walking. I love so much to obey her! When I was alone, I made some attempts by the edge of the bed; it hurt a great deal; I prayed to Sister Thérèse of the Child Jesus,[3] not to cure me but to give me the use of my legs, and I was able to walk. You'd really laugh if you saw me like a little old lady bent over my stick. Our good Mother takes me by the arm onto the terrace; I'm quite proud of my comings and goings; I'm longing to give you a demonstration; you'd surely get a good laugh, for I'm very funny, and I'm delighted to announce this good news to you, knowing it will make you very happy. Don't cry over your Sabeth; God will leave her with you a little while longer; and then, in Heaven, she will always be bending over her mother, this mother who is so good and whom she loves more and more.... Oh, darling Mama, let's look above, that gives rest to the soul; when you think that Heaven is the Father's House,[4] where He waits for us as for beloved children returning home after a time of exile, and that He makes Himself our traveling companion to lead us there! Live with Him in your soul, make acts of recollection in His presence; offer Him the sufferings you are going through with your health, for it's the best thing we can give Him. If we knew how to appreciate the happiness of suffering, we would yearn for it; keep in mind that it is thanks to it we can give something to God: Oh, let's not lose one opportunity for doing so; put all your joy into it.

But, for example, be very careful to obey your Carmelite; let yourself be pampered by our good Guiguite, who is so happy to do it; don't worry; this is a little crisis you're going through at the moment; rest on your Sabeth, who is praying so much for her darling little Mama. The good air will revive you; you must have some very fresh eggs in the country and some good milk for your poor stomach. I'll be delighted to see you again;[5] while we are waiting, let's always live together close to Him. Once I would have loved that little life you are leading in your convent;[6] the calm, the rest and your Guite's affection will revive you. Sabeth's poor little finger must hurt her.... I wish I could spend just a few minutes in the habit of the kind Sister who is caring for it; but no, I want to be the Angel of my little ones; an Angel does not touch, but is always there, and I too have my wings to cover them: prayer, suffering. I'm closing very quickly so my letter can be sent this evening; I kiss you with all the fullness of my heart overflowing with love for you; don't *be concerned* about my health, nor about yours. Our Mother loves you like a daughter and sends you all her heart; I have no more words for her kindness, there is too much of it.

Sabeth r.c.i.

[1] The envelope (5.9" x 4.8") is rather large, so the letter was folded only once (5.3" x 5" format), and is still preserved. The letter, postmarked in Dijon on "July 12, 1906," at 11 o'clock in the morning, was therefore written the day before. Moreover, she recounts the sudden improvement of July 8–9. In an undated note to Mme. Catez

that must have accompanied this letter, Mother Germaine writes: "Her general condition is the same, even seems to improve, since she is walking at present! Her stomach, however, still remains recalcitrant with respect to a very needed increase in food."

[2] July 8th or 9th. Cf. L 294, note l.

[3] It is not surprising that Elizabeth had recourse to her.

[4] Cf. Jn 14:2.

[5] Saturday, July 21. Cf. L 300.

[6] The envelope of this letter is addressed to "Madame Catez, at Sainte-Marie-sur-Ouche, Côte d'Or." The "convent" belonged to the Sisters of Providence (of Vitteaux). Forced by the anti-assembly laws to close their convent school, they lived in the neighboring house (to the left of the convent) and did not wear the religious habit, which Elizabeth seems to have forgotten when she speaks of "the habit." Undoubtedly Mme. Catez, with Guite and her children and also Mme. Guémard (cf. L 302), were lodged in the rooms of the convent school.

L 296   To Madame de Sourdon   [July 15, 1906][1]
J. M. + J. T.

Very dear Madame,

You can guess how much I am praying for our dear Marie-Louise during the great novena in preparation for Our Lady of Mount Carmel. Besides, I have been discussing Marie-Louise's concerns with the Blessed Virgin a long time now,[2] and you know that we never invoke her in vain; but God's thoughts are deep and are not our thoughts;[3] may we know how to wait for His hour and may our faith grow, if this were possible, to the height of His love. He is Father, and even if a mother would forget her child, He would never abandon us.[4] Dear Madame, believe that this grace won by suffering and by waiting in peace and trust will be all the greater and deeper because of it, and may all the prayers and sacrifices offered for your dear little one draw down very special blessings on her. I repeat once again how much I am praying for this intention; I would be *so happy* to have something to do with Marie-Louise's happiness. My health is still pretty much the same, but imagine, without getting any stronger, one fine day last week[5] I started to walk; I was urged to ask this of God, and I was answered immediately. On the other hand (I can tell you everything), I cannot ask to be cured, and everything seems to speak to me of a more or less imminent departure. Oh, how I will delight in the Father's House to draw down on you the graces my very grateful heart would love to obtain for you here on earth…. A Dieu, dear Madame, be assured of the affection of the little Carmelite who thinks of herself almost as your third daughter; she kisses you with all her heart.

Sr. M. E. of the Trinity r.c.i.

[1] The envelope addressed to the "Comtesse de Sourdon, chez M[e] la baronne d'Anthès, Avallon, Yonne" is still preserved. The Dijon postmark is illegible but must be the 16th, since the letter was stamped in Avallon on July 17 at 6:30. (Moreover, a postscript from Mother Germaine, mentioning that "The dear little one is about the same," speaks of the Benediction that ended on July 16.) But Elizabeth's letter (which undoubtedly remained on the Prioress's desk on that feast day) was well *before* the 16th, since it was written still "during the great novena in preparation for Our Lady of Mount Carmel." It can only be from *Sunday,* July 15; otherwise she would not have been able to say that the sudden improvement of July 8 or 9 occurred "last week." Mme. de Sourdon later fixed the date of "July 15, 1906."
[2] Still her concerns about marriage.
[3] Cf. Is 55:8.
[4] Cf. Is 49:15.
[5] July 8 or 9. Cf. L 294, note 1.

L 297   To Sister Marie of the Blessed Sacrament[1] [July 16, 1906][2]

J. M. + J. T. Amo Christum.

The entire soul of your little sister is united to yours on this vigil of the beautiful day when you are going to be clothed in the habit of the Virgin of Carmel, and I am happily taking advantage of this occasion to send you a little note from my heart, which is so touched by the kind lines you wrote to me. I am even more separated, more alone with the Alone,[3] and I can assure you that in my little heaven you are often the subject of conversation between Bridegroom and bride. All my sufferings, in a word, my whole day tomorrow will be for you; I am asking the Master to make you a bride according to His Heart, one of those souls like our holy Mother Teresa wanted, able to serve God and His Church,[3a] wholly passionate for His glory and His interests. Oh, isn't it beautiful in Carmel; I think I will soon leave it for Heaven,[4] but the transition seems very simple to me, and the waiting is truly very sweet for the bride who longs to see Him whom she loves in His great light! I must leave you, for I am very weak and my good Mother would scold me if I were too talkative. Ah! if you could see her at the bedside of her child! I could never say all that she is for me; but you know! Be assured that your little sister is using all her rights as bride over the Heart of the Master in your favor; like a little queen at the right hand of the King[5] of glory, she implores Him wholeheartedly that He might fill you with His fullness, root you in His charity,[6] and surround you with His strength to climb the austere mountain. I thank Him for you; I delight in your happiness, "for you are Christ's, and Christ is God's."[7] In Him, I love you and am your very affectionate little sister.

S. M. E. of the Trinity r.c.i.

I am not in a condition to write to your kind Mother, but I will make up for it before long,[8] ask a blessing from her for her little House of God.[9] My good infirmarian (Sister Anne of Jesus) asks me to tell you she is praying very much for you and remembers you often.

[1] This is Marie de Benoist, then 46 years old, whom Elizabeth knew well since she had often visited the Dijon Carmel. She entered the Carmel of Paray-le-Monial (PO 343) in March 1906.
[2] "On this vigil" of her clothing, July 17.
[3] Teresa of Avila. Cf. L 109, note 5.
[3a] Cf. L 299, note 12.
[4] Mother Germaine adds regarding this: "and I think so too: what a little saint!"
[5] Cf. Ps 44:10.
[6] Cf. Eph 3:17.
[7] 1 Cor 3:23.
[8] Cf. L 306.
[9] Allusion to her Hebrew name "Elizabeth."

L 298   To her sister   [July 16, 1906][1]
     J. M. + J. T.   "My vocation is love."[2]

Dear little sister,
     Your letter has been one more joy in my heaven where I keep you constantly with me. Today I gave you and the little angels to the Blessed Virgin. Oh! never have I loved her so much! I weep for joy when I think that this wholly serene, wholly luminous Creature is my Mother and I delight in her beauty like a child who loves its

mother; I feel strongly drawn to her, I've made her Queen and Guardian of my heaven, and of yours, for I do everything for both of us. Darling little sister, you must cross out the word "discouragement" from your dictionary of love; the more you feel your weakness, your difficulty in recollecting yourself, and the more hidden the Master seems, the more you must rejoice, for then you are giving to Him, and, when one loves, isn't it better to give than to receive?[3] God said to Saint Paul: "My grace is sufficient for you, for power is made perfect in weakness,"[4] and the great saint understood this so well that he cried out: "I boast of my infirmities, for when I am weak, the power of Jesus Christ dwells in me."[5] What does it matter what we feel; *He,* He is the Unchanging One, He who never changes: He loves you today as He loved you yesterday and will love you tomorrow. Even if you have caused Him pain, remember that abyss calls to another abyss[6] and that the abyss of your misery, little Guite, attracts the abyss of His mercy,[7] oh! you see, He is making me understand that so well, and it is for both of us. He is also drawing me very much toward suffering, the gift of self; it seems to me that this is the culmination of love. Little sister, let us overlook no sacrifice, there are so many we can gather up in one day: with the little ones you have many opportunities; oh, give everything to the Master. Don't you find that suffering binds us more closely to Him.... So, if He takes your sister, it would be in order to be even more yours. Little Guite, help me prepare for my eternity; I don't think I will live much longer; you love me enough to rejoice that I am going to rest there where I have already lived for a long time. I love to talk to you about these things, little sister, echo of my soul;[8] I am selfish, for I am perhaps going to hurt you, but I love to lead you above what dies, into the bosom of infinite Love. That is the homeland of the two little sisters, where they will always meet. Oh, Guite, as I write you this evening my soul is overflowing, for I feel the "exceeding love"[9] of my Master and wish I could make my soul pass into yours so you could believe in this love always, especially in your saddest times.

My little legs are making progress, and I am taking advantage of it to make visits in the little tribune, it's divine! I am God's little recluse,[10] and when I return to my dear cell to continue there the

conversation begun at the tribune, a divine joy takes hold of me; I
so love solitude with Him alone, and I lead a simple hermit's life that
is truly delightful. You know, it is far from being exempt from help-
lessness; I, too, need to seek my Master who hides Himself well; but
then I stir up my faith, and I am happier at not enjoying His presence so I can make Him enjoy my love. At night, when you awake,
unite yourself to me. I wish I could invite you here near me; it is so
mysterious, so silent, this little cell with its white walls that set off a
black wooden cross without a Corpus. It is mine, the place where I
must immolate myself at every moment to be conformed to my crucified Bridegroom. Saint Paul said: "what I want is to know Him,
Christ, to share in His sufferings, to become like Him in His
death." [11] By this is understood that mystical death by which the soul
annihilates itself and forgets itself so completely that it goes to die
in God in order to be transformed in Him. Little sister, that requires
suffering, for all that is us must be destroyed in order to put God
Himself in place. I've been thinking about Saint Margaret for a long
time, [12] and I think I can celebrate your feast better than anyone else,
for I am offering you nothing perishable, but rather something divine, eternal: I am preparing to celebrate your feast with a special
novena. I am saying SEXT for you every morning—that is the hour of
the Word—so He might imprint Himself so well in you that you
might be another Christ. And then NONE, which is the hour of the
Father, so He might possess you like a beloved daughter, that the
power of His right arm [13] might lead you in all your ways and guide
you ever more toward that abyss where He lives and where He wishes
to hide you away with Him.

   I am sending you this journal through the little ex-Carmelite; [14]
hide it well because of Mama; I'll send you a little holy card through
her. [15] Take good care of her, as you're doing. I imagine she won't
live much longer; oh, little Guite, make her last years the sweetest,
the brightest; she has suffered so much and is so good a mother; you
are her whole joy, give her every happiness for both of us. Keep me
informed about her health. A Dieu, what is Our Mother going to
say, she who protects me from tiring myself out? But with you I feel
only my love. May the Three bless my three little hosts [16] and make
their Heaven and their resting place in each one. [17] O Abyss, O Love!

That is our refrain on our lyre of praises of glory, and that is how I'll end this letter. What happiness that Sabeth's finger is getting better.[18]

    Your sister and your little mama,

                          Laudem Gloriae.

---

[1] During the "novena" preparing for Marguerite's feast, July 20th. "Today I gave you to the Blessed Virgin": thus July 16, Our Lady of Mount Carmel. Cf. also note 14.

[2] HA 208 [SS 194].

[3] Cf. Acts 20:35.

[4] 2 Cor 12:9.

[5] 2 Cor 12:9–10 (quoted rather freely).

[6] Ps 41:8. Recently read in Ruysbroeck (cf. L 292, note 2).

[7] The "misery-mercy" combination is found in Ru 2, quoted in HF 12 (Vol. I, p. 35). It also echoes Thérèse of Lisieux.

[8] "Echo of my soul": HA 315 (LT 89), a name that Elizabeth had already given Guite in L 204.

[9] Eph 2:4.

[10] The "little tribune" (cf. Plan 3, letter A) looking out on the chapel. Elizabeth alludes to the medieval "recluses" who sometimes lived in a little room off a church.

[11] Phil 3:10 (quoted rather freely).

[12] July 30.

[13] Cf. Ps 117:16.

[14] Clémence Blanc. She undoubtedly came that day to attend the solemnity of the feast of Our Lady of Mount Carmel.

[15] In L 300. The holy card has disappeared.

[16] Guite, Sabeth, and Odette.

[17] Cf. PN 15: "Make it Your heaven ... and Your resting place."

[18] Cf. L 295.

L 299   To a Carmelite Novice[1]   [around July 17, 1906][2]

    I give thanks to Him who has willed to unite us so closely in Himself and thank Him for having *grasped you with His right hand*[3] to lead you to the mountain of Carmel, which is wholly lighted by the very rays of the Sun of Justice.[4] There, following our holy Mother Teresa and all our saints, our two souls, which the Divine Master has consummated in Himself, must be transformed into that *praise of glory*[5] of which Saint Paul speaks.

    "I burn with zeal for the Lord God of hosts,"[6] this was the motto of all our saints; it made our holy Mother a *victim of charity,* as we sing in her beautiful Office. It seems to me that if God is still leaving me on earth, it is so I might also be that victim of love, wholly jealous for His honor.[7] Would you please obtain the grace for your sister to fully accomplish this divine plan; like you, she has a great desire to become a saint in order to give full glory to her adored Master!

Saint Paul, whose magnificent epistles I am reading a great deal, says "God chose us in Him before creation so we might be immaculate and holy in His presence, in love."[8] To live in the presence of God is a heritage Saint Elijah bequeathed to the children of Carmel, he who, in the ardor of his faith, cried out: "He lives, the Lord God, in whose presence I am."[9] If you wish, our souls, passing through space, will meet to sing in unison that great motto of our Father; we will ask him, on his feast day,[10] for the gift of prayer that is the essence of life in Carmel, that heart-to-heart that never ends, because, when we love, we belong no longer to ourselves but to the one we love, and we live more in Him than in ourselves.[11]

Our blessed Father Saint John of the Cross has written some divine pages on that in his *Canticle* and *Living Flame of Love;* this dearly loved book gives joy to my soul, which finds in it a wholly substantial nourishment.

I am happy thinking that the gates of the novitiate have opened for you, and I am asking the Queen of Carmel to give you the double spirit of our beloved holy Order; the spirit of prayer and penance; for, to live continually in contact with God, one must be entirely sacrificed and immolated. Let us have the ardor of our saints for suffering and, above all, let us know how to prove our love to God by fidelity to our holy Rule; let us have a holy passion for it; if we keep it, it will keep us and make us saints, that is, souls such as our seraphic Mother wanted, *able to serve God and His Church.*[12]

[1] S 194–96 (the text we're following, since the autograph letter has disappeared) gives no indication about this novice. Tradition affirms that he did not persevere. The monasteries of the two French provinces of Carmelite friars then in existence— Avignon and Aquitaine—were all expelled from France; they joined into a single province (named Avignon) on December 3, 1906; this explains why there were quite a lot of blanks in the lists of those times. This letter was probably sent to a Brother Bernard-Marie of the Cross (without other details) who belonged to the old province of Avignon and was making his novitiate in Taggia in Italy. He had already left the Order by 1909. We do not know how Elizabeth knew this "novice."

² The *Souvenirs* of 1909 place this letter in the context of 1906. "God is still leaving me on earth" implies she is already sick. "The feast day" of St. Elijah, July 20, is near.
³ Cf. Ps 138:10 (Eyragues trans.).
⁴ Mal 3:20.
⁵ Eph 1:12.
⁶ 1 Kgs 19:10.
⁷ Cf. L 156, note 4.
⁸ Eph 1:4.
⁹ 1 Kgs 17:1.
¹⁰ July 20.
¹¹ John of the Cross, to whom Elizabeth will refer, develops this theme, for example, in SC 34–35 (stanza 1) [K-RJ 1:13–14], 94–95 (stanza 9) [K-RJ 9:4–6], 323–25 (stanza 29) [K-RJ 29:9–10].
¹² Described thematically, for example, in the first three chapters of Teresa of Avila's *Way of Perfection*.

L 300   To her mother   [July 18, 1906]¹
          J. M. + J. T.

Darling little Mama,

I'm expecting you on Saturday at the time we arranged; I will go to receive you *on foot, without a cane.* I'm delighted about it! I was expecting you today, and here I see my Master wants to unite mother and child in suffering, since your dear health is the reason for the delay of your visit; I love you too much to be sad about it, for I understand better than ever how much God loves us when He tries us. What a relief for me to think of you looked after by our dear Guite; let yourself be cared for by her, *obey* her completely, won't you, little Mama.

The Blessed Virgin has not performed the miracle you desired. When, as you tell me in your dear, kind letter, you're afraid that I might be a victim marked out for suffering, I beg you not to be sad about it, that would be so beautiful; I don't feel worthy of it; think now, to have a share in the sufferings of my crucified Bridegroom, and to go with Him to my passion to be a redemptrix with Him…. Saint Paul says that those whom God foreknew, He predestined to be conformed to the image of His Son.² Rejoice in your mother's heart when you think that God has predestined me and has marked me with the seal of the Cross of His Christ.

My legs, however, are getting better; I can walk without a cane.

I've been given a very light robe, and this is what I wear when I make my little comings and goings, which consist in going out on the terrace and to the little tribune; can you imagine what a joy this is for my soul? Several times a day I make long visits to my Master, and I thank Him for having given me the use of my legs to go to Him. I am reading your dear book,[3] which is magnificent; you've made me a very precious gift, my dear Mama; I have it beside me on the little table that is so useful to me.[4] If you knew how well set up I am…. I think up something new every day, and my dear Mother smiles at my *"comforts."* How she cares for me and anticipates my every need; I had told her I had a bad taste in my mouth and she got some new candy for me to bring me more relief, and it's like that with everything; she has the intuitions of a mother. If you knew how she loves you; it was she who told me to write you right away, and I didn't have to be begged, as you can imagine. We've had a very beautiful feast of Our Lady of Mount Carmel,[5] I'll tell you all about it on Saturday. I'm giving you all my best wishes for my Guite; tell little Sabeth to give her this holy card and to kiss her for Tata. A Dieu, darling Mama, I gather all of you together to kiss you as I love you. Be very reasonable, listen well to your Guite to please me. Your daughter who loves you more than she can say.

M.E. of the Trinity r.c.i.
26 years old today.

[1] "26 years old today." The "July 18th" added after "Wednesday" is exact, but written by another hand.
[2] Cf. Rom 8:29.
[3] *Rusbrock l'Admirable.* Cf. above, L 288, note 7.
[4] A "little table" received from her mother, probably the little pedestal table seen in her last photograph on the terrace.
[5] The Chronicles of the Carmel mention that Bishop Dadolle not only presided at evening Benediction when he preached but also came to celebrate Mass and Communion in the morning.

L 301   To her mother   [around July 26, 1906][1]
    J. M. + J. T.   God is Love.[2]

My little Mama whom I love,
    How happy your nice letter made me…. I was anxiously wait-

ing for results of your visit to the doctor. I had had some dear news of you from Georges: they had called him on business, and after that Our Mother had him come up to the infirmary to see me;[3] it was Monday evening, so he was able to give me the latest news of my darling Mama. I was pleased to see *how concerned* he is about your health; he could not be more mindful of it if you were his own mother. He was worried that you were unable to eat, I'm glad you could get the chicken down. I am praying so much for you. Let your children take care of you, they do it with so much happiness and your Sabeth takes care of you too, in her own way. See how God wants to unite us by sending us sufferings that are rather alike:[4] it is the symbol for what must be taking place in our souls. Oh darling Mama, I can't tell you how much I am praying for you, I never stop; I have told my Master that I am offering all my sufferings for you, for, you see, I am jealous for the beauty of your soul; I feel He wants it for His own and all the trials He is making you pass through have been sent only for that. Yes, little Mama, take advantage of your solitude to recollect yourself with God; while your body is resting, think how He is the rest of your soul and how, just as a child loves to remain in the arms of its mother, you too may find rest in the arms of this God who surrounds you on all sides. We cannot leave Him, but alas!, sometimes we forget His holy presence and leave Him all alone to occupy ourselves with things that are not He. It's so simple, this intimacy with God; it gives rest rather than tires—like a child rests beneath the watchful eyes of its mother. Offer Him all your sufferings; that is a good way of uniting yourself to Him and a prayer that is very pleasing to Him. Tell kind Sister Marie-Philippe[5] that your little Carmelite is praying fervently for her. I love her without knowing her and I am so grateful to her for all the good care she is giving my little Mama; it is the Master whom she is caring for within you, and I am asking Him in turn to give Himself more and more to her soul. I'm delighted to see Guite and I'm hurrying to write you so she can take the letter to you from your little child. My health is still the same, but my little legs are quite sturdy; this morning I went as far as my good Mother's room without a cane.[6] If you knew how she thinks of you and prays for you, and if you saw her kindness to your child, to both of us! You see, we'll never love her enough. A

Dieu, darling Mama, I'm keeping a rendez-vous with you in the Master's sight, let us stay very close to Him, let us bring Him all our miseries of body and soul just as the sick once came to Him throughout all Judea: "a secret power"[7] will again go out from the Master, and even if we don't feel it, we will believe, won't we, darling Mama, in its effect, which is all love. I love you and I kiss you like a Mama, the best of mamas. Take good care of yourself.

Sabeth r.c.i.

[1] The convergence of several factors justify the approximate date: the increased strength in her legs described in the preceding letter of July 18, which allowed Elizabeth to go without a cane "out on the terrace and to the little tribune," continues; she has been able to go "without a cane" to the Mother Prioress's cell (cf. Plan 3); there is also an oral message for Sister Marie-Philippe (mentioned for the first time), to whom she will write on August 2; she is writing several days after "Monday," which must have been July 23: Mme. Catez came on Saturday, July 21 (cf. L 300); she is ill *(ibid.)* and must have told Elizabeth she was going to consult a doctor; Elizabeth "was anxiously waiting for the results of [her] visit to the doctor"; before her mother's letter arrives, she "had had" news already from Georges (on "Monday evening"), who was often commuting during these vacation months between Dijon and Sainte-Marie-sur-Ouche (as in 1903, cf. L 171).
[2] 1 Jn 4:16.
[3] Her brother-in-law Georges was very worried about the care given to Elizabeth and even had several doctors come. Mother Germaine had him note the progress of her legs. He "came up" to the outer parlor of the infirmary.
[4] Mme. Catez was also suffering from a stomach ailment and was eating poorly, as the letter indicated.
[5] Cf. L 303, note 1.
[6] Almost 100 feet to her office.
[7] Cf. Lk 6:19.

L 302   To her mother   [August 2, 1906]
J. M. + J. T.   August 2.[1]

My darling little Mama,

    You can guess with what joy I read your nice letter announcing the good news of your improved health. How I thanked God.... You see, you must listen to me and surrender your cares to me; with my Master we'll arrange everything so well! As for me, I can't give you better news; I still have the use of my little legs, but as for the rest I don't see any improvement, and if you knew how it delights me that God is letting me suffer and not you.... He could not satisfy me more. Tell Guite her cheese was very good, very thick, and that its taste was a nice change from what I usually have; would you thank her too for her good chocolate, which sometimes helps my digestion; I assure you I'm doing as much as I can, but my stomach refuses to listen. I haven't seen Doctor Morlot,[2] who has also upset Our Mother; I'm waiting for Doctor Barbier,[3] for it's his day; if I see him first, you can be sure I will give him your message.

Darling Mama, do you remember five years ago? I remember, and He does too!... He collected the blood from your mother's heart in a chalice that will weigh a great deal in the scales of His mercy! Last night I was recalling that last evening,[4] and as I wasn't able to sleep, I settled myself close to my window and stayed there until almost midnight, in prayer with my Master. I spent a heavenly evening; the sky was so blue, so calm, you could feel such a silence in the monastery; and I went back over these five years, so filled with graces. Oh, little Mama whom I love, don't regret the happiness you have given me; yes, thanks to your "fiat," I was able to enter into the holy dwelling and, alone with God alone, enjoy a foretaste of the Heaven that so draws my soul. Tonight I've offered again the sacrifice you made five years ago so that showers of blessings might fall on the FOUR[5] whom I love more than anyone!...

Darling Mama, live with Him. Ah, I wish I could tell all souls what sources of strength, of peace, and of happiness they would find if they would only consent to live in this intimacy. Only they don't know how to wait: if God does not give Himself in some perceptible way, they leave His holy presence, and when He comes to them laden with all His gifts, He finds no one there, the soul is outside in external things, it is not living in its depths! Recollect yourself from time to time, little Mama, and then you will be quite close to your Sabeth.

I saw Madame de Sourdon and Françoise, who gave me a supply of sour candy; I am very happy with Françoise. I have been waiting two days now for Madame de Vathaire, who had said she was coming; perhaps she is ill. The little ex-Carmelite[6] sent me two pretty postcards: the church and your house; she marked your room and the place in the garden where you stay, you can imagine how happy that made me; your set-up looks charming! I'm glad Madame Guémard is close to you; tell her I often think of her and her dear little ones; her beautiful picture[7] came with me to the infirmary; it does much good for my soul; I love to look at it night and day.

A Dieu, darling Mama, I gather you together with my beloved Guite and her little angels to send you all the love of my heart.

E. Trinity

Our Mother has seen the kind Sister who is taking care of you and who gave her much better news; that made her very happy; we talk together about you so much.... She too is always a mama for your Sabeth, whom she takes care of so well. You can be at peace, I assure you, with such a good Mother; so really take advantage of your stay with your Guite. We are having ten Masses every morning; it seems there are a great many priests for the congress;[8] you can imagine how happy I am to have the use of my legs to get me to my little tribune; you are there with me, for my little Mama, my Guite, and I are inseparable.

[1] Elizabeth underlines the date, because she has been in Carmel five years.
[2] Perhaps one of the doctors sent by Georges.
[3] The community's doctor. Elizabeth will address L 340 to him to thank him for his good care.
[4] Cf. the letter from Guite dated August 5, 1901, to Mlle. Forey (in PAT); "... I did not know where to hide myself to cry, it was a real agony; as for the last days, they were horrible, the last meal, the last evening!"
[5] Mme. Catez, Guite, and her two daughters.
[6] Clémence Blanc.
[7] The reproduction of Our Lady of Sorrows of which S 203–4 speaks, that is, the Virgin beneath the Cross, with John and Mary Magdalene.
[8] In 1906, the third "Social Week of France" took place in Dijon. The SRD of August 4 (21, pp. 497–99) writes: "There are about four hundred priests in Dijon who have come from all the dioceses of France.

L 303   To Sister Marie-Philippe[1]   [August 2, 1906][2]
J. M. + J. T.   Mihi vivere Christus est.[3]

My very dear Sister,

A little Carmelite who does not know you is coming beneath the gaze of the Master to pay you a little visit. I know how well you are taking care of my dear Mama and that is enough to draw my heart to yours, since the same Lord has chosen us to be His brides, and isn't that a very strong bond, a wholly divine knot? Even if we never meet here on earth, one day in the inheritance of the saints[4] we will meet among the procession of virgins, that generation as pure as light, and together we will sing canticles to the Lamb.[5] While waiting to follow Him everywhere in Heaven, dear Sister, let us follow Him now here on earth and let us live with the Divine Bridegroom in an uninterrupted heart-to-heart. Oh! how sweet it is to be His! I have been a prisoner of His love here for five years, and each day I understand my happiness better; Sister, we have chosen the better part, and I believe we will be able to spend our eternity singing with David the mercies of the Lord.[6] "He has loved exceedingly,"[7] Saint Paul says, and wasn't it this exceedingly great love that impelled Him to raise us to the dignity of brides? With you, my Sister, I adore Him and in Him am your little sister,

M. Eliz. of the Trinity r.c.i.

[1] From the convent of Sainte-Marie-sur-Ouche. Cf. L 295, note 6.
[2] "I have been ... here for five years" in Carmel, Elizabeth writes. The quotation in Latin is the same as in L 304 of August 2. The letter probably accompanied L 302 of that date.
[3] "For me, to live is Christ": Phil 1:21.
[4] Cf. Col 1:12.
[5] Combination of Rev 14:4 and 15:3.
[6] Cf. Ps 88:1.
[7] Eph 2:4.

L 304   To Père Vallée   [August 2, 1906]
        J. M. + J. T.   Mihi vivere Christus est.[1]
                                          Carmel, August 2nd

My Reverend Father,
        I really think that next year I will celebrate your feast with Saint Dominic[2] in "the inheritance of the saints in light";[3] this year, I am recollecting myself once again in the heaven of my soul to celebrate a very private feast day with you, and I need to tell you that; I need also, Father, to ask for your prayer, that I may be wholly faithful,

wholly attentive, and may ascend my Calvary as a bride of the Crucified. "Those whom God foreknew, He also predestined to be conformed to the image of His Divine Son."[4] Oh! how I love that
thought of the great Saint Paul! It gives rest to my soul. I think that
in His exceeding love, He has known, called, and justified me, and,
while waiting for Him to glorify me,[5] I want to be the unceasing
praise of His glory.[6] Father, ask that of Him for your little child. Do
you remember? Five years ago today I knocked on the door of
Carmel, and you were there[7] to bless my first steps into holy solitude;
now I am knocking on the eternal gates,[8] and I ask you to bend once
again over my soul and bless it on the threshold of the Father's
House. When I am in the great Furnace of love, in the bosom of the
Three toward whom you have directed my soul,[9] I will not forget all
you have been for me, and in return, ah! I would like to give to my
Father from whom I have received so much. Dare I tell you what I
wish? I would be so happy to receive a few lines from you[10] in which
you would tell me how I might accomplish the divine plan: to be
conformed to the image of the Crucified. A Dieu, my Reverend Father, I ask you to bless me in the name of the Three and to consecrate me to Them like a little sacrifice of praise.

S. M. Elizabeth of the Trinity r.c.i.

[1] Phil 1:21.
[2] The liturgical feast on August 4.
[3] Col 1:12.
[4] Rom 8:29.
[5] Cf. Rom 8:30.
[6] Cf. Eph 1:12.
[7] On August 2, 1901, P. Vallée celebrated Mass and was present at Elizabeth's entrance.
[8] Cf. Ps 23:7.
[9] In the first long meeting she had with him before she entered.
[10] He will do so on August 5. Elizabeth will quote his response several times (HF 20,
L 308). The letter was published in A. De Pitteurs, *Un grand precheur. Le R. P. Vallée* (A
Great Preacher, The Rev. Fr. Vallée) (Juvisy: Cer, 1934), 305–6.

*During these first days of August, Elizabeth begins to draft her first retreat,
Major Spiritual Writings, I, "Heaven in Faith" (cf. Vol. I).

L 305   To her mother   [August 13–14, 1906][1]
            J. M. + J. T.

My darling little Mama,
        Here is your Sabeth coming to jump into your arms to tell you
with a big kiss: "Happy and holy feast day." The Blessed Virgin has
been asked to pick my bouquet, so I suspect she is going to strip the
heavenly grounds bare to satisfy the desires of my heart, this heart
of a child who so loves her mother, a Mama so good, so good "that
there can be none better."[2] You can guess how my prayer for you is
rising, wholly ardent, wholly recollected, wholly confident, too, for
I know God answers the desires of little ones, and I am His child. He
acts like a mother full of tenderness with me. I am asking the Blessed
Virgin to obtain an ever-increasing improvement in your health, for
the other day[3] you were wholly transformed and I was so happy to
see you that way, darling Mama. You see, I would like to take on all
your sufferings; that is the first impulse of my heart; but I think that
would be selfish, for suffering is so precious a thing, and then, what
I want is to obtain for you the grace to endure it faithfully without
wasting any of it; the grace, too, to love it and receive each suffering
as a pledge of the heavenly Father's love. I read something so beautiful in Saint Paul: he wishes for his followers "that the Father might
strengthen them inwardly so Christ might dwell in their hearts
through faith and they might be rooted in love";[4] there is my bouquet for my little Mama; isn't that strong and magnificent? Oh, may
the Master reveal to you His divine presence, it is so pleasant and
sweet, it gives so much strength to the soul; to believe that God loves
us to the point of living in us, to become the Companion of our
exile, our Confidant, Friend at every moment.... But I must stop,
for it's getting dark and I can't see what I'm writing any more.
        Tuesday morning. I'm back, my dear Mama, to resume our con-
versation. I've had a visit from good Doctor Gautrelet,[5] whom I wel-
comed as warmly as possible so he won't have a poor impression of
Carmel: I love my Carmel so much, I want all who come near me to
share my feelings. He stayed a long time, but I don't think he's the
one who will bring me back to life; do you know what he advised me
to take so my stomach would recover: a good stew with bacon; I'll

bet you have about as much of an appetite for that as I do![5a] I did try to take a few spoonfuls more, and that upset my stomach, increased my vomiting and so forth; so I'm back to taking my little spoonful and that's all I can do.

Our Mother is always a mother, too, for your Sabeth. I think you would have been very moved if you had come to our cell at night before Matins and had seen her on her knees by my bed, massaging her child's legs like a mother rocking it to sleep, and also like the Master washing the feet of His apostles.[6] So don't worry AT ALL[7] about my health, for I'm being as well cared for as possible, and if God does not cure me, it is because it is His good pleasure to see His little victim in the state of immolation; I am as happy as He, and my darling Mama must do as much if she is to sing in unison. I've received a very long letter from the Canon, and a pretty postcard from Framboise.

A Dieu, little Mama whom I love, I'm keeping a rendez-vous with you close to Him, and there in a single embrace He holds mother and child close to His Heart and His love pours out in waves over them. I'm asking and delegating my little Sabeth to offer her grandmother the best wishes of her Carmelite, yet I think only God can carry this message, for the wishes of my heart are as infinite as He is Himself. I kiss you with all my love. Big kisses to Guite and her angels.

S. E. Trinity

Our Mother has a beautiful little nephew in Lausanne.[8]

I don't think your last trip[9] tired you out too much; rather, the happiness of the meeting *prevailed*. Greetings to Madame Guémard and the little ones.

---

[1] For her mother's "feast day," August 15. Continuing on "Tuesday morning," Elizabeth is thus writing on the 13th and 14th. In an undated note for Mme. Catez's feast day that must have accompanied this letter, Mother Germaine writes: "... may God still keep our dear little saint here for us! These stormy days, like the temperature, tire her a little more, but her general condition is still the same."

[2] Joinville, *Histoire de saint Louis*, chap. 4. Joinville defines God as "so good a thing that there can be none better."

[3] Since Mme. Catez was "wholly transformed," that "other day" cannot be July 21, when she was ill (cf. L 300–301). If the interval of visits ("every two weeks," cf. L 294,

note 1) remained regular, this must be Saturday, August 4. That was her seventh visit
to the patient.
⁴ Cf. Eph 3:16–17.
⁵ Probably sent by Georges. Cf. L 301, note 3.
⁵ᵃ Mme. Catez also suffered from a stomach ailment. Cf. L 301, note 4.
⁶ Cf. Jn 13:2–15.
⁷ Elizabeth underlines the words "at all" three times.
⁸ Just-Urbain-François Favier, born on August 12.
⁹ "Trip": probably the journey (about 13 miles) from Sainte-Marie-sur-Ouche to Dijon
and her return, for the "meeting" with Elizabeth. We do not know what other trip
the ill Mme. Catez would have undertaken. Mme. Guémard is on vacation near her
(cf. L 302).

L 306   To Mother Marie of Jesus   [August 14, 1906]¹
       J. M. + J. T.   "Deus ignis consumens."²

My Reverend and good Mother,

     Laudem gloriae is coming to sing very close to your soul on
the eve of your feast day. On her lyre is always the hymn of silence,
is that not the most beautiful of canticles, the one sung in the bosom of the Three?... My Mother, I enclose myself in this sacred
silence²ᵃ of the Holy Trinity so I can better celebrate your feast; today I had a visit from another little Praise of Glory,³ and we have
conspired to join each other in the same prayer for you. Our dear
Mother, who is also our consecrating Priest,⁴ will thus offer for your
intention her two little sacrifices of praise in the same chalice. Dear
Mother, I am delighted to meet you on my great journey.⁵ I leave
with the Blessed Virgin on the eve of her Assumption to prepare
myself for eternal life. Our Mother did me so much good by telling
me that this retreat would be my novitiate for Heaven, and that on
the 8th of December, if the Blessed Virgin sees I am ready, she will
clothe me in her mantle of glory.⁶ Beatitude attracts me more and
more; between my Master and me that is all we talk about, and His⁷
whole work is to prepare me for eternal life. I beg you, in the name
of that goodness, that motherly affection you have always shown me,
to help my Bridegroom enrich me with His graces. I am anxious for
His honor within me, for I so want the Father to be able to recognize in me the image of the One crucified by love, since Saint Paul,

my dear saint, says that in His foreknowledge God has predestined us to this resemblance and conformity.[8] My little infirmarian, the last victim you offered to the Lord in this monastery,[9] asks me to send you all the best wishes of her heart. As for me, my Mother, I am going to drink in long drafts at the fountain of Charity *for you,* and my little soul will meet yours there and will sing His canticle of praises while she waits for the Bridegroom to say to her: "Come, my praise of glory, you have sung enough here on earth, now chant your canticle in My eternal courts, beneath the rays of light streaming from My Face."[10] A Dieu, my Mother, I often think of the nice visits[11] you have paid to your little patient, she treasures your dear holy cards[12] and sends you all her heart.

Laudem gloriae +

[1] "Eve of your feastday," August 15. As we learn from a letter from Marie of Jesus to a niece on August 30, 1906 (Archives of the Carmel of Paray-le-Monial), she had recently visited the Carmel of Dijon and had spoken with Elizabeth. She recalls these words: "When I lie down on my little bed, I imagine I am climbing onto my altar and I say to Him: 'My God, do not hesitate!' Sometimes anguish comes, but then I very quietly calm down and tell Him: 'My God, that doesn't count' " (for the "bed" of suffering as an "altar," cf. L 294, note 4). In another undated letter, written from the Dijon Carmel to that of Paray, Marie of Jesus says: "This little Sister Elizabeth is a true little Saint." This visit is undoubtedly the reason for Elizabeth's letter.

[2] "God is a consuming Fire": Heb 12:29, quoting Dt 4:24.

[2a] "Sacred silence" (of the Trinity): Ru 29.

[3] Sister Anne-Marie.

[4] Cf. L 320, note 3.

[5] That is, her retreat, from the "evening of August 15" until August 31 (S 212–13). In her state of illness, her retreat could not be as perfectly solitary as her preceding ones. She will also receive a visit from her mother (cf. L 308, note 3).

[6] An allusion to her entrance into Heaven. The "8th of December" had been her clothing day, five years earlier. She will die one month before that anniversary.

[7] Elizabeth writes *son,* "His," for Christ is preparing her.

[8] Cf. Rom 8:29.

[9] This refers to Sister Marie of the Holy Spirit, a lay Sister who had made her profession on December 25, 1899, the last profession before the foundation of the Carmel of Paray-le-Monial.

[10] The quotation marks here do not indicate a quotation.

[11] During her recent stay in Dijon, cf. note 1.

[12] Several of them are in fact in her books.

L 307   **To Sister Agnès of Jesus-Mary**   [August 15, 1906][1]

      +   Janua Coeli,[2] ora pro nobis!

This evening, Laudem gloriae is entering the novitiate for Heaven to prepare to receive the habit of glory and is anxious to beg the help of her dear Sister Agnès. "Those whom God foreknew," Saint Paul tells us, "He also predestined to be conformed to the image of His divine Son."[3] This is what I am going to be taught: conformity, identity with my adored Master, the One crucified by love. Then I will be able to fulfill my work as praise of glory and sing even now the eternal Sanctus while waiting to go and chant it in the divine courts of the Father's house. My Sister, let us fix our eyes on our Master, and may that simple, loving gaze of faith separate us from everything and set a cloud between us and things here on earth. Our essence[4] is too rich for any creature to grasp it; let us keep [it] all for Him, and with David sing to the Lord on our lyre: "I shall keep my strength for You."[5]

---

[1] She "is entering the novitiate for Heaven" this evening: an allusion to her retreat, which begins on the evening of August 15 (cf. L 306, with note 5).

[2] "Gate of Heaven": the name Elizabeth very often gave to the Virgin at the end of her life (cf. S 204). S 197 recounts that Elizabeth gave Mother Germaine (on September 14, with P 113) a little cardboard citadel measuring about 4" x 2.25" (which has been preserved) with a little flag (also preserved) that carries in red ink, like P 113, the following words. On one side: "Citadel of suffering and of holy recollection" (an image inspired by SC 439 [cf. K-RJ 40:3], cf. L 284, note 6); and on the other: "Dwelling of Laudem gloriae while waiting for the Father's House." Near the closed door was a cut-out Virgin of Lourdes (not preserved) that represented *Janua Coeli*.

[3] Rom 8:29.

[4] A more philosophical term that Elizabeth might have encountered, for example, in John of the Cross or Ruysbroeck.

[5] Ps 59:10, according to the version from SC 313 [K-RJ 28:8].

---

* On August 16, Elizabeth begins to draft her Last Retreat, *Major Spiritual Writings* III (cf. Vol. I).

L 308   To her mother   [August 29, 1906][1]
        J. M. + J. T.
    "The entire will of God for our souls is one of love" (P. Vallée).[2]

My darling little Mama,
        Our nice parlor visits on Saturdays have left me with such a
delightful feeling, one that is still with me,[3] and we can be very grateful to the one[4] who, with such a delicate, motherly heart, arranges
these visits for us; they truly are real favors, for in my state of health
it is a real exception, which Our Mother is nevertheless happy to
make for you; she loves you so much, and I think your ears must buzz
a lot sometimes when we're together talking about you, darling
Mama. Oh, isn't it good to speak of Him and to rise above things
that have an end and pass away; above suffering and separation,
there where everything lasts. If you knew what a consolation it is for
your Sabeth to be able to talk with you about her plans for eternity;
don't forget you've promised me, at the Elevation of Holy Mass, to
place yourself with the Virgin at the foot of the Cross to offer *your
children* together to the heavenly Father, "whose entire will is one of
love"....[5]
        Darling Mama, rejoice in the thought that from all eternity we
have been known by the Father, as Saint Paul says, and that He
wishes to find once again in us the image of His crucified Son.[6] Oh,
if you knew how necessary suffering is so God's work can be done in
the soul.... God has an immense desire to enrich us with His graces,
but it is we who determine the amount to the extent that we know
how to let ourselves be immolated by Him, immolated in joy, in
thanksgiving, like the Master saying with Him: "Am I not to drink
the cup my Father has prepared for me?"[7] The Master called the
hour of His passion "His hour,"[8] the one He had come for, the one
He invoked with all His desire! When a great suffering or some very
little sacrifice is offered us, oh, let us think very quickly that "this is
our Hour," the hour when we are going to prove our love for Him
who has *"loved us exceedingly,"*[9] as Saint Paul says. So gather up everything, my little Mama, offer a beautiful bouquet by not overlooking
even the smallest sacrifice: in Heaven they will be like beautiful rubies enriching the crown your God is preparing for you. I will go to

help Him make the diadem and I will come with Him on the day of the great meeting to set it on my darling Mama's head.

Our Mother saw Marie-Louise de Sourdon, who dropped in to request a parlor visit, but Our Mother has promised instead a letter to Framboise,[10] for those visits are not in order and I can't manage them with the closed grille any more. I saw good Père Vergne[11] like that, and he told me some magnificent things, but I wasn't able to make myself understood and the good Father sent me away, finding me rather tired; I wish you would see him sometime, he would do you good. Our good Mother takes such good care of me, she knows that speaking tires me,[12] and I can say that I don't even see my Sisters at all, who, in their tender love for me, declare they love me like a true sister. Oh! what a Carmel! How the beautiful virtue so recommended by the Master reigns in it![13] My state of health is about the same, my stomach still can't take food. Our Mother has them buy the finest candy for me and has me take as much of it as I can, saying that there's always that; she knows only how to bring me relief, to urge me to take some nourishment, and, you know, mothers have an intuition about their children that others don't have. I wish I could tell you with what delicacy she lavishes her maternal care on me, but you know it, don't you, darling Mama, and I think you're at peace about me when you think of the wise and zealous care that everyone around me lavishes on me. I'm still making nice little visits to my Master to the dear little tribune off the infirmary; I have the consolation of being able to go there for the exercises when the community is in choir, and I thank God for giving back the use of my legs; I wonder how they can still hold me up, seeing what I take in nourishment. Continue to take care of yourself, my little Mama, so I can have the joy, on your next visit,[14] of seeing the most improvement ever. A Dieu, let us love Him in truth, by giving Him all the big and little sacrifices He asks of us, and let us draw strength in our union with Him. The soul who lives in God's sight is clothed with His strength and is valiant in suffering. I kiss you.

E. o. the Trinity

[1] Date deduced from note 3; the two letters must have been sent together. The date is corroborated by notes 10 and 12.

[2] In his reply to Elizabeth of August 5 (cf. L 304, note 10). Literally: "Remember that His entire will for us is one of love."

[3] August 29. Mother Germaine writes to Mme. Catez: "Your Elizabeth will write to you at length.... Sr. Elizabeth is not doing too poorly; she still remembers with delight her last parlor visit with her dear Mama. And I have a very sweet memory of it too. The fine weather allows her to go out onto the terrace, which does her good." So there was an eighth visit, on "Saturday," August 25 (or 18). In the same letter, Mother Germaine invites Guite to come on September 1 rather than on August 31: the noise from the parlor would interfere with adoration of the Blessed Sacrament exposed that day in the oratory below.

[4] Mother Germaine.

[5] Cf. note 2.

[6] Cf. Rom 8:29.

[7] Jn 18:11.

[8] Jn 12:27.

[9] Cf. Eph 2:4.

[10] That will be L 310.

[11] P. Vergne was the spiritual director for several Sisters. On the occasion of these visits, other Sisters could ask to speak with him. "The closed grille": cf. L 112, note 4.

[12] The weakness of her voice will become even more accentuated, cf. L 309, around September 9. Her handwriting shows physical exhaustion.

[13] Fraternal charity. Cf. Jn 13:34–35.

[14] September 14 (cf. L 309), but at this moment, Elizabeth is anticipating it earlier.

L 309   **To her mother**   [around September 9, 1906] [1]
J. M. + J. T.

"In my own flesh I make up what is lacking in the passion of Jesus
Christ for the sake of His body the Church" [2] (Saint Paul).

My darling little Mama,

I'm coming to tell you that I'm expecting you *Friday*, since that day is good for you and we don't have the Blessed Sacrament exposed; I am very tired, and between now and the 14th my voice will perhaps get a little stronger[3] for talking with my beloved mother. I nearly regret having told you that, for now, maybe, you'll go and worry, but I *forbid* you to do that, there's no reason for it: God is pleased to immolate His little sacrifice, but this Mass[4] He is saying with me, for which His love is the priest, may last a long time yet. To the little victim in the Hands of the Master who is sacrificing her, time does not seem long and she can say that, even if she passes through the way of suffering, she is still following the path of *true* happiness, darling Mama, a happiness no one can take from her.

"I rejoice," said Saint Paul, "to make up in my flesh what is lacking in the passion of Jesus Christ for the sake of His body the Church."[5] Oh, how your mother's heart should leap for divine joy in thinking that the Master has deigned to choose your daughter, the fruit of your womb, to associate her with His great work of redemption, and that He suffers in her, as it were, an extension of His passion. The bride belongs to the Bridegroom,[6] and mine has taken me, he wants me to be another humanity[7] for Him in which He can still suffer for the glory of His Father, to help the needs of His Church; this thought has done me so much good.... My darling Mother talks about it often with me and tells me such beautiful things about suffering.... I close my eyes and listen, and I forget that it's she, for it seems it's my Master who is beside me, coming to encourage me and teach me to carry His Cross. This good Mother, who is so inspiring about the ways of immolation, thinks of nothing but giving me comfort, which I often point out to her, but I let myself become like a little child, and the Master told our holy Mother Teresa He preferred her obedience to the penance of another saint.[8] So I accept the little favors, like the candy and chocolates when my stomach allows it, and that's what makes it suffer the least these days. Many thanks to Georges for the case of milk. I am deeply grateful to him for his kindness to his little sister; I like very much to have my soup with this milk, which doesn't curdle like the other, but I admit that digesting it is also painful: a single spoonful really hurts me, and if I try to force myself, it causes an attack. (Be careful about what you say to Georges about me.) I'm happy you can have peace of mind on that score, so I won't say any more about it since we'll be seeing each other in a few days. Thanks to Guite for her chocolate. Our Mother had them buy some Suchard for me, but I find it more sugary and sticky. I prefer Klauss, it makes me less nauseated; tell Guite that what she was kind enough to exchange is also very good; it burns more because it's stronger, but I alternate. You can see I'm attentive to my stomach and, for love of God, I do what I can to not let it die of hunger. Darling Mama, everything lies in the intention: how we can sanctify the smallest things, transform the most ordinary actions of life into divine actions! A soul who lives in union with God does nothing that is not supernatural, and the most common actions, instead of separating her from Him, on the contrary draw her ever nearer. Let us live like that, little Mama, and the Master will be happy, and at the evening of each day He will find a sheaf to harvest in our souls. I love you as the best of mamas, I repeat that you are to take good care of your stomach, leave all the suffering to me, and above all you are not to worry. Until Friday, the *14th.* Let us prepare a beautiful feast of the Cross by our generosity in sacrifice. Kiss my Guite, tell her she is my darling daughter; a kiss to the little angels whom I'll be so happy to see again.

You're afraid I am suffering from the heat. If you saw me with my two shawls you'd be very reassured. Do you still have my little cape from the Pyrenees? How I could use it if you could bring it to me! but only if that's no trouble for you, my little Mama; thanks in advance. I give you a big kiss.

Your happy daughter,

M. E. o. the Trinity.

Greetings to Madame Guémard and her little ones. Thanks to l'Abbé[9] for his postcard; may he pray for me.

[1] "I'm expecting you *Friday,*" "the 14th," "feast of [the Exaltation of] the Cross." That will be her ninth visit to her ill daughter. The letter may have been written anywhere from Friday the 7th to Wednesday, September 12.
[2] Col 1:24.
[3] Elizabeth has already indicated the weakness of her voice in L 308.
[4] Cf. L 294, note 6.
[5] Col 1:24.
[6] Cf. Jn 3:29.
[7] Mgsr. Gay's expression. Cf. PN 15, note 28.
[8] Cf. Teresa of Avila, *Relations,* 23 [K-RT vol. 1, *Spiritual Testimonies,* 19]. The "saint" is Doña Catalina de Cardona. This paragraph is connected to the spirituality of Mother Germaine's priesthood as Elizabeth sees it (cf. L 320, note 3).
[9] Very probably Abbé Anatole Contant, then parish priest of Sainte-Marie-sur-Ouche. He will send his condolences after Elizabeth's death.

L 310   To Françoise de Sourdon [around September 9, 1906][1]
      J. M. + J. T.

Here at last comes Sabeth to sit down by her dearest Framboise and visit—with her *pencil!* I say pencil, for the heart-to-heart communion was established long ago, and we are now as one. How I love our evening rendez-vous;[2] it is like the prelude of that communion from Heaven to earth that will be established between our souls. It seems to me that I am like a mother bending attentively over her favorite child: I raise my eyes and look at God, and then I lower them on you, exposing you to the rays of His Love. Framboise, I do not use words when I speak to Him of you but He understands me even better for He prefers my silence. My dearest child, I wish I were a saint so I could help you here below while waiting to do it from Heaven. What I would not endure to obtain for you the graces of strength that you need! I want to answer your questions....

* The rest of this letter is found in *Major Spiritual Writings,* II, "The Greatness of Our Vocation" (cf. Vol. I).

I wonder what our Reverend Mother is going to think when she sees this journal. She does not let me write any more because I am extremely weak, and I feel as if I would faint at any moment. This will probably be the last[3] letter from your Sabeth; it has taken her many days to write, and that explains its incoherence. And yet this evening I cannot bring myself to leave you. I am in solitude; it is seven-thirty, and the community is at recreation. As for me, I feel already as if I were almost in Heaven here in my little cell, alone with Him alone, bearing my cross with my Master. Framboise, my happiness increases along with my suffering! If you only knew how delicious the dregs are at the bottom of the chalice prepared by my Heavenly Father!

A Dieu, beloved Framboise; I cannot go on. And in the silence of our rendez-vous you will guess, you will understand, what I do not tell you. I send you a kiss. I love you as a mother loves her little child. A Dieu my little one. In the shadow of His wings may He guard you from all evil.[4]

S. M. Eliz. of the Trinity
Laudem gloriae.
(This will be my new name in Heaven.)

A very respectful and loving remembrance to your dear mama and regards to dear Marie-Louise.

[1] A letter announced in L 308 of August 29. Elizabeth must have delayed in writing: "Here ... at last...." She adds that it took her "many days to write." Françoise de Sourdon, who was not very precise in her dates, will note "September 11." That may serve as the latest approximate date.

[2] The "8 P.M. rendez-vous," as arranged in 1901 in L 98 and 105, and even earlier (cf. L 65).

[3] This was, in fact, the last.

[4] Cf. Ps 90:4 and 10.

L 311   To her sister   [September 14, 1906][1]
            J.M. + J.T.

My darling daughter,[2]

I'm very tired, I haven't the strength to hold my pencil, but I don't have the courage to let Mama leave without sending you a word from my heart. I love you more than ever. I cover you and your angels with my prayer and my sufferings; you can draw from the chalice of your Sabeth: all that is hers is yours. I've read something so beautiful, listen: "Where then did Jesus Christ dwell but in suffering?"[3] O little child, it seems to me that I have found my dwelling place: it is the immense suffering that was also the Master's; in a word, it is He Himself, the Man of sorrows.[4] I am begging Him to give you that love for the Cross that makes saints. Write me something of your interior life, little sister, I so love the story of your soul.

October 2 is the feast of the holy Angels, and in preparation I'm going to make a beautiful novena to the Angels for your little angels, so they might draw down on them the great light that comes from the Face of the Father and so your daughters might always walk in the bright splendor of God and be *contemplatives* like their little mama.

I give you all a big kiss.

                                        Your little mama Sabeth

[1] This letter, which surely dates from before September 23 (since Elizabeth says: "I'm going to make" a "novena" for "October 2nd"), was written on September 14, during the visit of her mother (cf. L 309); Elizabeth says: "I don't have the courage to let Mama leave without sending you a word from my heart." The date is corroborated by note 3. Another visit from her mother, after that of September 14 and before September 23, is ruled out. On Sunday the 23rd (or right at the beginning of the week: cf. L 315, note 2), Elizabeth affirmed that her mother "came to see me every two

weeks," and besides she "is returning this week from the country." This weekend (Saturday the 29th or Sunday the 30th) constitutes the normal interval of "two weeks" (one or two days more at the most) that separated the visits. There is no apparent reason an intermediate visit would have been inserted; besides, it was already a special concession on the part of the Carmel, breaking the rhythm of monthly visits. In addition, during this interval Elizabeth writes a letter (L 314, around the 21st) in which she expresses her joy at "seeing again" her family on their return from the country, thus at the end of September, without mentioning a possible visit from her mother in a day or two.

[2] Elizabeth feels like a "little [spiritual] mother" (L 239) to Guite, "my own little child" (L 233).

[3] Angela di Foligno, *Le livre des Visions et instructions* [The Book of Visions and Instructions] (Ang), p. 197. Elizabeth quotes the same sentence in P 113 and 114 from the same day (in all probability). The quotation recurs in L 312, 314, 315, 324, and on the holy card for Germaine de Gemeaux, cf. L 324, note 10. Note that Mother Germaine writes, also on September 14, to Marie Bouveret (ACD): "St. Angela di Foligno ends a superb chapter in which she speaks of the painful life of Christ with this exclamation: 'Where then did He dwell but in suffering?' What light this thought creates in the soul!" Was Elizabeth or her Prioress the first to discover it? We note again that September 14 is the feast of the Exaltation of the Cross.

[4] "Man of sorrows": Is 53:3. Cf. P 121.

L 312   To Madame d'Anthès   [September 18, 1906][1]
         J. M. + J. T.

Dear Madame,

I come to you by passing through the pierced Heart of the Mother of sorrows.[2] Along with her, you have consummated your sacrifice, and I am begging her to pour out in your soul the calm, peace, and strength that always accompanied her during her cruel martyrdom. One saint, speaking of the Master, said: "Where then did He dwell but in suffering?"[3] Any soul immersed in suffering, then, lives beside Him; she dwells with Jesus Christ in that immensity of suffering sung by the prophet;[4] the dwelling place of those predestined, those whom the "Father has known and wishes to be conformed to His divine Son, the Crucified";[5] Saint Paul says that. Dear Madame, I believe that soon I will go to be with your dear daughter; while waiting, I am giving her and those she left behind a large share of my prayers and sufferings. The veil has been lifted for her, and in God's light she sees that "suffering passes away, but the experience of having suffered endures forever." I leave you, dear

Madame, since I am too weak to write. Please forgive these lines in pencil and see only a heart very united with yours who begs God and the Mother of sorrows to bind the wound of your maternal heart. Be assured of my respectful affection and allow me to kiss you.

S. E. of the Trinity

[1] The envelope has been preserved, postmarked Dijon, "9–18, 1906, at 8 P.M." We can assume that the other little L 313 to Mme. de Sourdon left the same day. Baroness d'Anthès was the mother of the deceased, Mme. de Maizières, the sister of Mme. de Sourdon.
[2] The feast of Our Lady of Sorrows was celebrated on the third Sunday of September; in 1906, this was the 16th.
[3] Ang 197. Cf. L 311, note 3.
[4] Distantly reminiscent of Lam 1:12 (cf. P 113, note 6), but the direct source was the recent reading of Ang 199, 201, 202, where we find the expression "immense suffering," already quoted in L 311 of September 14.
[5] Cf. Rom 8:29.

L 313   To Madame de Sourdon   [September 18, 1906][1]
J. M. + J. T.

Dear Madame,

Although I am very ill, our Reverend Mother is allowing me to send you a few lines, for it would be too great a sacrifice for my heart to keep silence in the face of the trial that has struck your family so profoundly. Would you please have the kindness to tell Monsieur Joseph and his sisters[2] how much I am praying for them, how much I share their grief, and that I am too weak to tell them so myself. I think I will be going soon to join their dear departed one. Dear Madame, she has gone to Life, to Light, to Love[3] after having passed through the "great tribulation,"[4] and these are the ones who have traveled the royal way[5] whom Saint John shows us with "palm in hand, serving God day and night in His temple, while He wipes every tear from their eyes"![6] Never have I understood so well that suffering is the greatest pledge of love that God can give His creatures, and I did not suspect that just such sweetness was hidden at the bottom of the chalice for the one who drank it to the dregs. Dear Madame, it is a fatherly hand, a hand of infinite tenderness that metes out suffering to us. Oh, may we know how to go beyond the bitterness of that suffering to find our rest in it. I am praying for your intentions and I love you like a mother; you are so much like one to me!...

Sr. M. E. of the Trinity r.c.i.

Our Reverend Mother has asked me to express to you as well as to Madame d'Anthès how much she shares in your sorrow.

[1] Cf. L 312, note 1.
[2] Joseph de Maizières, husband of the deceased.
[3] Three key words in Saint John. These will be the last intelligible words that the dying Elizabeth will pronounce (cf. S 258).
[4] Rev 7:14.
[5] *Imitation of Christ,* book II, chap. XII, note 6 (in the *Manual,* p. 58). Elizabeth might also have read the expression in Angela di Foligno (Ang 208), whom she quotes the same day in L 312. SC 58 [cf. K-RJ 3:5] speaks of the "royal road of the cross."
[6] Combination of Rev 7:9, 15, and 17.

L 314   To her mother   [around September 21, 1906][1]
J. M. + J. T.

My darling little Mama,

I was very touched when I received your beautiful samples:[2] they seemed to carry your whole heart to me. Be very reassured about me, you know what a Mother watches over all my needs; when it concerns me there is no question of holy poverty but only of charity. I have a little earthenware stove in our cell; they wanted to light it for me, but I begged them to wait a little, for I'll no longer be able to leave the fireside once I'm settled there, and then adieu, my dear little tribune I love so much!

As for my clothes, our Reverend Mother had our supplier send a beautiful piece of quilted material the same color as our habits, and they will make the warmest possible robe[3] for me: you see that Our Mother spares nothing, and I'm a little embarrassed by it; that kind Mother thought this would be even more practical than your cloak. Since you want so much to make something for me, Our Mother thought you could make me a petticoat with that material; the one Guite gave me[4] is very worn out, it hardly keeps me warm and weighs a lot; the one you would make me would have the advantage of being warm and light, and then your Sabeth would be so happy to have something made by her darling Mama. Could you make it a little longer, *37.5"* or thereabouts; I took out as well as I could the belt pattern of my little gray petticoat, you could put it on something similar, closing it with two buttons; or I could even place them just to fit my size. Do exactly as you wish, with these few directions. Thanks in advance, my darling Mama; while you go to busy yourself with clothing me, I'll also go to work for your soul. More and more I am drawn to suffering; this desire almost surpasses the one for Heaven, though that was very strong. Never has God made me understand so well that suffering is the greatest pledge of love He can give His creature. Oh, you see, with each new suffering, I kiss the Cross of my Master, and I say to Him: "Thank you, I am not worthy of it,"[5] for I think how suffering was the companion of His life,[6] and I do not deserve to be treated as His Father treated Him. In speaking of Jesus Christ, one saint wrote: "Where, then, did He dwell but in suffering?"[7] and David sang that this suffering was as immense as the sea.[8] Every soul crushed by suffering, in whatever form it may occur, can tell itself: I dwell with Jesus Christ, we are living in intimacy, the same dwelling shelters us! The saint of whom I just spoke says that the sign by which we recognize that God is in us and His love possesses us is that we receive not only patiently but gratefully whatever wounds us and makes us suffer. To reach that state, we must contemplate the God crucified by love, and that contemplation, if it is true, never fails to end in the love of suffering.[9] Darling Mama, receive every trial, every annoyance, every lack of courtesy in the light that springs from the Cross; that is how we please God, how we advance in the ways of love. Oh, thank Him for me; I am *very, very happy....* I wish I could sow a little of my happiness in those I love.

My stomach still makes me suffer; it is nourished by your good chocolate, which I alternate with the kind Our good Mother got for me; that is enough to increase the pains; in the evening I take a few spoonfuls of soup (and cheese) with the milk from Georges,[10] and I offer my digestion to God.

Tell my Guite to take care of herself, to rest in the morning without any scruples, for it is her little mama Sabeth who tells her to do it and I don't want to see her looking ill. And the little ones? Does Odette have her beautiful rosy cheeks back? I'm very delighted to see them again,[11] they will have changed, since it's been so long since I've seen them. Kiss them for me as well as my darling Guite. Please give all my greetings to Madame Guémard and her little ones; I'm delighted about and join in your nice reunion with our dear friends the d'Avout family; tell them that.

I learned by telegram of Madame de Maizières's death; I wrote a few lines to her poor mother and to Madame de Sourdon.

A Dieu, I can't hold my pencil any longer, but my heart doesn't leave you. Thank you a thousand times for the petticoat; you'll find the belt in my letter; as for the length, if you can: *37.5″*. I kiss you as the best of mamas. Remember that another mama is caring for me more than I can say, and be very much at peace about me. I'm keeping a rendez-vous with you in the shadow of the Cross to learn the science of suffering. Your happy daughter,

E. o. the Trinity r.c.i.

---

[1] Elizabeth had already "written" L 312 and 313 of September 18. Mother Germaine adds in a postscript: "The dear little one could no longer see last night to tell you how much we were united to the dear Pilgrim of Our Lady of Lourdes, and how much we are praying with him for his so lovable household. [This is referring to Georges.] Quickly, it's time. A Dieu, dear Madame, we will see you soon, won't we?" If this "last night" of the letter could be September 18 at the latest, Mother Germaine's "soon," together with Elizabeth's joy at the thought of the return of Guite and her little ones, suggest rather that the end of the stay in the country (cf. L 311, note l) is approaching. We can only date this approximately.

[2] Samples of material for the new "petticoat" in question. Suffering from the cold, Elizabeth had asked her Mother for her "cape from the Pyrenees" around September 9 (L 309). During her visit on the 14th, Mme. Catez gave her the "cloak" spoken of in the letter and then sent some samples because she wanted to make something for her daughter. Elizabeth asks her to make a "petticoat" of that warm "material" and gives the measurements.

[3] Which she is wearing in her last photograph, on the terrace. She would put it on for the first time on October 4, as S 236 tells us: "In the afternoon of that day, she took the opportunity of putting on a new habit to ask to renew the ceremony of her clothing. Everything took place near the tribune that was close to the tabernacle. With what a spirit of faith she observed the least details of our ceremonial, not dispensing herself even from the great prostration."

[4] Cf. L 221, and note 6.

[5] Perhaps inspired by Angela di Foligno, who wrote: "And if you catch fire in that furnace, you will accept every tribulation as a consolation of which you are not worthy" (Ang 181).

[6] Cf. Ang 196: "The third companion of Jesus Christ: suffering."
[7] Ang 197.
[8] It was not "David," but cf. Lam 2:13.
[9] In this passage, Elizabeth alludes to chap. 61 of Angela di Foligno, "the saint" (Ang 250–56), on "The Ways of Love." She summarizes in a very personal way.
[10] Cf. L 309 of September 9.
[11] According to L 315, the family "is returning this week from the country," that is, between September 23 and 29. There could be no visits on Sunday, the 30th. So Elizabeth is waiting for hers during the first days in October. In fact, in L 322 of October 7, she indicates that her mother has come: this was her tenth visit. According to RB 2 (PAT), the family came back from the country "during the first days of October." But Elizabeth's information, much closer to the fact, seems more certain, unless they decided at the last minute to stay several days longer in Sainte-Marie-sur-Ouche.

L 315   To Madame Gout de Bize[1] [around September 23, 1906][2]
J. M. + J. T.

Very dear Madame,

It is said that the Master, having loved His own who were in the world, loved them to the end,[3] and never was His Heart so overflowing with love, it seems, than at the supreme hour when He passed from this world to His Father. It seems to me that something similar is taking place in your little Elizabeth. The evening of her life has arrived, the evening that precedes the eternal day, and she feels an even stronger overflowing of love in the depths of her heart. Do you know what I mean? Feel all my affection conveyed through these lines; if this letter were not for you, so beloved of my heart, I would not have the strength to hold a pencil, I am so weak, but instead of putting it in my hand, I have put it in my heart, and now I can!...

If you only knew how well cared for I am in my dear Carmel.... I imagine that interests you, since you have wanted very much to give me a large place in your heart. Our Reverend Mother is a real mother to me; her heart has all the tenderness and intuitions of a mother; during the day and also at night, she comes rushing to my bed, for her maternal heart is so good; I believe God has made nothing better here on earth! My dear Mama is very courageous, and God's grace sustains her visibly. Won't you help her mount her Calvary, you who know what it is to give God your children. Oh, dear

Madame, how well I understand the value of suffering; I did not believe that such sweetness lay hidden at the bottom of the chalice, and I often repeat to my good Mother that the great, true happiness I have found in Carmel increases in proportion to the suffering.[4] That is because in our dear solitude, living in continual contact with God, we see everything in His light, the only true one; and that light shows us that suffering, in whatever form it may take, is the greatest pledge of love God can give His creature. Saint Paul says that "those whom God foreknew, He also predestined to be conformed to the image of His divine Son, the Crucified."[5] Dear Madame, both of us have been among those *foreknown,* oh let us not scorn our happiness! Undoubtedly our nature can be distressed in the face of suffering—the Master willed to know that humiliation—the will must come to dominate all these sensations and say to the Heavenly Father: "May Your will be done and not mine."[6] One saint, speaking of Christ, said: "Where, then, did He dwell but in suffering?"[7] Every soul visited by suffering, therefore, dwells with Him. I am keeping a rendez-vous with you in that dwelling place: there, if you wish, dear Madame, we will pray together for your dear Jaja. I so wish to draw down some happiness upon her, and I have entrusted her to the Blessed Virgin: she is Mother! We can speak with her of Jaja's future,[8] and on earth or in Heaven, I won't give the good Virgin any rest until she sends my little Jaja the husband who will make her happy!

I must leave you despite my happiness in being close to you, but my heart is not separated from yours. Could I venture to tell you a wish? In Carmel we are allowed to have a photograph[9] of those we love, and before leaving for Heaven, your little patient would love so to see once again your dear picture and that of Jaja; so that my joy might be complete, Madame de Guardia could add hers to it and also Margot.[10] Send them soon, before my departure! Up above I won't forget you, for I think the heart does not change but only expands in its contact with the Heart of God. How much I will pray for you! I beg too for a remembrance in your prayers and a *thank you* to Him who has chosen for me a part that is so beautiful, so brightened by His ray of love. I kiss you with all the tenderness of my heart, as well as Jaja and dear Madame de Guardia, if she would allow it. Tell her I still have sweet memories of the nice vacations at Saint-Cyprien.

Your little Elizabeth of the Trinity r.c.i.

My dear Mama is returning this week from the country, from which she was coming to see me every two weeks. Our kind Mother gives every consolation to that poor heart and lets her take advantage of the last days of her daughter; she is *herself* such a mother.

---

[1] Mme. Gout de Bize is "my dear Madame Berthe whom I love so much" of L 97. Before entering Carmel, Elizabeth had known her well and had confided in her about her vocation: cf. the letter of Mme. Gout de Bize to Mother Germaine of February 25, 1907 (PAT). In it, she explains: "I heard that dear child on February 22, 1905, and through the grilles of Carmel I found again her perfect heart. The love of God enveloped her completely, but she was able to tell me such tender things.... She had such feelings of affection for her mother that I cried."

[2] In her letter of September 30, Elizabeth thanks her friend who has sent the photos in question "so quickly." It took about four days for the round trip of the correspondence. She may also have written on Sunday, September 23 (or on the 24th or the 25th).

[3] Cf. Jn 13:1.

[4] On her happiness in suffering, cf. L 309.

[5] Cf. Rom 8:29.

[6] Mk 14:36.

[7] Ang 197.

[8] In her letters to Mme. de Sourdon, Elizabeth often showed her interest in the future of her elder daughter Marie-Louise. She willingly spoke to the Blessed Virgin about it, cf. L 246 and 296. It was the same with her other friends. Anne-Marie d'Avout, then 21 years old, recounts that Elizabeth, already very ill, said to her during their last meeting at Carmel: "I will send you a fine husband" (PA 646).

[9] She kept some, for example, in her *Manual*, cf. L 243.

[10] Mme. Gout de Bize's other daughter (already married in 1905) was the sister-in-law of Mme. de Guardia.

L 316   To Mother Germaine of Jesus   [September 24, 1906][1]
Ecce Mater tua.[2]

It was in my arms that Jesus made His first oblation to the Father when entering the world, and He is sending me to receive yours!...[3] I am bringing you a scapular[4] as a pledge of my protection and my love, and also as a *"sign"* of the mystery that is going to be worked in you. My *daughter,* I am coming to finish *"clothing you with*

Jesus Christ,"⁵ so "*you may walk in Him,*"⁶ the royal Way, the luminous Road; so you may be "*rooted in Him,*" in the depths of the Abyss, with the Father and the Spirit of love; so you may be "*built up on Him,*" "your Rock,"⁷ your "Fortress,"⁸ so you may be "*strengthened in your faith,*" faith in the immense Love that is rushing from the great Furnace into the depths of your soul. My daughter, that all-powerful Love *will do great things for you:*⁹ believe my word, that of a Mother, and this Mother leaps with joy to see with what *particular tenderness* you are loved. Oh, remain in the depths of your soul: *here He is,* the one who comes with all His gifts. The abyss of His love surrounds her like a garment: it is the Bridegroom!

    Silence!...

    Silence!...

    Silence!...¹⁰

¹ The Prioress recalled the precise date, which she placed on the autograph, the day of the twelfth anniversary of her profession, the feast of Our Lady of Ransom. Throughout the letter the Blessed Virgin is addressing Mother Germaine. The autograph carries on the first page a little picture of the Virgin with the Child Jesus (1.25" x .75") surrounded by the quotation.

² "Behold your Mother," Jn 19:27.

³ An allusion to Mother Germaine's profession and to her continuing oblation.

⁴ A little something Elizabeth would have made for the Prioress.

⁵ Gal 3:27.

⁶ Col 2:6. Elizabeth immediately quotes verse 7, divided into pieces: "Rooted in him, built up on him, strengthened in faith." She recently commented on these verses in two of her Spiritual Writings: GV 10–11 and LR 33–34.

⁷ Ps 61:3 (Eyragues trans.).

⁸ Cf. L 284, note 6.

⁹ Cf. Lk 1:49. Perhaps at the same time an echo of the message of Angela di Foligno that Elizabeth quotes in LL 7 (and that Mother Germaine is then supposed to know): "I will do great things for you" (Ang 61).

¹⁰ The repeated "Silence! Silence!" is also found in Ang, for example on pp. 77, 84, 171. A little more elaborated, too, in Ru 107–8.

L 317   To her mother   [end of September 1906]¹

    J. M. + J. T.

My darling little Mama,

    Our kind Mother wants very much for me to send you a note from my heart, and you can guess how happy that makes me. Thanks in advance for your beautiful petticoat; I will be so happy to have something you made. When you come to see me, I'll receive you in the splendor of my beautiful habit:[2] Our Mother is spoiling me! I would be glad to see Guite, and I share your joy about keeping the little ones.[3] Darling Mama, I am acquiring a taste for my dear Calvary, and I am asking the Master to set up a tent there next to His own;[4] I am very absorbed in the passion,[5] and when you see all He suffered for us in His heart, in His soul, and in His body, you have, as it were, a need to give all that back to Him in return; it's as if you wish to suffer all that He suffered. I cannot say I love suffering in itself, but I love it because it conforms me to Him who is my Bridegroom and my Love. Oh, you see, that bestows such sweet peace, such profound joy on the soul, and you end up putting your happiness in everything that is irritating. Little Mama, try to put joy—not the joy you can feel but the joy of your will—into every irritation, every sacrifice, and say to the Master: "I am not worthy to suffer that for you, I do not deserve that conformity with you." You'll see that my recipe is excellent, it puts a delightful peace in the depths of the heart and draws you closer to God.

I'm leaving you, for I'm very tired and we'll see each other soon. What happiness that you're doing better; I can't say as much, but it's better all the same, since it is what He wants. My happiness is immense when I see my dear Mama cling in advance to all that God wills; what rest for my heart! Our Mother, despite the beautiful sun and my supplications, has given the order for them to make me a fire.[6] While waiting for my habit, I look like a Poor Clare in a housecoat of gray flannel. Be at peace about me, you know Our Mother; if you could see her coming with new varieties of chocolate to try to nourish my poor stomach!... Little Fléville has bought me a supply of delicate candies; I was touched by her kind heart; tell her so. *Thanks for your work*, darling Mama; I think it is your heart that plies the needle, mine feels that. I kiss you.

Sabeth

[1] Shortly before her mother returns from the country. The "petticoat" requested around September 21 (L 314) has not yet arrived. Elizabeth is rejoicing over her mother's visit at the beginning of October (cf. L 314, note 11).
[2] Cf. L 314, note 3.

[3] She may want to see Guite separately.
[4] An allusion to the Transfiguration on Mt. Tabor, cf. Mt 17:4, only Tabor has become Calvary.
[5] Particularly through Angela di Foligno, as we see from her quotations.
[6] Cf. L 314.

L 318   To Madame Gout de Bize

[September 30, 1906][1]

J. M. + J. T.

Sunday the 30th

Dear Madame,

It's a shame you can't see into the holy cloister and up to the infirmary of your little Elizabeth to witness her happiness at receiving the much-desired photographs!... My dear Mother, who was near me, was delighted over my joy; she loves her little patient so much, and you can imagine how glad I was to introduce you to her. You have conquered her heart, a heart I like to compare with yours in its warmth, breadth, and height.[2] How good it is to meet such hearts and to be loved by them! I found you and your beautiful Margot still the same. Could I be so bold to say I have a weakness for Jaja; she is charming and one's heart is quite drawn to her. I cannot tell you to what an extent her sweet picture haunts me; I have placed it before the Blessed Virgin of my childhood, the one that belongs to Mama that she sent to keep me company in my dear solitude in the infirmary,[3] and we are plotting together.[4] I have begun a novena,[5] and perhaps soon, according to the inspiration of the Blessed Virgin, I will try to send you a little note. I have a dream! I know a person who is so noble,[6] of so fine a character, so worthy of your Jaja, and I wish my Heavenly Mother would give him to her to make her happy—that happiness won by all your sufferings, and also, I HOPE, by mine. Yes, I am very ill these days, and I am very happy if the Virgin wants a drop of my blood to use for the success of my novena. I am leaving you, I'm too tired. I read something this morning that did me some good and that I send to you: "God so loved the company of suffering that He chose it for His Son, and the Son lay down on this bed, and He agreed with the Father in that love."[7] Oh, dear Madame, let us too agree in that love in which I am keeping a rendez-vous with you. Thanks again for having fulfilled my wish so quickly. I kiss you as well as my very dear Jaja.

S. E. o. the Trinity r.c.i.

[1] "Sunday the 30th" of September in 1906.
[2] Cf. Eph 3:18. Mother Germaine is for Elizabeth an image of "the breadth and ... the height ... of the charity of Jesus Christ."
[3] Cf. S 204: "Remembering a statue of the Virgin of Lourdes before which, as a young girl, she had received many graces, Sister Elizabeth asked her mother for it, so that she who had watched over her entrance [into Carmel] *might also protect her leaving.* From then on she only called it *Janua Coeli* [Gate of Heaven]."
[4] Cf. L 315, note 8. This refers to the 24-year-old Jaja's marriage.
[5] In preparation for the feast of Our Lady of the Rosary, then celebrated on the first Sunday of October, which in 1906 fell on October 7.
[6] Elizabeth names him (Robert de Saint-Seine) only in her next letter to Madame Gout de Bize (cf. L 322, note 4).
[7] The source is unidentified.

L 319　　To Mother Germaine of Jesus　　　[September 30, 1906][1]
11 o'clock

+ My darling Mother,

　　Your little praise of glory is suffering very much, very much; it is the "exceeding love," [2] the divine dispensation of pain.[3] She thinks that between now and the 9th she has just enough time to make you a novena of suffering with her Master. My Mother, please make her heart happy by accepting it. I have taken complete refuge in the prayer of my Master and I have complete confidence in its all-powerful efficacy!...

[1] "Between now and the 9th ... a novena." It is 11 o'clock (in the *evening:* cf. the following note). October 9th will be the fifth anniversary of the Prioress's election. In S 220, Mother Germaine also indicates the date to be September 30.
[2] Cf. Eph 2:4.
[3] Cf. Ang 201: "A divine dispensation, prior to our thoughts, superior to our words, he [Jesus] dispensed suffering."

L 320   To Mother Germaine of Jesus   [October 1906][1]
      11 o'clock. From the palace[2] of suffering and beatitude.
                       +

My darling Mother, my beloved priest,[3]
    Your little praise of glory cannot sleep, she is suffering; but in her soul, although the anguish penetrates there too, she feels so much peace, and it is your visit that has brought her this Heavenly peace. Her little heart needs to tell you this, and in her tender gratitude she is praying and suffering unceasingly for you! Oh, help me climb my Calvary; I feel the power of your priesthood over my soul so strongly, and I need you so much. My Mother, I feel my Three so close to me; I am more overwhelmed by happiness than by pain: my Master has reminded me that it is my dwelling place and I am not to choose my sufferings; so I immerse myself with Him into immense suffering,[4] with much fear and anguish.

---

[1] The echoes of St. Angela di Foligno (cf. notes 2 and 4) prove that we are surely after September 14 (cf. L 311, note 3), probably already in October (cf. note 2).
[2] The word "palace" (found also in L 323a, P 113 and 120) like the words "dwelling place" (or residence) in this letter (and in L 315, 323, 323a, 324, and P 120) are inspired by the "dwelling place" (habitation) of Jesus, a term found in P 120, but especially in L 311 and P 114, both from September 14, which reveal their source by quoting Ang 197: "Where did He live but in suffering?" The three terms are used, one after the other, in P 120 of October 3.
[3] "Priest": toward the end of her life, Elizabeth loved to give this title to Mother Germaine (S 240). As Prioress, Germaine had received Elizabeth's oblation to God through her religious vows; again as Prioress, she is helping the dying nun to offer her life to the Lord, for the Church. The name was already introduced in P 100 ("And He consecrated you so that you might be the Priest / The Sacrificer who offers me to Love") for the feast of June 15, also in P 113 from September 14, and it is the central theme of P 121, which was composed during the same period as L 320. In L 306 to Mother Marie of Jesus (who understood this language well), Elizabeth had already named her Prioress a "consecrating Pontiff." Mother Germaine was conscious of "having, as it were, a priesthood to exercise" over Elizabeth, cf. her letter quoted in L 271, note 1.
[4] "Immense suffering" (Angela di Foligno), cf. L 312, note 4.

L 321   To Mother Germaine of Jesus
[October (4th or 9th), 1906][1]

+ My beloved priest,

I do not know what is happening. My Master caught hold of me and made me understand that today the Mother and child are beginning a new life, "wholly present to Love, wholly within pure Love." At Mass, the Sovereign Priest is going to deliver up His priest and His two victims,[2] and it will be full possession by Love! Oh, I cannot say what I feel, my Mother. How great it is!

+

---

[1] There is something solemn about this "today" when Mother Germaine and Elizabeth "are beginning a new life." Could it be October 4, when the feast of Saint Teresa of Avila was celebrated by a community act: Elizabeth would go down to the choir, the one time during her illness (cf. S 236-37)? Or the 9th, the fifth anniversary of the Prioress's election?

[2] Elizabeth and Sister Anne-Marie.

L 322   To Madame Gout de Bize   [October 7, 1906][1]
J. M. + J. T.

Under the inspiration of the Blessed Virgin and urged by her, I am sending you this little note. I was wondering how to get it to you, and here my Heavenly Mother has sent me my earthly mother,[2] and we have done our little plotting together,[3] for our kind Mother gives me any permission for my dear Mama; she has enough confidence in her little child and I don't think I am abusing it under the circumstances. I don't think you would feel as free to talk with me in all simplicity if you thought my dear Mother was reading our letters; this is why: it is one of her brothers whom the Blessed Virgin has in mind for our little Jaja. Oh, you see, it seems to me this marriage would be *ideal*. Monsieur Robert de Saint-Seine[4] is someone with such a fine character and such lofty sentiments, so profoundly Christian, he is one of those young men of a "stock" one scarcely finds any more, it seems to me. I do not know if my dream will be fulfilled (but I can say all the same that the good Virgin let me dream it), but I think these two are worthy of each other, and in

God's mind I believe I can see them "two in one."[5] So, I will admit to you that before my departure for Heaven, I am fancying that the Virgin will yet give me the joy of seeing this union. I am speaking to you with an open heart, as if I were near you, knitted to your heart in your dear Boaça[6] where I remember the past with so much sweetness. Answer me just as simply, through Mama if you want to be freer. Mama will give you details about Monsieur de Saint-Seine that I don't have the strength to write. There is only one thing, he does not have any money outside his pay as an officer; I think Jaja would have enough for her to make this sacrifice; you can tell me all that. How happy her sweet letter made me! May I dare say I feel a mother's tenderness for her in my heart? Isn't everything permitted a soul on the threshold of paradise?... How happy I would be, before going there, to see her become the little sister-in-law of my darling Mother! Oh, what a Mother! Mama can tell you about her. Her heart makes me think of yours: God must have created them, animated them with the same breath, and her brother is also one of those hearts; oh, how well it would go with the heart of my Jaja!...

A Dieu, dear Madame, I had no more strength left when I took up my pencil, and I think I have recovered some near you! I throw myself into your arms to kiss you and find my dear Jaja in that motherly heart. Oh, thanks for the photographs; if you knew the happiness they brought my heart....

Your little Eliz. of the Trinity r.c.i.

(I haven't told you anything about the Saint-Seine family, the lords of Burgundy: I'll leave the earthly side to *Mama*.)

---

[1] "Under the inspiration of the Blessed Virgin": at the end of her novena, and so October 7 (cf. L 318 note 5). The autographs of L 318 and the first part of this letter form two halves of the same sheet.

[2] Mme. Catez, in her tenth visit during these first days of October.

[3] Elizabeth has handed her letter to her mother (cf. "how to get it to you"); Mme. Catez would also write to her friend, who would be able to address her answer to her; all of which results from this L 322. From whom did the initiative spring (cf. L 325, note 7)?

[4] Younger brother of Mother Germaine. He was 34 years old at that time. Someone else (undoubtedly Mother Germaine?) later erased this name as well as the words "Saint-Seine ... lords of Burgundy," but they can still be read.

[5] Cf. Gen 2:24, taken up again in Mt 19:5.

[6] Her chateau in Alénya (Eastern Pyrenees). On Elizabeth's confidences, cf. the letter from Mme. Gout de Bize of February 25, 1907, in PAT. Elizabeth loves the expression "knitted," which she found in Saint John of the Cross, cf. L 209, note 5.

L 323   To Madame de Sourdon   [October 9, 1906][1]
        J. M. + J. T.

Very dear Madame,

My heart is making this pencil move, for my fingers do not have the strength, and yet I want to answer your touching letter, to tell you I am praying for your intentions, for your dear Marie-Louise, for your dear departed one,[2] that the God who is rich in mercy might lead her into her glorious heritage,[3] for one must be so pure to contemplate His Face!... You ask me to get into contact with her.... Oh, if you knew how we live by faith in Carmel, how imagination and feeling are excluded from our relationship with God.... I was astonished that you would say that to me, but I thought I might have misinterpreted the meaning of your words. Oh, yes, very willingly I unite myself with the dear deceased, I enter into communion with her, I find her once more in Him by whom alone she lives: and so each time I draw near to God, faith tells me that I am also drawing close to her. Now, whether she is already in the City of saints[4] or still in that place where the soul completes the work of being purified to contemplate the divine beauty and be transformed in His own Image,[5] as Saint Paul says: in whichever of these she may be, she is held firm in pure love, nothing distracts her from God, and that is what makes me feel closer to the dead than to the living. For, dear Madame, when we want to find a beloved soul again, do we know if at every moment it is dwelling in God?[5a] Alas, here below, so many things make us wander!... Oh, do not be discouraged about our little Marie-Louise;[6] you haven't yet read what is in the great Heart of God, you do not know all the love it contains and how, in His fatherliness, he is *looking after* and thinking about you. Oh, believe me and leave everything to me; I do not forget you, I assure you, on my cross where I taste unknown joys. I understand that suffering is the revelation of Love, and I rush to it: it is my beloved dwelling place where I find peace and rest, where I am sure to meet my Master and dwell with Him. A Dieu, dear Madame, this time I don't think He will be much longer in coming to seek me;[7] you are part of my heart, so I bring you with me, that you might be unceasingly present before the Face of God. I kiss you as a beloved mother.

S. E.[8]

Remember me to the dear little de Maizières.

[1] The envelope; addressed to the "Comtesse de Sourdon, c/o Mme. la baronne d'Anthès, Avallon, Yonne," is postmarked at Dijon on "10-10-06," at 11 o'clock (in the morning).

[2] Her sister, Mme. de Maizières.

[3] Cf. Eph 2:4 and 1:18.

[4] Cf. Eph 2:19.

[5] Cf. 2 Cor 3:18.

[5a] Elizabeth means: If we want to "find a beloved soul again" *here on earth,* is this soul in fact *at this moment* united to God? Wanting to reply to the request that she "get in contact" with someone, she has already insisted on faith and here proposes union with God *at this moment* as the means of spiritual communication.

[6] Marie-Louise will finally marry on May 7, 1907.

[7] In a note that accompanied this letter, Mother Germaine writes "Dear Madame, our child speaks very truthfully: I think the last 'veni' will not be long in coming; she is really going downhill, the little saint. Another month, six weeks perhaps.... Her poor Mother is admirably prepared for it: she finds her changed, actually it is very perceptible."

[8] Elizabeth draws a little triangle, the symbol of the Trinity, after her name.

L 323a   To Madame de Vathaire[1]   [around October 10, 1906][2]

... David said about Jesus Christ: "His suffering is immense."[3] I have fixed my dwelling place in that immensity, it is the royal palace where I live with my crucified Bridegroom; I am keeping a rendez-vous there with you, for your soul knows how to appreciate the happiness of suffering and to regard it as the revelation of the "exceeding love"[4] Saint Paul speaks of. Oh! how I love it! It has become my peace, my repose; pray that God might increase my capacity for suffering.

[1] The autograph of this letter has disappeared (which is why it escaped our attention for a long time). The extract we are reproducing is found in *Circ* 9 and, with one

sentence from L 314, in S 197–98. The recipient is "a friend" *(Circ 9)*, "a soul capable of understanding it" (S 197). By a process of elimination we conclude that this refers to Mme. de Vathaire: a) We cannot see why the *known* correspondents would have omitted this beautiful letter from their collection; b) Mme. de Vathaire visited Elizabeth during her illness, and Elizabeth wrote to her (cf. note 11 of L 287); c) Even before she entered Carmel, Elizabeth had intimate conversations with her, notably about suffering (cf. her RB in PAT); d) As she wanted to remain unknown in that RB, a desire that Mother Germaine always respected (but we were nevertheless able to reveal, cf. PAT), she would not have kept Elizabeth's correspondence.
[2] The use of such terms as "palace" and "dwelling place" (cf. note 2 of L 320) and particularly the similarity with the end of L 323 (suffering as "peace," "joy," and the "revelation" of love) suggest the approximate date.
[3] As in L 314, and it is not "David" but Lam 2:13.
[4] Eph 2:4.

L 324   To Germaine de Gemeaux   [around October 10, 1906][1]
J. M. + J. T.   God alone suffices!

My dear little sister Germaine,

Oh! if you knew what heavenly days your friend is spending in Carmel! I am growing weaker day by day, and I feel the Master will not delay much longer in coming to seek me. I am tasting, experiencing unknown joys. The joy of pain, oh! little Germaine, how pleasant and sweet it is!... Before I die, I dream of being transformed into Jesus Crucified, and that gives me so much strength in suffering.... Little sister, we should have no other ideal but to be conformed to that divine Model; then what eagerness we would have in sacrifice, in contempt of ourselves, if the eyes of our heart[2] were always focused on Him.

One saint wrote, in speaking of the Master: "Where, then, did He live but in suffering?"[3] In fact, it was His dwelling place during the thirty-three years He spent on earth, and it is only with privileged ones that He shares it. If you knew what ineffable happiness my soul tastes when I think that the Father predestined me to be conformed to His crucified Son....[4] Saint Paul informs us of that divine election that seems to be my share!...

Little sister of my soul, in the light of eternity God makes me understand many things, and I come to tell you as if it were coming from Him not to be afraid of sacrifice, of struggle, but rather to rejoice in it. If your nature is a subject of combat, a battlefield, oh, do not be discouraged, do not become sad. I would gladly say to you: love your misery, for that is where God exercises His mercy, and when the sight of it throws you into sadness that makes you withdraw into yourself, that is self-love! When you find yourself faltering, go take refuge in the prayer of your Master; yes, little sister, on His Cross He saw you and prayed for you, and that prayer is eternally living and present before His Father; that prayer will save you from your miseries.[5] The more you feel your weakness, the more your confidence must grow, for you must depend on Him alone. So don't believe that He won't take you because of that;[5a] it is a huge temptation.

How happy I was about Albert's fine success;[6] please be my little messenger to your dear parents, they know my deep affection and will not doubt the union of my heart with theirs under these circumstances. Tell them, too, that I won't forget them or dear Yvonne in Heaven.

We are going to have very beautiful feast days in honor of our blessed martyrs of Compiègne on Saturday, Sunday, and Monday.[7] I will be able to attend them in a little tribune, for Sister Thérèse of the Child Jesus granted my prayer three months ago[8] by giving me the strength to take a few steps, which had been impossible for me. That is a great consolation to me, for I can spend many hours in the dear little tribune, which has a grille opening on the sanctuary; I go to seek strength there, close to Him who has suffered so much because "He loved us exceedingly,"[9] as the Apostle says.

A Dieu, little sister, let us ask for the strength of love that burned in the hearts of our blesseds so we too might be martyrs of that love like our holy Mother Teresa. I'm sending you a holy card[10] our kind Mother, who cares for me like a true mama, gave me for you. Courage, let us look at the Crucified and be conformed to that divine image. I kiss you.

S. M. E. o. the Trinity, r.c.i.

[1] A few days before "Saturday, Sunday, Monday," October 13-15 (cf. note 7).
[2] "Eyes of the heart": Eph 1:18.
[3] Ang 197.
[4] Cf. Rom 8:29.
[5] Cf. Heb 7:25
[5a] "Take" into the convent.

[6] Her brother, in his examinations: cf. L 278.

[7] October 13–15. Cf. the report in SRD 21, pp. 690–93 (signed by "A witness," who is Mother Germaine: cf. P 123, note 1). The first two evenings P. Vallée preached at Benediction; on the 15th, feast of St. Teresa (after having celebrated a pontifical Mass in the morning), it was Bishop Dadolle.

[8] Cf. L 295.

[9] Eph 2:4.

[10] A holy card commemorating the martyrdom of the sixteen Carmelites of Compiègne. On the back, Elizabeth writes: "Where, then, did Jesus Christ live but in suffering? S.M.E. of the Trinity, r.c.i." This refers to Ang 197, which has appeared so often since L 311.

L 325   To her mother   [October 14, 1906][1]

+

My darling little Mama,

Our Mother had me taste the chocolates, which I found very good; the pistachio flavor is a nice little change for me, but I'm suffering so much from my stomach that everything makes me a little sick; in any case this still goes down, and I would be grateful if you'd send me some. Our Mother wants me to take *eight* [2] of them a day; well, I'll try to take what I can. Thanks for the Kalougas, which are better than anything else for my stomach; I'll be happy to have some, made by my darling little Mama whom I love more and more. Yesterday I spent the evening in the little tribune, and I attended the concert. Our Mother spoiled me, she opened the grille for me[3] and I had the joy of seeing you; I was wholly united with you. Oh, if you knew, when I compared myself to Guite, I felt *my happiness* more than *ever*. I was suffering a lot, I was thinking that soon perhaps earth would no longer be for me, for truly my poor body is very sick, and I said to myself: "You are the happy one." I spent a heavenly evening like that, overwhelmed by my happiness. Darling Mama, yes, renew your sacrifice; that is so pleasing to God, and you draw down for me graces of strength for suffering, which I love more and more and which my Master does not spare me.

A Dieu, let us be united during these three days,[4] thanks for the sweets, I love you and kiss you. I am exceedingly happy to have you for a mother.

+

Our good Mother sees the manifestation of God's will in Madame Berthe's reply,[5] and that is all she needs to find her pleasure in it; she is so above human views…. As for me, I must admit I feel a real sacrifice[6] and I'm very sure you feel quite the same. Who knows? Maybe later…. We can't know, but for the time being it is completely impossible. Our Mother's brother can do much better! Alas, that wretched money, as soon as it's lacking…. Don't feel sorry[7] for my dear Mother, she was half expecting it and sees only God's will.

[1] "Yesterday" "evening" was "the concert" in which Guite participated. This refers to Benediction on October 13. Very good musicians, Guite and Georges lent "their musical assistance to feast days" (S 237). "Let us be united during these three days" implies that Elizabeth is not writing on the last day, the 15th.

[2] Written first as "10"!

[3] That is, the inner frame covered by a veil. From her little tribune (see Plan 2, 1, letter b), Elizabeth can see her mother, who was in the outer tribune on the other side (*ibid.,* letter d).

[4] The Triduum at the Carmel that Mme. Catez attended.

[5] The negative response concerning the marriage proposed in L 322.

[6] "A real sacrifice": Elizabeth's reaction is always lively in such cases; it was the same for Marie-Louise de Sourdon ("I am as interested in her future as if she were my little sister," L 206) when a marriage possibility vanished: "I'm sorry he does not have another name, for I imagine this is what he lacks. It's a shame, I admit" (L 167); and, on another occasion: "Believe that my disappointment was great" (L 262). Here, instead of the "name," "wretched money" seems to be at least the reason given for the refusal.

[7] As planned in L 322, Mme. Catez undoubtedly had the negative reply delivered to Elizabeth (at the same time as "the chocolates"), as the present letter implies. Has Mme. Catez expressed her "sorrow"? As for Mother Germaine, who seems to have been outside the "little plotting" of Elizabeth and her mother in the beginning (L 322), she had known about it for some time since "she was half expecting it."

L 326   To Madame Farrat   [around October 18, 1906][1]
J. M. + J. T.

Very dear Madame,

I cannot find words to express how touched I was by your thoughtfulness: it seemed to me that the pretty box of Kalougas brought me your heart! Your delicious candy arrived just at the right moment! I have been suffering more for several days, and your good Kalougas are so soothing…. And then there is such a variety of them, which is another advantage for a poor stomach tired of everything.

A thousand thanks for the relief you are giving this little patient, who is nonetheless so happy to suffer for her Master. Yes, dear Madame, my happiness has never been so great, so true as it has since God deigned to associate me with the sufferings of the divine Crucified, so "I might suffer in my flesh what is lacking in His passion,"[2] as Saint Paul said. I think I will soon be going to join your little Cécile[3] in the bosom of Light and Love. Together, we will turn God's graces and gifts in your direction.... We will watch over your dear son so He may keep him wholly pure, wholly worthy of the home where God has willed to shelter him; and also our little Marie-Madeleine, your beautiful little lily so beloved of my heart. For you, dear Madame, we will ask, if you allow, those graces of union with the Master that give so much strength to the soul for passing through any trial and that transform life through continual contact with Him! If you knew how well cared for I am in my dear Carmel, what a Mother I have unceasingly near me.... She is a true mama for her little patient. You would have tears in your eyes if you could see through the grilles the goodness lavished on me by this heart whom God has made so motherly. A Dieu, dear Madame, and thanks again. I have given my gratitude to the Master: may He tell you too about the very deep affection of your little Carmelite friend,

S. E. o. the [4]

---

[1] Approximate date deduced from L 327, in which Elizabeth recounts the news of the "pretty box of Kalougas" received.
[2] Col 1:24.
[3] The granddaughter Mme. Farrat had lost.
[4] The signature is followed by a triangle.

L 327   To her mother   [around October 20, 1906][1]
            J.M. + J.T.

My darling little Mama,
      How could I not come to thank you for your treats, which touch me to the depths of my heart! Your Kalougas are excellent, that is a nice little change for me, for now I have continual nausea; I am losing my sense of smell a little. Madame Farrat sent me a pretty

box containing 30 Kalougas of different kinds, some pistachio, others fruit, and there are some coffee ones that are not any better than yours, I couldn't tell them apart: you see, you rival the *"specialists"!...* I'm sorry about all these sweets for my wretched palate,[2] which doesn't even taste them any more; but my heart is grateful to my darling little Mama. Our Mother told me how happy you were to make me these candies; how many times we speak of you together!... I attended the rehearsal,[3] and I'm sure my niece Sabeth wanted to take part in the concert, am I wrong? I am *counting on the iron* for Monday morning;[4] thanks for the collar; our little Sister[5] is superb, I've already tried her headdress. Oh darling Mama, that has brought back some memories!...[6]

There is a Being who is Love and who wishes us to live in communion[7] with Him. Oh Mama, it is delightful, for He is there keeping me company, helping me to suffer, urging me to go beyond my suffering to rest in Him; do as I do, you will see how that transforms everything.

A very warm thank you to my darling Guite for everything. I kiss her, tell her I'll be fused into one with her at the ceremony on Monday. I bless the little angels. For you, all my love.

+

[1] Date deduced from note 4.

[2] After having recounted the clothing of October 22, Mme. Catez testifies: "Her tongue and her palate were on fire, speaking was excruciating for her, but she still addressed affectionate words to friends, who left her weeping ..." (RB 2 in PAT). Also S 241: "At this time (October 22), a great interior inflammation increased her sufferings even more; she was literally burning to death and could speak only with difficulty, but the greatest joy shone on her face." And a priest who took her Communion "three weeks before her death": "Even though I had been warned, when I saw that tongue, red as fire, I was so affected that my hand trembled" (S 241). That condition kept on getting worse: "Toward the end of October, her stomach, which was nearly consumed, would accept only a few pieces of barley sugar; after All Saints' Day, it was a complete fast; Sister Elizabeth of the Trinity could not even take a drop of water without experiencing acute pains; her mouth, already on fire for three weeks, continued to dry up. The scorching thirst, the torment of which we could not relieve, was particularly painful for her" (S 249–50).

[3] For the next clothing, preceded by Benediction in which Guite participated musically (cf. the end of the letter).

[4] Monday, October 22. "The collar," "the iron" to press with, "the headdress": "A white-veil [lay] postulant, her companion in the novitiate, was going to receive the holy habit; she [Elizabeth] offered to prepare her white dress and put her heart and

the last of her strength into this work…. The exhaustion of that poor body, which was like a skeleton and demanded all the strength of her will to make the least movement, foretold well that the end was near. Her fingers, which could hardly make out the hem of the dress she was trying to work on, sometimes fell to the floor; the poor child would smile, but would not hear of anyone else replacing her; her great charity sustained her, for she knew that her work would be the joy of her happy little sister" (S 239–40).

[5] Sister (Thérèse) Marie-Joseph of Our Lady of Grace (Marie Passieux), 25 years old. She must have entered the year before; she did not persevere.

[6] Of her own clothing, December 8, 1901.

[7] Cf. 1 Jn 1:3.

L 328   To Sister Louise de Gonzague
[(around October 20?), 1906][1]

How can I express my gratitude for the happiness you gave me this morning? I will offer my Communion for you to Him who is a consuming Fire,[2] so He might transform you always more into Himself, so you might give Him all glory. Union, and a big thanks.

[1] The great change in her handwriting indicates the time of her illness. The recipient was in charge of the habit room: without doubt the "happiness" of "this morning" had to do with the clothing of October 22 that Elizabeth was preparing for (cf. L 327, note 4). See also note 2.

[2] Cf. Heb 12:29, quoting Dt 4:24. Cf. S 241 speaking of her physical sufferings around October 22: *"God is a consuming fire,* she said; it is to His action that I am submitting."

L 328a   To Anne-Marie d'Avout   [around October 21, 1906][1]

My dear Anne-Marie,

I am so weak I can hardly hold a pencil and yet I need to thank you from my heart, which was so deeply touched by your thoughtfulness. I award you a diploma in candy making: your kalougas are so good! How pretty they are in their little box! I have quite a supply of chocolates of every kind; everything makes me suffer, but yours, on the contrary, soothe me; it is surely your heart that has placed a special essence in these pretty candies. A thousand thanks. I am not forgetting you on my cross, where I taste unknown joys, and when I am in Heaven, your names and your memories, which are so well engraved in the depths of my heart, will be constantly present there before God. I am very happy, little Anne-Marie!... If you saw how my dear Mother takes care of me.... For a Carmelite used to mortification, I am ashamed of my comfort, but where I am concerned, the only consideration is one of charity, of goodness that is so maternal! A Dieu, little one, I love you and your family a lot, and I kiss you all. Thanks again.

S. E. of the Trinity r.c.i.

[1] In pencil. Approximate date deduced from L 330 of October 23, which recounts how her "friends" are getting "chocolates of every kind" for her (the same expression she uses here). Anne-Marie might have heard about the "kalougas" given by Mme. Farrat (L 326) and Mme. Catez (L 327). Hers will soon be surpassed by those of Mme. Gout de Bize (L 330).

L 329   To Mother Germaine of Jesus [October 22, 1906][1]
11 o'clock

My beloved priest,
    Your little victim is suffering very, very much, it is a kind of physical agony. She feels so cowardly, cowardly enough to scream![2] But the Being who is the Fullness[3] of Love visits her, keeps her company, makes her enter into communion[4] with Him, while He makes her understand that as long as He leaves her on earth, He will measure out suffering to her.[5] Darling Mother, if you will allow it, I feel moved to prepare for your feast on All Saints, so you might be rooted in pure love[6] like the glorified, by beginning a novena of suffering for you during which we[7] will go to visit you every night,[8] while you're asleep, with the Fullness of love! Excuse Laudem gloriae, she loves you so much. Next to Him, you are everything to her.

+

[1] Written "in the evening of that day," "October 22," says the recipient in S 240. The time of a "novena" for the "feast of All Saints."
[2] Cf. the testimony of Mother Germaine (PO 64): "One day, at the end of a conversation, in which she had shown the same serenity as usual, she said to me as I was leaving, pointing to the window quite close to her bed: 'My Mother, are you at peace leaving me all alone like this?' As I looked at her in surprise at this questioning, she added: 'I'm suffering so much that I now understand suicide. But be at peace: God is

there, and He protects me.' And yet, in the course of the conversation, she had, as always, testified to her happiness at suffering."

³ Cf. Jn 1:16: "We have all received of His fullness."

⁴ Cf. 1 Jn 1:3.

⁵ Vocabulary inspired by Angela di Foligno, cf. L 319, note 3.

⁶ Cf. Eph 3:17.

⁷ "We": God, into whom Elizabeth knows she has been assumed. Several days later, this unitary manner of speaking will be even more manifest in LL.

⁸ Referring to the month of August, S 188 speaks already of "painful insomnias."

L 330   To Madame Gout de Bize   [October 23, 1906]¹

　　　 J. M. + J. T.   "God is Love"!²

Very dear Madame,

　　In your dear little note you call me "my child." Oh, how sweet that sounded to the ear of my heart and how grateful I am for the affection you have given so freely to the little Carmelite who loves you so much! If you knew how often we speak of you with my darling and venerated Mother.... She is letting me be the little glutton today, for the dear Mother thinks only of soothing her child, and with wholly filial simplicity I am responding to the gracious desire of your kind heart by coming to confide to you that your good chocolates (especially the pistachio ones) are the *only* things that suit my stomach. Mama, my friends, not to mention my kind Mother, are supplying me with chocolates of every kind, but they burn me or make me sick, and yours soothe me while taking away the nausea that is becoming constant, and they are more mellow too. I suspect that will make you happy, for I know the heart of my dear Madame Berthe.

　　I am *praying,* I am *immolating* myself for your little Jaja. Perhaps God is waiting for me to go to Heaven to arrange her future with the Blessed Virgin. He is all-powerful, and what seems unattainable to us can become attainable when He so wishes.³ Oh, believe that up above, in the Furnace of love, I will be *actively* ³ᵃ thinking of you. I will ask, if you wish—and that will be the sign that I have entered Heaven—a grace of union for you, of intimacy with the Master; I confide to you what has made my life an anticipated Heaven: believing that a Being called Love dwells in us at every moment of the day and night and that He asks us to live in communion with Him, to receive every joy, like every suffering, equally as coming directly from His love; that raises the soul beyond what passes away, beyond what crushes, and gives it rest in the peace, the preferential love of the children of God. Oh, dear Madame, what waves of tenderness I feel rising from my heart toward yours.... I feel as if little Elizabeth were once again back in those days when she strolled beside you along the avenues of Boaça. Go and meditate in one of them and there, in the sight of God, you will feel her whole soul close to yours, for in Him we will be *one* [4] for time and eternity!... I kiss you as well as my Jaja.

> Your little E. o. the Trinity r.c.i.

If my darling Mother permits you to love her? Oh yes, your hearts are so well made to *go together.*[5]

---

[1] Date deduced from a letter of Mother Germaine to Mme. Gout de Bize on "October 23, 1906," that accompanied the present letter; she gives the "permission" Elizabeth speaks of (cf. note 5), and, above all, adds a postscript "for the chocolates" offered for her patient. Mother Germaine adds, "What a service you are rendering to that poor stomach that we no longer know how to nourish, since it is so exhausted and quickly sickened by everything!"

[2] 1 Jn 4:16.

[3] Jaja will marry only in 1919 (at 37 years of age) and will die the following year in childbirth.

[3a] This word, which Elizabeth underlines, may be connected with the promise of Thérèse of Lisieux: "I really count on not remaining inactive in heaven" (HA 236 [LT 254]). In any case, within a few days Mother Germaine and Elizabeth will discuss explicitly her posthumous mission, "following the example of the Little Thérèse" (cf. the end of our General Introduction, Vol. I). Cf. also Ru 146: "Love cannot be inactive."

[4] Elizabeth circles the word *one,* here in italics.

[5] In the letter quoted in note 1, Mother Germaine expresses herself personally: "The permission you request has so overcome my heart that it is anxious to declare itself wholly yours. Our angelic Elizabeth will be taken by God, as a sign and proof of that union long prepared by the outpouring of her heart, which is so filial and grateful to her dear 'Madame Berthe'." Mme. Gout de Bize did not misunderstand the marriage plans Elizabeth dreamed of for Jaja, as is evident in her letter to Guite, April 20, 1927 (ACD): "I had kept all the letters written by your dear Saint! I have found them again and am sending them to you with the thought that they might help you if you want to write her life! They would prove once again how great, profound, and sincere Elizabeth's faith was."

L 331   To Clémence Blanc   [October 1906][1]
            J.M. + J.T.

Dear little sister,

Your little Angel[2] is sending you a note from her heart before going away to Him who was already her All here on earth. The heart of Christ was never so overflowing with love as at the moment He was going to leave His own.[3] Nor have I, little sister, ever felt such a need to cover you with prayer. When my sufferings become more acute, I feel so urged to offer them for you that I cannot do otherwise. Do you have some pressing need? Are you suffering? Oh! little sister, I give you all of mine, they are completely at your disposal. If you knew how happy I am to think my Master is coming to seek me! How ideal death is for those whom God has protected and "who have not sought what is visible, because it is passing, but what is invisible, for it is eternal"[4] (Saint Paul).

In Heaven, I will be your Angel more than ever. I know how well my little sister needs protection in the midst of Paris, where her life is being spent. Saint Paul says that "God chose us in Him before the creation so we might be pure, immaculate in His presence, in love."[5] Ah! how I will ask Him to accomplish this great decree of His will[6] in you! For that purpose, listen to the advice of the same apostle: "Walk in Jesus Christ, rooted in Him, built up on Him, strengthened in faith and growing more and more in Him."[7] While contemplating Ideal Beauty in its great brightness, I will ask Him to imprint it on your soul, so that already here on this earth, where everything is soiled, you might be beautiful with His beauty, luminous with His light.

A Dieu, thank Him for me, for my happiness is immense. I am keeping a rendez-vous with you in the inheritance of the saints.[7a] There, among the choir of virgins, that generation that is as pure as light, we will sing the beautiful canticle of the Lamb,[8] the eternal Sanctus, beneath the radiant light of God's Face. Then, Saint Paul says, "we will be transformed into the same Image, from brightness to brightness."[9] I kiss you with all the love of my heart and am your Angel for all eternity.

                              M. Elizabeth of the Trinity r.c.i.

¹ This and the next two letters, which are undated, belong to the series of goodbye letters, letter-testaments, like L 335 and 336, that date with certainty from October 28. "We are coming to (Elizabeth's) last weeks," S 228 says, stating that "We are grouping together here her last letters"; L 331 and 333 are a part of them, but L 293 to Clémence Blanc should not have been. L 331 is clearly later than L 293 from July, since Clémence now lives "in Paris," and Elizabeth no longer calls her her "Tobias," as she had in July when Clémence's return to Carmel was still possible.
² Cf. L 87, note 9, and L 293.
³ Cf. Jn 13:1.
⁴ 2 Cor 4:18.
⁵ Eph 1:4.
⁶ Cf. Eph 1:11.
⁷ Col 2:6–7.
^{7a} Cf. Col 1:12.
⁸ Cf. Rev 14:3-4.
⁹ 2 Cor 3:18.

L 332   To Marthe Weishardt¹   [October 1906]²

How closely your little soul sister is united to you during these wholly heavenly days, in which "exceeding love"³ is overflowing in waves within her heart! Oh, you see, sometimes I think He is going to come and take me to carry me off where He is in dazzling Light. Even now in the night of faith, the union is so profound, the embraces so heavenly! What will it be, in that first face-to-face, in God's great light, that first meeting with divine Beauty! Thus will I flow out into the infinity of Mystery and contemplate the wonders of the Divine Being. It seems to me we will be even more consummated in the One, and we will always sing in unison that "Canticum magnum"⁴ Saint Paul speaks of. Thanks for your dear letter, it made me so happy! Thanks for all you have given of God to your little sister; He has united us so closely! Let us hide ourselves in eternal silence, may our simple gaze upon Him separate us from everything and fix us in the unfathomable depths of the mystery of the Three, while we await the Bridegroom's "Veni." Your *real little* sister,

> M. Elizabeth of the Trinity
> "Laudem gloriae."

¹ Before entering Carmel, Elizabeth had known Marthe, a former novice in Carmel, very well. Cf. L 50, note 2; also L 140.
² Cf. the preceding letter, note 1. The copy given to the Dijon Carmel in 1958 men-

tions "a letter written by Elizabeth during the last days of her illness." A characteristic mistake ("inssondable" instead of "insondable") testifies to the authenticity of this late copy.
[3] Cf. Eph 2:4.
[4] "Great canticle," but "Saint Paul" never uses this expression. There is the "canticum novum" in St. John, Rev 14:3 and 5:9.

L 333   To Madame de Bobet   [end of October(?), 1906][1]
      J. M. + J. T.   "Deus Charitas est."[2]

My very dear Antoinette,

    The hour is drawing near when I am going to pass from this world to my Father, and before leaving I want to send you a note from my heart, a testament from my soul. Never was the Heart of the Master so overflowing with love as at the supreme moment when He was going to leave His own![3] It seems to me as if something similar is happening in His little bride at the evening of her life, and I feel as if a wave were rising from my heart to yours!...Dear Antoinette, in the light of eternity the soul sees things as they really are. Oh! how empty is all that has not been done for God and with God! I beg you, oh, mark everything with the seal of love! It alone endures. How serious life is: each minute is given us in order to "root"[4] us deeper in God, as Saint Paul says, so the resemblance to our divine Model may be more striking, the union more intimate. But to accomplish this plan, which is that of God Himself, here is the secret: forget self, give up self, ignore self, look at the Master, look only at Him, accept as coming directly from His love both joy and suffering; this places the soul on such serene heights!...

    My beloved Antoinette, I leave you my faith in the presence of God, of the God who is all Love dwelling in our souls. I confide to you: it is this intimacy with Him "within" that has been the beautiful sun illuminating my life, making it already an anticipated Heaven; it is what sustains me today in my suffering. I do not fear my weakness; that's what gives me confidence. For the Strong One is within me[5] and His power is almighty. It is able to do, says the Apostle, abundantly more than we can hope for![6] A Dieu, my Antoinette, when I am up above, will you let me help you, scold you even, if I see you are not giving everything to the Master? because I love you! I will protect your two dear treasures and will ask that you be granted everything needed to make them two beautiful souls, daughters of love! May He keep you wholly His, wholly faithful; in Him I will always be WHOLLY YOURS.[7]

Sr. M.E. of the Trinity r.c.i.

I am never without your dear rosary,[8] day or night.

[1] Cf. L 331, note l. Elizabeth is now sure of dying soon and is writing this "testament."
[2] "God is Love": 1 Jn 4:16.
[3] Cf. Jn 13:1.
[4] Col 2:7 and Eph 3:17.
[5] Cf. 2 Cor 12:9.
[6] Cf. Eph 3:20.
[7] Elizabeth underlines this twice.
[8] Cf. L 261.

L 334   To Madame Gout de Bize   [end(?) of October 1906][1]
J. M. + J. T.

Very dear Madame,
    With what happiness my dear Mother has given a taste of your delicious chocolates to her little patient, whose wretched stomach will no longer agree to anything! You understand that it can only love what comes from its dear Madame Berthe. Your candies have a delightful taste that is a nice change from the Swiss chocolate I suck on and is about all I can eat. You can see that this is hardly a hearty meal, and I'm still suffering a lot!... I am *moved* to tears by the way you spoil me, and even though very tired, I very quickly send you thanks from my heart, which is *so, so grateful!*... Ah, you know I love you like a true mama, and know that this will be so in Heaven, too. Oh, how I will ask God for our dear Jaja's happiness; I would so like to see that before my departure; but my dream is not really attainable *now*. May the Virgin, who is also a Mother, send our dear little one that husband who is to make her happy; I love your Jaja so much. I love to speak with my darling Mother[2] about you while looking at your dear pictures.[3] How your thoughtfulness toward her spoiled child has rejoiced her wholly motherly heart.... If you knew

what she means to me! A Dieu, and please excuse this scribbling. The little Carmelite is very tired and her heart cannot remain silent; she is sending you all of it, all overflowing with tender affection; thanks again.

E. o. the Trinity

[1] The alteration in the handwriting here is the most marked of the five letters to Mme. Gout de Bize. Elizabeth is thanking her for the "delicious chocolates" requested on October 23. But her "wretched stomach" is increasingly unwilling.
[2] Mother Germaine.
[3] The photographs received, cf. L 318.

L 335   To Sister Marie-Odile[1]   [October 28, 1906]
   J. M. + J. T.   Our God is a consuming Fire.

Before flying away to Heaven, dear little Sister Marie-Odile, I want to send you a little note from my soul, for I am anxious for you to know that in the Father's House I will pray especially for you. I am keeping a rendez-vous with you in the Furnace of love; my eternity will be spent there, and you can begin it already here on earth. Dear Sister, I will be jealous for the beauty of your soul, for, as you know, my little heart loves you very much, and when one loves, one desires the best for the beloved. I think that in Heaven my mission[2] will be to draw souls by helping them go out of themselves to cling to God by a wholly simple and loving movement, and to keep them in this great silence within that will allow God to communicate Himself to them and transform them into Himself. Dear little sister of my soul, it seems to me I now see everything in God's light, and if I started my life over again, oh, I would wish not to waste one instant! He does not allow us, His brides in Carmel, to devote ourselves to anything but love, but the divine, and if by chance, in the radiance of His Light, I see you leave that sole occupation, I will come very quickly to call you to order; you would want that, wouldn't you?

Pray for me, help me prepare for the wedding feast of the Lamb.[3] Death entails a great deal of suffering, and I am counting on you to help me. In return, I will come to help you at your death.

My Master urges me on, He speaks to me of nothing but the eternity of love. It is so grave, so serious; I wish to live each moment fully. A Dieu, I don't have the strength or the permission to write at length, but you know Saint Paul's words: "Our conversation is in Heaven."[4] Beloved little sister, let us live by love so we may die of love and glorify the God Who is all Love.

"Laudem gloriae,"
October 28, 1906.

[1] Elizabeth had known her very well, first as the extern Sister at Dijon, then for another two months as a lay sister inside the Carmel. She then left for the new foundation at Paray-le-Monial. Elizabeth wrote her several times. Sister Marie-Odile later said: "I burned all her letters, I kept only the last.... Because it was the last" (cf. EP in PAT). This letter is dated.

[2] On the expression "mission" and the influence of Thérèse of Lisieux, cf. Vol. I, pp. 28–32.

[3] Cf. Rev 19:9.

[4] Phil 3:20.

L 336   To Sister Anne of Saint Bartholomew[1] [October 28, 1906]

The last wish of Laudem gloriae for her dear little Sister Anne of Saint Bartholomew; as she leaves for the great Furnace of love, she promises to help her achieve it. Yes, surrender yourself to this Fullness of Love, this "living Being" who wants to live in communion[2] with you!

October 28, 1906 +

[1] One copy, made while Mother Germaine was alive, mentions: "On the back of a holy card" (that has disappeared). The recipient is Marie-Odile's sister. Elizabeth did not know her as well, since she entered Carmel a little after Sister Anne left for Paray-le-Monial.

[2] Cf. 1 Jn 1:3.

L 337   To Mother Germaine of Jesus [last days of October 1906]

The text of this letter constitutes *Major Spiritual Writings*, IV, "Let Yourself Be Loved" (cf. Vol. I).

L 338   To Madame de Sourdon[1]   [October 30, 1906]

I the undersigned declare that although I possess nothing, since I have previously disposed[2] of everything that belonged to me, I nevertheless appoint as my sole heir Madame la comtesse Georges de Sourdon, resident of Dijon.

Elizabeth Catez
October 30, 1906

[1] What at first glance looks like an official will in reality constitutes a true message of friendship—and that is why we have placed it among the Letters—an astounding gesture of kindness and even of gaiety in this totally exhausted young woman, who is going to collapse that very evening (cf. L 339, note 1) and die ten days later. Written on paper, stamped, signed, and dated, this fictitious testament is valid to the extent that it would have been open to the Tribunal's legal interpretation, but that would only have declared it pointless since it did not revoke the first testament (cf. note 2) but, on the contrary, confirmed it. Elizabeth only wanted to tell the one she called her "second mama" and who was an excellent friend of her mother: "As I was dying I thought of you, and even though I have nothing, I give you my entire confidence." Did she wish, by doing so at this time, to entrust her mother to this faithful friend?
[2] The night before she entered Carmel, Elizabeth had made her real will, which reads: "Dijon, August 1st, 1901. This is my will and testament. I the undersigned, Marie Elizabeth Catez, residing in Dijon, département of Côte d'Or, have made my will as follows: I declare that I appoint as my sole heir my sister Marie Marguerite Raymonde Catez, asking that she have Masses said for the repose of my soul. Elizabeth Catez. Dijon, August 1st, 1901."

L 339   To Sister Marie-Xavier of Jesus   [October 30, 1906][1]

Abscondita in Deo.[2]

[1] Cf. S 253: "After Elizabeth had one day confided (to Sister Marie-Xavier) the grace she found in her name *Laudem gloriae,* the latter asked her for a name for herself, one that would give her strength and direction, and on October 30, Sister Elizabeth had this little note placed in her cell: *Abscondita in Deo.*" Sister Marie-Xavier (PO 107) says that Elizabeth had brought this note herself: "On October 30, 1906, she could still drag herself along with difficulty and came to place this simple note at the door of our cell." According to the same testimony (PO 108), Elizabeth had wanted to write more: "It is Jesus Himself who has named you. I would have liked to leave you in writing what beauty is contained in this name; but I had to tear up my paper, for there was no soul in it." According to S 246–47, on October 30th Elizabeth "could no longer leave the infirmary"; "that very evening ... she had been seized by a great trem-

bling that shook her in bed.... Her weakness was extreme, so she received the grace of the last Sacraments again on the morning of October 31." She would remain in bed from then on.
[2] "Hidden in God": cf. Col 3:3.

L 340   To Doctor Barbier[1]   [first days of November 1906][2]
+

My good Doctor,
    My heart is borrowing the hand of my Mother to tell you again one last time how grateful it is to you for the good care you have lavished on me during these months of sufferings that have been months of blessings, profound joys unknown by the world.
    I also want to tell you that it is my turn now; I feel my mission is beginning on your behalf. Yes, God is entrusting you to your little patient, and she is to be the invisible Angel, close to Him, who will lead you, by the path of duty, to the goal of every creature born of God. In this last hour of my exile, in this beautiful evening of life, how solemn everything looks to me in the light coming to me from eternity.... I wish I could make souls understand, tell them the vanity, the emptiness of anything not done for God. At least I am sure you understand me, dear Doctor, for you have always understood me; I felt it very much and it made me so happy in the depths of my heart. Oh! frequently go back over the things we've talked about together, and let your soul resonate under the action of the grace they will bring to it; but do that to conform your will faithfully to what God asks, through His law and through His Holy Church. It made me so happy to see you appreciate my dear Saint Paul that I am asking you, so as to complete my happiness, to accept as a last goodbye from your little patient, a last testimony of her affectionate gratitude, the book of those Epistles from which my soul has drawn so much strength for the trial. We will meet in the light these pages bring to those who read them with the faith of the children of God; in this light that for me will soon have no shadow, I will remember you and will pray to Him, who was so merciful to me, to keep you for Himself until all eternity, where I want to meet you one day, good Doctor. A Dieu, and thank you again. I am signing by this little cross.
+

[1] Letter dictated by Elizabeth, written by the hand of Mother Germaine, who added later: "First days of Nov. 1906."
[2] In sending this letter, on November 16, Mother Germaine writes: "She could hardly speak,... she placed a little + there for her signature."

L 341   To Madame Hallo   [November 1906][1]

+ My second Mama,

My hand can no longer hold a pen, but the heart of your daughter still leads it, passing through the heart of her Mother. I believe that the great day, so ardently desired, of my meeting with the only beloved, *adored*, Bridegroom is here.

This evening I hope to be in "that great multitude" that Saint John saw before the throne of the Lamb, serving Him day and night in His temple.[2] I am keeping a rendez-vous with you in that beautiful chapter of Revelation and in the last, which carries the soul off so well up above the earth into the Vision in which I am going to lose myself forever! How I will think of you, dear Mama, and of my little sister Marie-Louise in the light of that Furnace of love! You will be very present to me there, and my happiness will grow in interceding for you whom I love so much. Pray very much for your little Elizabeth; do not leave her waiting too long for the divine fusion. A Dieu, to Heaven! I am carrying you away with me and am entrusting to you my dear Mama, whom God is sustaining admirably well and for whom He is reserving so many graces in return for her generous sacrifice.

Your Elizabeth of the Trinity r.c.i.

[1] In a letter of October 14, 1962 (ACD), Marie-Louise Hallo confirms what has always been said at the Dijon Carmel and L 341 and 342 make clear: "The last two [letters] to Mama and Charles, dictated to Mother Germaine, are precious souvenirs." "Before her death," adds RB 7 (cf. PAT); thus in the weakness of the last days. "Shortly before her death," as Charles Hallo writes, on May 1, 1963 (ACD). "She could only sign with a cross," he further adds (PA 791).
[2] Cf. Rev 7:9, 15.

L 342   To Charles Hallo   [November 1906][1]

+ My little brother,

Before going to Heaven your Elizabeth wants to tell you once more of her deep affection for you and her plan to help you, day by day, until you join her in Heaven. My darling Charles, I want you to walk in the footsteps of your father, in the valiant faith that keeps the will always faithful. You will have battles to fight, my little brother, you will encounter obstacles on the path of life, but do not be discouraged, call me. Yes, call your little sister; in this way you will increase her happiness in Heaven; she will be so glad to help you triumph, to remain worthy of God, of your venerable father, of your mother, whose joy you must be. I no longer have the strength to dictate these last wishes of a very loving sister. When I am close to God, recollect yourself in prayer and we will meet each other in an even deeper way. I am leaving you a medal from my rosary; wear it always in memory of your Elizabeth who will love you even more in Heaven!

[1] Cf. L 341, note 1.

Elizabeth as novice, with her mother and sister (Guite), on December 22, 1902, the day of her canonical examination before profession of vows.

Appendix

Chronology

(A more detailed chronology will be found in PAT.)

1880   *July 18:* Elizabeth Catez's birth at the camp of Avor in the
             district of Farges-en-Septain (Cher).
             July 22: baptism at the camp chapel.

1881   *Around May 10:* family settles in Auxonne.

1882   *May 9:* death of her grandmother, Mme. Rolland, at Saint-
             Hilaire.
             Around November 1: another move; the Catez family goes to
             live in Dijon, on rue Lamartine.

1883   *February 20:* birth of her sister Marguerite.

1885   *June 2:* Captain Catez retires.

1887   *January 24:* death of her grandfather, M. Rolland, who was
             living in their home.
             October 2: death of her father.
             Shortly after: move to rue Prieur-de-la-Côte-d'Or, near the
             Carmel.
             During this year: first confession.
             During this year: first French lessons from Mlle. Grémaux.

1888   *During this year or the preceding one:* while on a trip in the
            south of France, Elizabeth confides her religious
            vocation to Abbé Angles.
            October: first enrollment at the Conservatory of Dijon.

1891   *April 19:* First Communion at Saint-Michel.
            June 8: Confirmation at Notre-Dame.

1893   *July 18:* first prize in higher fundamentals of music at the
            Conservatory.
            July 25: first prize at the piano.
            August–beginning of October: vacation at Gemeaux (Côte-
            d'Or) in the Vosges and the Jura.

1894   *Spring-Summer:* private vow of perpetual virginity. Interior
            call to Carmel.
            July: at the Conservatory, the prize for excellence was
            taken away from her unjustly (cf. L 7).
            Vacation: in the south of France.
            August 11: "My first poems."

1895   *January 11:* certificate of merit for harmony at the
            Conservatory.
            Vacation: in the Vosges, and at length in the Jura.

1896   *Vacation:* in the south of France.
            October: visit to Lourdes.

1897   *Vacation:* in the Vosges (and perhaps elsewhere).

1898   *Vacation:* in the south of France. Visit to Lourdes. Return by
            way of Marseille, Grenoble, Annecy, and Geneva.

1899 *January 24 (evening)–January 28:* retreat preached by Père
  Chesnay, S.J.
  January 30: begins the part of her *Diary* still preserved.
  March 4: beginning of the mission preached in Dijon.
  March 26: Mme. Catez agrees to let her daughter enter
   Carmel when she reaches the age of 21.
  April 2 (Easter): end of the mission preached in Dijon.
  June 20: first visit to the parlor of the Carmel (after her
   mother's consent).
  Vacation: in the Jura, three weeks in Switzerland (Fleurier),
   then in the Vosges.
  During the year: reads [St. Thérèse of Lisieux's] *Histoire d'une
   Ame* (Story of a Soul)

1900 *January 23 (evening)–27:* retreat preached by Père
  Hoppenot, S.J.
  First half of the year: first meeting with Père Vallée, O.P.
  Vacation: in the south of France: Tarbes, Biarritz, Lourdes,
   Carlipa. Then in Charentes and in Paris.

1901 *August 2:* enters Carmel.
  October 9: Sister Germaine of Jesus is elected Prioress of the
   Carmel; she is also Mistress of Novices.
  November: eight-day community retreat preached by Père
   Vergne, S.J.
  December 5–7: three day retreat in preparation for her
   clothing.
  December 8: clothing; Bishop Le Nordez presides over the
   ceremony; sermon by Père Vallée.

1902 *May 9–17:* "Cenacle" retreat: annual days of silence between
   Ascension and Pentecost.
  October 7–14: community retreat preached by Père Vallée.
  October 15: marriage of her sister Marguerite to Georges
   Chevignard.
  December 22: canonical examination. Elizabeth spends
   several hours outside the enclosure with her mother
   and sister.

1903   *January 1–10:* personal retreat in preparation for her
             profession.
             January 11 (Epiphany Sunday): profession.
             January 21: veiling.
             Shortly after her profession: second portress (inside enclosure).
             May 22–30: "Cenacle" days of silence.

1904   *March 11:* birth of her first niece, Elizabeth Chevignard.
             May 13–21: "Cenacle" days of silence.
             September 26–October 5: personal retreat.
             October 10: reelection of Mother Germaine as Prioress; she
             remains Mistress of Novices.
             November 12 (evening)–20: community retreat preached by
             Père Fages, O.P.
             November 21: Elizabeth writes her prayer, "O My God,
             Trinity Whom I Adore"

1905   *Lent (March 8–April 22):* first symptoms of illness;
             dispensations from observance of the Rule.
             April 19: birth of her second niece, Odette Chevignard.
             June 2–10: "Cenacle" days of silence.
             Mid-August: Elizabeth, weakened, is dispensed from her
             office as second portress.
             October 9–18: personal retreat.

1906   *January 15–23:* community retreat preached by Père
             Rollin, S.J.
             Before the end of March: Elizabeth enters the infirmary.
             April 8: dying. Extreme Unction.
             April 14: sudden improvement.
             May 13: new, serious attack.
             May 25–June 2: "Cenacle" days of silence.
             July 8 or 9: after having invoked Thérèse of Lisieux,
             Elizabeth can again stand.

First half of August: Elizabeth writes *Heaven in Faith.*
August 16–31: personal retreat. She writes her *Last Retreat.*
Evening of October 30: she is confined to bed.
October 31: receives Extreme Unction for the second time.
November 1: last Communion.
November 9: death.
November 12: burial.

Horaria of the Carmel

The *summer horarium* (from Easter until the eve of the Exaltation of the Cross, on September 14) was different from the *winter horarium* (September 14 to Holy Saturday).

Here is the summer horarium (which Elizabeth speaks of in L 168):

4:45 A.M.	Rise.
5:00	One hour of silent prayer.
6:00	Little hours (Prime, Tierce, Sext, and None).
7:00	Mass and thanksgiving (about 15 minutes).
8:00	(Never any breakfast.)

The novices (the Sisters remained in the "novitiate" three years after their final profession) gathered in the novitiate for "visits" (several prayers, particularly to the saints); each novice saw the Novice Mistress for a few minutes to give an account of her prayer.

During the morning (preferably at the beginning), the Sisters, and particularly the novices, did "a quarter-hour's reading"; 15 minutes of reading in the *Manual,* Gospels, Epistles, Psalms, the *Imitation of Christ;* usually a little from each was read.

Work.

10:00	Examination of conscience (in the choir, about 10 minutes).
10:15	Meal, always in silence, accompanied by reading aloud. Perpetual abstinence from meat (except for the sick).
11:00	Recreation in common.
12:00 P.M.	"Silence" (= free time, siesta).
1:00	Work.
2:00	Vespers.
2:30	Spiritual reading.

The novices gathered in the novitiate where it was usually the Mistress of Novices who gave a reading with commentary or a conference.

3:00	Work.
5:00	One hour of silent prayer.
6:05	Meal (called "collation" on the days when the *fast of the Order* applied, for example on the vigils of feasts and all during the winter horarium, except on Sundays; collation was still more reduced on days when the *fast of the Church* applied).
6:40	Recreation in common.
7:40	Compline.
8:00	"Silence" (as at noon).
9:00	Matins and Lauds (which usually lasted an hour and twenty minutes, or even an hour and forty minutes on feast days).

Examination of conscience (15 minutes).

Reading of the point of prayer for the next day (about 5 minutes).

Prioress's blessing at the doors of the cells.

10:50	Bed (later on feast days).

During the winter horarium, rising and everything that followed until after recreation was one hour later. The midday "silence" was removed, and from 1 P.M. on, the horarium was the same as in summer. In Lent, however, the sisters recited Vespers at 11:00 A.M. (in the morning!), before the meal at 11:30, recreation at noon, and work at 1 P.M. At 2 P.M., there was an hour of spiritual reading; the novices gathered in the novitiate from 2 o'clock until 3.

Mail

The sisters could request permission to write:
- *every month* to their parents, brothers, and sisters, *when* they had not seen them in the parlor;
- *every three months* to other relatives and friends, *when* they had not visited them in the parlor.

During Advent and Lent, no correspondence (in either sense) was allowed. Exceptions were possible. According to the custom of the time, both outgoing and incoming mail was read by the Prioress, except for mail to the spiritual director (if they had one) and to ecclesiastical Superiors.

Visits to the Parlor

The Sisters could receive visits in the parlor:
- *every month,* for 30 minutes, from their parents, brothers, and sisters; at that time, the grilles would be "opened" (cf. below) and the visitors could *see* the Carmelite;
- *every three months,* for 30 minutes, from other relatives and friends: the grille was not opened, and the visitors could only *hear* the Carmelite.

During Advent and Lent, no visits to the parlor were allowed. Exceptions were possible. If the visitors (particularly relatives) came from a great distance, the length of the visit could be prolonged and even repeated the same day. According to the custom of the time, another Sister (the "tierce") was always present, back in a corner, during these visits.

A double *grille* separated the religious from visitors: one of iron (in little squares) and the other in wood (vertical bars). On the inner side, there was also a wooden frame covered with a black veil. "To open the grille" meant that this frame was opened. In the choir, there were the same grilles as in the parlor and a wooden frame covered with a black veil. For Mass and adoration of the Blessed Sacrament during exposition, this frame was opened, but a very light veil of transparent black remained, which was drawn back only at the time of consecration and during very solemn exposition (for example, during Forty Hours and the Octave of Corpus Christi). In all cases, the shutters of the *windows* of the choir were closed. During Mass, Holy Communion was received through a window in another grille to one side: the "communion window" (cf. Plan 1, Chapel, c).

For very exceptional occasions (clothing, veiling, funeral), the second, wooden grille (with vertical bars) was also opened, so that the family could follow the ceremony. The shutters of the windows remained open; the Sisters, however, wore large black veils.

A Brief History of the Carmel of Dijon

The Carmel of Dijon was founded on September 21, 1605. It was the third foundation in France after Paris (1604) and Pontoise (1605). The foundress and first Prioress for fifteen months (until her departure for the foundation in Brussels) was Venerable Mother Anne of Jesus, companion of Saint Teresa of Avila and spiritual daughter of Saint John of the Cross, who wrote the commentary on his *Spiritual Canticle* for her. It was at Dijon, on November 1, 1605, that the first French professed nun, Marie of the Trinity, pronounced her vows.

Since the house, on rue Charbonnerie (now rue de la Préfecture) was soon too small, the Carmelites built a new monastery, on rue Sainte-Anne, which they occupied in 1613. The Sisters were dispersed into public life by the revolutionary laws of 1790.

In January 1866, however, the Carmelites returned to Dijon, after an unsuccessful attempt in Strasbourg. The foundress was then Mother Marie of the Trinity, Sub-Prioress of the Carmel of rue de Messine in Paris. They lived first in a little house, and then built a new monastery on the adjoining property. The blessing of the foundation-stone took place on July 25, 1868. It was this monastery,

4 boulevard Carnot, that Elizabeth entered more than thirty years later.

For reasons of the greatest importance, the Sisters moved again on March 17, 1979, in order to settle into their new monastery of Flavignerot, some eight miles southwest of Dijon.

Dijon Carmel

PLAN OF THE GROUND FLOOR

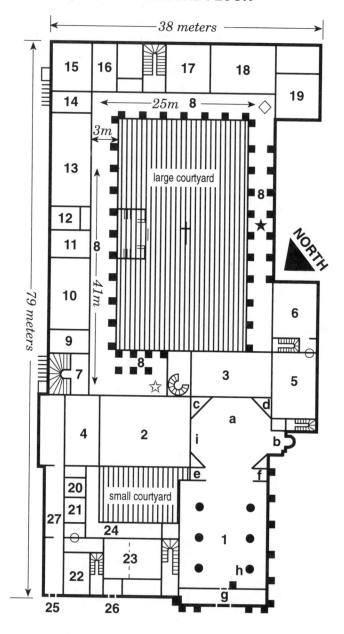

1. Chapel
2. Choir
3. Oratory
4. Preparatory
5. Outer sacristy
6. Inner sacristy with "turn" (a kind of revolving cupboard)
7. Large staircase
8. Cloisters (pillars ■)
9. Storeroom
   (bursar's office)

☆ Our Lady of Grace
★ Cloister with the Stations of the Cross
◇ Our Lady of Sorrows

10. Library
11. Pantry (supply of bread and water)
12. Refectory for the sick (small refectory)
13. Large refectory
14. Provisory – tableware
15. Kitchen
16. Dish closet
17. Linen room
18. Recreational room
19. Novitiate
20. Storage
21. Inner "turn" with round ⊖ "turn":
    where one could communicate with the outside
22. Outer "turn"
23. Large parlor (St. Teresa's parlor)
24. Covered passageway
25. Enclosure door
26. Door entering from the outer ("extern") part of the house
27. Passageway

CHAPEL:

a. Altar
b. Altar of the Blessed Virgin
c. Communion grille
d. Sisters' confessional
e. Altar of St. Teresa
f. Altar of St. Joseph
g. Chapel porch
h. Outer confessional
i. Choir grille

Dijon Carmel

PLAN OF THE SECOND FLOOR

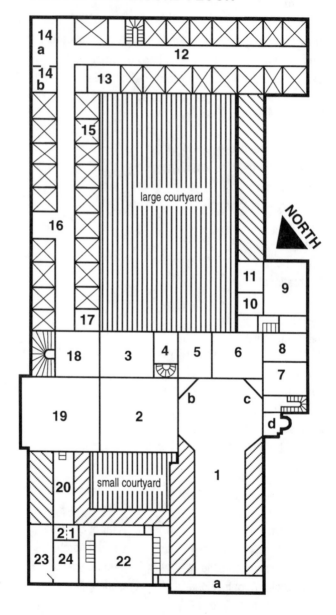

1. Chapel
2. Choir (takes full height of ground floor & second floor)
3. Terrace
4. Small infirmary cell
5. Prioress's infirmary
6. Infirmary parlor
7. Outer room
8. Infirmary parlor (outer side)
9. Infirmary cell (large infirmary)
10. Small pharmacy
11. Infirmary cell where Sr. Elizabeth died
12. Small corridor of cells (☒ = cell)
13. Tunic room
14. Habit room; (14a) small habit room
15. Cell of Elizabeth of the Trinity
16. Large corridor of cells (☒ = cell)
17. Prioress's office
18. Large staircase and bell landing (under the bell tower)
19. Chapter room
20. Small attic
21. Small parlor (of St. John of the Cross)
22. Room of the extern Sisters
23. & 24. Guest rooms

☒ Dimensions of one cell: 10'6" long; 9'1" wide and high

CHAPEL:
    a. Tribune
    b. Infirmary tribune where Sr. Elizabeth prayed
    c. Communion grille and infirmary tribune
    d. Tribune outside enclosure above the altar of the Blessed Virgin

 metal roof

slate roof

Dijon Carmel

PLAN OF THE INFIRMARY AND SURROUNDINGS

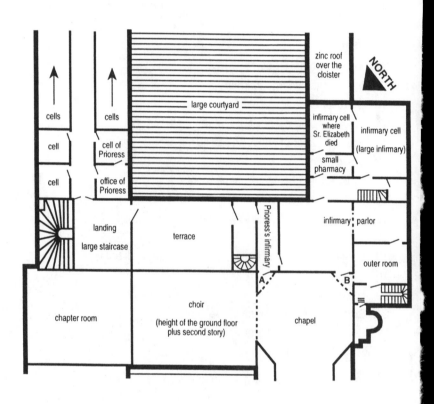

A. infirmary tribune where Sr. Elizabeth came to pray

B. infirmary tribune and communion grille for the sick sisters

⌐ door

┊ grille

Last photo of Elizabeth alive, about one month before her death, on terrace near infirmary. She holds the rosary given her by Antoinette de Bobet (see L 261 and L 333) and a volume of St. John of the Cross containing the *Spiritual Canticle* and *Living Flame.* Nearby is the statue of Our Lady of Lourdes (see L 188) that she called "Janua Coeli" (Gate of Heaven).

The Institute of Carmelite Studies promotes research and publication in the field of Carmelite spirituality. Its members are Discalced Carmelites, part of a Roman Catholic community—friars, nuns, and laity—who are heirs to the teaching and way of life of Teresa of Jesus and John of the Cross, men and women dedicated to contemplation and to ministry in the church and the world. Information concerning their way of life is available through local diocesan Vocation Offices, or from the Vocation Director's Office, 1525 Carmel Road, Hubertus, WI, 53033.